Criminal Law

3rd Edition

Diana Roe

D0432934

Hodder Arnold

A MEMBER OF THE HODDER HEADLINE GROUP

Orders: please contact Bookpoint Ltd, 130 Milton Park,
Abingdon, Oxon OX14 4SB. Telephone: (44) 01235
827720. Fax: (44) 01235 400454. Lines are open from
9.00 - 6.00, Monday to Saturday, with a 24-hour message
answering service. You can also order through our
website www.hoddereducation.co.uk

If you have any comments to make
about this, or any of our other titles,
please send them to
educationenquiries@hodder.co.uk

British Library Cataloguing in Publication Data
A catalogue record for this title is available from the
British Library

ISBN-10: 0 340 90047 4
ISBN-13: 978 0 340 90047 5

First Edition Published 1999
Second Edition Published 2002
This Edition Published 2005
Impression number   10 9 8 7 6 5 4 3 2
Year   2010 2009 2008 2007 2006 2005

Hodder Headline's policy is to use papers that are
natural, renewable and recyclable products and made
from wood grown in sustainable forests. The logging
and manufacturing processes are expected to conform to
the environmental regulations of the country of origin.

Typeset by Dorchester Typesetting, Dorchester, Dorset
Printed in Great Britain for Hodder Arnold, an imprint
of Hodder Education, a member of the Hodder Headline
Group, 338 Euston Road, London NW1 3BH
by Martins the Printers, Berwick upon Tweed

CONTENTS

Criminal Law

PREFACE

Welcome to the third edition of this textbook and to your study of Criminal Law. This enthralling subject affects all our lives in one way or another and, hopefully, you will be looking forward to studying it.

My main objective in writing this book is to try to ensure that your study of Criminal Law is both interesting and enjoyable. I aim to set out the subject matter as clearly and simply as possible, while maintaining sufficient depth to enable you to gain the highest grades. There are several different types of work set throughout the following chapters that are carefully designed to assist students of all abilities and with varying amounts of time.

While this book will be of value to students studying for an ILEX qualification or the Common Professional Examination and those on law degree courses, **it is primarily designed for students studying Criminal Law in their A Level courses.** It acts as a companion volume to Jacqueline Martin's best selling book on the English Legal System. The following grid should help you to identify the topics set by your particular board

You will immediately note with relief that you are not required to study **every** criminal offence known to English law. There are many thousands of these and it is obviously unrealistic, at this point in your studies, to expect you to have knowledge of them all. Indeed, very few barristers and solicitors would have such wide-ranging information. At best, they would know where to find the appropriate rules, should this be necessary. Law courses, therefore, are selective in the choice of crimes to be studied in their syllabuses. This book aims to cover the criminal law subjects of the three major A Level boards. It is set out in the way shown opposite:

EXAM BOARD SPECIFICATIONS				
for CRIMINAL LAW ELEMENTS				
		A Q A	O C R	W J E C
ELS Summary	Chapter 1	YES	YES	YES
Actus Reus	Chapter 2	YES	YES	YES
Mens Rea	Chapter 2	YES	YES	YES
Strict Liability	Chapter 2	YES	YES	YES
Murder	Chapter 3	YES	YES	YES
Voluntary Manslaughter	Chapter 4	YES	YES	YES
Involuntary Manslaughter	Chapter 5	YES	YES	YES
Non-fatal offences against the Person	Chapter 6	YES	YES	YES
Consent	Chapter 6	YES	YES	NO
Theft	Chapter 7	YES	YES	NO
Robbery	Chapter 7	YES	YES	NO
Burrglary	Chapter 7	YES	YES	NO
Making Off	Chapter 8	YES	YES	NO
Deception	Chapter 8	YES	NO	NO
Criminal Damage	Chapter 9	YES	YES	NO
General Defences	Chapter 10	YES	YES	YES
General Defences	Chapter 11	YES	YES	YES
Parties to a crime	Chapter 12	NO	YES	NO
Inchoate Offences	Chapter 13	NO	YES	NO

- Chapter 1 gives general information on the criminal law, its sources and the different types of criminal courts
- Chapter 2 discusses the two different elements of a crime, looking at the conduct of the accused and his state of mind when the offence was committed. It also examines at strict liability offences
- Chapters 3 to 6 describe offences against the person, from murder down to a simple assault. Chapter 3 looks at the crime of murder, while Chapters 4 and 5 deal with manslaughter. Chapter 6 sets out the non-fatal offences against the person and examines the limited defence of consent
- Chapters 7 to 9 examine property offences. Chapter 7 deals with theft, robbery and burglary. Chapter 8 sets out the law on making off without payment and describes the deception offences in the Theft Acts 1968 and 1978. Chapter 9 looks at offences relating to criminal damage
- Chapters 10 and 11 investigate the general defences a defendant could use to enable him to escape liability
- Chapter 12 looks at crimes committed by more than one person and how to decide whether the participant is a principal offender or merely an accomplice
- Chapter 13 deals with those who attempt to commit crimes but are unsuccessful, those who conspire with others in relation to a criminal offence and those who may not be actively involved in the crime but incite others to engage in criminal activity. Collectively, these are known as inchoate (or incomplete) offences
- Chapter 14 gives guidance on the synoptic modules set by the three A Level examination boards, while Chapter 15 ties everything up, gives examples of past

examination questions and helps with revision and examination technique

HOW TO USE THIS BOOK

It is suggested that you approach your study of criminal law by using this book in the following way:

✔ **Select a particular topic**
Your chosen examination board will have laid down the subject matter covered in your three modules. Read through the material to get an overview of the topic and then go back and study it in greater depth.

✔ **Read any accompanying Comments**
These might shed further light on a controversial or topical subject.

✔ **Study the Key Facts Chart on this part of the law**
These charts are vital as they summarize the current state of the law, giving relevant cases and/or statutes in support.

✔ **Tackle the Activity Sections.**
Before undertaking these tasks, it would be a very good move to examine the sections on essay writing and problem solving, to be found in Chapter 15. You will also see examples of past examination questions there. Armed with this extra knowledge, you should then be equipped to deal with the various discussions, essay questions and problem scenarios set under these headings.

✔ **Deal with the rest of the topics**
Go on through the rest of the chapter in a similar way.

✔ **Answer the Ten Self-Assessment Questions at the end of each chapter**
These questions are designed to test your understanding of the whole chapter. If you have dealt with these questions well, you would be ready to move on to the next complete area of law.

TABLE OF STATUTES AND STATUTORY INSTRUMENTS

TABLE OF CASES

Criminal Law

ACKNOWLEDGEMENTS

As mentioned in the last two editions, every writer on Criminal Law owes a great debt of gratitude to the late Sir John Smith for his extensive knowledge and incomparable analysis of this subject. In addition, I would like to thank the other contributors mentioned in this 3rd edition.

Many thanks also to the great team at Hodder, particularly Alexia Chan for her continuing faith in this series and Jaimee Biggins as Desk Editor for all her hard work. I would also like to thank my students for their enthusiastic support, my dear mother who inspired in us all the love of education, education, education and Peter, whose love, support and practical help is infinitely greater than that given by most husbands.

The author and publishers would like to thank Pat Murray for the cartoons and the following for their permission to reproduce copyright material:

APACS, p.173; © Assessment and Qualification Alliance for AQA examination questions, pp. 290-93; © *The Daily Mail*, p.78; © *The Daily Telegraph*, pp.12, 104, 201; © *Evening Standard*, pp.11, 53, 91, 123, 139-40, 184, 233-34, 241, 245; © Guardian Newspapers Limited 2004, p.161; © OCR for examination questions, pp.285, 288-89; © *The Times*, pp.20, 57, 111-12; © Welsh Joint Education Committee for WJEC examination questions, pp.286, 295-96.

The publishers apologise if inadvertently any sources remain unacknowledged and will be glad to make the necessary arrangements at the earliest opportunity.

INTRODUCTION TO CRIMINAL LAW

1.1 INTRODUCTION

Before undertaking any in-depth study of criminal law, it is important to remind ourselves of aspects of the English Legal System that relate specifically to this subject. The first chapter therefore, deals with the following preliminary material:

✔ The nature and definition of a crime
✔ The various sources of criminal law
✔ The system of binding precedent in English law
✔ The interpretation of statutes
✔ The different ways of reforming criminal law
✔ The prosecution process
✔ The courts in which such offences are tried.

1.2 THE NATURE AND DEFINITION OF A CRIME

One of the most important differences between civil and criminal law is that, under the latter, the State plays a major role in the proceedings. It will be noted later in this chapter that nearly all prosecutions are initiated by the State in one form or another. Criminal wrongs are dealt with by the State for one or more of the following reasons:

● In many instances the events are so serious, both in relation to the victim and to the public at large, that the matter cannot, and should not, be left to the individuals concerned to take action against the perpetrator.
● It may well be necessary to render the aggressor less of a threat to the general

public. This can be done by providing treatment for him or placing him within the confines of a prison or other institution.
● A claim for monetary compensation alone may not suffice. Some form of retribution may be considered desirable.
● Even where the matter could be dealt with by way of compensation, it might be unfair for the victim to bear the expense and trauma of such a move.
● Conversely, with some of the minor public order offences, there may be too little interest on the part of individuals in getting the matter dealt with and it will be necessary for the State to ensure that standards are kept high.

The State, therefore, enforces the rules of criminal law. It now needs to be established which wrongs fall into this category.

1.2.1 THE DEFINITION OF A CRIME

There have been many attempts to define the meaning of a crime, most of them extremely lengthy. My own definition is as follows:

● A crime is a wrong against the State
● either by commission or omission
● classified by the State as criminal
● and one to which a punishment has been attached.

Many offences also involve moral wrongs, such as the crimes of murder and theft, but crime and morality do not always combine in such a definite way. A large section of the community would argue that it is morally wrong to tell lies or commit adultery but, unless the lies are told under oath or the adultery committed in public so as to offend against public decency, the criminal law would not become involved. Conversely, illegal parking or drinking after hours, while thought to be anti-social and thoughtless acts, would not normally be regarded as moral wrongs. A study of criminal law will also show that, while certain crimes remain constant, views about other behaviour may change over the years. For example, certain acts classed as criminal offences 50 years ago are no longer crimes today, such as suicide, which was decriminalised in 1961 and homosexual acts between consenting adults for which the law changed in 1967. The Wolfenden Committee in 1957 decided that it was not the function of the criminal law to interfere into the private lives of citizens in order to try to impose certain standards of behaviour more than was considered necessary. It was felt that this should only be done:

> *to preserve public order and decency, to protect the citizen from what is offensive or injurious, and to provide sufficient safeguards against exploitation and corruption of others, particularly those who are especially vulnerable.*

The law, however, did not change until 10 years later, and even then there was still a continuing debate as to whether the age limit imposed by the State should remain as it was in order to protect the young or, instead, be lowered to give the latter more freedom of choice.

The **Sexual Offences (Amendment) Act 2000** had a very rough ride through Parliament but eventually the latter route was chosen, with some safeguards built into the Act to protect more vulnerable groups. **S1 of the Act lowers the age of consent from 18 to 16 in England, Wales and Scotland and from 18 to 17 in Northern Ireland, equalising it with the relevant age of consent for heterosexual activity in these countries**.

1.3 SOURCES OF CRIMINAL LAW

Criminal law is an uneasy mixture of common law rules, i.e. rules laid down by the judges over the years, and legislation. The latter is the law coming from Parliament in the form of Acts of Parliament and delegated legislation. Some statutes are of very ancient origin; for example, the **Treason Act** was passed in 1351. Before the last century, however, the law coming from Parliament was fairly limited and large areas of the criminal law were developed by the judges. Much of this has subsequently been put into statutory form, such as the law of theft, which is now to be found in the **Theft Act 1968**. In addition our judges decided in the case of **Knuller v DPP 1973**, that it is not now their province to make new law so this will normally be done by Parliament.

Between 30 to 80 new Acts of Parliament are therefore enacted every year. One with far-reaching consequences for criminal law and even more for criminal procedure, is the **Human Rights Act 1998**. This incorporated the provisions of the **European Convention on Human Rights** into English law, helping to protect certain fundamental freedoms. A glance through the criminal appeal reports shows that defendants are not being slow to invoke appropriate sections of this Act, although the move was unsuccessful in the case of the late **Diane Pretty**, described in Chapter 3. On the other hand, the **Terrorism Act 2000** and subsequent legislation contain controversial provisions restricting personal freedoms and create several new criminal offences.

1.3.1 A MIX OF JUDGE-MADE LAW AND LEGISLATION

Although large pockets of criminal law still remain largely judge-made, Parliament might decide to amend some of the provisions.

A notable example of this interaction between the judges and later Parliamentary intervention can be seen in the crimes of murder and voluntary manslaughter. For example, until the middle of the twentieth century, the death penalty was imposed for the crime of murder. Parliament then stepped in with the **Murder (Abolition of Death Penalty) Act 1965**, which suspended the death penalty for murder, except for treason and certain forms of piracy. A later piece of delegated legislation made this permanent. The **Crime and Disorder Act 1998** then removed the death penalty for treason and piracy. In addition, there is no Act of Parliament laying down a definition of murder; instead, the judges developed this offence over the years. Their definition originally stated that death had to occur within a year and a day. This prevailed until 1996 when Parliament abolished it by passing the **Law Reform (Year and a Day Rule) Act 1996.** With regard to voluntary manslaughter, this, originally, was curtailed strictly by the judges. The **Homicide Act 1957** then extended it by reducing the charge from murder to manslaughter where the defendant could establish that he was suffering from diminished responsibility at the time of the killing, had been provoked in some way or was the survivor of a suicide pact. In contrast, the law on involuntary manslaughter remains completely judge-made.

Discovering the source of much of criminal law is not, therefore, an easy process. There have been many calls for a complete statutory code to deal with this problem. A draft code was put before Parliament as long ago as 1878 and, again, in the following two years but was never brought into law. A similar fate seems to await the **Draft Criminal Code** drawn up in 1989, discussed later in this chapter, although it now appears that some of its provisions may be enacted in a more piece-meal fashion.

1.4 THE OPERATION OF BINDING PRECEDENT IN CRIMINAL LAW

Most of you will be studying the rules relating to the English legal system as part of your course and will learn of the importance of the doctrine of precedent in English law. Our system differs from that in many other countries in Europe in that the decisions of some courts are binding on others.

The general rule is that the decisions of the higher courts will bind the courts lower in the hierarchy, but the system is not as simple as this.

1.4.1 THE DIVISIONAL COURT OF QUEEN'S BENCH

Each of the three divisions of the High Court has, in addition to its court of trial, a Divisional Court, which hears limited appeals to take some of the load from the Court of Appeal. The busiest of these is the Divisional Court of Queen's Bench Division, which, in addition to its supervisory role over government departments and inferior courts and tribunals, also hears appeals on points of law from the magistrates' courts. The decisions it makes are then binding on the latter court. The Divisional Court, in turn, is bound by all the higher courts and must generally follow its own earlier decisions. As with the Court of Appeal, however, it can utilise the exceptions laid down in **Young's case** (see below) and also refuse to follow one of its own earlier decisions if this is clearly thought to be wrong.

1.4.2 THE COURT OF APPEAL

The decisions of this court bind the Crown Court and, where applicable, the magistrates' courts. In turn, it is bound by precedents laid down by the House of Lords and also its own earlier decisions, unless one of the three limited exceptions laid down in **Young v Bristol Aeroplane 1944** can be put forward:

- **If there are two conflicting earlier decisions of the Court of Appeal, the court may choose which of the earlier cases to follow.**
- **If the earlier Court of Appeal decision expressly or impliedly conflicts with one laid down by the House of Lords, it should not be followed.**
- **If the earlier Court of Appeal decision was made 'per incuriam', i.e. by mistake, because a relevant precedent or statutory provision was not brought to the court's attention, it should be disregarded.**

The following additional points apply to the Criminal Division of the Court of Appeal:

- **It may depart from its own earlier decisions if they are believed to be based on a misapplication of the law. This was stated in Taylor 1950.**
- **A full court of five judges may overrule an earlier decision made by three judges, as in the case of Palmer 2003.**

It should be noted that the Court of Appeal is not bound by decisions of the Judicial Committee of the Privy Council. This body sits to hear appeals from other Commonwealth countries, which still retain this court for their final appeals. The precedents set by the Privy Council are highly persuasive as, in many cases, the judges are the same as those who sit in the House of Lords, but they are not binding.

1.4.3 THE HOUSE OF LORDS

This is the final appeal court in criminal matters, unless Community Law is involved. The House of Lords binds all the courts below it and, until 1966, was bound by its own earlier decisions. Lord Gardiner then issued his famous Practice Statement, declaring that while their Lordships still considered the doctrine of binding precedent to be an essential part of English law, the House

of Lords from that time on would be prepared to depart from its own earlier decisions **'when it appears right to do so'**. Lord Gardiner did go on to say that the new freedom would only be used sparingly and that House would bear in mind **'the especial need for certainty as to the criminal law'**, a statement that might have come back to haunt him after some later decisions of the Lords rendered the law anything but certain!

The advantages of binding precedent include the following:

- **Certainty**

  Legal advisors and others are able to assume that like cases will be treated in a similar way, thus making it easier to predict the possible outcome. It is also felt to be fair and just that like cases should be decided in a similar way.

- **Time saving**

  If existing precedents are clear, the arguments originally put forward do not have to be re-argued every time a similar case goes to court.

- **Cost-saving**

  Members of the legal profession are better able to advise their clients on the possible outcome of a case if they are aware of existing precedents.

- **Decisions are made by superior judges**

  Judges of the lower courts cannot overrule decisions made earlier by higher-ranking judges. It can be argued that the latter have more expertise.

- **The doctrine is followed by others**

  Although countries in continental Europe follow a system of Roman law and do not have a system of binding precedent, many Commonwealth countries and the USA follow English law and have adopted a common law system of law and a similar method of binding precedent.

- Greater flexibility than it appears

There are limited ways to avoid an unwelcome precedent, such as where it can be distinguished. The judge might decide that the facts of the case are not materially the same as those in the case laying down the precedent and thus refuse to follow it. In addition, one of the parties could appeal to a higher court in the hope that the lower court's decision will be reversed. Normally, this will be the defendant but it should be remembered that the prosecution can appeal from the magistrates' court on a point of law. In other cases, a party may be bound by a decision made earlier in a different case. If he appeals to a higher court than the one laying down the precedent, this court could decide to overrule the earlier decision and therefore set a new precedent on the subject. In addition, we noted above that the Court of Appeal has limited methods of avoiding its own earlier decisions. We also noted that, since 1966, the House of Lords has had the power to overrule its own, earlier precedents, in addition to overruling those laid down by lower courts. Should all these points fail, it is still possible for Parliament to step in and overrule a precedent by passing a statute in conflict with it.

Some of the disadvantages of binding precedent are as follows:

- Rigidity

    Judges bound by precedents of which they disapprove, will nevertheless find it difficult to overrule earlier decisions, even where they are convinced that they are wrong. The fact that the Court of Appeal is normally bound by its own earlier decisions exacerbates the problem. This argument was taken up by the late Lord Denning, who wanted the Court of Appeal to be given the same freedom as that possessed by the House of Lords, to overrule its own earlier precedents, where this was felt to be just. He was not successful in his attempts.

- Cost

    A party wishing to challenge an existing precedent may have to appeal to the Court of Appeal or the House of Lords, which could incur high costs, either for the defendant or for the taxpayer, as well as being time-consuming and traumatic for the parties involved.

- Bulk

    There are hundreds of thousands of precedents and the amount is growing all the time. In some areas of law, this might necessitate research into many different cases, a very time-consuming process. Conversely, in a more obscure subject, a precedent could be overlooked. In addition, despite the advent of the computer, there is still a storage problem for all the paper information.

- Complexity

    It is sometimes difficult to extract the precedent from the judgment. The judges do not specifically announce the point at which they are laying down the precedent. The problem is compounded when the case is decided by more than one judge and they have different views on the matter, as seen in Re A 2000, in Chapter 3.

- Uneven growth

    Different areas of the law could grow at different speeds, depending on the volume of cases coming to court on the particular subject.

- Illogical distinguishing

    Too much distinguishing can make the law look very odd, as seemingly similar cases are dealt with in different ways.

- The doctrine is out of line with other EU countries.

    Countries such as France and Germany have their law laid down in very large Codes, which set out general principles of law. The judges may have to interpret these rules and, when doing so, are given more flexibility than that possessed by English judges. Precedents laid down by other judges may be of persuasive value but there is no compulsion to follow them.

1.4.4 CITING CASES

The operation of the doctrine of binding precedent explains why the citing, (or quoting), of cases is so important in criminal law. Certain cases lay down precedents that the later courts must follow. The facts of the case are relatively unimportant, although often very interesting; it is the precedent or principle of law coming from the case that will be binding on other judges.

Most criminal cases start with the word **Regina** (the Latin for Queen), or **R v the defendant.** When this is the case, only the defendant's name will be shown in this book. If the case involves a prosecutor's name, this will be included in the citing. If the case concerns the Attorney General, the Director of Public Prosecutions or the Metropolitan Police Commissioner, the initials will indicate this. It should also be noted that, when an appeal is made, the defendant becomes known as the appellant. For ease, however, I have retained the words **'defendant'** or **'accused'**.

1.5 THE INTERPRETATION OF STATUTES

Because we live in a democracy, legislation will always take priority over case law. The judges, however, can exert influence over statute law in cases where the legislation is ambiguous or where the words are capable of having more than one meaning. If a problem over the interpretation of a statute comes to court, often by the defendant seeking to exploit some weakness in the Act, the judge must resolve this. Rather strangely, there are no hard and fast rules to

assist him in this task, just various presumptions and guidelines that have been formulated by the judges themselves. The latter have vastly different views over their power to interpret legislation. Some take a very restrictive approach and believe that the words laid down in the statute should be followed whatever the outcome, as noted in **R v Judge of the City of London Court 1892**, even if this would produce an absurd or unjust result. They believe if a problem arises – '**the remedy lies in an amending act**' – to quote the words of Lord Simonds. Use of the 'literal rule' can be seen in the cases of **LNER v Berriman 1946** and **Fisher v Bell 1960**.

If the case leads to an obviously absurd or repugnant result, some judges are prepared to use the 'golden rule', which allows the judge to modify the words so as to achieve a sensible or fairer result. This approach can be seen in **Allen 1872** and **Re Sigsworth 1935**.

Many judges are now going further. They are extending the use of the 'mischief rule', laid down in **Heydon's Case 1584**, and used in the famous case of **Smith v Hughes 1960**, and taking a wider purposive approach to statutory interpretation, as seen in **Royal College of Nursing v DHSS 1981**. To try to discover the meaning of a statute, they are prepared to look at reports before a Bill is introduced and even Hansard, the daily report of Parliament's activities, in limited circumstances, as seen in **Pepper v Hart 1993**, a House of Lords' decision. To a layman, this might seem the most obvious method to use, but it should be borne in mind that it is more subjective and could lead to uncertainty in the law. Despite the problems, however, this seems to be the way forward. Widespread use of the literal rule was criticized by the Law Commission as long ago as 1969 and now that we are a member of the European Union, our judges are becoming more ready to adopt a more dynamic approach to statutory interpretation.

1.6 REFORMING CRIMINAL LAW

The main law-making body in the twenty-first century is, of course, Parliament but, before Parliament can legislate, someone must have made the decision that the law needs to be changed.

1.6.1 THE GOVERNMENT OF THE DAY

Successive governments will introduce legislation reforming criminal law. The changes often involve procedural matters or sentencing, the **Criminal Justice Act 2003** being an example, or are in response to a particular problem, as shown by the **Dangerous Dogs Act 1991** and the **Protection from Harassment Act 1997**. The government may also decide to take up and adopt a private Member's Bill, as seen with the controversial Mental Capacity Bill, going through Parliament at the time of writing.

1.6.2 ROYAL COMMISSIONS

These ad hoc bodies are set up for a specific purpose, often after concern has been expressed about the matter to be examined. They are usually made up of a wide cross-section of people who are independent, non-political and have expertise in the particular field. The members are allowed to commission research and consult with interested parties. After reaching their conclusions, they will publish a report containing detailed recommendations, which they hope that Parliament will go on to implement.

Examples include the Beeching Commission, which resulted in the creation of the Crown Court, the Royal Commission on Criminal Procedure which led to the passing of the **Police and Criminal Evidence Act 1984,** and the Royal Commission on Criminal Justice. The latter was instrumental in the setting up of the Criminal Cases Review Committee, which made it easier to deal with possible miscarriages of justice.

1.6.3 THE CRIMINAL LAW REVISION COMMITTEE

This part-time body was set up in 1957 and has instigated several important reforms. One such example led to the passing of the **Theft Act 1968.**

1.6.4 THE LAW COMMISSION

In 1965, it was decided that a full-time body should be set up to undertake more comprehensive law reform, (both civil and criminal), and the Law Commission was created. Its remit is extensive and laid down in **s3 Law Commissions Act 1965** (there was a separate one for Scotland). The two Law Commissions were charged with keeping:

under review all the law, ... with a view to its systematic development and reform, including in particular the codification of such law, the elimination of anomalies, the repeal of obsolete and unnecessary enactments, the reduction of the number of separate enactments and generally the simplification and modernisation of the law.

The English Law Commission saw the codification of the criminal law as a pressing issue. It recognised that the rules are an untidy mixture of judge-made rules and statutory provisions, and that even where legislation existed, some of this was deficient because of its age and style of language, the **Offences Against the Person Act 1861** being a prime example. A great deal of work, therefore, went into producing a Draft Code in 1989, along with a Bill to implement its proposals. This Code is referred to in the following chapters, in cases where other reforms have not overtaken it. Unfortunately, successive governments made little effort to implement it. The Law Commission then tried to effect changes in key areas in a more piece-meal fashion. This, too, was unsuccessful and in 1993, the Commission launched a stinging attack on the government of the day, roundly declaring that the failure by Parliament to implement any of the reforms was **'a disgrace'**.

In August 1999, the late Sir John Smith, a key figure in producing the Draft Criminal Code, also felt a pressing need to remind Parliament of its role, when he argued that:

Major parts of English criminal law are in a thoroughly unsatisfactory state – the criticisms that the law is archaic, obscure, incoherent and inconsistent are familiar and have been rehearsed on numerous occasions. The law is increasingly inefficient, and is increasingly failing to deliver justice. The case for a modern criminal code, a strong one when first made by the Law Commission in 1968, is overwhelming thirty years on.

Eventually, there was a response from government, though hardly dramatic. In 2001, it produced a paper called 'Criminal Justice: The Way Ahead' in which it indicated that codification was among its aims in improving the effectiveness of the criminal law.

The Law Commission has had greater success with more piece-meal reform of the law, such as repealing old acts and making limited reforms in Contract Law, Land Law, Family Law and the Law of Tort. In criminal law, its work can be seen in the **Criminal Attempts Act 1981**, the **Public Order Act 1986,** the **Computer Misuse Act 1990** and the **Law Reform (Year and a Day Rule) Act 1996.**

1.7 THE PROSECUTION PROCESS AND CLASSIFICATION OF OFFENCES

1.7.1 THE DECISION TO PROSECUTE

As stated earlier in this chapter, the decision to prosecute comes from the State via the Director of Public Prosecutions, who is the head of the Crown Prosecution Service. In most cases, the police will start the investigations and until 1985, they carried on to prosecute. The **Prosecution of Offences Act 1985** changed the position because it was believed that a separate body should be involved in this process. Despite this laudable aim, the CPS has had a poor press, with complaints being made about poor administration and the quality of its lawyers, although certain important reforms have since been made. The CPS is not the only body involved in the process; officials from local authorities, such as Trading Standards Officers, the NSPCC and the Serious Fraud Office may decide to start a prosecution. In addition, a private prosecution may be launched, although these are rare. With regard to serious offences under the **Official Secrets Acts**, the Attorney-General must give permission for these to progress.

When making the decision to prosecute, regard must be given to the evidence available, which needs to be substantial and reliable, and whether it is in the public interest to do so. When there is doubt, the accused should be given the benefit of it, which inevitably means that some offenders are never brought to trial.

1.7.2 THE CLASSIFICATION OF OFFENCES

Offences are put into two broad categories, summary offences, the more minor ones, and indictable offences, which are more serious. The James' Committee later recommended dividing cases into three: offences triable summarily, offences to be tried on indictment only and a third category of cases that could be tried either way.

Summary offences

These offences must be tried in the magistrates' court because an Act of Parliament decrees that they will be dealt with summarily. Normally three lay magistrates try the case although, in some of the larger towns, a legally qualified, paid magistrate, now called a District Judge (Magistrates' Court), will decide the case alone. If the defendant pleads not guilty, the magistrates act as both judge and jury, deciding the matter of guilt or innocence and fixing the sentence. Most of these offences are fairly minor but, periodically, they are added to by Parliament and more serious ones have been included. The following are examples:

- **Speeding**
- **Careless driving**
- **Assaulting a police officer in the execution of his duty**
- **Minor criminal damage**
- **Assault and battery**
- **Driving or being in control of a vehicle with excess alcohol in the blood.**

Indictable offences

Offences tried on indictment are the more serious or complicated ones which must be dealt with by the Crown Court. Such offences include:

- **Murder**
- **Manslaughter**
- **Rape**
- **Robbery**
- **Arson**
- **Causing death by dangerous driving.**

The case will normally start in the magistrates' court, but will then be transferred for trial in the Crown Court.

The magistrates still have the important task of deciding whether the accused will be remanded in custody or released on bail until his trial takes place. **The Bail Act 1976, as amended,** states that everyone has a general right to bail, unless the offence is a serious violent or sexual one, in which case the magistrates must state in open court why they are giving bail. In most other cases, bail will be allowed unless there is a good reason why it should be refused, such as the likelihood of the defendant committing further offences or absconding.

Offences triable either way

As the name suggests, it is possible for such offences to be tried summarily in the magistrates' courts or on indictment in the Crown Court. If it is decided that the case is more suitable for trial on indictment, then it must be dealt with in this way; the accused has no say in the matter. If, however, the magistrates decide that they have enough power to try the case, the defendant, if pleading not guilty, may choose whether he wants this form of trial or would prefer to take his case to the Crown Court. The vast majority of offenders choose summary trial but in a dangerous driving or theft case, the accused may believe (often wrongly) that a jury trial will give him a better chance of an acquittal. If he chooses such a trial, committal proceedings will take place and the case will be set down for trial in the Crown Court.

If he chooses magistrates' court trial, he must first be warned that the magistrates still retain the power to send him to the Crown Court for sentencing, if they have found him guilty and believe that their powers are insufficient to deal with him. It should be remembered that magistrates only have the power to impose a fine of £5000 or less and/or a sentence of imprisonment of twelve months for any one offence.

Examples of triable either way offences include:

- **Theft**
- **Dangerous driving**
- **Burglary**
- **Actual bodily harm**
- **Criminal damage over £5000**
- **Obtaining property or services by deception.**

The current government tried to abolish jury trial in such cases but twice faced defeat in the House of Lords.

1.8 THE SYSTEM OF CRIMINAL COURTS

1.8.1 COURTS OF FIRST INSTANCE

These are the magistrates' courts and the Crown Court with over 90 branches. Magistrates' courts deal with all the summary offences and with the triable either way offences where the defendant has chosen summary trial or has pleaded guilty. The Crown Court is reserved for indictable offences and those triable either way offences where the magistrates decide that they have insufficient power to deal with them or where the accused opts for this form of trial. Trial in the Crown Court will be conducted by a single judge, if the defendant pleads guilty, or by judge and jury if the defendant pleads not guilty. In the latter case, a jury of twelve, who are selected at random, will decide upon the verdict, after listening to the facts and hearing advice on the points of law involved from the judge. The latter will be a circuit judge or a recorder (a part-time judge) for the less serious indictable or triable either way cases dealt with in this court. For the most serious cases, a High Court judge will officiate. This judge normally sits in the Queen's

Bench Division of the High Court but makes periodical visits to the branches of the Crown Court on his circuit. He is sometimes known as the 'Red Judge', because of the colour of his robe.

Deliberations in the jury room are secret and, when they are complete, the foreman delivers the verdict in open court. Majority verdicts, of 11–1 or 10–2, are now accepted. If the defendant is acquitted, he will walk free from the court and, except in exceptional circumstances, cannot be retried for the same offence. If the jury finds the defendant guilty, the judge will do the sentencing. Most offences have a maximum sentence laid down, but no minimum, giving the judge a large measure of discretion. Exceptions to this are certain forms of treason and piracy and the crime of murder, which have a fixed sentence of life imprisonment. Until 1998, the first two crimes were, theoretically, punishable by death but this position changed with the passing of the **Crime and Disorder Act 1998.**

Possible reform of the criminal courts

The eagerly awaited Auld Report, published in October 2001, suggested major changes to the courts of first instance, recommending the insertion of a middle tier of courts, where a tribunal would decide the issue. It remains to be seen whether such sweeping changes will ever be adopted.

1.8.2 THE APPEAL COURTS IN CRIMINAL LAW

Appeals from the magistrates' courts

There are two main ways to appeal. The normal appeal route allows the defendant to appeal to the Crown Court against the verdict or the sentence decided by the magistrates. There will be a complete rehearing of the case by a circuit judge and magistrates. Only the accused is permitted to appeal by this method. The verdict may be affirmed or changed. The sentence may

Stone loses his appeal over Russell murders

By Paul Cheston

Michael Stone failed today to convince a court that he was innocent of the murders of Lin and Megan Russell.

He will return to Long Sutton high-security prison to continue his life sentence for savagely beating to death 45-year-old Dr Russell and her six-year-old daughter Megan.

The attack took place in woods at the village of Chillenden near Canterbury nine years ago.

Dr Russell's nine-year-old daughter Josie was left for dead with severe head injuries but made a miraculous recovery. Today's ruling by three Appeal Court judges confirms two previous jury verdicts on 44-year-old Stone. He was found guilty at his original trial and the verdict was upheld at a retrial.

For two days his lawyers argued that he had been framed by fellow prisoner Damien Daley, who had provided the key evidence of Stone's prison confession to smashing his victims' skulls like 'eggs'.

Today's decision will be greeted with relief by Josie, who is now 17 and living in North Wales with her father Shaun.

Mark Stephens, solicitor for Mr Russell and one of Josie's trustees, later issued a statement on behalf of Mr Russell.

It said: 'I am satisfied that Kent police did the best possible job given the difficult circumstances surrounding our case. The justice system has taken its course and as far as I can see it has been fair to all parties. Josie and I have made an effort to put our memories of this terrible affair behind us, especially as nothing can bring back Josie's mother Lin and sister Megan.

'We would be grateful if we could be left in peace with our happy memories of the ones we have lost, and get on with our lives in as undisturbed a way as possible.'

Stone's sister, Barbara, pledged to fight on with a possible appeal to the House of Lords. 'There's not a scrap of evidence against him, only the word of one heroin-addict lying person – that's the only piece of evidence and I just don't believe it,' she said.

Evening Standard, 19 January 2005

---

be increased or (perhaps more often) decreased.

The other route only concerns points of law or claims that the magistrates have acted '*ultra vires*', i.e. outside the scope of their powers. Either the prosecution or defence may appeal by way of 'case stated', i.e. by a written statement asking for an opinion on the point of law involved, to the Divisional Court of Queen's Bench Division. Two or three judges of the court will give their view of the law, which will then be followed by the lower court. If the case has reached the Crown Court, this court, too, may make such an appeal if the parties require advice on a point of law. There is a further appeal from the Divisional Court straight to the House of Lords.

Appeals from the Crown Court

Such appeals are made to the Court of Appeal (Criminal Division), which sits in the Royal Courts of Justice in the Strand. The main rules are to be found in the **Criminal Appeal Act 1995**, which simplified the existing system.

Against sentence

Leave to appeal is needed from the Court of Appeal or the trial judge. Such appeals are normally made by the defendant to have his sentence reduced but, since 1988, the Attorney-General, on behalf of the prosecution, can also appeal against an unduly lenient sentence.

Court dishes out justice to men and their best friends

By John Steele

When the Criminal Cases Review Commission was established by law in 1997, as a result of disquiet in legal and political circles over a series of alleged miscarriages of justice, Parliament did not define its potential 'clients' in a way that excluded convicts with four paws and shaggy coats.

The CCRC has, however, generally asked the Court of Appeal to consider the cases of convicted murderers, rapists, terrorists and others found guilty of serious criminal offices, some of them since dead.

Yesterday, though, Dino – a seven-year-old German Shepherd that bit a woman – joined a list of beneficiaries of CCRC referrals which has included Sion Jenkins, the deputy headmaster who won a retrial over the murder of Billie-Jo Jenkins, Sally Clark, who was cleared of killing her two children, and Danny McNamee, whose conviction as an alleged IRA bomber was quashed.

Posthumous cases where the Court of Appeal has quashed a conviction on a referral from the CCRC have included that of Derek Bentley, the 19-year-old hanged in 1953 for his alleged part in the murder of a police officer. There is no time limit on the cases it can consider.

The CCRC has justified its role in the case of Dino by arguing that it was not set up solely to deal with serious cases, though they are the norm.

The CCRC is, in its own words, an 'independent public body set up to review suspected miscarriages of justice and decide if they should be referred to an appeal court'.

'We do not consider innocence or guilt, but whether there is new evidence or argument which may cast doubt on the safety of an original decision,' the CCRC says.

It began life in April 1997 and took over the responsibility for assessing alleged miscarriages from the Home Office. Its creation followed a decade which had seen the overturning of a series of convictions for alleged IRA terrorism, including the Birmingham Six, the Guildford Four – and the linked Maguire case – as well as the case of Judith Ward.

There was a consensus that the job of investigating suspected miscarriages should be given to an independent body, in order to restore confidence in the criminal justice system.

Most cases sent to the CCRC by solicitors do not pass its tests. Referrals to the Court of Appeal also fail. Posthumously, the convictions of James Hanratty and Ruth Ellis were upheld.

In total, the CCRC has received 6,957 applications for review. It has completed 6,292 reviews and referred 194 to the Appeal Court, which quashed convictions in 133 cases.

Daily Telegraph, 19 January 2005

Against the verdict

Only the defendant may challenge the actual verdict in a case, except in exceptional cases where the prosecution can show that the jury has been '**nobbled**' or has reached a perverse verdict (**Criminal Justice Act 2003**). The defendant may appeal, either on a point of law, or because there are other reasons to suggest that the verdict may be 'unsafe'. It has now become easier to bring such evidence before the court, as noted below.

Leave is required for this. You will discover as you progress through this book that most appeals are on the grounds that the judge has misdirected the jury in some material way on the law relating to the crime in question.

The Court of Appeal may allow the appeal, order a retrial, or dismiss it as shown in the newspaper article on page 11.

While the prosecution cannot overturn an acquittal, the Attorney General has power to ask the Court of Appeal to look at the point of law involved and set a precedent for the future. The original acquittal will not be touched.

The Criminal Cases Review Commission

Following concern about miscarriages of justice and the report from the Runciman Commission, the Criminal Cases Review Commission was set up by the **Criminal Appeal Act 1995** to make it easier for such cases to be investigated. This became operational in April 1997. This Commission will investigate possible miscarriages of justice and if they are felt to have merit, will refer them back to the Court of Appeal. The article opposite shows examples of its work.

Appeals to the House of Lords

Either the prosecution or the defence may appeal from the Court of Appeal to the House of Lords if a point of law has been certified as one of general public importance. Such appeals rarely reach double figures each year, but have a very important influence on the law.

Self-assessment questions on Chapter 1

1 Define a crime. Give two examples where the criminal law seems to combine with more general views of morality and two instances where there may be a conflict.

2 Describe two sources of criminal law, giving examples to support your answer.

3 Discuss the position of the House of Lords and the Court of Appeal with regard to their own earlier precedents.

4 Give four points in favour of the doctrine of binding precedent and four against it.

5 Describe the purposive approach to statutory interpretation.

6 Note three bodies, other than Parliament, which are instrumental in reforming the law and give an example of their work.

7 What was the effect of the **Prosecution of Offences Act 1985**?

8 Give two examples of a summary offence, a triable either way offence and an indictable offence and state where and by whom such offences are tried.

9 To which court will a defendant in a magistrates' court appeal against a) the sentence or verdict or b), on a point of law?

10 To which courts may an appeal be made from the Crown Court and when will this be possible?

Chapter 2

THE ELEMENTS OF A CRIME

2.1 INTRODUCTION

Before we start our study of certain specific criminal offences in Chapters 3–9, we need first to ascertain whether the defendant in question actually possesses criminal liability. We therefore need to see how such liability arises and what normally has to be proved. In most cases, the constituents of the offence must be satisfied, plus the necessary state of mind for committing such a crime. There are, however, a limited number of offences, often of a regulatory nature where the defendant can be convicted without the prosecution having to establish blame. These are known as offences of strict liability. This chapter, therefore, looks at the following issues:

✔ The burden of proof in criminal law
✔ The two different elements of a crime
✔ The *actus reus* of a criminal offence, (the factual elements that have to be shown)
✔ The *mens rea* of a crime, (the mental element that has to be proved)
✔ Offences of strict liability

2.2 THE BURDEN OF PROOF IN CRIMINAL LAW

Before a person can be convicted of a wrong against the State, the prosecution must satisfy the jury that he has committed the wrong of which he is accused. **In criminal law, the burden of proof is a strong one; the prosecution must establish this beyond reasonable doubt.** This point was made clear by the House of Lords in **Woolmington v DPP 1935.**

In the above quoted case, the defendant claimed that he took a gun with him to the home of the victim's mother, not for any criminal intent, but to demonstrate to his estranged wife that he planned to commit suicide if she failed to return to him. He alleged that the gun then went off by accident, as he was showing it to her. Despite this claim, the defendant was convicted of murder.

The House of Lords allowed the appeal on the grounds that the judge had misdirected the jury by suggesting that it was necessary for the defendant to prove that the killing had been accidental, rather than for the prosecution to establish that the killing had been intentional.

2.3 THE ELEMENTS OF A CRIME

When trying to establish whether the accused is criminally liable, the prosecution will normally have to prove two things:

● that the defendant has actually committed the crime in question. This is known as the *actus reus* of the offence
● that the defendant had committed the wrong with the degree of blameworthiness required by the law, i.e. with the necessary 'guilty mind'. This element of the offence is known as the *mens rea*.

Figure 2.1 might help you recognize the difference between the two terms.

2.4 THE *ACTUS REUS* OF A CRIME

The existence of the *actus reus* is essential for criminal liability. Each crime has its own *actus reus*, laid down by statute or by the judges. For

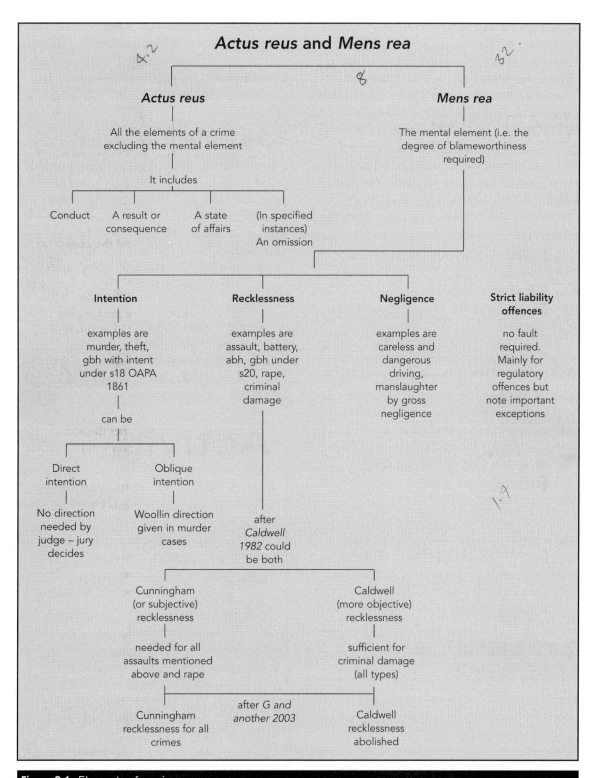

Actus reus and *Mens rea*

Actus reus — All the elements of a crime excluding the mental element

It includes
- Conduct
- A result or consequence
- A state of affairs
- (In specified instances) An omission

Mens rea — The mental element (i.e. the degree of blameworthiness required)

Intention — examples are murder, theft, gbh with intent under s18 OAPA 1861

can be:
- **Direct intention** — No direction needed by judge – jury decides
- **Oblique intention** — Woollin direction given in murder cases

Recklessness — examples are assault, battery, abh, gbh under s20, rape, criminal damage

after *Caldwell 1982* could be both
- Cunningham (or subjective) recklessness — needed for all assaults mentioned above and rape
- Caldwell (more objective) recklessness — sufficient for criminal damage (all types)

after *G and another 2003*
- Cunningham recklessness for all crimes
- Caldwell recklessness abolished

Negligence — examples are careless and dangerous driving, manslaughter by gross negligence

Strict liability offences — no fault required. Mainly for regulatory offences but note important exceptions

Figure 2.1 Elements of a crime

example, the *actus reus* of **s18 Offences Against the Person Act 1861** occurs where a person unlawfully wounds or causes grievous bodily harm to another. The *actus reus* of theft under the **Theft Act 1968** arises when a party '**appropriates property belonging to another**'. At common law (i.e. where the criminal offence has been developed by the judges, rather than by Parliament), the *actus reus* of murder has been established as '**the unlawful killing of a person in being under the Queen's peace**'. These definitions will be explained in detail when the relevant offences are dealt with later in this book.

In many cases, the actions of the accused will speak for themselves and the *actus reus* will be easy to establish but occasionally the matter is more complex as can be seen in the following subsections.

2.4.1 CONDUCT

In many instances, the mere conduct of the accused may be enough to show that the *actus reus* has been committed. A classic example of this is perjury, i.e. lying under oath. Another example is the conduct of '**appropriating property belonging to another**' as laid down in the crime of theft.

Once a person has taken property belonging to someone else, the *actus reus* of the offence will have been established. If he has done this dishonestly with the intention of permanently depriving the other person of the goods, he will also have the necessary guilty mind.

2.4.2 A RESULT OR CONSEQUENCE

For the commission of some crimes, however, it is necessary to show more than just conduct; the result or consequence of that conduct must also be assessed. For example, in the crime of murder, the defendant's violent act must have resulted in an unlawful killing.

Similarly, under **s20 Sexual Offences Act 1956**, it was an offence to take an unmarried girl out of the possession of her parent or guardian without lawful authority. Should this have occurred, the *actus reus* of the crime would have been established.

2.4.3 A STATE OF AFFAIRS

In rare cases, the unfortunate defendant may be found guilty of a crime simply by being in a particular place when this state of affairs has been declared to be wrong. An example is the case of **Larsonneur 1933**. The defendant had gone to Ireland when her permission to be in the UK had expired. She was then deported from Ireland and brought back to England against her will by the police.

Despite the fact that she had no wish to return to this country, she was found guilty of 'being an alien to whom leave to land in the United Kingdom has been refused', which was an offence under the Aliens' Order 1920.

Activity

- Read the following extract and decide how the *actus reus* of the crime was established by the prosecution:

In **Winzar v Chief Constable of Kent 1983**, the defendant had been taken to hospital, but once there it was discovered that he was not ill, merely drunk. He was therefore requested to leave the premises. He failed to comply with this order and was later found in a corridor of the hospital. The police were called and he was removed from the premises against his will and taken to a police car on the highway. He was then charged with being found drunk in the highway.

Despite widespread criticism of the unfairness of this decision, certain later Acts of Parliament have also adopted this strict approach. A modern example is **s4 Road Traffic Act 1988**, under which it is an offence to be in charge of a motor vehicle on a road or public place while unfit to drive through drink or drugs. The *actus reus* of the offence will be present even if the defendant has decided not to drive the vehicle in question and has planned to sleep in the car instead. The state of affairs of being in charge of the vehicle is enough to establish liability under this section of the Act.

2.4.4 AN OMISSION

The first point to note is that normally, in English law, a person will not be found to be criminally liable merely because he has failed to act.

Stephen L J made this position clear back in the nineteenth century, when he stated:

It is not a crime to cause death or bodily injury, even intentionally, by any omission.

He went on to describe the situation where a person sees another man drowning but does nothing to help him, even though, if he had merely reached out his hand, the man who could not swim would have been saved. Under English law, the person failing to act has committed no crime.

There are, however, limited exceptions to this rule where the law has decided that a person should be criminally liable for failing to act. They include the following situations:

● **Where a statute lays this down**
A limited number of statutory provisions create liability for omissions in specified circumstances. The following are examples under the **Road Traffic Act 1988, as amended**: (i) Failing to provide a breath specimen as required; (ii) Failing to give details to someone entitled to receive them, after a traffic accident; (iii) Failing to report an accident as required.

It is also a statutory offence under the **Children and Young Person's Act 1933** to fail to provide a child with adequate food, clothing, housing or medical help.

● **Where there is a contractual duty to act in a particular way**
There may be a specific duty to act laid down in a person's contract. For example, a lifeguard is employed to save lives, so would obviously be failing in his duty if he observed someone in difficulties but took no steps to save him from drowning. The same rules would apply to a person employed to guard a level crossing, as the defendant in **Pittwood 1902** discovered to his cost. He was a railway employee who had opened the level crossing gates to let a cart pass across the line, but had failed to shut the gates again before going off to have his lunch. A few minutes later, a passing train hit a hay-cart crossing the track and the driver of this latter vehicle was killed.

The defendant was found guilty of 'gross and criminal negligence' after the judge made it clear that 'a man might incur criminal liability from a duty arising out of contract'.

● **Where there is a duty imposed by law**
The judges themselves have imposed liability for omissions in certain situations.

(i) **Where the person is guilty of misconduct in a public office**
In **Dytham 1979**, a police officer stood by while a man was kicked to death.

The Court of Appeal upheld his criminal conviction for misconduct in a public office.

(ii) **Where there is a special relationship between the parties**
A party may be found guilty of failing to act if there is a duty imposed upon him by virtue of the special relationship between him and the victim. An early case on this subject was **Instan 1893**, where a niece failed

to obtain help for her aunt, with whom she was living. The aunt contracted gangrene in her leg and died.

The niece's conviction for manslaughter was upheld. The appeal court held that English law would be 'hopelessly deficient if the judges were unable to base liability on the common duty of care owed by one relative to another'.

Another case illustrating this is **Gibbins and Proctor 1918**, where a man and his common law wife were found guilty of homicide, when they failed to feed the man's child and she died from starvation.

The father obviously had a duty to look after his child. The woman was held to be liable because even though the child was not hers, she was living with the man and had accepted his money for food.

In **Khan 1998**, however, it was decided that drug dealers are not normally under any special duty to look after their clients, so a manslaughter conviction was quashed.

(iii) **Where the defendant has voluntarily accepted responsibility for the other**

This often overlaps with the duty imposed by a special relationship, mentioned above, but is wider in that the law can impose liability in any case where the victim has relied upon the defendant and the latter then fails to help.

A particularly gruesome example of this was the case of **Stone and Dobinson 1977**. The sister of an elderly man came to stay with him and his woman friend. The man's sight, hearing and sense of smell were all deficient and his woman companion was of low intelligence. Fanny, the sister, was said to be **'morbidly obsessed'** with putting on weight. She refused to eat, became bed-bound and developed serious bedsores that became very badly infected. The couple made half-hearted attempts to get help for her but failed to obtain the proper medical aid and Fanny died.

The couple's conviction for

manslaughter was upheld. The Court of Appeal decided that they had assumed a duty to care for the sister, they knew that she was relying on them and they had failed to get her the assistance that she needed.

(iv) **Where there is a dangerous situation caused by the defendant and he has failed to put this right**

In the case of **Miller 1983** a squatter had fallen asleep while smoking and his cigarette caused the mattress to catch fire. The flames awoke him but instead of putting out the fire, Miller merely moved to another room and went back to sleep. The house was badly damaged and the defendant's conviction for arson was upheld.

The House of Lords decided that 'failing to take measures that lie within one's power to counteract a danger that one has oneself created' could, in circumstances like this, create liability.

● **Liability under a continuous act**
In some instances, the courts will avoid the difficulties of trying to establish liability for omissions and impose liability in another way. An example was the case of **Fagan v MPC 1969**.

Comment

Some legal writers, among them Professor Glanville Williams, favour retaining a restrictive approach to imposing liability for omissions. Other academics, including Professor Ashworth, have taken an opposing view and believe that the proposed reforms do not go far enough, as wider policy issues are involved.

People taking the latter stance are dissatisfied with the current state of English law, which normally absolves a party from blame when he fails to help, even in extreme situations, such as where he stands watching, while a child drowns in a shallow pool of water. They would argue that there has been an unwelcome increase in the principle of non-involvement in the affairs of strangers, even when it is patently obvious that help is urgently needed. Harrowing reports of people ignoring cries for help from victims of muggers or rapists or closing their ears to the sounds of children being ill-treated are, unfortunately, all too common.

Whether they would advocate going as far as the French courts appear to be doing, as noted in the article overleaf, is debatable.

Education in good citizenship might be an alternative approach to creating further criminal offences.

Activity

- In groups or in written form, decide whether the right balance has been struck concerning liability for omissions.
- Ascertain whether the *actus reus* of a crime has been established in the following unrelated situations. Give cases to support your findings:

Sue was in the habit of feeding her bedridden grandmother at lunchtime, before going to her part-time job. She was promoted suddenly, necessitating far greater hours at her place of work and totally forgot her grandmother's needs. Her grandmother has just died of starvation.

Gary noticed that the wheel of the car in front of him was wobbling dangerously but failed to inform the driver because he was late for an appointment and did not wish to become involved. The wheel came off the car and the driver was killed.

Gaby was staying illegally in college accommodation. She fell asleep while the bath was running and the bath water overflowed. She woke up, decided that the water was now too cold and went to bed, leaving the water running in the bathroom. The resulting flood seriously damaged the lower two floors of the college building.

Ian, an electrician employed by the local council, went off for his tea break, leaving all the wires exposed. Murray, the supervisor was electrocuted.

The defendant had been told to stop his car and pull in to the kerb. As he did so, he accidentally drove on to the policeman's foot. When he was shouted at to remove the car, the defendant swore at the policeman, told him he could wait and switched off the ignition. He was convicted of assaulting a police constable in the execution of his duty but later appealed stating that no liability could be incurred by merely failing to act.

The Court of Appeal held differently. The judges decided that driving onto the

Couple face prison after drunken dinner guest killed four in crash

By Charles Bremner

A crackdown on drink-driving in France entered new territory yesterday when a couple went on trial for allowing an intoxicated dinner guest to drive away from their home and cause a crash that killed him and four others.

The case of Angélique and Jean-Sebastien Fraisse, who face up to five years in jail and a £50,000 fine, is being closely watched because a conviction could open the way to a flood of prosecutions and civil actions for indirect involvement in drink-driving.

Safety campaigners are hailing the case as a sign that the state is getting serious with the alcoholic driving that plagues France. Motoring organisations are depicting the Fraisses as victims of a new 'blame culture'.

The defendants' situation is particularly poignant because they met at a rehabilitation centre after they had both been victims of drink-drivers. Mme Fraisse, 29, has been confined to a wheelchair since being run over at 16. Her husband, 30, an unemployed metal worker, recovered from his injuries.

The couple are charged with 'failing to prevent a crime or lesser offence causing bodily injury'. The prosecution arose from a night in February 2000 when Frédéric Colin drove away at 3.45am from dinner at the Fraisse's home at Maizieres-les-Metz in Lorraine.

He went the wrong way up a motorway and collided with a car carrying a family of five. M Colin died, along with the parents and two children in the other car. The grandparents of a surviving five-year-old boy applied for proceedings against the Fraisses when Colin was found to have a blood alcohol level of 2.4 grams a litre. The legal maximum is 0.5. An investigating judge later dropped the case, but it was reinstated by an appeal court.

The Fraisses said that they did all they could to prevent their friend driving home. 'We tried to take his keys but he wouldn't let us,' Mme Fraisse said. 'I suggested that he spend the night with us, but he didn't want to. The prosecutors think I should have called the police but that is not realistic. I understand the suffering of the grandparents of the victims. I also hated the reckless driver who made me a paraplegic at 16. I have started having atrocious nightmares in whch I see car accidents and I wake up screaming.'

Bruno Zillig, the couple's lawyer, said that they were faulted for not notifying the police after their friend left. 'This type of denunciation does not exist in French law,' he said. 'This is the first time that people are being asked to be responsible for others' behaviour.' The couple could be found guilty only if they knew that their friend intended to cause bodily harm, which was clearly not the case, he added. Lawyers for the victim's family said that they had brought the case to prove the principle of responsibility.

Genevieve Jurdensen, a leading road safety campaigner, called for a guilty verdict that would set a precedent, even if the sentence was light. 'It is a good thing that the case was brought. It will open a debate on the question of whether we are responsible for the acts of others. Should this couple have done more to prevent that man from taking his car?'

Christiane Cellier, the president of another road safety foundation, said: 'It is high time that everyone realised that even if we do not drive while drunk, we are responsible if we let others do so.'

French road deaths have dropped by 15 per cent over the past two years in a national drive to curb France's culture of dangerous driving. But the death toll remains one of Europe's highest.

The authorities have been displaying a new toughness. A woman in Lyons was fined £14 last month for smoking a cigarette while driving because she had only one hand on the wheel. A café owner in Burgundy was given a two-month suspended prison sentence last year for 'complicity in drunk-driving' because he had served a bottle of wine to a client who was intoxicated. The man later caused a fatal accident.

The Times, 6 October 2004

FIVE KEY FACTS ON THE *ACTUS REUS*

- The *actus reus* comprises all the elements of a crime except the mental element.
- The *actus reus* may consist of conduct (as in appropriating property in theft), a result or consequence (e.g. a death in murder), or a state of affairs as in **Larsonneur 1933, Winzar 1983**.
- Generally, there is no liability in criminal law for omissions, as stated by Stephen L J.
- There are limited exceptions to this rule, as where statute imposes liability (e.g. **Road Traffic Act 1988**), a contract of employment (**Pittwood 1902**), or a public duty (**Dytham 1979**). Liability may also be imposed where there is a special relationship between the parties (**Instan 1893, Gibbins and Proctor 1918**), where one party voluntarily accepts liability (**Stone and Dobinson 1977**), or where there is a dangerous situation that the person creating the danger fails to put right (**Miller 1983**).
- If liability cannot be imposed in this way, the courts may be prepared to say that there is a continuing act rather than a later omission (**Fagan v MPC 1969**).

---

policeman's foot and then keeping the car there was one continuous act, not an act followed by an omission i.e. a failure to put right the wrong. Fagan's conviction, therefore, was upheld.

2.4.5 SUGGESTED REFORM

The various bodies who seek to reform criminal law appear to be very undecided on the subject of liability for omissions. In 1980, the Criminal Law Revision Committee recommended that liability for omissions for offences against the person should be restricted to serious crimes. In 1989, however, the Law Commission took the opposite approach and suggested widening liability for omissions, proposing that some offences could be redrafted to allow for this.

The latest recommendations are in a Law Commission Report of 1993 *(No. 218)*. Attached to this report is the *Draft Criminal Law Bill*, ready to be put before Parliament. This ignores the earlier proposals of the Commission to widen liability and follows instead the reforms suggested in 1980!

Clause 19 of the Bill states that a party may be liable for omissions in the range of situations already laid down by the judges, but confines liability to serious offences, such as intentional serious injury, torture, unlawful detention, kidnapping, abduction and aggravated abduction.

The *Draft Criminal Law Bill*, therefore, would not provide for more general liability for omissions. It does, however, recognise the '**Miller** principle', in *Clause 23. This clause states that a person will commit an offence where he fails to act, which may not at that stage be unlawful, but then fails to take reasonable steps to deal with the results of that act.*

2.5 THE *MENS REA* OF A CRIME

In addition to proving that the *actus reus* exists, in most cases it will also be necessary to show that the defendant has committed the offence with the relevant *mens rea*, i.e. the degree of blameworthiness required by the offence in question. It will be noted towards the end of this chapter, however, that some offences, usually those of a regulatory nature, do not require fault to be proved. These are offences of strict liability. The latter crimes are increasing but are still in the minority. In the case of other offences, some form of *mens rea* will have to be established before guilt can be shown.

2.5.1 THE DIFFERENT DEGREES OF *MENS REA*

In relation to the most serious criminal offences, the prosecution will normally need to prove a high degree of blameworthiness. The defendant will only be found guilty if it is shown that he intended to commit the crime in question. This form of *mens rea* is necessary before the offence of murder is established. The accused will only be convicted if the jury is convinced that he intended to kill or cause grievous bodily harm. Under **s18 Offences Against the Person Act 1861**, the accused can only be convicted for this most serious of non-fatal offences if he maliciously wounds another or causes grievous bodily harm, **'with intent to do some grievous bodily harm'**. Intention is also needed for the crime of theft. The defendant will not be guilty of this offence unless it is shown that he appropriated property belonging to another, **'with the intention of permanently depriving the other of it'**.

Specific intent crimes

The above-mentioned crimes are all examples of specific intent crimes. Apart from the crime of murder, which appears to be in a class of its own, they require some extra intent, (sometimes called an ulterior intent), to be shown before the crime is committed. For example, under **s18**, not only must grievous bodily harm or malicious wounding be established, it must also be proved that the defendant intended to inflict serious harm (gbh).

Basic intent crimes

Other crimes do not necessarily require such a high degree of fault. They can be committed either intentionally or recklessly. The other non-fatal offences against the person noted in Chapter 6 all come into this category. These are the offences of assault, battery, assault occasioning actual bodily harm and malicious wounding or grievous bodily harm under **s20 Offences Against the Person Act**; other crimes are rape and basic criminal damage.

In a small number of cases, it is even enough to establish mere negligence. This is comparatively common in civil law, which has laid down a duty not to be negligent in a wide variety of situations. In criminal law the defendant will not normally be liable for careless acts, even where these cause harm to another person. There are, however, notable exceptions to this general rule, where criminal liability has been imposed. One example is driving without due care or attention. A much more serious offence that can be committed negligently is manslaughter although, as will be seen in Chapter 5 on involuntary manslaughter, the negligence in such a case must be 'gross'.

The difference between basic and specific intent crimes is important when deciding whether the defence of intoxication can be pleaded and will be examined more fully in Chapter 10, It is now necessary to look at these three states of mind, intention, recklessness and negligence, in more detail.

2.5.2 INTENTION

We have noted that liability for crimes like murder and theft can only be established if the jury is satisfied that the defendant intended to commit the offence. Unfortunately there is no statutory definition of the word 'intention' and it is the jury that has to decide whether this state of mind exists. This can be a difficult task because it is obviously impossible to crawl inside the mind of the offender to ascertain his thinking at the time of the crime. Instead, all the evidence must be examined and an opinion reached.

The difference between intention, motive and desire

What has been made clear by the judges is that the word 'intention' is not to be equated with the word 'desire' or the word 'motive'.

We might perhaps consider robbing a bank should we be faced with severe financial problems and might even have the desire to inflict injury on those we feel responsible for our predicament. Provided that these remain as mere thoughts, we cannot be brought before a court of law, no matter how strong the desire may be. **It was clearly stated in Cunliffe v Goodman 1950 that intention is a state of affairs 'that a person does more than merely contemplate'.**

In addition, the intention to commit a crime should not normally be confused with the motive for doing this. The defendant might feel quite justified in acting as he did but, provided that the intention to commit the crime is present, the *mens rea* will have been established and his motive is irrelevant at this point. The defendant will have to hope that his reason for committing the offence is taken into account at the sentencing process.

In **Chandler v DPP 1964**, the defendant was very much opposed to the use of nuclear weapons and had been involved in a 'sit in' at a military base with the purpose of preventing aircraft containing such missiles from taking off. He was charged with breaking into a prohibited place with a purpose prejudicial to the safety and interests of the state but argued that he did not have the appropriate *mens rea* for this offence. He claimed that his purpose was to save the State from the dangers of nuclear weapons.

The case reached the House of Lords, where it was established that the defendant's motive was irrelevant. The immediate purpose of the offender was to break into the airfield and cause an obstruction.

In the earlier case of **Steane 1947** the courts had been more prepared to consider the motive of the defendant. The latter had appealed against a conviction for doing acts with the intention of assisting the enemy during the Second World War. He had broadcast favourable propaganda for the Nazi regime but argued that he had only done this after being beaten and after threats that he and his family would be sent to a concentration camp if he refused to help.

His conviction was quashed, despite the fact that his immediate purpose had been to help the enemy. Lord Goddard was obviously sympathetic and compared the defendant's action to those of prisoners of war who are also forced to do unpleasant acts to assist the captors.

Despite this case, which has not been expressly overruled, the current approach is to separate motive and intention, in all but 'racially aggravated offences' and to use other methods, such as the defence of duress or a reduced sentence, to ensure that any special circumstances are taken into account.

Direct intention

In many cases it will not be too difficult for the jurors to decide whether the defendant had the required *mens rea* – they can deduce this from the circumstances. For example, if a leader of a gang took a gun with him, that he had deliberately loaded, and fired it point blank at a rival gang leader at an arranged meeting, it would be obvious that he intended to kill or at least cause serious injury to that other person. A suicide bomber, with explosives strapped to her waist, driving her car straight at a crowd, would also be seen as having such an intent, whatever her motives for committing such a crime. Most jurors would have little difficulty in finding the necessary intention in such circumstances, if she survived the attack.

Such an intention is referred to in law as **'direct intent'**. In such cases, the judges have made it clear that the jury requires no extra help from the trial judge.

Oblique intention

This form of intent has caused great problems in this area of law. This could arise where the purpose of the offender in committing the crime is different to the result. For example, a pensioner facing extreme poverty because of the unwise dealings of his pension provider, might decide to start a fire in the latter's building in the early hours of the morning, with the purpose of drawing attention to his plight. Unbeknown to him, three cleaners working throughout the night perish in the blaze. Should the arsonist also be found guilty of murder? Some would take the view that any reasonable person would have given thought to the possibility of people still being in the building and that the answer should be a resounding 'yes'. Others would argue that it is what was in the defendant's mind that is important and that he should not be found guilty of murder unless it can be shown that he foresaw the possible results of his action. Although, ultimately, it is up to the jury to decide on this matter, the judges have decided that, in this type of situation, some guidance in reaching their decision, should be given to the jurors. Unfortunately for law students, the form this guidance has taken has varied greatly over the years, ranging from the objective approach taken in the case of **DPP v Smith 1961**, to a more subjective one. The latter approach takes the state of mind of the defendant into account, as seen in the cases of **Nedrick 1986** and **Woollin 1998**. The current guidance in cases of oblique intent is stated below but we also need to understand how this position came to be established. It shows that the judges themselves have difficulties in deciding such complex issues.

The current state of the law on oblique intention in murder cases

This was expressed by the House of Lords in the case of Woollin 1998. Their Lordships clearly affirmed that it is the jury's task to determine whether the defendant intended to kill or cause serious bodily harm. In cases of oblique intent, however, the jury should be further directed that they are not entitled to find the necessary intention unless they feel sure that death or serious bodily harm was a virtually certain result of the defendant's action (barring some unforeseen intervention) and the defendant had appreciated this fact.

To understand how this direction was eventually reached, we need to look at six major cases starting back in 1961, where the defendant was charged with murder but alleged that it was not his purpose to commit such a crime.

The early view of intention

In **DPP v Smith 1961**, the defendant had been ordered to leave his car, which contained stolen goods. Instead, he accelerated sharply and drove off at great speed with the policeman clinging to the vehicle. The officer was thrown off and into the path of an oncoming car and died from his injuries. Smith was charged with murder and convicted.

The House of Lords upheld the conviction, deciding that the defendant had the necessary intention for murder if an ordinary responsible man, in similar circumstances would have contemplated the end result.

At this stage, therefore, an objective test had been laid down for establishing intention in murder cases, a view that was strongly criticised by academics and later led to intervention from the newly formed **Law Commission**. On the advice of this body, **s8 Criminal Justice Act 1967** was enacted.

S8 states that the jury is not bound in law to infer that the defendant intended or foresaw a result of his actions just because it was a natural and probable consequence of them. It should, instead, make the decision about whether he did have such an intention or foresight by looking at all the evidence and drawing the proper conclusions from that.

It can be seen therefore, that others are not supposed to tell the jury what it must do in such a situation. The jurors must, instead look at the matter in a more subjective way and after looking at all the evidence decide what the actual defendant intended or foresaw, not look at the matter from the viewpoint of the reasonable man, as suggested in **Smith**.

In the case of **Hyam v DPP 1975**, the defendant became very jealous when another woman took her place in the affections of her man friend. In the early hours of the morning, she poured petrol through this woman's letterbox and set fire to it. In the resulting blaze, two children died.

Hyam argued that she never had any intention to kill, she merely intended to frighten the other woman. Her case reached the House of Lords, which rejected her appeal.

The judges varied in their reasons for dismissing the appeal but two of them at least gave the impression that intention was established if it was shown that the defendant foresaw the result as **highly probable**. Lord Hailsham did not subscribe to this view and his words were picked up by judges of the Court of Appeal in two non-fatal injury cases, that of **Mohan 1976** and **Belfon 1976**.

These judges decided that mere foresight that death or personal injury was highly probable was not the same as having the intention to cause the act in question. Instead, it was merely evidence for the jury to look at, when deciding whether an intention was present.

The meaning of the word 'intention' resurfaced in the case of **Moloney 1985**. The defendant had been drinking late at night with his stepfather at a Ruby Wedding anniversary celebration. Evidence showed that the parties were on good terms but, later, a disagreement broke out over which of them could load a shotgun in the fastest time. The stepson won this argument and then claimed that his stepfather dared him to pull the trigger. He did so and the stepfather was killed.

Moloney was convicted of murder but the House of Lords changed the verdict to manslaughter. Lord Bridge delivered the main judgment. He stated:

> *The golden rule should be that, when directing a jury on the mental element necessary in a crime of specific intent, the judge should avoid any elaboration or paraphrase of what it meant by intent, and leave it to the jury's good sense to decide whether the accused acted with the necessary intent, unless the judge is convinced that . . . some further explanation or elaboration is strictly necessary to avoid misunderstanding.*

He went on to say that he thought that such cases would be very rare, even where the death is more indirect.

This part of his judgment was approved of in later cases but problems arose over the form the direction to the jury should take when those 'rare occurrences' arose. He said that the jury should be asked to decide on two matters:

> *First, was death or really serious injury in a murder case . . . a natural consequence of the defendant's act? Secondly, did the defendant foresee that consequence as being a natural consequence of his act? The jury should then be told that if they answer yes to both questions it is a proper inference for them to draw that he intended that consequence.*

These complicated 'Moloney guidelines' as they came to be called were criticised in the case of **Hancock and Shankland 1986**. The case concerned two striking miners who were bitterly angry when another miner went back to work. They pushed a heavy concrete block and post from a bridge onto the motorway in front of the taxi and police escort taking the miner to work. The taxi driver was killed. The trial judge diligently recited the Moloney guidelines to the jury and the defendants were convicted of murder. The Court of Appeal quashed the conviction arguing that the Moloney guidelines were deficient.

In the House of Lords, Lord Scarman agreed with this and stated that the Moloney guidelines were 'unsafe and misleading'. He declined to put others in their place, even though the Lord Chief Justice in the Court of Appeal had suggested rather lengthy ones! He did go on to reiterate, however, that it was the jurors who should decide whether the intention to kill existed, after looking at all the evidence in the case.

This case established that the Moloney guidelines should no longer be used. Both the appeal courts also stressed that even where there is a belief that the defendant must have known that the consequences of his act were virtually certain, this is not the same as saying that he has an intention to kill. The members of the jury must still decide on this point.

The matter came up again in the case of **Nedrick 1986**, a case with very similar facts to **Hyam**. The defendant poured petrol through a letterbox and set it alight and the death of an innocent child resulted. The jury convicted Nedrick of murder. The trial at first instance was heard before the case of **Moloney** reached the House of Lords and, was, of course, also before the modifications made in **Hancock and Shankland**. The judge had therefore directed the jury in a way that followed the House of Lords' decision in **Hyam**. The appeal against the conviction for murder was accepted because of the later changes that had been made in this area of law.

Lord Lane decided that the correct direction to the jurors should now be to tell them that:

> *if they are satisfied that at the material time the defendant recognised that death or serious injury would be virtually certain, (barring some unforeseen intervention) to result from his voluntary act, then that is a fact from which they may find it easy to*

> *infer that he intended to kill or do serious bodily harm, even though he may not have had any desire to achieve that result.*

Lord Lane also stated more forcibly, later in his judgment, that 'Where the charge is murder and in the rare cases where the simple direction is not enough, the jury should be directed that they are not entitled to infer the necessary intention unless they feel sure that death or serious bodily harm was a virtual certainty (barring some unforeseen intervention) as a result of the defendant's actions and that the defendant appreciated that this was the case.'

This appeared to be the clearest statement so far and, as will be seen, was the one that came to be favoured. In the meantime, however, certain decisions continued to cause confusion.

In **Walker and Hayles 1990**, an attempted murder case, the conviction was upheld, even though it was claimed that the judge had misdirected the jurors on the lines that they could also infer the necessary intention if the defendant foresaw the consequences of his act as being 'highly probable'. The Court of Appeal stated:

> *once one departs from absolute certainty, there is bound to be a question of degree. We do not regard the difference of degree, if there is one, between a very high degree of probability on the one hand and virtual certainty on the other as being sufficient to render what the recorder said a misdirection.*

The court did, however, go on to state that it would prefer the words 'virtually certain' to be used.

The leading case of Woollin

The House of Lords then became involved again in the case of **Woollin 1998**. The defendant was alleged to have violently shaken his three-month-old baby and then thrown him across the room in the direction of his pram four or five feet away. Woollin admitted in later interviews that the baby had hit the floor hard but claimed that he 'did not think it would kill him', although he accepted that there was a risk of injury.

In addition to giving the model direction in **Nedrick**, the trial judge had later told the jurors that they might infer intention '**if they were satisfied that when the defendant threw the child he appreciated that there was a substantial risk that he would cause serious harm to it**'. The defence claimed in the appeal that such a direction 'might therefore have served to confuse or mislead the jury as to the degree of foresight required'.

The Court of Appeal decided that there was no misdirection. The issue was then referred to the House of Lords and, as already noted, their Lordships disagreed with the Court of Appeal's decision. The point of law put before that court was quite a narrow one. It concerned murder cases where there is no direct evidence that D's purpose was to kill or inflict serious injury on V and asked:

> . . . is it necessary to direct the jury that they may only infer an intent to do serious injury if they are satisfied (a) that serious bodily harm was a virtually certain consequence of D's voluntary act and (b) that D appreciated that fact?

The answer was in the affirmative although Lord Steyn decided that the word 'find' should be used instead of the word 'infer'. Apart from this modification therefore, the middle part of the judgment of the Court of Appeal in Nedrick was considered to be a correct statement of the law. The jurors will still decide the issue but, where the charge is murder, their discretion has been fettered and they can only find intention when they are satisfied that death or serious bodily harm was virtually certain (barring some unforeseen intervention) and the defendant appreciated this fact.

Woollin's conviction for murder therefore, was quashed and one of manslaughter

substituted instead. Even though the judge had, at an earlier time, given a correct direction under the Nedrick guidelines, the House of Lords decided that he had later confused the jury by his comments the next day concerning 'a substantial risk', thus giving a wider direction. As it was impossible to know which of the two statements the jury had followed, this must therefore be considered a material misdirection that could not be cured by the inclusion of the earlier correct statement of the law.

◀ *Comment*

The decision in **Woollin** has made the law more certain in some respects but, unfortunately, leaves other issues unresolved.

Plus points

- The new direction concerning oblique intention in murder cases is mercifully brief and easy for a jury to understand. Their Lordships had stressed the need for any direction to be '**clear and simple and expressed in as few words as possible**'. This modification by them of the middle part of the judgment in **Nedrick** has this advantage, particularly when compared to the lengthy statements formulated by Lord Bridge in **Moloney** and those suggested by the Court of Appeal in **Hankcock v Shankland**, which could well have confused a jury.
- The line between intention and recklessness has now been firmly drawn. The fact that death or serious injury might have been '**highly probable**' or '**a substantial risk**' is no longer sufficient in cases of murder.
- There are now clear instructions as to what the members of the jury cannot do

in cases of murder, i.e. they are not entitled to find a person guilty of murder unless they are sure that death or serious bodily harm was virtually certain and the defendant appreciated this fact.

- It appears that the case of **Hyam** has at last been put to rest. The late Sir John Smith stated forcefully:

  > *Their Lordships have often been unnecessarily – and dangerously – coy about declaring that their brethren or predecessors have got it wrong. Lord Steyn now recognises the truth about Hyam. It was not materially different from Nedrick; and in Nedrick the conviction was rightly quashed.*

Areas of confusion

- It is unclear whether the modified direction in **Woollin** had the endorsement of all five Law Lords. While two of the judges expressly agreed with the judgment of Lord Steyn, Lord Browne-Wilkinson and Lord Goff only agreed that the appeal should be allowed, thus suggesting that they might not have agreed with all of Lord Steyn's reasoning.

- The point of law certified for the House of Lords only related to the crime of murder and Lord Steyn stated that a different approach to the word 'intention' could be taken where other offences were concerned. This matter needs clarification.

- With regard to the crime of attempted murder, the case of **Walker & Hayles** was not expressly overruled. It would be strange however, if a different standard were to apply to this lesser

crime and an offender found guilty if he foresaw the consequences of his actions as being **'highly probable'**. It is a matter of regret that such a simple issue was not addressed by their Lordships.

- There is still some debate as to whether the foresight of a consequence as being virtually certain actually amounts to intention, thus giving the jury no discretion on the matter or whether it is still only evidence from which the jury can make the ultimate decision. In **Nedrick**, the Court of Appeal's final direction appeared to be that foresight of a consequence as being virtually certain was not the same as intention. Part of the direction stated that the jury was merely entitled to infer intention if death or serious bodily harm was a virtual certainty. **From this, it can be presumed that they were not compelled to do so. It is submitted that, following the statements made in the cases of Woollin and Matthews and Alleye, (mentioned below), the latter view is the current state of the law.**

In **Woollin**, Lord Steyn appeared to accept this fact by retaining the word **'entitled'** in his revised direction. The amended direction states that the jurors are not entitled to find intention unless they are sure that the defendant foresaw that death or serious injury was virtually certain. Nevertheless, once they have decided on this issue, they appear to have some discretion about their eventual decision. **It would appear from this that foresight of virtually certain consequences is not therefore the same as intention. It is still only evidence on which the jury may find it.**

Others would point to the fact that Lord Steyn changed the word 'infer' which appeared in the **Nedrick** direction, to that of 'find', and thus by this action was acknowledging the concerns expressed by academics like Glanville Williams and Ashworth over the use of the former word. They would go on to argue that it follows from this that the House of Lords is now accepting the view that foresight that a consequence is a virtual certainty actually equates to intention. To support this, they would draw our attention to the fact that Lord Steyn quoted with apparent approval a statement in **Nedrick** declaring that '**A result foreseen as virtually certain is an intended result**'.

This is in line with a view expressed earlier by Professor Glanville Williams. He stated back in 1989 that:

> *The proper view is that intention includes not only desire of consequence (purpose) but also foresight of certainty of the consequence, as a matter of legal definition.*

The late Sir John Smith also endorsed this approach. He stated in his commentary on the case:

> *If that is right, the only question for the jury is 'Did the defendant foresee the result as virtually certain? If he did, he intended it.' That, it is submitted is what the law should be; and it now seems that we have at last moved substantially in that direction.*

Be that as it may, I would argue that we have not reached that destination. The matter came to the fore again in the case of **Matthews and Alleyne 2003**. The defendants had been convicted of murder, after throwing the victim from a bridge. The Court of Appeal was called upon to decide whether the trial judge had misdirected the jury with his guidelines on the meaning of intention. He stated that the prosecution will only prove such an intent either:

> (i) *by making you sure that this specific intention was actually in the minds of the defendants, or*
> (ii) (a) *by making you sure that the deceased's death was a virtual certainty (barring some attempts to save him), and*
> (b) *the defendant whose case you are considering appreciated at the time the deceased was thrown off the bridge that this was the case and he then had no intention of saving him, and knew or realised that the others did not intend to save him either*

The defendants had appealed on the grounds that this was a misdirection, arguing that the second point was stated by the judge as a rule of law, rather than a mere rule of evidence that the jury should take into account.

The Court of Appeal stated clearly that acting deliberately, appreciating that death was virtually certain, did not in itself amount to an intent to kill. It noted, instead, that it was evidence from which an intent to kill could be inferred. (A point of interest is that the Court of Appeal has resurrected the word 'inferred' here, rather than using the word 'find', which was preferred by the House of Lords in

Woollin.) Despite this, the appeals were dismissed. The court took the view that if the jury were sure that the appellants appreciated the virtual certainty of death when they threw the victim over the bridge, and also that they had no intention of saving him from such death, it was impossible to see how they could not have found that the appellants intended the victim to die.

The Court of Appeal then added that if what was required was an appreciation of virtual certainty of death, and not some lesser foresight of merely probable consequences, there was very little to choose between a rule of evidence and one of substantive law. It did not, however, state that foresight of a consequence as being virtually certain actually amounts to intention. Further cases on this subject are almost inevitable.

In view of all the problems caused by trying to give additional guidance to the jury, it could be argued that it would be better to leave the matter completely to them, after drawing their attention to s8 **Criminal Justice Act 1967**.

A more effective move might be to put pressure on Parliament to formulate a statutory definition of intention, perhaps on the lines suggested below. This would deal with the issue as a matter of law and take the pressure off the jury. The latter could then do the task asked of them, which is to apply the law to the facts, after a suitable direction on it has been given to them by the judge.

Activity

- In essay form or in group discussion, assess the truth of the following statement:

  'foresight of a consequence as being virtually certain is not the same as intention'.

- Brigitte belonged to a fringe animal rights group. She was very upset when a Private Member's Bill outlawing fishing was defeated in the House of Commons. She therefore decided to set fire to the building to draw attention to the cause. There was a late night sitting in Parliament at the time and two MPs were overcome with smoke and died. Brigitte has been charged with the crime of murder.

Advise the judge and jury how they should approach the subject of deciding whether Brigitte had the necessary *mens rea* for this offence.

TEN KEY FACTS ON INTENTION

- The *mens rea* of an offence usually consists of intention or recklessness, although in a small percentage of crimes, mere negligence will suffice. Manslaughter is one such crime, provided that the negligence is gross. In a small amount of criminal offences, often ones of a regulatory nature, liability might be strict.

- The word 'intention' is not defined by statute although there have been repeated calls for reform.

- The judges have made it clear that the word 'intention' is not normally to be equated with the words 'desire' (**Cunliffe v Goodman 1950**), or 'motive' (**Chandler v DPP 1964**), but note the new 'racially aggravated' offences under the **Crime and Disorder Act 1998**, under which the defendant's motive may well be a factor.

- **S8 Criminal Justice Act 1967** tells the jury that they should make the decision about whether the defendant had the necessary intention or foresight by looking at all the evidence and drawing the proper conclusions from that.

- Where it is obviously the purpose of the defendant to achieve the intended result he is stated to have a direct intent to commit the crime in question. In other cases, the actual consequence may not have been his original purpose. These are known as cases of oblique intent.

- In cases of direct intent, the jury will be asked to decide whether the defendant had the intention to commit the crime without any additional guidance from the judge. In cases where the defendant is claiming that it was not his purpose to kill or seriously injure the victim or cause him other harm but where nonetheless this has happened, a further direction from the judge may be deemed to be necessary (**Moloney 1986**).

- The wording of such a direction has changed several times, as seen in cases such as **Smith, Hyam, Maloney, Hancock and Shankland** and **Nedrick**. Part of the direction in the latter case was approved of, with some modification, by the House of Lords in **Woollin 1998**. This amended direction states that, in cases where the charge is murder, the jury is not entitled to find intention unless it is sure that death or serious bodily harm was a virtual certainty and the defendant appreciated this fact. This is very similar to the direction suggested by Lord Lane in **Nedrick**, except that he used the word 'infer'. This has now been changed to the word 'find', which appears to give the jury less choice in the matter.

- In cases of murder it is not now sufficient to show a lesser degree of blameworthiness, such as the defendant being aware that death or serious bodily harm was 'highly probable' (**Walker and Hayles 1990**) or that he appreciated 'that there was a substantial risk' of this consequence (**Woollin 1998**). The **Nedrick** wording, as modified by the House of Lords in **Woollin**, must be used. The blurring of the lines between intention and recklessness has therefore been halted.

- There has been considerable debate as to whether foresight of a consequence as virtually certain actually amounts to intention as a matter of law or merely permits the jury to find intention once this has been established. The latter view seems to prevail (**Matthews and Alleyne 2003**). Other problems with the **Woollin** direction should also be noted.

- **In Woollin**, the House of Lords made it clear that the word 'intent' need not necessarily have the same meaning in lesser crimes.

Suggested reform of intention

There have been three reports on this, a Law Commission Report in 1989, with the *Draft Criminal Code*, a report from the Select Committee of the House of Lords on *Murder and Life Imprisonment*, which echoed the views of the Commission and, finally the definition of intention in the Law Commission's report *'Legislating the Criminal Code: Offences Against the Person and General Principles' (Law Com No. 218 1993)*. The latter only applies to non-fatal offences but it is assumed that the same definition would be used for fatal offences. This states that a person is classed as acting 'intentionally' when 'it is his purpose to cause it, or, although it is not his purpose to cause that result, he knows it would occur in the ordinary course of events if he were to succeed in his purpose of causing some other result'.

2.5.3 RECKLESSNESS

The preceding part of this chapter showed how difficult it can be in some cases to prove that the defendant intended to commit the crime in question. **For many offences, however, it is not necessary to show such a high degree of blameworthiness; it is sufficient to prove that the accused has been reckless as to whether the crime was committed**.

What is recklessness?

Recklessness is the taking of an unjustifiable risk. Not all risks come into this category. For example, a surgeon may decide to perform a delicate operation on a patient, which only has a 50:50 chance of success but knowing that it will give that patient a much better quality of life if it succeeds. Provided that the patient consents, there is obvious social utility in allowing the doctor to proceed without the fear of facing criminal liability if the operation is a failure.

Other actions demonstrate clearly that the risk is unjustifiable. The throwing of a firework into a crowd of people would be such a case; the offender would be taking an unjustifiable risk that someone in the crowd might be harmed and it would be felt right for such a person to face criminal charges if that happened.

The two types of recklessness

Confusion has arisen over the legal definition of the word '**reckless**' because of the different opinions as to the degree of recklessness to be shown.

- **Some would argue that a defendant should only be liable if he had actually foreseen that he was taking an unjustified risk. (This takes a subjective view of the matter; if the defendant did not foresee that he was acting recklessly, he must be acquitted.)**
- **Others are of the belief that the defendant could also be convicted if he ought to have foreseen such a risk, i.e. if a reasonable man would have foreseen that the risk was unjustifiable. (This takes a more objective view of the circumstances, making it easier to establish guilt.)**

These two types of recklessness are known respectively as **Cunningham** and **Caldwell** recklessness, after cases of those names, which laid down different types of recklessness for different crimes. **The current state of the law is to be found in the case of G and another 2003, a House of Lords decision. Their Lordships decided that Cunningham recklessness, the more subjective form of recklessness, is the one to be used for crimes where recklessness is part of the *mens rea*.** We need, however, to investigate how the law on this subject developed.

Cunningham recklessness

Before the case of **Caldwell 1982**, the judges had decided that the more subjective approach was the one to be used, i.e. **before the defendant could be said to be liable, he must have been aware that he was taking an unjustifiable risk**.

This was established in the case of **Cunningham 1957**. It was stated that this type of recklessness had to be shown in any case where the old-fashioned word 'malicious' was used. The offence of malicious wounding is an example and another is shown in the case of **Cunnningham** itself, i.e. the strangely worded crime of **'maliciously administering a noxious thing so as to endanger life'**, contrary to **s3 Offences Against the Person Act 1861**.

The defendant stole money from a gas meter and in so doing, tore the meter from the wall and left the gas pipes exposed. Gas then seeped through the porous walls into the basement of the house next door and affected a woman living there. Cunningham was convicted but made a successful appeal. It was held that the judge had misdirected the jury by telling them that the word 'malicious' simply meant 'wicked', instead of giving it its more precise legal meaning.

The Appeal Court stated that when the word 'malicious' was used in a statute, it was necessary to establish that the defendant had either intended to cause the harm in question or he had foreseen that such an event would occur.

On this test, Cunningham could only be convicted if he knew of the risk from the gas but, nevertheless, went on to take it. It was not enough that he ought to have foreseen such a risk; the test was subjective. This ruling was therefore held to apply to all cases that had the word **'malicious'** in the offence and in **Parmenter 1991**, a conviction for malicious wounding was quashed because such a direction had not been given.

For several years, this test was also felt to be of a more general application, even in newer statutes where the word **'reckless'** was used, as in the case of the **Criminal Damage Act 1971**. In this statute, the word **'reckless'** had replaced the word **'malicious'** which had been used in the **Malicious Damage Act 1861** preceding it. Before the new act was put before Parliament, the Law Commission had considered the mental element needed for this offence and had decided that the old law was satisfactory in this respect, although it needed to be expressed more clearly. This was effected by using the words **'intentionally'** and **'recklessly'**, instead of the word **'maliciously'**. **No definition of recklessness was provided in the Act, so it was therefore believed that the law remained substantially the same, despite the change in wording, i.e. it was believed that the Cunningham test continued to apply.**

This view was followed in the case of **Stephenson 1979**. The defendant was a schizophrenic and had decided to sleep in a haystack. He lit a fire to keep himself warm and caused £300 worth of damage. Such a result would obviously have been foreseen by an ordinary **'reasonable'** man, but the Court of Appeal quashed the conviction.

Lord Lane was emphatic that the test was subjective: 'we wish to make it clear that the test remains subjective, that the knowledge or appreciation of risk of some damage must have entered the defendant's mind even though he may have suppressed it'.

Caldwell recklessness

This then was the position until the cases of **Caldwell** and **Lawrence**, in **1982**. These two cases were decided by the House of Lords on the same day and, together, they introduced a high degree of uncertainty into this area of law.

In **Caldwell 1982**, the defendant had been engaged to work for the proprietor of a residential hotel but had been dismissed and nursed a grievance against the owner. When he was very drunk, Caldwell broke a window in the hotel and started a fire on the ground floor. Fortunately, this was discovered and put out quite quickly and no serious harm was done, either in the form of personal injury to the ten people residing in the hotel, or in the form of property damage.

Caldwell was prepared to admit to the lesser charge of criminal damage but fiercely resisted the more serious charge of causing criminal damage with intent to endanger life or being reckless as to whether life would be endangered. Despite this, the jury found him guilty and he was sentenced to three years' imprisonment.

The case eventually reached the House of Lords where Lord Diplock gave the main speech and changed the law on recklessness, at least for the crime of criminal damage. Diplock argued:

> *that the only person who knows what the accused's mental processes were at the time of committing the crime is the accused himself and probably not even he can recall them accurately when the rage or excitement under which he acted has passed or he has sobered up if he were under the influence of drink at the end of the relevant time.*

He therefore believed that the test for recklessness should be widened to encompass a wider range of situations. He decided that a person is reckless under the Criminal Damage Act 1971 if:

1 **He does an act which in fact creates an obvious risk that property will be destroyed or damaged, and**

2 **when he does the act he either has not given any thought to the possibility of there being any such risk or has recognised that there was some risk involved and has nonetheless gone on to do it.**

Caldwell's appeal therefore was dismissed and a wider test of recklessness had emerged on a three to two majority. Lord Edmund Davies and Lord Wilberforce dissented on this point but upheld the conviction.

It should be noted, however, that **Cunningham** recklessness had not disappeared in this new test; it is included in the second half of point two, i.e. the defendant has recognised that there may be some risk involved but has nonetheless gone on to take it. It was the other part of the test which has the effect of widening liability substantially. It included situations where there was a risk, which would have been obvious to a reasonable man, but the defendant in question had not given any thought to it.

Lord Diplock believed that such an extension of liability was both necessary and justifiable, because of the difficulties of trying to gauge the state of the defendant's mind. He argued that **Cunningham**-style recklessness had been developed for a special purpose, i.e. to deal with statutes containing the word '**malicious**', which seemed to indicate some foreseeability on the part of the defendant. The **Criminal Damage Act**, on the other hand, had substituted the word '**reckless**', so he argued that the same approach was not necessary. He also stated that it was not helpful to classify types of recklessness into subjective and objective categories but, despite this plea, that is exactly what had happened.

Judgment in the case of **Lawrence** was also given by the House of Lords on the same day as **Caldwell** but after that decision, and by a differently constituted court, although Lord Diplock was included in both sittings. In **Lawrence**, the House, in a reckless driving case, upheld the wider definition of recklessness, laid down in **Caldwell**.

A motorcyclist had collided with and killed a pedestrian and the House held that there had been an obvious and serious risk, to which Lawrence had failed to advert. His conviction, therefore, was upheld.

Later cases followed this new approach. In **Reid 1992**, discussed more fully below, Lord Keith stated that the:

> *'absence of something from a person's state of mind is as much part of his state of mind as is its presence'.*

Criticisms of the decision in Caldwell

Lord Diplock's attempt to clarify the law on recklessness and, arguably, to make his new test one of universal application, attracted great criticism from both judges and academics. It was said that the change in the law was 'regrettable' (Professor Glanville Williams), that the test was 'not very helpful' (Lord Browne-Wilkinson) and was one which made the eyes of the jury 'glaze over' when it was put to them (the late Sir John Smith).

Caldwell recklessness, therefore, far from becoming of universal application, was attacked from the beginning and its use has been increasingly restricted. The Court of Appeal confirmed that the more subjective Cunningham recklessness was the test to use for offences containing the word 'malicious', as in the offence of malicious wounding. This was seen in W (a minor) v Dolbey 1989, where a boy of fifteen wounded another with an airgun. The boy argued that he thought the gun was unloaded.

His conviction for unlawful wounding was quashed because the more objective test had been applied and this was held to be incorrect for this type of offence.

In Savage and Parmenter 1992, the House of Lords also agreed that Cunningham recklessness was necessary for cases of assault, as will be noted in Chapter 6.

Over time, it was decided that Cunningham, rather than Caldwell recklessness, was necessary for a conviction in cases of rape, attempted rape, different types of assault and for any cases where the word 'malicious' appears in the definition of the offence. In addition, the Caldwell test no longer had any application in driving offences because reckless driving had been replaced by dangerous driving. It will be noted in Chapter 5 that reckless manslaughter, for which Caldwell recklessness would have sufficed, has also disappeared and been replaced by manslaughter by gross negligence.

When did Caldwell recklessness still apply?

Caldwell recklessness appeared to be limited to criminal damage, as discussed in Chapter 9, i.e.

basic criminal damage, criminal damage with intent to endanger life or being reckless as to whether life will be endangered, and arson, i.e. basic or aggravated criminal damage caused by fire. In these cases the more objective test in Caldwell was strictly applied, sometimes with unjust results.

In Elliott v C (a minor) 1983, the defendant was only 14 and of low intelligence. She stayed out all night without sleep and entered a garden shed, where she poured white spirit over a carpet and set light to it and the whole shed was destroyed.

The Divisional Court reluctantly upheld her conviction for criminal damage, because the court was bound by the precedent set in Caldwell, concerning the test of recklessness. There was an obvious risk of fire, even though the girl herself might not have appreciated this fact. Goff L J stated, however: 'I would be lacking in candour if I were to conceal my unhappiness about the conclusion which I feel compelled to reach.'

A similar view was taken in Coles 1995, where a 15 year old boy with learning difficulties set a haystack alight. His conviction under s1(1) and s1(3) of the Criminal Damage Act 1971 was upheld by the Court of Appeal.

A possible loophole in Caldwell recklessness?

It was clear that the test of Caldwell recklessness, when it applied, was a strict one and its use made more offenders liable. It was argued, however, that a possible loophole, or lacuna as it came to be called, existed, through which some offenders might be able to escape conviction. This, it was suggested, could arise where the defendant had considered the possibility of a risk, concluded that none existed and therefore gone ahead with his action.

The matter was considered in the case of Chief Constable of Avon and Somerset v Shimmen 1987. The defendant possessed skills in martial arts and was demonstrating these to his friends.

He intended to land a kick falling just short of a shop window, but his skills were not as great as he imagined and he put his leg through the window. The magistrates were not prepared to convict and the prosecution appealed to the Divisional Court. **The appeal court decided that the lacuna did not apply in this case. The judges decided that the facts showed, instead, that he had perceived that there was at least some risk but had gone ahead anyway; he had not decided that no risk at all existed.**

The Court of Appeal took a similar view in the case of **Merrick 1995**, where the defendant had gained permission to remove some old electrical equipment from a house and in so doing, had left a live cable exposed for six minutes before burying it. He argued that he had believed that there was no risk.

Once again, the judges preferred to take the view that he must have known that there was some risk in the period while the cable was exposed but had thought that the risk was worth taking.

Eventually, the House of Lords was called on to consider this problem. In **Reid 1992**, the defendant was driving in the centre of London and tried to overtake on an inside lane. This narrowed considerably near a junction to allow for a taxi driver's hut. Reid struck this hut and his passenger was killed. He appealed against his conviction for causing death by dangerous driving.

The House of Lords rejected his appeal but went on to discuss certain limited situations in a driving case where someone might not be liable under the Caldwell/Lawrence test:

● **Where the driver acted under an understandable or excusable mistake of fact, (as, for example, overtaking on a hill when driving a left-hand drive vehicle and being misinformed about the safety of such an act, or where a safe manoeuvre suddenly became unsafe because of a fuel blockage).**

● **Where the driver's ability to recognise a possible risk had been affected by a condition which was not his fault, (as, for example, illness or shock).**
● **Where the driver was acting under duress.**

Back to Cunningham recklessness

The case of **G and another 2003** was very similar to the cases of **Elliott** and **Coles,** mentioned above, but eventually a very different decision was reached, despite the fact that the damage was substantial. In the early hours of the morning, two boys, aged 10 and 11, entered the back yard of a Co-op shop, set alight some newspapers they found there and threw them under a wheelie-bin. They then left the premises without waiting to see whether the fire went out. Instead, the fire escalated and travelled to the shop and adjoining buildings, resulting in damage in the region of £1,000,000. Despite the misgivings of both the trial judge and the jury, the boys were found guilty of criminal damage, after the definition of **Caldwell** recklessness had been duly cited. The Court of Appeal, being bound by the latter case, upheld the convictions. The following point of law was then put to the House of Lords:

Can a defendant properly be convicted under s1 of the Criminal Damage Act 1971 on the basis that he was reckless as to whether property was destroyed or damaged when he gave no thought to the risk, but by reason of his age and/or personal characteristics the risk would not have been obvious to him, even if he had thought about it?

The House of Lords decided that the answer was 'no', reversed the decision of the Court of Appeal and reverted to the subjective form of recklessness affirmed in Cunningham, which stated that foresight of the consequences was a necessary ingredient of recklessness. Under this test, if a defendant genuinely failed to appreciate the risk because of his young age or some other characteristic, he should not be found guilty. The case of Caldwell and subsequent ones like Elliott, were overruled.

The decision in more detail

Hopefully all students will remember that, in 1966, the House of Lords, via a Practice Statement, decided that it would no longer be bound by one of its own earlier decisions if the latter was felt to be unjust or unduly restrict the development of the law. It was, however, stressed that the House still supported the doctrine of binding precedent and would only use its new freedom to depart from previous precedents in a very sparing way.

Despite this, all five Law Lords agreed that the case of **Caldwell** should be overruled. Lord Steyn stated that the '**very high threshold for departing from a previous decision**' had been satisfied. Lord Bingham gave the main judgment, with which the other four Law Lords, Lord Browne-Wilkinson, Lord Hutton, Lord Steyn and Lord Rodger concurred.

Lord Bingham gave four reasons for overruling **Caldwell**:

- He believed that the majority of the Law Lords had misinterpreted **s1 Criminal Damage Act** and the meaning of the word 'reckless'. He stated that the judges had 'fallen into understandable but clearly demonstrable error', (very tactful!), by not considering both the Working Paper and the Report of the Law Commission preceding the introduction of the Bill into Parliament. In these preparatory papers, it was made clear that Cunningham recklessness should remain. He felt that this error should not be left to Parliament to correct because the misrepresentation was 'offensive to principle' and liable to cause injustice.

- He argued that it was a necessary ingredient of serious criminal offences that the defendant should only be culpable, if he intended to commit the crime in question or

knew that he was taking an unjustifiable risk. Those who were merely stupid or without imagination, he said, should not be classed as criminal.

- He stressed that the model direction in **Caldwell** could lead to unfairness, as shown in **Elliott** and **Coles** and had been questioned by both trial judges and juries. He commented that, in the current case, the two boys could well have been convicted of damage to the wheelie-bins if the charge had indicated this, because they must have realised that some damage could occur. He strongly argued, however, that it was wrong to adopt an objective approach in relation to the greater damage to the commercial premises, stating:

  > *It is neither moral nor just to convict a defendant (least of all a child) on the strength of what someone else would have apprehended if the defendant himself had no such apprehension. Nor, the defendant having been convicted, is the problem cured by the imposition of a nominal penalty.*

- He noted that the decision in **Caldwell** had led to 'reasoned and outspoken' criticism from many leading academics, such as the late Sir John Smith and Professor Glanville Williams. The highly respected Lord Lords, Lord Edmund-Davies and Lord Wilberforce had also expressed serious misgivings, as had Lords Justices Robert Goff and Ackner and the editors of Archbold.

Lord Steyn was just as forthright. He thought that, in **Caldwell**, the law had taken a wrong turn and that the case for departing from the decision was 'irresistible'. He stated categorically that the majority in **Caldwell** should have accepted 'the overwhelming evidence' that Parliament did not intend to alter the existing meaning of recklessness. He, too, pointed out that the decision in **Caldwell** had been sharply criticised by academics, practitioners, judges and juries and noted that the trend in modern times had swung towards a subjective approach when establishing criminal liability. He also believed that it was now against the Convention on the Rights of a Child, which the UK had ratified in 1990, to ignore the special position of children in the criminal justice system.

Lord Steyn, along with Lord Bingham, did not believe that the **Cunningham** test would allow wrongdoers to escape conviction more easily, arguing that cases before **Caldwell** did not support this view. He went on: 'One can trust the realism of trial judges, who direct juries, to guide juries to sensible verdicts and juries can in turn be relied on to apply robust common sense to the evaluation of ridiculous defences'.

Lord Rodger of Earlsferry added that the test in **Caldwell** was 'notoriously difficult to interpret' and any attempts merely to modify the direction in relation to children would cause even greater confusion. He therefore felt that **Caldwell** should be overruled and the law put 'back on the track that Parliament originally intended'. If the latter body objected to the subjective approach regarding recklessness in cases of criminal damage, it was then up to Parliament to legislate accordingly.

Comment

- The return to **Cunningham** recklessness for offences of criminal damage will be welcomed by many, including most law students! It allows a standard test to be used for all cases including recklessness in their *mens rea*. The **Caldwell** test had introduced a lack of uniformity over criminal liability and blurred what was formerly a clear distinction between recklessness and negligence. It was also very difficult for juries to understand.
- The new test brings the law on this subject in line with current opinion, as expressed by academics, earlier judges and the general public. In addition, all five Law Lords in **G and another** were strongly of the opinion that **Caldwell** was wrong and that Lord Diplock had wrongly interpreted the wishes of the Law Commission and Parliament by introducing a more objective test.

One can perhaps understand why Lord Diplock wished to introduce a wider test for criminal damage when looking at the circumstances in **Caldwell.** It would, however, have caused much less disruption to the law if he had merely decided that drunkenness could not be used as a defence in cases of basic intent and left the *mens rea* for criminal damage as it was.

Activity

- In groups or individually, obtain and read the judgments of the Law Lords in **G and another** and analyse their reasons for overruling **Caldwell**.
- David, aged 14, but with a mental age of 11, ran away from home. As the weather deteriorated, he decided to sleep in the doorway of a furniture store. He made a small fire in order to keep warm and fell asleep. The wind became stronger and the fire spread to a stack of wooden pallets nearby and then to the building itself. By mid-morning when David awoke, much of the furniture inside the shop was ablaze and the staff had to be evacuated.

Advise David, who has been charged with aggravated criminal damage caused by fire.

While use of an objective test might not be too worrying in cases of low-value basic criminal damage, it is a very different matter when the charge is aggravated criminal damage. Here, the maximum sentence is life imprisonment. Past experience shows that the judges are prepared to sentence up to the maximum, especially in cases of arson, and it is highly questionable whether an objective test should be used to decide on the defendant's guilt. In other serious offences where the maximum sentence is life, a subjective approach to liability is taken.

- Another area of great concern was the use of the test for children or those with learning or other difficulties. They were then judged by the standard of the reasonable adult. There was much criticism over the decisions in **Elliott** and **Coles.**

- On the other hand, the use of a subjective test could well make it more difficult for prosecutors to obtain a conviction. The Law Lords were not unduly concerned about this. They pinned their faith on the ability of trial judges and juries to differentiate between genuine and fake defences. Use of the subjective test will, however, place a greater burden on both these groups. It could also result in the CPS 'playing safe' and framing a less serious charge than the events actually warrant. Time will tell!

FIVE KEY FACTS ON RECKLESSNESS

- Recklessness is the taking of an unjustifiable risk. Before 1982, **Cunningham**, or subjective recklessness, was the test to be applied in all cases (**Cunningham 1957**). It seeks to discover whether the defendant was aware that there was an unjustified risk. A subjective approach is taken. Since the important House of Lords' decision in **G and another 2003**, this test is now of universal application.

- Earlier House of Lords' decisions on the same day in **Caldwell** and **Lawrence 1982** had restated the law and laid down a different test in cases of criminal damage and what was then reckless driving. This said that a person was reckless when he did an act which created an obvious risk, in circumstances where he had either not given any thought to the possibility that a risk existed or had given the matter some thought but nevertheless had gone on to take the unjustifiable risk. This introduced a more objective element into the test as shown in **Elliot v C (a minor) 1983** and **Coles 1995**.

- It was suggested that the test should apply to all cases but, with the demise of reckless driving and reckless manslaughter and the refusal of later judges to use it for offences against the person, it came to be restricted to offences of criminal damage.

- The subjective, **Cunningham** test was still used for cases of rape, malicious wounding (**W (a minor) v Dolbey 1989**), assault (**Parmenter 1991**).

- The use of a possible lacuna in the **Caldwell** test, where a person was held to have considered whether a risk existed but then decided that one did not exist, was recognised by the House of Lords but was strictly contained (**Reid 1992**). Now that **Caldwell** has been overruled, this no longer has any part to play.

Possible Reform of Recklessness

The Law Commission, in the *Draft Code* and in later Bills had already suggested a return to subjective recklessness. It proposed that a person acts recklessly with respect to:

(i) a circumstance, when he is aware of a risk that it exists or will exist; and

(ii) a result, when he is aware of a risk that it will occur, and it is unreasonable, having regard to the circumstances known to him, to take that risk.

2.5.4 NEGLIGENCE

Negligence occurs when a person acts in a way that falls below the standard expected of the reasonable person in the same situation as the accused. Such carelessness often incurs liability in civil law but, in addition, there are certain situations where a person would also be liable under the criminal law.

As discovered in the last section, the distinction originally between recklessness and negligence was clearly defined, the former being the deliberate taking of an unjustifiable risk, while the latter was inadvertent risk taking. After the decisions in **Caldwell** and **Lawrence,** however, the line between the two forms of blameworthiness became more blurred. The case of **G and another 2003**, has now restored the earlier position.

Criminal negligence

Negligent acts may suffice to incur liability in driving offences. In **McRone v Riding 1938**, the defendant was a learner driver but, nonetheless, it was decided that he could be convicted of careless driving if his standard fell below that of a reasonably competent driver.

Negligence, albeit negligence of a higher degree, will also suffice for the more serious offences of dangerous driving and causing death by dangerous driving. These offences were introduced by the **Road Traffic Act 1991**, which substituted new sections in to the **Road Traffic Act 1988**, and, at the same time, abolished the offences of reckless driving and causing death by reckless driving.

The new **s2A Road Traffic Act 1988** states that a person will be guilty of dangerous driving if the way he drives falls far below what would be expected of a competent and careful driver and it would be obvious to the latter that driving in that way would be dangerous. He would also be driving dangerously if it would be obvious to a competent and careful driver that driving a vehicle in its current state would be dangerous. Unlike recklessness, therefore, the test is objective, i.e. would a competent and careful person drive in such a way?

Gross negligence manslaughter

In addition to these serious driving offences, grossly negligent behaviour that leads to a death may result in a manslaughter charge. This area of law will be examined more fully in Chapter 5.

2.5.5 THE DOCTRINE OF TRANSFERRED MALICE

Before leaving the subject of *mens rea*, it should be noted that if the defendant has the *mens rea* for one offence, it can then be transferred to another offence of the same type. The case of **Latimer 1886**, provides an example. The defendant, a soldier, hit a customer in a pub with his belt after an attack by that other. The belt rebounded off the first victim and hit a woman, cutting her face open in the process.

The court held that the *mens rea* from the first attack could be transferred to the second offence.

The position would have been different if another type of offence had been planned in the first instance as, for example, criminal damage. In such a case, the *mens rea* of that offence could not be transferred. The case of **Pembliton 1874** illustrates this. The defendant intended to throw a stone at a fighting crowd but accidentally broke a window instead. He could not be found guilty of this offence under the doctrine of transferred malice; it would have to be the subject of a separate charge.

The House of Lords was not prepared to accept the doctrine of transferred malice in **Attorney General's Reference (No 3 of 1994) 1998.** A man had stabbed his girlfriend in the stomach. The girl was over five months' pregnant, a fact known to the accused. It later came to light that in addition to the injuries to the girlfriend, the foetus had also been penetrated by the weapon. The baby was born very early and only lived for a few months. The man was convicted of grievous bodily harm in relation to the mother and was later charged with the murder of the baby.

The trial judge decided that there could not be a conviction for either murder or manslaughter in such circumstances and the man faced no further action on this charge. The Attorney General submitted a reference to the Court of Appeal. This court decided that, under the doctrine of transferred malice, the acts against the mother could be transferred to the child and charges of both murder and manslaughter were sustainable. The court decided that it was immaterial that the child had not yet been born.

The House of Lords took a different view and decided that only a manslaughter conviction could be obtained, due to an unlawful and dangerous act that caused a death, (as will be noted in Chapter 5 on Involuntary Manslaughter). The top appeal court judges did not approve of the attempt to extend the doctrine of transferred malice to a case such as this.

2.5.6 THE NEED FOR THE *ACTUS REUS* AND THE *MENS REA* TO COINCIDE

We have noted that, for the vast majority of offences, two elements have to be established before a crime can be committed, the *actus reus* and the requisite *mens rea*. Normally, these two elements should coincide. In a small minority of cases, however, the courts have been willing to accept that the *actus reus* can be a continuing act, as decided in the case of **Fagan**, mentioned earlier. **They may, instead, use the concept of a series of acts in which the *mens rea* may have been present some of the time.** The case of **Thabo Meli 1954** provides an illustration of this.

A gang had severely beaten the victim and, believing him to be dead, had thrown him over a cliff. At that time, he was still alive but he died later from exposure. The defendants tried to argue that they had not possessed the appropriate *mens rea* at the time of the victim's death.

Despite this, the Privy Council upheld the conviction for murder. It decided that the mental requirement for murder had existed at the beginning of the sequence of events and this was sufficient to constitute liability.

A similar view was taken in **Le Brun 1991** where the defendant was alleged to have quarrelled with his wife and knocked her out. While trying to remove her from the scene, he dropped her, causing her death as she hit her head on a kerbstone.

The Court of Appeal upheld the husband's conviction for manslaughter, deciding that the original attack and the subsequent blow causing the death were part of the same sequence of events.

2.6 OFFENCES OF STRICT LIABILITY

There are many offences, often of a regulatory nature (but not necessarily so), which have been created as offences of strict liability. Most have been laid down by statute, but there are limited common law examples such as public nuisance and criminal libel.

This last offence had lain practically dormant for many decades but was dramatically resurrected in the case of **Lemon 1979**, when the newspaper in question was convicted of blasphemous libel. The poem causing all the trouble had described various homosexual acts being performed on the body of Jesus Christ after his death. The editor and publisher appealed against the conviction, arguing that the blasphemous libel had to be proved.

The case reached the House of Lords, which affirmed the decision of the lower courts that the liability in such cases was strict.

It is commonly stated that no *mens rea* is needed for strict liability offences. This is not quite accurate; **what should be stated is that *mens rea* does not have to be proved with regard to one or more of the elements of the *actus reus*.** In most offences, it is obvious that *mens rea* is required. The words, **'intention'** or **'recklessness'**, laid down for many offences, signify the degree of blameworthiness required. Other crimes will only be committed if the defendant acts **'wilfully'**, **'knowingly'** or **'dishonestly'**. He cannot, therefore, be convicted if such states of mind cannot be shown. Should the offence be one of strict liability, however, the defendant may well be held to be criminally liable without any proof of fault on his part.

An early example of liability without fault is illustrated in the case of **Prince 1875**. The defendant was charged under **s55 Offences Against the Person Act 1861**, with unlawfully taking an unmarried girl under the age of 16 out of the possession of her parents. Prince was found guilty, despite the fact that the girl looked much older than her 13 years and had convinced Prince that she was 18.

The court stressed that the relevant section did not contain the words 'knowingly' or 'maliciously', so liability arose when Prince merely committed the act.

It will be noted below that this decision, which acted as an important precedent for well over 100 years has recently been affected by the case of **B (a minor) v DPP 2000** and while not officially overruled, has been discredited.

2.6.1 THE DIFFERENT TYPES OF STRICT LIABILITY OFFENCES

Regulatory offences

There are several hundred of these. **In some, a defence of 'due diligence' may exist in the statute, as seen in Tesco v Natrass, mentioned in Chapter 4. In such a case, the defendant may have a defence if he can show that he took all possible care to avoid the commission of the offence. In other cases however, where no such defence has been laid down, the liability is absolute.** An early example can be seen in the case of **Cundy v Le Cocq 1884**. The unfortunate publican in this case was convicted of selling intoxicating liquor to someone who was drunk, contrary to **s13 Licensing Act 1872**, despite his claim that the customer showed no sign of this. On appeal, the judges were unsympathetic, stating:

the object of this part of the Act is to prevent the sale of intoxicating liquor to drunken persons and it is perfectly natural to carry that out by throwing on the publican the responsibility of determining whether the person comes within that category.

The appeal courts are quite prepared to strike an equally uncompromising attitude today, as can be seen in **London Borough of Harrow v Shah & Shah 2000**. The defendants were charged with selling a National Lottery ticket to a boy under the age of 16, despite the fact that they had not been present when the transaction took place and they had also put up clear notices in the store warning employees not to sell tickets to under-age buyers, as well as warning them verbally. The employee who sold the offending ticket believed the boy to be over the requisite age limit. The magistrates dismissed the charge but the local authority then appealed against this decision.

The Divisional Court of Queen's Bench Division allowed this appeal. The court decided that liability under s13 National Lottery Act 1993 and its attendant regulations was strict and that no defence of 'reasonable diligence' appeared in the section. The prosecution, therefore, did not have to prove that the defendant knew of the buyer's age or was reckless about this. It also claimed that the matter was not 'truly criminal in character' but dealt instead with a matter of social concern, i.e. access to gambling by young people. The judges therefore took the view that the imposition of strict liability would encourage greater vigilance in preventing the commission of such an offence, even in cases like this. The point of law was referred back to the magistrates to continue with the hearing but with an expectation that they would deal with the case in a lenient way.

We will see many similar '**regulatory**' cases below, detailed in the arguments for and against the imposition of strict liability.

'Truly criminal' offences

With regard to more serious offences, where the stigma of a conviction is greater, the House of Lords is now far less ready to impose strict liability unless this has been clearly stated by Parliament. Three important cases illustrate this.

In **Sweet v Parsley 1970**, a teacher leased a farmhouse near Oxford, which she then rented out to students, while retaining a room for her occasional use. These students indulged in the use of recreational drugs and this resulted in Sweet being convicted of being concerned in the management of premises which were being used for the purpose of smoking cannabis, contrary to **s5 Dangerous Drugs Act 1965**. This section was silent on the matter of *mens rea* and both the court of first instance and the Divisional Court of Queen's Bench Division decided that she was

strictly liable. Her case then reached the House of Lords.

Lord Reid made a clear distinction between regulatory criminal offences and ones which he decided were more 'truly criminal acts'. He acknowledged that the imposition of strict liability might well be appropriate for the former type of offence but felt that there was a strong presumption that *mens rea* was needed for the latter type of crime. Sweet's conviction was therefore quashed.

Following this, the **Dangerous Drugs Act** was replaced by the **Misuse of Drugs Act** and the section corresponding to the one affecting **Sweet** now requires knowledge before liability is imposed.

In **B (a minor) v DPP 2000,** the appeal concerned a boy of 15, who was charged with inciting a girl under the age of 14 to perform an act of gross indecency with him. The Youth Court sought the advice of the Divisional Court on a point of law as to whether the boy would have a defence if he genuinely believed that the girl was over the age of 14. The relevant section of the **Indecency with Children Act 1960** made no mention of this. The appeal court decided that the case was one of strict liability. There was a further appeal to the House of Lords, where a markedly different approach was taken.

Their Lordships noted that the relevant section of the Indecency with Children Act 1960 made no mention of *mens rea*. They decided therefore, that their starting point should be the common law presumption that *mens rea* was an essential ingredient of an offence unless Parliament had expressly or by implication indicated otherwise. Their Lordships quoted with approval the case of Sweet v Parsley 1970, just discussed. They argued that there was no general consensus of opinion that strict liability was necessary to the enforcement of the law in sexual matters so took the view that, if the interpretation of the current offence was being gleaned from an interpretation in another statute (in this case the Sexual

Offences Act 1956), that other act had to 'give compelling guidance' on the matter. In this case it did not. Steyn went on to state robustly that Prince 'is a relic from an age dead and gone'.

The House of Lords decided, therefore, that the prosecution needed to prove that the offence had taken place and to do this had to show an absence of genuine belief by the defendant that the girl was 14 or over. When deciding on this second issue there was another important development. The judges followed cases like Morgan and decided that such a belief did not have to be reasonably held.

They decided that there had been several cases in recent years where the courts had departed from the traditional view that if the defence of mistake was put forward, it had to be shown that the honest mistake was reasonably held. The judges in the current case came to the conclusion that when *mens rea* was ousted by a mistaken belief, it was as well ousted by an unreasonable belief as by a reasonable one. This issue will be looked at more fully under General Defences in Chapter 11.

► Comment

The late Sir John Smith thoroughly approved of the width of the decision in **B**. He believed that it helped to counter the House of Lords' 'dismal record in criminal cases' and hailed it as a 'good start to the new millennium'. He noted that, while the precedent set in **Prince**, mentioned earlier, was not expressly overruled, it was 'severely shaken as authority'.

In **K 2001**, the House of Lords took a similar view and decided that the decision in **Prince** was 'discredited'. **K** was another complicated case where the defendant was charged with indecent assault on a girl under the age of 16, contrary to s14 Sexual Offences Act 1956. As in the previous case, the section in question did not mention *mens rea*. The 26 year-old defendant argued that he honestly believed the 14 year-old girl's assertion that she was 16 and alleged that she had consented to the sexual activities. On a preliminary point of law, the trial judge had decided that the prosecution needed to prove that the defendant did not possess this belief. The prosecution appealed, stating that the section in question made no mention of this. The act in question was confusing because, in addition to dealing with an offence of indecent assault on a child under s14(2), with which the defendant was charged, it also imposed similar liability in relation to an indecent assault on a 'defective' of any age under s14(4). Under this section, however, the defendant was allowed a defence if he did not know of her disability, as would a man, under s14(3), who had unknowingly contracted a marriage with an underage girl. There was no mention of such a defence in s14(1). The Court of Appeal therefore took the view that liability was strict and distinguished the case of **B v DPP 2000**. It did, however, certify two points of law for the House of Lords to consider:

- Is the defendant entitled to an acquittal if he honestly believed that the girl in question was over the age of 16?
- Did his belief have to be reasonably held?

The House of Lords answered 'yes' to the first question and 'no' to the second. The following reasons were given:

- The court noted that the Sexual Offences Act was merely a consolidating Act, bringing together several different offences under one umbrella. It had not, therefore, been specifically enacted as a whole, so it was not as odd as first appeared that a defence was not provided under s14(I) but was allowed under ss14(3) and (4).
- It would be unjust to impose strict liability under s14(I) for indecent assault when, in cases of unlawful sexual intercourse under the same act, a defence was permitted.

- In B (a minor) v DPP, it had been suggested that the range of provisions relating to sexual offences in relation to children should be taken as a whole and treated in the same way. Therefore, as the judges had decided that s1 Indecency with Children Act 1960 allowed a defence of honest belief, the same view should be taken in the current dispute.
- It had also been strongly affirmed in earlier cases that a presumption of *mens rea* existed, which needed clear words or 'necessary implication' to rebut. In this case, neither of these points had been established.

◀ *Comment* _____

K2001, coming hot on the heels of **B (a minor) v DPP**, demonstrates an unwillingness on the part of the highest court to impose strict liability in unclear cases where the offence is felt to be 'truly criminal'. In cases where the statute is merely silent as to whether or not *mens rea* has to be proved, therefore, the presumption that some form of *mens rea* is necessary appears to be a strong one.

Since these cases were heard, the **Sexual Offences Act 2003** has been passed. A Level students do not have to study this large new enactment but it should be noted that it clarifies and simplifies many aspects of the law in this area. Ironically, it has also taken the approach that any belief by the defendant must be reasonably held.

The imposition of strict liability still remains for many different types of regulatory offences. Several more examples of such offences and the merits and failings of this are considered below.

2.6.2 TEN ARGUMENTS IN FAVOUR OF RETAINING STRICT LIABILITY OFFENCES

- **The public is protected against the selling of unfit food**
  Strict liability is imposed in such cases to ensure that the providers of food maintain control of their checking procedures and keep their standards high.

  In **Callow v Tillstone 1900**, a butcher was convicted of selling meat which was held to be unfit for public consumption, even though a vet had declared the meat to be safe. Similarly, in **Smedleys v Breed 1974**, the manufacturer's conviction for selling unfit food was upheld by the House of Lords, when four tins of peas were found to contain caterpillars.

  Their Lordships were unimpressed with the argument that over three million tins of uncontaminated peas had been sold.

- **The public gains greater protection from pollution**
  In **Alphacell v Woodward 1972**, the defendant's conviction for causing polluted matter to enter a river was upheld, despite the claims that the company was unaware of any obstruction to its pumps.

  Lord Salmon stated that, if the offence were not one of strict liability, 'a great deal of pollution would go unpunished and undeterred to the relief of many riparian factory owners. As a result many rivers which are now filthy would become filthier still and many rivers which are now clean would lose their cleanliness'. Fighting words!

- **The countryside is better protected**
  In **Kirkland v Robinson 1987,** the Divisional Court of Queen's Bench refused to accept the defendant's claim that he was

unaware he was in possession of wild birds, contrary to the **Wildlife and Countryside Act 1981**.

The court decided that the protection of the environment was of 'outstanding social importance'.

- **People are deterred from holding unlawful weapons**
  Both Parliament and the courts believe that the holding of weapons capable of causing harm should be strictly controlled even if this should result in occasional injustice. In **Howells 1977**, the defendant's conviction for failing to obtain a firearms certificate was upheld, despite the fact that he believed that his gun was an antique one and therefore did not need such certification. In **Bradish 1990**, the defendant argued that he was unaware that a canister in his possession contained prohibited CS gas. Once again, the conviction was upheld.

- **There is greater protection from illegal broadcasts**
  In the case of **Blake 1997**, a conviction under the **Wireless Telegraphy Act 1949** was upheld, when the defendant operated a radio station without a licence, despite his claim that he thought he was merely making demonstration tapes.

  The court decided that the Act had been designed to deter such practices, which might otherwise interfere with emergency communications.

- **There is more effective protection against dangerous drugs**
  Strict liability is imposed in some drug offences, both to protect the public and to make it more difficult for offenders to evade liability by arguing that they did not know the drugs were in their possession. In **Warner v MPC 1969**, the defendant had taken possession of some boxes, left for him at a café. He sold perfume as a sideline and

argued that he thought that this was what the boxes contained. In fact, prohibited drugs were found.

Despite his allegations, the House of Lords upheld his conviction.

- **The public is protected from unsafe buildings**
  In **Atkinson v Sir Alfred McAlpine 1974**, a building company was convicted under the **Asbestos Regulations 1969** for failing to state that it was using crocidolite, even though it was unaware of this fact. Similarly in **Gammon v AG for Hong Kong 1984**, the defendants were found liable when part of the building they were helping to construct collapsed, even though the company was unaware that the plans were not being followed.

  The Privy Council stressed that the main reason for enforcing strict liability in cases such as this was to protect the public.

- **Higher standards will be obtained**
  In the above case, the Privy Council also went on to state that strict liability was necessary 'to encourage greater vigilance to prevent the commission of the prohibited act'. Manufacturers, builders, providers of food all know that they must keep to the highest standards or face possible prosecution.

- **A successful prosecution has a powerful deterrent value**
  Any commercial enterprises found to be liable are likely to take stringent measures to try to prevent a recurrence of the problem. Any publicity arising from the conviction might also alert other businesses and ensure that their standards are kept high.

- **It allows a prosecution to be brought in difficult cases**
  It would be much harder in some cases to obtain a conviction if *mens rea* had to be

proved. This might seem unfair but it should be noted that, while liability is strict, it is not always absolute. This means that the defendant could be allowed a limited defence, such as the 'due diligence' defence, noted in **Tesco v Natrass**, or where he is acting under duress.

2.6.3 TEN ARGUMENTS AGAINST THE IMPOSITION OF STRICT LIABILITY

- **It can be unjust**
  One of the main principles of criminal law is that a person or a company should only be liable if they are at fault in some way. In many of the cases described, the defendants were completely unaware that an offence was being committed. For example, in **Pharmaceutical Society of Great Britain v Storkwain Ltd 1986**, a pharmacist's conviction for supplying drugs without a valid prescription was upheld, even though he did not know that the signature was forged. It could be argued that it would be fairer in such cases only to impose liability for negligent behaviour, giving the truly innocent a defence.

- **It may not succeed in raising standards**
  It is impossible to take steps to raise standards if a party is unaware of any wrongdoing.

- **There is little concrete proof that strict liability works in other cases**
  It could, instead, foster feelings of resentment and injustice, which might lead to a loss of respect for the law.

- **The courts often face difficulties in identifying such offences**
  In many statutes, it is not always clear whether a strict liability offence has been created. Some guidance on this was given in the case of **Gammon v AG for Hong Kong 1984**, mentioned earlier.

The Court of Appeal reiterated the view expressed in Sweet v Parsley that crimes could be divided into ones which are 'purely criminal' in character and those that were merely regulatory.

- In truly criminal cases, a presumption clearly exists that *mens rea* is required before an individual or company can be convicted.

- With regulatory offences, there is also a presumption that *mens rea* is necessary, which normally would predominate unless, however, an issue of social concern, such as public safety, is involved. It may then be necessary to impose liability in order to encourage greater vigilance and higher standards.

- **The courts have been inconsistent in their attitude towards strict liability offences**
  In some instances they take a very harsh approach, as in **Cundy v Le Cocq 1884**, described earlier, whereas in similar cases, more tolerance has been displayed. In **Sherras v De Rutzen 1895**, a publican's conviction for serving alcohol to a police officer was quashed by the Divisional Court. The officer had not worn an armband, which would have identified him as being on duty.

  As noted earlier, in **Warner v MPC 1969**, the House of Lords upheld the conviction of a defendant for being in possession of drugs.

  In Sweet v Parsley 1970, however, the same court quashed a similar conviction and stated that where a section in an act is silent on the matter of *mens rea*, it should be presumed. The latter approach has been supported more recently by the Law Lords in the cases of B (a minor) v DPP 2000 and K 2001 so, hopefully, such a view will now prevail in 'truly criminal' cases.

- **There may also be a lack of clarity in some judgments**

  The courts may struggle to justify the imposition of liability and, in so doing, arrive at decisions which affront notions of common sense and simple justice. The case of **Warner** was the first case on strict liability to go to the House of Lords. Smith and Hogan, in the Eighth Edition of their book stated that '**The five speeches delivered in Warner differ so greatly and it is so difficult to make sense of parts of them that courts in later cases have found it impossible to extract a ratio decidendi.**'

- **Legal academics may criticise the decisions made by the judges**

  The late Sir John Smith called the judgment in **Warner 'another calamitous decision by the House'**!

- **Such decisions may also have the opposite effect of what is intended**

  They could lead to later action by Parliament, allowing a defence in some situations, as in the **Misuse of Drugs Act 1971.**

- **A criminal conviction is imposed**

  Probably the most important argument against the creation of strict liability offences is that the stigma of a criminal conviction is imposed on the individual or company, sometimes for an act which he could not have foreseen or prevented.

- **The penalties for such infringement may be very severe**

  Even though offences are often of a regulatory nature, with fairly minor fines, this is not always the case. In the case of **Gammon,** the maximum penalty was a $250,000 fine and imprisonment for three years. The offence committed in **Shah 2000,** if tried on indictment, carried a maximum sentence of two years' imprisonment. In more **'truly criminal'** cases, even lengthier sentences are possible.

FIVE KEY FACTS ON STRICT LIABILITY

- These offences are ones for which no fault has to be shown for one or more parts of the *actus reus*. They are nearly always created by statute although public nuisance and criminal libel are common law examples.

- Such offences can be divided into regulatory offences and more 'truly criminal' acts (**Gammon v AG for Hong Kong 1985**).

- In relation to the latter group of offences, the House of Lords has made it clear that the presumption that *mens rea* has to be shown before liability is imposed is a strong one that will not lightly be ignored. The decisions in **Sweet v Parsley 1970, B (a minor) v DPP 2000** and **K 2001** illustrate this. The long established precedent in **Prince**, though not expressly overruled, has now been discredited.

- Strict liability offences may still be needed to protect the environment and to protect the public from unfit food, unsafe buildings, unnecessary pollution, unlawful weapons and drugs and illegal broadcasts. They may act as a deterrent to others and thus help to raise standards.

- On the negative side they can be unjust, ineffective, difficult to identify and lead to confusion. The stigma of a criminal conviction should not be underestimated.

2.6.4 POSSIBLE REFORM OF STRICT LIABILITY OFFENCES

Reform of this area is indirectly incorporated into the Draft Criminal Code. The Code, if ever enacted, would lay down a general presumption that all offences require either intention, recklessness or knowledge and, if offences are felt to be necessary which create liability for negligence or seek to impose strict liability, then Parliament must clearly state this in the relevant provision.

Activity

- On paper or in general debate, discuss the following proposition: In a just society, criminal liability should never be imposed without some degree of blameworthiness.
- The (fictitous) Regulation of Salsa Dancing Act 2005 states that it is a criminal offence, punishable by a fine of £500, to fail to display a certificate awarded by the Department of Entertainment, indicating that the premises have been declared fit for dancing.

  Bruce, the owner of the Salsa Is Cool Club duly obtained such a certificate and believed that it was hanging in the foyer. Unbeknown to him, it had been taken down when the walls were repainted. A rival club owner has reported him and he faces prosecution. Advise Bruce.

Self-assessment questions on Chapter 2

1 Define the term 'actus reus' and give three examples.
2 State the general rule in English law relating to omissions. Give four exceptions to this, quoting cases or statutes as appropriate.
3 Describe the two types of intention in English law.
4 What help should the judge now give the jury in cases of murder, where the accused is arguing that it was not his purpose to kill? Give three arguments in favour of the modified direction and three problems that might arise.
5 What is meant by the term 'recklessness'?
6 Define the two types of recklessness in English law, developed by the courts, with cases illustrating each. Describe the current position.
7 Give two examples where negligence will suffice for liability in criminal law.
8 Define a strict liability offence and state why the case of **B (a minor) v DPP 2000** is an important one.
9 Give five points in favour of retaining strict liability offences and five arguments against this.
10 How was sufficient criminal liability established in the cases of **Latimer 1886**, **Thabo Meli 1954**, **Fagan 1969** and **Le Brun 1991**?

Chapter 3

UNLAWFUL KILLING I: MURDER

3.1 INTRODUCTION

Having discovered the elements that are necessary before a crime is committed, it is now necessary to examine some of the most important crimes in more detail. **These are known as substantive offences and in the following four chapters we shall be looking at offences against the person, starting with the most serious of these where a death results.**

This chapter concentrates on the crime of murder and is divided into the following main areas:

✔ General information on homicide
✔ The crime of murder
✔ Possible reform of the crime of murder
✔ The chain of causation in criminal offences.

3.2 GENERAL INFORMATION ON HOMICIDE

Firstly, it is important to realise that killing can be either lawful or unlawful. The diagram on the next page gives illustrations of each type.

3.2.1 THE DISTINCTION BETWEEN MURDER AND MANSLAUGHTER

Murder is the 'killing of a human being with malice aforethought', i.e. with the intention to kill or cause serious harm. This definition is examined in more detail below.

Manslaughter can be voluntary or involuntary:

● Voluntary manslaughter arises where the definition of murder appears to have been satisfied but one of three possible defences granted by statute can be pleaded, which will reduce the offence from murder to manslaughter. These are diminished responsibility, provocation and the survivor of a suicide pact. This subject will be examined in Chapter 4.

● Involuntary manslaughter occurs where there is no malice aforethought but a death results because of an unlawful act or gross negligence. This type of manslaughter will be discussed in Chapter 5.

3.2.2 THE *ACTUS REUS* AND *MENS REA* OF THESE CRIMES

Murder and manslaughter share the same *actus reus*, which is the unlawful killing of a human being. The *mens rea* for murder and voluntary manslaughter is killing with malice aforethought. The *mens rea* for involuntary manslaughter varies, as will be noted in Chapter 5.

3.3 MURDER

Murder is a common law offence, that is a crime developed by the judges, not one laid down by statute. It is one of the oldest and most reviled of crimes. Until the middle of the twentieth century, a person convicted of murder was sentenced to be hanged by the neck until dead.

The death penalty was at first suspended and then abolished altogether by the **Murder (Abolition of Death Penalty) Act 1965**. Now, following a conviction for murder, the judge will impose a mandatory sentence of life imprisonment.

It should be noted that, while the sentence

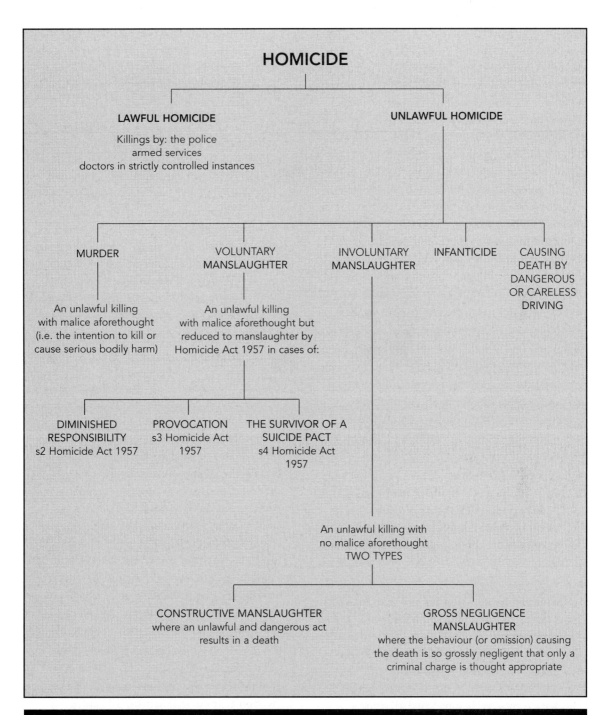

Figure 3.1 Information on homicide

lasts for a lifetime, in many cases the defendant would not spend all his life behind bars. Instead, he might be released on licence after a number of years in jail, if the Parole Board believes that he is no longer a threat to society. The judges have played their part when sentencing by recommending the minimum number of years that should be served before the defendant is considered for such release. Lord Woolf, the Lord Chief Justice, has laid down new guidelines on the procedure for passing mandatory life sentences. These were in response to **s269 Criminal Justice Act 2003.** This stated that all courts passing a mandatory life sentence must either announce in open court the minimum term the prisoner must serve before the Parole Board should consider his release on licence, or announce that the offence is so grave that life really should mean life. The article opposite shows an example of such a decision.

Under the new guidelines, there are three main starting points in deciding how long a person should stay in prison before being considered for release, a 'whole life order', a term of 30 years or a term of 15 years:

- **A 'whole life order'**
  In awarding such an order, the judge will be of the opinion that the defendant should never be considered for early release. The gravity of the offence must be 'exceptionally high' and the defendant must be over 21.

- **A 30 year order**
  This can be imposed for a defendant of 18 or over, in cases where the offence is not so serious as to require a "whole life order", but is still considered to be particularly grave. This would also be used for defendants over 18 but under 21 who would otherwise have qualified for a 'whole life order'.

- **A 15 year order**
  This can be considered for any defendants over the age of 18 where the offence is not quite so grave as in the first two categories.

The starting point for defendants under the age of 18, who are detained during her Majesty's pleasure, is always 12 years.

The judge has a discretion not to follow these guidelines if he feels that to do so would cause injustice in a particular case but is under a duty to state his reasons for failing to comply with them. In addition, it is important to remember that the above are only starting points. The guidelines then state that, as a second step, the judge should take into account any aggravating or mitigating factors that might justify a departure from the starting point. His final move would be to deduct any time remanded in custody before the trial, except, of course, in the case of a 'whole life order'. The minimum sentence that the judge has arrived at would then be read out in open court.

◀ *Comment*

Despite the flexibility given by the above with regard to the time spent in prison, it is important to stress that a judge has no discretion over the passing of a mandatory life sentence on a charge of murder. This fixed sentence has attracted great criticism. Prima facie, a sadistic multiple murderer and a mercy killer would be treated the same way and both would be sentenced to life imprisonment, even though, hopefully, their time spent in jail would vary greatly. In English law, there are no degrees of murder as exist in other jurisdictions.

In 1989, a Select Committee of the House of Lords decided that changes were overdue but decided against having different degrees of murder. Lord Nathan, who chaired the Committee, made the following comment: **'To divide unlawful killing into categories is going the wrong route. You should give the judges discretion for the penalty'**. The Committee therefore recommended scrapping the mandatory life sentence but this has not yet been acted upon.

Teenager gets life for murder of friend, 14

By Paul Cheston

A teenager obsessed with a violent video game battered to death a younger friend in a 'prolonged, vicious and murderous attack'. He was ordered to be detained for life today.

Warren Leblanc lured Stefan Pakeerah to a park armed with a knife and claw hammer in February.

The 17-year-old claimed he planned to rob the boy, but his victim's parents blamed the violent computer game Manhunt, in which players win points for stealth killings.

Leblanc's onslaught in Stokes Wood Park, Leicester, left the 14-year-old with at least 50 injuries.

Judge Michael Stokes QC ordered Leblanc to serve a minimum of 13 years when he sentenced him today at Leicester Crown Court.

The claimed link with computer games was not brought up in court evidence.

Roderick Price QC, defending, said both Leblanc and his victim were 'victims of a gang culture'.

He claimed the 17-year-old was in 'a blind panic' because he feared being attacked by a gang called the Crusaders to whom he owed £75.

Evening Standard, 3 September 2004

3.3.1 THE ORIGINAL DEFINITION OF MURDER

In Coke's Institute, an early work, the famous judge and former Lord Chief Justice of England laid down his definition of murder. This was said to arise where:

> *a man of sound memory and the age of discretion unlawfully killed within any county of the realm any reasonable creature in* **rerum natura** *under the King's peace, with malice aforethought, either expressed by the party or implied by law, so that the party wounded or hurt etc. die of the wound or hurt etc. within a year and a day after the same.*

This lengthy definition has been altered and in some respects simplified over the years.

The criminal liability of children has been extended

The term 'a man of sound memory and the age of discretion' covers people of either sex and includes all those who are not insane or allowed some other defence. The term also applies to children between the ages of 10 and 14. Until very recently, such children were presumed not to have criminal liability unless it could be proved that they knew that they were doing something seriously wrong. **Since October 1998, this presumption has been removed and children of this age have the same liability as adults, although normally they will be treated differently in court and when sentenced.** (There will be a fuller discussion on this in Chapter 10 on General Defences.)

The 'year and a day rule' has been abolished

Another very important change in Coke's definition was the removal in 1996 of what is called 'the year and a day rule'. This ancient rule decreed that a charge of murder or manslaughter could not be brought if the victim survived for longer than a year and a day.

The rule was developed in earlier times to avoid the difficulties of proving whether the injury inflicted by the accused had caused the death or whether such a death had resulted from a later illness or accident. In more recent times where medical science makes it easier to pinpoint the reason for the mortality, there were repeated calls for the abolition of the rule.

Its limitations can be seen in the sad case of **Dyson 1908**. The defendant assaulted his baby daughter on 13 November 1906 and again on 29 December 1907. She eventually died on 5 March 1908. At first instance, Dyson was convicted of manslaughter after the trial judge informed the jury that a conviction could be secured if the baby's death had resulted from **either** of these injuries.

On appeal, the conviction for manslaughter had to be quashed because of this misdirection by the trial judge of the 'year and a day rule'.

There was also injustice where victims of violent attacks survived for longer than a year and a day, sometimes for many years on life support machines, before eventually dying, and the offender could not be charged with murder. Further calls for the rule to be reconsidered were made but were rejected by the Criminal Law Revision Committee.

The Law Commission reopened the debate in its *Consultation Paper No. 136 (1994),* in which it favoured abolishing the rule, so as to follow the lead given by other jurisdictions. Their proposals were introduced into Parliament via a Private Member's Bill in December 1995. The Bill passed through all its later stages in one single day without opposition and emerged in June as the **Law Reform (Year and a Day Rule) Act 1996**.

3.3.2 THE CURRENT DEFINITION OF MURDER

After the modifications are taken into account, the current definition of murder can be said to be:

- the unlawful killing
- of a human being
- under the Queen's peace
- with malice aforethought.

This revised definition of murder needs to be examined in more detail.

'The unlawful killing'

The death must be the result of an unlawful act. As noted below, certain killings will not attract criminal liability.

Killings conducted by an executioner

If the death penalty were to be returned, a defendant convicted of murder could be lawfully killed by the process agreed upon. In other jurisdictions, various methods have been adopted, including electrocution, gassing, shooting, hanging, administering a lethal injection and even stoning.

Killings by the police or the armed forces

A soldier or policeman who kills in the lawful exercise of his duty will obviously not be guilty of murder. Should he exceed the powers given to him, however, he could face criminal proceedings, as is shown in the cases of **Clegg 1995** and other soldiers in Northern Ireland who were all originally convicted of murder. This subject is discussed more fully in Chapter 10, where the defences of self-defence and prevention of crime are explored.

Certain deaths accelerated by the medical profession

Doctors, too, may be allowed to shorten life in very limited circumstances. They have to be careful to operate within the current state of the law and are not normally permitted to accelerate the death of a patient without the judge's permission. The doctor may wish to end the suffering of a terminally ill patient but, if he intends to kill that person, his acts will come within the definition of murder and he could well face life imprisonment. He is accelerating the death of a human being and this is not allowed.

In **Adams 1957**, this fact was made clear to the

jury by Devlin J who stated that:

If life were cut short by weeks or months it was just as much murder as if it were cut short by years.

This view of the law was affirmed in the case of **Cox 1992**, where a doctor was convicted of attempted murder, despite the fact that the patient and her family wanted him to end her suffering.

Exceptions

- **Where the acceleration is minimal**

   Under what is called the 'de minimus rule', a doctor would not face criminal proceedings if he gave an injection towards the very end of a patient's life, to ease his suffering, even if it was known that this might well accelerate the death by a very small degree. In the case of **Adams**, mentioned above, Devlin J did go on to qualify the statement that he made. He added:

   But that does not mean that a doctor aiding the sick or dying has to calculate in minutes or hours, or perhaps in days or weeks, the effect on a patient's life of the medicines he administers. If the first purpose of medicine – the restoration of health – can no longer be achieved, there is still much for the doctor to do, and he is entitled to do all that is proper and necessary to relieve pain and suffering even if measures he takes may incidentally shorten life.

- **Where the patient is in a persistent vegetative state**
   A medical practitioner may, in very limited circumstances, cease to provide treatment or food even though in other cases liability for gross negligence could arise, as shown in Chapter 2.

   The landmark case of **Airedale National**

Health Trust v Bland 1993 concerned 17-year-old Tony Bland, who was crushed in the terrible Hillsborough disaster. He was put onto a life support system but after a period of three years there was no sign that he would ever recover.

The House of Lords affirmed that the parties involved, the NHS trust and the boy's parents, would not face criminal liability if the life support machine were turned off. The action was likened to an omission. When dealing with the uncomfortable fact that the turning off of a life support machine could be seen as a more positive act, Lord Goff argued robustly that 'discontinuation of life support is, for the present purposes, no different from not initiating life support in the first place'.

A similar view was taken by the Court of Appeal in the case of Frenchay Healthcare NHS Trust v S 1994. If, however, the doctors and the close relatives of the patient do not agree on such a course of action (or inaction) the courts may be called upon to make the final decision, as can be seen in the case of Re A (children) 2000, described below. It is perhaps inevitable that some rulings will lead to further anguish and recriminations, as noted in the baby Charlotte decision in October 2004, and that of baby Luke, noted in the newspaper article on page 57.

- **Where the defence of necessity can be pleaded**

   In **Re A (children) 2000**, lawful homicide by doctors was extended when this very unusual case came before the courts. Jodie and Mary, (not their real names), were conjoined twins. Mary's heart and lungs were too deficient to sustain life and if she had been born apart from Jodie, she would have died soon after birth. She stayed alive because a common artery enabled Jodie to circulate the blood for both of them. Jodie was in a healthier condition than Mary but the doctors believed that if she were not soon separated from Mary she too, would die. The doctors wished to perform the operation but faced a dilemma. If they went ahead with the operation, Mary would die and that arguably, could be seen as murder, following the principles laid down in **Woollin**, mentioned in the last chapter. If the doctors did nothing and allowed their patient Jodie to die, they could be guilty of gross negligence manslaughter. The hospital therefore, against the wishes of the parents, sought a declaration that the doctors would be acting lawfully if they proceeded. They were successful but the parents appealed.

The Court of Appeal decided that the doctors would not be acting unlawfully, although the three judges faced some difficulty in arriving at this conclusion. First, they rejected the trial judge's arguments by which he had arrived at a similar answer. He had decided that the operation should not be classed as a positive act, but merely a withdrawal of Mary's blood supply. Secondly, he had taken the view that the operation that would result in her death was in her best interests. The Court of Appeal held that the operation must be seen as a positive act and as Ward L J accepted, one consisting of 'a number of invasions of Mary's body . . . before the positive step was taken of clamping the aorta and bringing about Mary's death'. Because of the decision in **Woollin 1998**, therefore, the act would be murder, unless a suitable defence could be found. The doctors would know that even though it was not their purpose to kill Mary, her death would be a virtually certain consequence of their actions.

By a majority, the Court of Appeal used the defence of utilitarian necessity to decide that the doctors would not be acting unlawfully, although the possibility of private defence was also argued. These issues will be returned to more fully in Chapter 11. The court made it clear that the judgment was to be restricted to similar cases, but after this decision, it can now be said that the circumstances in which a doctor will still be within the limits of lawful homicide have been increased. The late Sir John Smith stated

this new principle in his commentary on the case of Re A:

> *where A is, as the defendant knows, doomed to die in the near future but even the short continuation of his life will inevitably kill B as well, it is lawful to kill A, however free of fault he may be.*

It remains to be seen how such a principle will be used in future cases.

● **Where the patient wants to die?**
In November 2001, the House of Lords made it clear that the law was not ready to countenance mercy killings, even when the patient is a willing victim. This issue arose in the tragic case of Diane Pretty, a terminally ill motor neurone sufferer. She had a great fear of choking to death and wanted 'to die with dignity'. She wanted her husband to assist her in ending her life at a time of her choosing, without the fear of him being prosecuted, and challenged the refusal of the DPP to offer such immunity.

While the House of Lords clearly sympathised with her plight, her appeal was dismissed (she later died naturally, fortunately without choking). Their Lordships decided that the Human Rights Act 1998 only bestowed a right to live with dignity, and could not be interpreted as 'conferring a right to die or to enlist the aid of another in bringing about one's own death'. Lord Bingham clearly affirmed that 'Mercy killing is in law, killing'.

If, therefore, the person helping does the actual killing, he normally would be liable for murder and face life imprisonment. The law is a little more lenient if the helper also intends to die, as in a suicide pact. Here his liability would be reduced to manslaughter, should he survive, and the judges have much more discretion over the sentence. This can be seen in the case of Blackburn 2005, noted in Chapter 4.

Mrs Pretty's case would have involved a non-medical third party assisting in a death and the

Inquiry call over baby death

By Russell Jenkins

Police were asked last night to investigate the death of a terminally ill baby whose life-saving treatment was withheld by a High Court order.

Luke Winston-Jones, aged ten months, died yesterday after suffering from a rare genetic disorder known as Edwards's syndrome. Doctors at Alder Hey hospital in Liverpool successfully argued in court that Luke's treatment should be withheld if his condition deteriorated.

That moment arrived early yesterday but Luke's mother has now made a formal complaint to Merseyside Police about the treatment her son received in his final hours.

Ruth Winston-Jones, 34, who described her baby as her 'little fighter', was said yesterday to be severely traumatised by the turn of events and has accused hospital staff of not doing enough in the final hours to save Luke. She said: 'It is the end of my world. I have lost my precious little boy.'

The child's death has done nothing to heal the rift between Mrs Winston-Jones from Holyhead, North Wales, and medical staff at Alder Hey.

Mrs Winston-Jones has always insisted that doctors had written off her son's chances too early in his life. She fought a joint application to the High Court by Gwynedd Hospital, in Bangor, and Alder Hey requesting permission to withhold treatment if Luke's condition deteriorated. The case came only two weeks after a High Court judge ruled that another terminally ill baby, Charlotte Wyatt, from Portsmouth, should be allowed to die.

At the hearing before Dame Elizabeth Butler-Sloss, President of the Family Division, doctors agreed that Luke should not be resuscitated by mechanical ventilation but that he could be given cardiac massage.

Luke was born five weeks prematurely at Gwynedd Hospital. Once Edwards's syndrome, a chromosome condition, was diagnosed, doctors expected him to live for a few weeks or months. His mother refused to believe the dire prognosis. She had hoped that Luke would one day be well enough to be cared for at home, but he was never able to leave hospital.

Jacqui Kirkwood, Luke's aunt, who was with him when he died, claimed that doctors did not give him the treatment that the court had ordered was acceptable. 'The whole family is grieving but we are also angry because of the actions of the medical staff. This is exactly what we did not want to happen,' she said.

Mrs Kirkwood said that doctors refused to carry out procedures that the family believed would have prolonged Luke's life. She said: 'Ruth had left Luke at 12.20 last night and he was fine. She was called back an hour later after he developed a slight temperature. We want a full inquiry into what happened. We will not let this rest.'

The medical staff insist that they did more than was demanded by the courts. A hospital trust spokeswoman said that senior clinicians attempted to resuscitate Luke during the early hours of the morning.

She said: 'Luke's condition had significantly deteriorated over the past 48 hours and so, despite extensive resuscitation lasting over an hour, we were unsuccessful. The trust is confident that it has always acted in the best interests of Luke and has fully complied with the recent ruling.'

Police have referred Luke's death to the coroner. Chief Superintendent Mike Langdon, area commander for North Liverpool, said: 'Merseyside Police will be liaising with other agencies, and gathering information under our comprehensive protocols for infant deaths which are already in place. This information will then be presented to the coroner.'

The Times, 13 November 2004

courts are not ready to countenance such a practice. In March 2002, in the case of **B**, a 43 year-old paralysed social worker, wanted her doctors to turn off her ventilator,

Dame Butler-Sloss decided that a 'mentally competent' patient's desire not to extend her life in such circumstances should be allowed to prevail over the 'benevolent paternalism' of the doctors who wished to keep her alive.

The Mental Capacity Bill which, at the time of writing, is having a stormy passage through Parliament, will, if passed, enable people to make 'living wills', laying down their wishes if they become unable to make their own decisions. More controversially, they may also be allowed to name others to act on their behalf. It has been stressed, however, that the Bill does not promote euthanasia.

'Of a human being'

This will usually be obvious but certain points need to be addressed.

- **The victim must be human**
  A person will not commit murder or manslaughter if he kills an animal intentionally, although he may well be liable for other offences. The term 'human' would, however, cover tragic cases where the newborn baby is hardly recognisable as a human being, as can occur after the mother's exposure to radiation or drug abuse. Some would argue strongly that it should not be regarded as murder if such a child were allowed to die. Current legal and medical opinion, however, appears to favour the view that any offspring of a human mother should be protected by the law, as was indicated in **Rance v Mid Downs Health Authority 1991.**

- **The courts must decide when life begins**
  Normally, a foetus must have been expelled from the mother's womb and have an independent existence, a view affirmed by the Criminal Law Revision Committee. In **Rance v Mid-Downs Health Authority** it was stated, that a baby is capable of being born alive if it can breathe through its own lungs.

An attack on an unborn child, therefore, either by the mother herself or by another, would normally only result in a charge of abortion or child destruction. In **Attorney General's Reference (No. 3 of 1994) 1998**, however, already noted in Chapter 2 , it had to be decided whether a charge of homicide could be sustained in a case where the foetus was injured but not destroyed, a live birth then resulted, but the baby subsequently died of the injuries that had been inflicted in the womb.

The defendant, despite knowing that his girlfriend was pregnant, stabbed her in the stomach. The knife penetrated the uterus and abdomen of the foetus, although this fact was not discovered until later. The woman gave birth prematurely. The baby was born alive but died four months later. The Attorney General required the opinion of the appeal courts as to whether the man, in addition to his crime against the woman, should have faced liability for the murder or manslaughter of the baby.

Their Lordships decided that a murder charge could not be sustained in such a case, as this would strain existing principles. It was, however, decided that a case of manslaughter could be brought in such circumstances.

- **The courts must decide when death occurs**
  The old medical view was that death occurred when the heart stopped beating and breathing ceased. In 1976, the concept of brain death was adopted by the world of medicine and a person was pronounced dead where irremediable structural brain damage was shown.

The courts have not expressly adopted this test. In **Malcherek and Steel 1981**, however, the Court of Appeal accepted that:

there is a body of opinion in the medical profession that there is only one true test of death and this is irreversible death of the brain stem, which controls the basic functions of the body such as breathing.

Activity

Topsy went into a hospital ward and switched off a life support machine connected to her friend, Tim. She could not bear to see him continue in this state. Discuss her possible liability. Would your answer be any different if Tim's parents and doctors decided that Tim should no longer be kept alive?

'Under the Queen's peace'

Most victims would come under this umbrella, including prisoners of war. The phrase would not, however, cover enemy aliens who are killed in the process of warfare.

'With malice aforethought'

This is a very archaic expression and has been criticised as being misleading in its present context. The word 'malice' seems to suggest that some sort of illwill must exist but this is not necessary. **The expression 'malice aforethought' merely means that the accused must have the intention to cause death or grievous bodily harm.** The latter was defined in **DPP v Smith 1961** as meaning really serious harm but in cases since then as, for example, **Saunders 1985**, it has also been stated that the word 'really' need not be added. **Currently, therefore, the phrase 'malice aforethought' merely means the intention to cause death or serious injury.** Before 1982, there was some doubt as to whether the

intention to cause grievous bodily harm was sufficient intention for murder or whether an intention to cause death was necessary. In **Cunningham 1982, the House of Lords made it clear that the intention to cause serious harm was enough**.

The accused attacked his victim in a pub, hitting him many times with a chair. The victim subsequently died of the injuries inflected. The accused appealed, stating that the judge had misdirected the jury by saying that the defendant was guilty of murder if he intended to cause serious harm.

The House of Lords was unanimous in its opinion that the intention to cause grievous bodily harm constituted enough blameworthiness to amount to malice aforethought.

The different types of malice

The word 'malice' needs to be examined further. If a person intends to kill another human being, he is said to have express malice. If, however, he merely intends to cause serious harm he has implied malice. Before the **Homicide Act 1957**, a third category of malice existed, which was known as constructive malice. Under this head, a person could be found guilty of murder if he killed in the furtherance of a felony (i.e. in the furtherance of a serious crime, such as rape or burglary) provided that he had the intention to commit the lesser crime. A murder charge was also possible if the defendant killed while intending to prevent a lawful arrest (either his own or that of another person) or to escape from lawful arrest or custody. The prosecution did not need to prove that he possessed the extra *mens rea* of intending to kill or cause grievous bodily harm.

S1 Homicide Act 1957 abolished liability for murder in these situations although the defendant would almost certainly face other charges, such as involuntary manslaughter, as discussed in Chapter Five.

FIVE KEY FACTS ON MURDER

- Murder is the most serious form of unlawful homicide. Less serious forms of homicide are voluntary and involuntary manslaughter which are dealt with in subsequent chapters.

- The current definition of murder is the unlawful killing of a human being with malice aforethought, i.e. with intent to cause death (express malice), or grievous bodily harm (implied malice) (**Cunningham 1982**). Constructive malice was abolished by **s1 Homicide Act 1957** and the 'year and a day rule' by the **Law Reform (Year and a Day Rule) Act 1996**.

- Certain killings can be lawful as, for example, those sanctioned by the State or by the judges (**Airedale NHS Trust v Bland 1993**) or where a full defence is possible (**Re A (children) 2000**). In other killings the charge may be reduced to manslaughter.

- A victim is considered to be a human being when he has an existence independent of his mother. It is not certain whether he must have drawn breath, although this would be the medical view. A victim is probably considered to be dead when he is brain dead.

- It appears that there could be an injury to a human being, even if this injury occurred before birth, if the baby was born alive but subsequently died (**AG's Reference [No. 3 of 1994] 1998**). It seems unlikely that liability for murder would result even if the accused intended to harm the foetus. It is clear that the offender could be charged with involuntary manslaughter, if there had been an unlawful act against the mother, a live birth and then the subsequent death of the baby.

The meaning of the word "intention"

As noted in Chapter 2, it is the task of the jury to decide whether the accused intended to cause death or serious harm. After the decision in **Woollin 1998,** however, they are not entitled to find such an intention unless death or serious injury was virtually certain and the defendant was aware of this.

3.4 POSSIBLE REFORM

The *Draft Criminal Code Bill,* prepared by the Law Commission in 1989, suggests that the *mens rea* of murder should be reformed. It states in *Clause 54* that the mental element should only be present in cases where a person kills intending to cause death or intending to cause serious harm and being aware that it may cause death.

If this were enacted, it would narrow the liability for murder. Under current law, there is no requirement that the defendant must have a foresight of death occurring; it is enough that he intends to cause grievous bodily harm.

3.5 THE CHAIN OF CAUSATION

Before we leave the subject of murder, it is important to stress that the death must have been caused by the unlawful act of the defendant. In some cases, the defendant might not have been directly responsible for the final act that caused the death but will still be liable for the homicide because he set in motion the chain of events leading up to it. This subject of causation is also applicable to other offences but will be examined in this chapter because many of the cases on causation have involved fatal offences against the person, in the form of murder or manslaughter.

3.5.1 ESTABLISHING THE CHAIN OF CAUSATION

There are no rules laid down by statute concerning the problems of causation; instead, various principles have been established by case law, as problem areas have come before the courts.

In most cases, it is not difficult to discover whether the defendant's conduct caused the death in question although the jury, of course, has to be convinced of this beyond reasonable doubt. In some trials however, the defendant will be arguing that someone else caused the death, or at least contributed to it, or that the death was the victim's own fault in some way and these matters need to be explored. When ascertaining whether the defendant is the person on whom to fix liability, the courts will look at two issues:

- **Did the conduct of the accused cause the resulting harm (i.e. what was the factual cause of the death?)**
- **Was the defendant also liable in law?**

It will be the jury's task to look at the facts of the case but when deciding on the second question, the jurors will have to apply the legal principles explained to them by the judge. Both these issues will be examined further in the following paragraphs.

3.5.2 THE FACTUAL CAUSE OF DEATH

It should first be noted that the defendant would only be criminally liable if his conduct made a significant contribution to the death. This was not established in the case of **White 1910**. The accused had intended to murder his mother; he had poison in a glass ready for her but she suddenly died, instead, of heart failure.

The accused was found liable for attempted murder but it is clear that he had not caused her death, however much he had desired it to happen. He could not, therefore, be found guilty of murder.

The 'but for' test

When deciding on the factual cause of death, the courts use the 'but for' test, i.e. but for the act of the defendant, the death would not have occurred. It can be seen in the above case that this test was not satisfied, as the mother would have died anyway.

A more difficult case for the jury was the early case of **Dalloway 1847**. A driver of a cart was not using his reins as he proceeded along a road. A three-year-old child then ran into the path of the cart and was killed. It could have been argued that, but for the driver travelling along this road, the child's death would not have happened.

The courts required the passing of a more stringent test, i.e. had the prosecution established that, but for the driver's negligence in failing to use his reins, the death would not have happened. As the answer was 'no', the charge could not be sustained.

3.5.3 THE LEGAL CAUSE OF DEATH

After satisfying the test for factual causation, it still needs to be shown that the defendant's act was a significant cause of the death and that no intervening act had broken the chain of causation.

The defendant's act must be a significant cause of the death

Many would argue that the defendant should only be liable if he makes a major contribution to the victim's death and, indeed, in earlier cases it was stated that the act of the accused had to be **substantial**. Cases like **Benge**, discussed below, support this.

The current view, however, is that liability might arise where the defendant has made a significant contribution to the death.

This point was confirmed in **Cato 1976**, a view which was later supported in the case of

Malcherek, discussed below. In **Kimsey 1971**, it was not considered to be a misdirection by the trial judge when he stated that the contribution must merely be something more than 'a slight or trifling link'.

An example of only 'a slight or trifling link' would be where two mountaineers were roped together and one fell over a cliff. If the other were to cut the rope to save himself from a similar fate, he would certainly be accelerating the death of the other mountaineer but this would only be by a fractional period of time. **It would not be significant enough to make him criminally liable for the other's death.**

The contribution must therefore be significant enough to contribute to the victim's death. In addition, nothing later must have occurred to break the chain of causation.

A *novus actus interveniens* must not have arisen

This means that no intervening act must have arisen to break the chain of causation leading from the defendant's act to the actual death. The defendant would be able to escape liability if he could prove that some other act had caused the death, not his own act of violence or his own omission. In the following wide range of situations, the defendants have tried to argue such a point, nearly always unsuccessfully.

Claims by the defendant that the chain of causation has been broken

1   Claims that the accused did not directly cause the death

    If the defendant put in motion the chain of events leading to the death, he will usually be unsuccessful in his claim that he should not be liable. Any supervening act must be something unforeseeable in order to remove the liability of the first party. If, therefore, the defendant had knocked the victim unconscious and then left him on the seashore near to the water's edge and he

was later drowned by the incoming tide, such an event should have been anticipated by the assailant and his liability would remain.

A more controversial situation occurred in **Pagett 1983**. The accused was being pursued by the police and had forcibly taken his pregnant girlfriend captive after injuring her mother and stepfather. He later came out of one of the flats, using his girlfriend as a human shield. He then fired his shotgun at two officers.

The policemen fired back instinctively and the girl was hit by three bullets and killed.

The defendant was found guilty of her manslaughter but appealed against this, arguing that the judge had misdirected the jury by stating that he had been the cause of the victim's death, not the police officers who had fired the bullets.

The Court of Appeal found that there was no misdirection. Goff L J compared the situation to one where the victim acts in self preservation but his attempt fails and, instead, causes or contributes to his death, as in the case of Pitts, discussed below. He went on to say:

> *Now one form of self preservation is self-defence; for present purposes, we can see no distinction in principle between an attempt to escape the consequences of the accused's act and a response which takes the form of self-defence. Furthermore, in our judgment, if a reasonable act of self-defence against the act of the accused causes the death of a third party, we can see no reason in principle why the act of self-defence, being an involuntary act caused by the act of the accused, should relieve the accused from criminal responsibility for the death of the third party.*

2   Claims that the victim harmed himself

In some cases a death has occurred because the victim has tried to escape from the violent actions of the accused. **Once again, the defendant will find it difficult to escape liability if he put in motion the chain of events which led to the accused having to take evasive action through fear for his safety.** A *novus actus interveniens* would only arise if the reaction of the victim was considered to be something totally unexpected, or, as stated in **Roberts 1971**, something so 'daft', when compared to how a reasonable man in the same situation might have acted.

The victim's reaction was considered to have been reasonable in **Pitts 1842**, when he jumped into a river to escape further violent assaults. **The defendant was held to be responsible for his death**.

In **Mackie 1973, a manslaughter conviction was upheld when a father frightened his three-year-old son so severely that the boy fell down the stairs and was killed.**

In **DPP v Daley 1980, Lord Keith stated that, in cases such as these, the prosecution had to establish that the victim was in fear of being hurt physically and this fear had caused him to try to escape and thereby meet his death. The conduct of the accused had to be unlawful and of a type which any reasonable and sober person would recognise as likely to subject the victim to at least the risk of some harm resulting from it, albeit not serious harm.**

In **Williams 1992**, the prosecution claimed that the deceased had jumped from a moving car because he was in fear of being robbed. To support this contention, it was alleged that his wallet had flown into the air as he had jumped. The victim had been travelling to a festival in Glastonbury and had 'hitched' a lift from the defendants. He had jumped out five miles further on and been killed. The occupants were originally held to be liable for his death but appealed.

The Court of Appeal stressed that the conduct of the victim had to be proportionate to the threat of harm and:

> *within the ambit of reasonableness and not so daft as to make his own voluntary act one which amounted to a novus actus interveniens and consequently broke the chain of causation.*

The conviction was quashed because the trial judge had not directed the jury in this fashion. The Court of Appeal did, however, go on to state that:

> *It should of course be borne in mind that a victim may in the agony of the moment do the wrong thing . . . and . . . may act without thought or deliberation.*

3   Claims that others were involved in the death

In some situations there may be more than one party involved in the chain of events; others may well have contributed to the outcome. **Nevertheless, the party starting the action will usually retain his liability, provided that, as mentioned before, his act was a significant factor in causing the death.**

In **Benge 1865**, a foreman plate-layer had misread a timetable so that the track had not been re-laid by the time a train arrived. The defendant had also failed to put any fog signals into place and had positioned a flagman only 540 yards away, instead of the required 1000 yards. The driver of the train failed to stop and an accident occurred causing many deaths. The foreman was charged with manslaughter. His defence tried to argue that the accident would not have occurred without the contributory negligence of the other people who were also involved.

The judge ruled that, provided that the defendant's negligence had been the main or a substantial cause of the accident, it was no defence to state that the deaths might have been avoided if the others had played their part correctly.

In **Towers 1874**, a young girl screamed very loudly when she was assaulted by the accused. At the time of the attack, she was holding a young baby in her arms who was so frightened by the screams that she went black in the face, had convulsions from that moment on and died four weeks later.

It was decided that the girl's attacker could be charged with the manslaughter of the baby.

In **Malcherek and Steel 1981**, the two appellants had injured their victims so severely that they had to be put on life support machines. When these machines were switched off by doctors, the defendants tried to argue that this action constituted a *novus actus interveniens*. Their appeals failed.

The Lord Chief Justice stated that where the medical treatment is given by:

competent and careful medical practitioners, then evidence will not be admissible to show that the treatment would not have been administered in the same way by other medical practitioners.

In these two cases, there was no doubt that the original injuries inflicted by the stab wounds were still operating. **Cheshire** and **McKechnie**, mentioned below, are more controversial.

4   **Where the victim has a pre-existing medical condition**
In both criminal law and in the law of tort,

there is a rule that the perpetrator of an act must 'take his victim as he finds him'. This is also known as the 'eggshell skull' rule. **The courts will not allow the defendant to escape liability just because the victim is more susceptible to harm than the normal person or is unusually sensitive in some other way.**

In **Hayward 1908**, the defendant had indicated that he was going to harm his wife. An argument developed and the woman ran into the road, followed by her husband who was still making threats against her. The woman then collapsed and died. She had a condition affecting her thyrus gland that would not normally have caused problems but the unusual physical exertion and the fright caused by her husband's treatment had caused her to collapse.

The husband was held to be liable for her death because her demise had been accelerated by his actions.

5   **Claims that the victim has aggravated his condition or refused medical treatment**
This overlaps in some measure with the above rule. **The defendant will not escape liability just because the victim takes an ill-advised course of action to relieve his pain or refuses to undergo the treatment suggested for his injuries, either through fear or because of religious objections.**

In **Wall's Case 1802**, the Governor of Goree had inflicted an illegal flogging of 800 lashes on the deceased and was charged with his murder. He tried to argue that the victim had aggravated his condition by consuming strong alcohol to deaden the pain of the punishment.

The judge refused to entertain such a notion.

Another early case, this time illustrating the victim's reluctance to undergo further treatment, is that of **Holland 1841**. The victim's hand had been severely cut by Holland, who had attacked him with an iron bar. Blood poisoning had then set in. The victim was advised to have his finger amputated but he refused to do this; lockjaw developed and he died.

Despite an assertion by a surgeon that the amputation would probably have saved the victim's life, the defendant was found guilty of his murder.

A more recent case illustrating the same point was **Blaue 1975**. The victim had been stabbed by the defendant, but, because of her religious beliefs as a Jehovah's Witness, she refused to have a blood transfusion which would probably have saved her life.

The Court of Appeal upheld Blaue's conviction for manslaughter on the grounds of diminished responsibility, even though the Crown had conceded that the girl may well have survived if the transfusion had been permitted.

Lawton L J stated:

It has long been the policy of the law that those who use violence on other people must take their victims as they find them. This in our judgment means the whole man, not just the physical man. It does not lie in the mouth of the assailant to say that his victim's religious beliefs which inhibited him from accepting certain kinds of treatment were unreasonable. The question for decision is what caused her death. The answer is the stab wound. The fact that the victim refused to stop this end coming about did not break the causal connection between the act and the death.

The Court of Appeal upheld the principles stated in **Blaue** in the cases of **McKechnie 1992** and **Dear 1996**. In the first case the victim was in hospital after a very

severe attack on him by the defendant and while there was discovered to have an ulcer. Because of his serious condition caused by the attack, the ulcer could not be operated upon. It burst and the victim died. As the jury had been correctly directed about the issues, the conviction was upheld.

In the second case, the victim indecently assaulted Dear's 12-year-old daughter and the defendant later attacked him, slashing him with a Stanley knife. The victim died two days later from the wounds but apparently had done nothing to staunch the flow of blood. It was suggested that he had actually reopened the wounds himself. Despite this, the defendant's conviction was upheld.

The Court of Appeal stressed that the question to be asked of the jury was 'whether the injuries inflicted by the defendant were an operating and significant cause of the death'. If the jury believed that this was the case, they were entitled to find the defendant guilty whether or not the victim had neglected the wounds or had even deliberately made them worse.

6   Claims that the medical treatment (or lack of it) actually caused the death
In the cases just discussed, medical treatment was actually refused by the victim or considered to be unwise by the doctors. In the following cases, treatment was given but was either wrong or, at best, given in a very negligent way. The courts had to decide whether this was enough to break the chain of causation. **In line with the situations already examined, it will be noted that the courts are very reluctant to allow this to happen and, in most cases, the liability of the person starting the injuries leading to the death will remain.**

The law on this subject is complicated by the case of **Jordan 1956**, which took a contrary approach, but, although this decision has not been overruled, it appears that it will not be followed in the future, unless the new circumstances are very similar to those in that case.

The victim had been stabbed. He was admitted to hospital but died eight days later. The defendant was convicted of murder. Later, evidence came to light that the medical treatment had been 'palpably wrong'. This showed that the victim had been given terramycin, to which he had proved allergic. It had then been withdrawn but inadvertently reintroduced later by another doctor. Large quantities of liquid had also been given intravenously and broncho-pneumonia had set in. On the other hand, at the time of his death, the stab wounds had nearly healed.

The conviction, therefore, was quashed, Hallett J stated:

Not only one feature but two separate and independent features of treatment were, in the opinion of the doctors, palpably wrong and these produced the symptoms discovered at the post-mortem examination which were the direct and immediate cause of death . . .

The court did, however, take pains to point out that in cases where normal treatment was given, the original injury would be considered to have caused the death.

The decision in **Jordan** caused concern among members of the medical profession who felt that wrongdoers might escape liability if it could be shown that any treatment given to try to save the victim was abnormal in some way.

The doctors need not have worried. The case of **Jordan** was later distinguished in **Smith 1959**, although, in this case too, the treatment given left a lot to be desired.

The victim had been stabbed twice in a barrack room fight between soldiers of different regiments. While being carried to the medical reception centre, the injured man was dropped twice. When he reached his destination, the doctor on duty failed to realise the seriousness of his injuries and administered treatment which was said at the trial to be 'thoroughly bad and might well have affected his chances of recovery'. An hour later, the victim died.

The defendant was still found guilty of murder and this was upheld by the Courts-Martial Appeal Court. It was stated that provided that the original wound was still an operating and substantial cause at the time of the death, the defendant would still be liable even though some other cause of death was also operating. Lord Parker went on to say:

Only if it can be said that the original wound is merely the setting in which another cause operates can it be said that the death did not result from the wound.

In the case of **Malcherek**, mentioned above, the Court of Appeal believed that the decision in **Smith** was preferable to that in **Jordan,** but decided not to overrule the latter because of the different facts.

The matter was raised again in the case of **Cheshire 1991**, where the statements made in **Smith 1959**, appear to have been taken a step further.

The victim was shot in the stomach and the leg by the accused, during an argument in a fish and chip shop. He was operated upon but later developed breathing difficulties and had to have a tracheotomy tube inserted. He died two months later. It was discovered that his windpipe had narrowed and this had caused the severe breathing problems. It was argued that this was due to the negligence of the hospital when the tracheotomy tube was fitted and that this, therefore, had broken the chain of causation. The trial judge directed the jury that a *novus actus interveniens* would only have occurred if the doctors had acted recklessly and the defendant was found guilty. He appealed against his conviction.

The Court of Appeal criticised the trial judge's reference to recklessness but still upheld the conviction. The court came to this conclusion despite the fact that the immediate cause of the victim's death was due to the possible negligence of the doctors, not from the gunshot wounds. The court stated that this would not excuse the defendant from liability unless the negligent treatment:

> *. . . was so independent of his acts, and in itself so potent in causing death, that they regard the contribution made by his acts as insignificant.*

◀ Comment

It has been shown from the many cases on this subject, that an offender is going to find it very difficult to prove that the chain of causation has been broken, even in cases where the intervening act appears to be substantial and the negligence of a third party is of a high degree. Some would argue that such a step is to be commended because the victim would not have met his death or other fate if the accused had not put in motion the chain of events leading to the death. Others would argue that in some instances, particularly those involving gross negligence by medical staff, where the original wounds seem to be healing well, it could be unjust to hold the original attacker liable for the full resulting death.

The principles developed in Smith and Cheshire were reinforced in Mellor 1996. He had been beaten by the defendant, resulting in bruising round his eyes, a painful shoulder and chest pain. He developed broncho-pneumonia and died two days later. The defendant tried to argue that the victim would not have died if he had been given sufficient oxygen and evidence given by experts supported this. Despite this, he was found guilty of murder and the conviction was upheld.

Activity

- In group discussion or in essay form, decide whether the rules of causation are now weighted too far against the interests of the defendant.
- Bart made an unprovoked attack on Homer during half-time at a football match and seriously injured him. Homer's friends took him to the first aid centre in the ground to receive attention but, because of the crush, they twice dropped him on the way. The centre was crowded with other people needing attention and Homer was not treated until two hours' later because the paramedic had not believed that his condition was life-threatening. In fact, Homer was a haemophiliac and was bleeding to death and, when this was discovered, it was too late to save him.

Advise Bart who has been charged with Homer's murder.

FIVE KEY FACTS ON CAUSATION

- There is no legislation on this subject, only case law. When deciding on the factual cause of death, the courts use the 'but for' test, i.e. but for the defendant's act, the death would not have happened (**Dalloway 1847, White 1910**).

- When deciding upon the legal cause of death two further issues are examined. The first is did the act of the defendant play a significant part in causing the death of the victim? (the term significant meaning more than a minimal role), and has any other event occurred to break the chain of causation?

- It has been decided that such an event must be something completely unforeseeable.

- It is not considered unforeseeable that the police might return the fire of a gunman (**Pagett 1983**), or that the victim might try to escape (**Pitts 1842, Roberts 1971, Mackie 1973, DPP v Daley 1980** and **Williams 1992**). It is foreseeable that others might be involved in the death (**Benge 1865, Towers 1874**), that the victims might already have a pre-existing medical condition (**Hayward 1908**), might refuse treatment (**Holland 1841** and **Blaue 1975**) or that they themselves might aggravate their injuries (**Wall's Case 1802** and **Dear 1996**). It is possible that doctors might have to switch off life support machines (**Malcherek and Steel 1981**), or refuse to operate because of the dangers involved (**McKechnie 1992**). Lastly, it is not unforeseeable that, on some occasions, the medical treatment might be negligently given or even be thoroughly bad (**Smith 1959, Cheshire 1991** and **Mellor 1996**).

- It will only be an accepted as a *novus actus interveniens* if the new act is completely independent and in itself 'so potent in causing death' that the original defendant's acts are insignificant (**Cheshire 1991**). The case of **Jordan 1956** provided an example of this but such cases are rare.

Self-assessment questions on Chapter 3

1   What is the *actus reus* of the crime of murder?
2   Define the *mens rea* and show how this is established.
3   Describe the 'year and a day rule' and explain what has happened to it.
4   Using cases or examples to illustrate your answer, describe three situations where a doctor may lawfully kill a patient.
5   What is the definition of a human being? When does his life end?
6   With reference to decided cases, describe the 'but for' test.
7   What is the meaning of the expressions:
    a) *novus actus interveniens*?
    b) the 'eggshell-skull rule'?
8   Why were the convictions upheld in the cases of **Pagett, Roberts, Pitts** and **Mackie**, even though the defendants had not physically committed the harm?
9   Describe the principles laid down in the cases of **Blaue**, **McKechnie** and **Dear**.
10 Giving cases to support your findings, explain the attitude the courts take when the defendant claims that the negligent medical treatment was responsible for the death, rather than his own actions.

Chapter 4

UNLAWFUL KILLING II: VOLUNTARY MANSLAUGHTER

4.1 INTRODUCTION

In **Andrews v DPP 1937**, Lord Atkin stated:

. . . of all crimes manslaughter appears to afford most difficulties of definition, for it concerns homicide in so many and so varying conditions.

We noted in Chapter 3 that manslaughter falls into two main categories, voluntary and involuntary manslaughter. This chapter is concerned with voluntary manslaughter and looks at the following things:

✔ **General information on voluntary manslaughter**
✔ **Diminished responsibility under s2 Homicide Act 1957**
✔ **Provocation under s3 Homicide Act 1957**
✔ **The survivor of a suicide pact under s4 Homicide Act 1957**
✔ **Infanticide (WJEC only).**

4.2 THE CRIME OF VOLUNTARY MANSLAUGHTER

This crime is similar to murder in that an unlawful homicide has taken place, with the requisite malice aforethought on the defendant's part, but here special circumstances exist which permit the less serious verdict of manslaughter to be brought in, with more discretion allowed to the judge on sentencing.

● **The maximum sentence is life imprisonment**
● **The minimum is an absolute discharge.**

The law on voluntary manslaughter was first formulated by the judges but only in relation to provocation. This was redefined in the **Homicide Act 1957** and two further defences were added, diminished responsibility and the survivor of a suicide pact. If one of these three defences is successfully established, the crime will be reduced from murder to voluntary manslaughter. These three defences are illustrated in the following diagram:

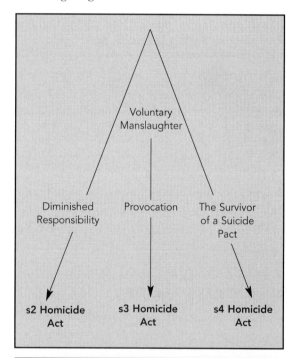

Figure 4.1 Types of voluntary manslaughter

It is very important to realise that the defences are only applicable to the crime of murder, and to appreciate that they only reduce the offence from murder to manslaughter. These partial defences now need to be examined in turn.

4.3 DIMINISHED RESPONSIBILITY

S2 Homicide Act 1957 states that a person may be found guilty of the lesser offence of voluntary manslaughter, rather than murder, if:

- he was suffering from an abnormality of mind
- caused by an inside source
- that substantially affected his responsibility for his actions.

The precise wording is to be found in **s2(1)**. This states:

Where a person kills or is a party to the killing of another, he shall not be convicted of murder if he was suffering from such abnormality of mind (whether arising from a condition of arrested or retarded development of mind or any inherent causes or induced by disease or injury) as substantially impaired his mental responsibility for his acts and omissions in doing or being a party to the killing.

S2(2) puts the burden of proof on the defendant; he will have to prove his abnormality of mind on a balance of probabilities and generally he must be the one to raise the defence.

Can the defence be used on appeal if a not guilty plea fails?

This will only be possible if strong evidence is produced. Two examples of this are **Borthwick 1997** and **Martin 2001**.

In the former case, the victim had been discovered in Borthwick's flat, with the latter's dressing gown cord around his throat. Despite this, Borthwick pleaded not guilty. The jury did not believe his story and convicted him of murder. He later admitted the killing to a psychiatrist, alleging that the death was accidental and had been caused by a bungled bondage session. This same doctor found that he was suffering from a form of mental illness, which could amount to paranoid schizophrenia and affect the sufferer's understanding, judgement and perception. The Crown tried to argue that it was the defendant's own fault that such evidence was not made available at the trial.

The Court of Appeal decided that if there was overwhelming evidence that a plea of diminished responsibility would have succeeded at the trial and it was the mental illness itself that caused the defence not to be put forward, then the appeal should be allowed.

Similarly in **Martin 2001,** the Court of Appeal accepted fresh evidence that the Norfolk farmer, who had shot dead a burglar, was suffering from a paranoid personality disorder. Lord Woolf decided that if this had been pleaded, rather than self-defence, it would have led to a finding of manslaughter on the grounds of diminished responsibility, rather than a murder conviction. The matter will be discussed more fully in Chapter 11.

The differences between diminished responsibility and insanity

It will be seen that the defence of diminished responsibility is wider in the range of abnormal states of mind it covers, than is allowed under the general defence of insanity under the **M'Naghten** rules, which are examined in Chapter 10. On the other hand the defence under **s2** is more limited in that it is only a partial defence, reducing a charge of murder to manslaughter. A finding of insanity is a complete defence.

The elements of diminished responsibility

As mentioned earlier, three important points have to be established before the defence will succeed. There has to be an abnormality of mind, arising from an inside source, that substantially affects the defendant's mental responsibility for his actions.

4.3.1 AN ABNORMALITY OF MIND

This is a state of mind a reasonable man would find abnormal. It is the task of the jury to decide this, not the medical experts, although the jury will obviously take notice of medical opinion. The jurors will also be influenced by the summing up of the judge. It is therefore vital that this gives the correct statement of the law. This was not held to be the case in **Byrne 1960**. He had strangled a young girl living in a YWCA hostel and then carried out horrific mutilations on her body. He claimed that he was suffering from diminished responsibility and had killed the girl while in the grip of an irresistible impulse caused by his perverted sexual desires. Three medical experts had testified that he was, indeed, a sexual psychopath. The judge told the jury that **s2** was not there to give protection **'where there is nothing else than what is vicious and depraved'** and had earlier given the impression that a difficulty or even inability of the defendant to control his acts would not amount to an abnormality of mind. The jury then convicted him of murder.

The Court of Appeal quashed the murder conviction, believing that, if properly directed, the jury would certainly have found that the defence of diminished responsibility had been made out. Lord Parker stated that the term 'abnormality of mind' included a lack of ability to form a rational judgement or exercise the necessary willpower to control one's acts. He said that the term was:

> *wide enough to cover the mind's activities in all its aspects, not only the perception of physical acts and matters and the ability to form a rational judgement whether an act is right or wrong, but also the ability to exercise willpower to control physical acts in accordance with that rational judgement.*

As stated, the appeal against the murder conviction was allowed and a verdict of manslaughter substituted. The sentence of life imprisonment was not, however, disturbed.

It has been noted that the defence of **s2** covers 'the mind's activities in all its aspects'.

In Hobson 1998, the Court of Appeal held that the cumulative effects of 'battered woman's syndrome' could lead to an abnormality of mind, thus affording a defence to a charge of murder if the abused woman turned on her tormentor and killed him.

Evidence of diminished responsibility in respect of such physical abuse was accepted in the retrials of two battered wives, **Ahluwalia** and **Thornton**. These cases will be discussed more fully under provocation.

4.3.2 CAUSED BY AN INSIDE SOURCE

The second element of the defence states that the abnormality must be caused by 'arrested or retarded development of mind or any inherent causes or induced by disease or injury'. This means that the abnormality must have been caused by an inside source, i.e. some malfunctioning of the mind. Evidence, therefore, of mere intoxication, caused by drinking or drug taking (i.e. outside sources), will not, on its own, be sufficient.

In **Tandy 1989** the female defendant was an alcoholic who, on the day in question, drank almost a whole bottle of vodka. Her normal drink was said to be Cinzano, which is less potent. She then strangled her 11-year-old daughter with whom she had quarrelled. The accused made the significant admission that her drinking was not totally involuntary and that she did initially have some control over her choice of drink and over the time she started drinking. The judge then withdrew the defence of diminished responsibility from the jury and she was convicted of murder.

The Court of Appeal upheld the conviction stating that, for the defence to succeed, it was necessary for the abnormality of mind to be induced by the alcoholism. It was decided that this would only have arisen if the defendant's mind had been damaged or there was evidence that she had no control over her drinking at the outset.

In **O'Connell 1997**, a similar approach was taken in relation to a prescribed drug called Halcion, which was alleged to have adversely affected the mind of the defendant. It was noted that the drug was absorbed very rapidly into the system and that its effects wore off very quickly.

The Court of Appeal took the view that its effect was similar to that induced by alcohol and could not therefore come under the definition of an abnormality of mind 'induced by disease or injury'.

As noted below, a different decision was arrived at in **Sanderson 1994,** because the Court of Appeal believed that the mental illness might well have existed before the sustained cocaine abuse.

This latter point had to be considered by the House of Lords in **Dietschmann 2003.** The defendant admitted that he had punched and kicked the victim, thus causing his death. He had been heavily intoxicated at the time but was also held to have an abnormality of the mind. This was described as an adjustment disorder arising from a depressed grief reaction to the death of an aunt, with whom he had sustained a close emotional and physical relationship. After a direction of the trial judge about intoxication, the jury had taken the view that the defendant would not have killed if he had not been drinking and convicted him of murder.

The House of Lords was asked to consider whether someone who had been drinking heavily prior to the killing, and who sought to use the defence of diminished responsibility, had to prove that if he had not been drinking he would still have killed and would have been under diminished responsibility when he did so.

Their Lordships made the following observations:

- S2(1) Homicide Act 1957 did not require the abnormality of the mind to be the sole cause of the defendant's acts in doing the killing.
- Even if the defendant would not have killed if he had not been drinking, the causative effect of the drink did not necessarily prevent any abnormality of the defendant's mind from substantially impairing his responsibility for the fatal acts.
- Therefore even if the jury had answered 'No' to the question 'have the defence satisfied you on a balance of probabilities that, if the defendant had not taken drink, he would have killed as he in fact did?', it was still open to the jury to find the defence of diminished responsibility had been established. The defendant's drinking was to be left out of the account in so far as it exacerbated his abnormality of mind.
- The judge's direction to the jury was therefore felt to be wrong and the case was referred back to the Court of Appeal to decide whether to order a new trial or whether to substitute a verdict of manslaughter.

◀ *Comment*

This decision of the House of Lords appears to widen still further the situations where diminished responsibility can be pleaded. The Court of Appeal in **Seers 1984** already had established that the defendant does not have to be insane to use the defence. **Byrne** decided that the defence could also cover the irresistible impulse type of situation. Perhaps more controversially, it has been used by someone who killed while in a fit of jealousy (**Miller 1972**), by women suffering from post menstrual tension (**Smith 1982** and **Reynolds 1988),** and by those suffering from chronic depression, as in **Gittens 1984.** After **Dietschmann,** it could also cover those with an abnormality of mind that they have made worse through drink or drugs.

In **Sanderson 1994,** the Court of Appeal decided that, in the majority of cases, it would not be helpful merely to quote the whole of **s2** to the jury as this could cause confusion. Instead, the trial judge should 'tailor his directions to suit the facts of the particular case'. This puts a lot of responsibility on his shoulders and may make it even harder for the jury to reach a decision as the direction may not always be clear. This was the case in **Sanderson** and the murder conviction had to be quashed.

4.3.3 WHICH SUBSTANTIALLY AFFECTED HIS MENTAL RESPONSIBILITY

The defendant's abnormality of mind must be shown to be substantially greater than would have been experienced by an ordinary person. The impairment need not be total but must be more than trivial, as stated in **Simcox 1964**. There should be medical evidence to support this contention. Generally, the jury will accept such evidence, but it need not if there is other evidence available to suggest a more calculated killing as in **Sanders 1991**.

In **Campbell 1997**, the defendant did succeed in pleading diminished responsibility at his second appeal. He had picked up a female hitchhiker and attacked her when she refused his advances. When he discovered that she was not dead, he tried to

FIVE KEY FACTS ON DIMINISHED RESPONSIBILITY

- The defence is to be found in **s2 Homicide Act 1957**. It is only a partial defence, reducing the conviction from murder to manslaughter. In cases of homicide, it has largely replaced the general defence of insanity.

- Three elements have to be proved before the defence will succeed: an abnormality of mind, caused by an inside source, which substantially impairs the defendant's mental responsibility for his actions.

- The term 'abnormality of mind' encompasses a greater variety of situations than the general defence of insanity. It covers a person's inability to distinguish right from wrong but also includes the 'irresistible impulse' situation, as in **Byrne 1960**.

- The abnormality must derive from the mind itself, although the accused need not be insane (**Seers 1984, Sanderson 1994, Martin 2001**). Those suffering from alcoholism which is shown to have affected the mind, battered woman's syndrome (**Ahluwalia 1992, Thornton (No. 2) 1996**), depression (**Seers, Gittens,** both **1984**), epilepsy (**Campbell 1997**), fits of jealousy (**Miller 1972**), and post menstrual tension (**Smith 1982, Reynolds 1988**), have all been able to use the defence. Those suffering from temporary intoxication cannot (**Tandy 1989**) although the defence can be used if the condition existed before the intoxication, even if the latter has made the situation worse (**Dietschmann 2003**).

- The abnormality must be great enough to substantially reduce the defendant's mental responsibility for his acts and the jury will be the body to decide this after listening to the evidence of doctors (**Sanders 1991** and **Campbell 1997**).

Comment

- There are mixed reactions to the defence of diminished responsibility. It is felt by many that those who are not totally responsible for their actions should not be convicted of murder. If the defendant is a danger, the judge still has the power to sentence him to life imprisonment or to be detained in a secure mental institution.

- Others would argue that the defence dilutes the seriousness of intentional killing. The decision in **Dietschmann 2003** may cause additional concern. It could be considered unjust that this partial defence should be available to those who exacerbate their mental condition through drink or drugs and go on to kill. On the other hand, the approach of the House of Lords in **Dietschmann** follows that taken by the same court in Smith in relation to provocation, in that the whole picture should be looked before a decision is arrived at.

- Women's groups have argued that the defence of diminished responsibility is too readily available for male defendants who kill their partners and then produce medical evidence of long-term depression caused by emotional problems. They are angered that the victim's character can be attacked when she is no longer able to defend it. In their review of this defence, the Law Commission declared itself surprised at the number of successful pleas on the grounds of depression, but went on to note that in a large proportion of these, there was a history of previous mental illness or particular mitigating circumstances. The Law Commision also noted that, in reality, successful pleas of diminished responsibility have declined in recent years. Home Office statistics show that there were 171 successful pleas between 1997 and 2001 but following this there was a falling off.

- Another claim, that the defence is less available for female offenders, has been addressed to some extent, as seen in the courts' recognition that severe pre-menstrual tension might result in an abnormality of mind. The judges have also accepted that mental and physical abuse over a long period, a condition known as 'battered woman syndrome', might reduce a woman's mental responsibility and cause her to kill her abuser.

- Other jurisdictions have not favoured a separate defence. James Chambers in his article in the Criminal Law Review 2004, 198, noted that the drafters of the US Model Penal Code were hostile to the concept of a separate partial defence of diminished responsibility. They stated in their Commentary 'By evaluating the abnormal individual on his own terms, it decreases the incentives for him to behave as if he were normal. It blurs the law's message that there are certain minimal standards of conduct to which every member of society must conform'.

strangle her and eventually hit her across the throat with his hockey stick. He maintained that he was suffering from diminished responsibility caused by his epilepsy and frontal lobe damage.

The Court of Appeal heard the evidence of two eminent psychiatrists in this field. Lord Bingham C J stated:

> *Having studied the available evidence of what the appellant did and said at the time, both doctors were of the clear opinion that at the time of the killing the appellant had been suffering an abnormality of mind of such significance as seriously to diminish his responsibility for the act he carried out.*

A retrial was therefore ordered, although it was made clear that this could not lead to an acquittal.

4.3.4 POSSIBLE REFORM OF DIMINISHED RESPONSIBILITY

The *Draft Criminal Code* wishes to alter the wording of this defence to 'Such mental abnormality as would be substantial enough to reduce the charge of murder to manslaughter'. To date, there have been no moves to put this change into effect. Instead, in October 2003, the Law Commission published a Consultation Paper entitled **'Partial Defences to Murder',** in which various suggestions were put forward for consideration, including a possible merger of the pleas of diminished responsibility and provocation. Some of the points made are dealt with here, others at the end of the section on provocation. The Law Commission noted the following criticisms of the defence of diminished responsibility:

- The defence is not available for all crimes, only as a defence to murder. It could be argued that a better solution would be to abolish the mandatory life sentence for murder and allow defendants, who at present try to plead diminished responsibility, to have these factors taken into account as mitigating circumstances when charged with the offence of murder

- The defence of diminished responsibility is said to be an "ill-defined compromise", that was brought in to help plug loopholes in the ancient common law defence of insanity, (discussed in Chapter 10). Its existence encourages mentally ill defendants to use this defence and face a manslaughter conviction, rather than putting forward the plea of insanity that might result in help being given.

- The defence of diminished responsibility is open to manipulation. For example, it has been used in cases of mercy killings where no mental abnormality existed.

On the other hand, the following points were advanced in favour of leaving things as they are:

- Even though the defence has flaws, the alternative noted in the first point above would result in the defendant being labelled a murderer, even though his sentence might be reduced.

- The verdict of 'not guilty by reason of insanity' might become a more attractive option for appropriate defendants, if the provision were to be removed that they always had to be detained indefinitely in a mental institution.

- It is argued that, in general, the defence of diminished responsibility works well in practice. The fact that it has been used to prevent mercy killers facing a sentence of life imprisonment, is not sufficient a reason to abolish it. It could be argued, instead, that while such an approach stretches the law on this subject, it could help to prevent a greater injustice.

On 1 May 2004, the Law Commission gave its Provisional Conclusions on Consultation Paper No 173. In relation to diminished responsibility, the Commissioners stated: 'From the evidence we have obtained, we are not presently persuaded that we should recommend any radical enlargement or reduction, of the scope of the defence.'

The Commissioners stated that the wording of **s2** had attracted much criticism but also noted that none of the alternative forms of wording that they had put forward had gained much support. They declared that they would think further about the wording but stressed that they would not be making any radical changes pending any wider review of the law of murder. There was also concern that **s2** was framed with adult offenders in mind and was therefore unsatisfactory in relation to children. Once again, however, it was decided that while this matter should be reviewed, such changes would not form part of this particular project.

Activity

Max has a severe persecution complex, which has been made worse by his excessive consumption of alcohol. He is convinced that his science teacher is a reincarnation of the Devil, come temporarily to Earth to ensure that Max fails his exams. On receiving an 'E' grade for a project that he believed was excellent, Max downed seven whiskys and then put poison in the teacher's coffee, causing the latter to suffer an agonising death. Max has been charged with murder but wishes to use the defence of diminished responsibility. Advise him, quoting relevant cases to support your answer.

4.4 PROVOCATION

It has been suggested that as many as 45 per cent of all killings are committed by people who lose their temper. The defence of provocation may be available if this loss of control has been caused by the provocative act of the other party.

The defence at common law

The defence of provocation has existed for many years, at least for men. The judges developed it in cases where the defendant had been provoked after being subjected to a violent physical attack. Provocation was also allowed for a man who discovered his wife committing adultery, as in **Maddy 1671**, and killed her or the lover or both. It was even suggested in Blackstone's Commentaries that such a crime was of 'the lowest degree of manslaughter', hopefully a view to which few would now subscribe! The defence was at first limited to husbands but, as the cases of **Larkin 1943** and **Gauthier** of the same year illustrate, it was extended to men killing their mistresses in similar circumstances. In **Fisher 1837**, a father who killed a man he discovered in the act of sodomy with his son was also entitled to the defence. It can be seen from these circumstances that, at common law, there had to be a provocative **act** of some sort; mere words were not enough. In **Lesbini 1914**, the defence was not available for a man who shot and killed a girl in charge of a firing range in an amusement arcade, after she had made derogatory remarks about him. In **Holmes v DPP 1946**, the House of Lords held that the defence could not be used by a husband who killed his wife after hearing her verbal confession of adultery. This can be contrasted with the current position as seen in **Parnham 2002**, where the jury accepted a manslaughter verdict when a teacher killed after his wife threatened to leave him (see overleaf).

Six years for teacher who killed his wife in an 'animal frenzy'

By Graham Keeley

A teacher who bludgeoned his wife to death over her affair with a colleague was jailed for six years yesterday.

Jillian Parnham was found with 30 wounds to her head after husband Mark hit her with a metal bar in a frenzied attack.

The information technology teacher admitted turning into a 'crazed animal' after confronting his 38-year-old wife about the staff room love triangle with her fellow maths teacher Christopher Worth. Yesterday Parnham, 37, who has two children by his wife, was convicted of manslaughter by a jury after a five day trial at Lewes Crown Court. He had denied murder

Judge Richard Brown told him: 'That was a horrendous attack on your wife and this court has to reflect the public horror in taking a life in this way. No sentence will ever reflect the value of the life you took and cannot restore a loved one to her family and a mother to her children.'

Mrs Parnham began an affair with 47-year-old Mr Worth after they played together in a school band for a Christmas Pantomime at Millais Comprehensive, a girls' school in Horsham, West Sussex, the jury was told.

The couple became lovers the day after Valentine's Day last Year, and their final encounter took place days before her death in March.

To many the Parnhams appeared devoted to each other. But her first marriage had collapsed more than 15 years earlier after her then husband suspected her of an affair with another married teacher at the same school.

She joined Millais in 1985, two years after marrying Chris Beeching at university.

A friend said: 'He became suspicious because Jillian always used to go jogging with this one teacher.

'At one point, she was supposed to be going away sailing with friends. But her husband had to ring the hotel where she was supposed to be for some reason and then found out she wasn't even booked in there.

'But she would never admit anything.'

The couple divorced two years later, and she met Parnham when he joined the school the same year.

They married in 1989 and had two sons, David, four, and 16-month-old Alexander. Family friend Neil Harding said: 'She never gave any hint of having a roving eye. She seemed very much in love. He worshipped her.

But another friend said: 'It was telling about their relationship that you would always see Mark down at the supermarket while she was off riding her horse. She wore the trousers.'

Already increasingly suspicious, Parnham finally confronted her after discovering contraceptive pills in her handbag.

Her husband told police that on the night of her death, Mrs Parnham had told him she wanted to leave him, and take the children and their four bedroom house in Ashington.

Initially Parnham claimed she had been killed by masked robbers before admitting his wife died at his hands.

Parnham will almost certainly be barred from future contact with his sons, the court was told.

He has seen them only once since his arrest to try to explain to the older boy what had happened, his solicitor said yesterday.

Daily Mail, 12 January 2002

The extended defence under s3 Homicide Act

The restrictive nature of the common law defence was lifted in 1957. Under **s3 Homicide Act 1957** it states:

Where, on a charge of murder, there is evidence on which the jury can find that the person charged was provoked (whether by things done or by things said or by both together) to lose his self-control, the question whether the provocation was enough to make a reasonable man do as he did shall be left to be determined by the jury.

This section of the **Homicide Act** clearly recognises and builds upon the common law defence of provocation. There has to be evidence of provocation but it now clearly states that this can arise from '**things said**' in addition to '**things done**'. It also reaffirms the position that it is the jury who will decide the issue, by measuring the conduct of the accused by the standard of the reasonable man, a concept first introduced in this context at common law in the case of **Welsh 1869.**

Under the **Homicide Act 1957**, therefore, the revised defence of provocation has three elements to it which have to be satisfied:

- There must be evidence that the defendant was provoked.
- He must then have lost his self-control.
- The jury must be satisfied that a reasonable man might have acted in a similar way.

4.4.1 THERE HAS TO BE EVIDENCE OF PROVOCATION

Initially, it is the judge who will decide whether there is enough evidence to be put before the jury. As mentioned earlier, the provocation can, under **s3 Homicide Act**, arise from either things done or things said. In addition, the words or actions do not need to have come from the deceased, as was the case at common law, nor need they be directed at the defendant. In **Davies 1975**, the action of the wife's lover, of walking towards her place of work to meet her, was taken into account when the husband lost control and killed his wife. In **Doughty 1986**, the Court of Appeal surprisingly held that even the continuous crying of a very young baby should have been considered by the jury as a possible provoking event, even though it was obviously not directed at the accused. Similarly, in **Pearson 1992**, the ill-treatment meted out over a period of eight years by the victim, had not been principally directed at the defendant but towards his brother.

The Court of Appeal decided that this was still an act of provocation, which the accused could use in his defence after he killed his father with a sledgehammer.

Self-induced provocation

To stop the possibility of a later appeal therefore it may be wise to put any form of provoking event before the jury. This even includes cases where the accused himself has started the trouble, which in law is known as 'self-induced provocation'. A case illustrating this is **Johnson 1989**. The accused started an argument in a night club, during which he made threats against the victim and his woman friend. A fight developed in the course of which the victim was fatally stabbed. The accused alleged that he was provoked by the fear of being 'glassed' by the victim but the judge declined to put this matter before the jury.

The Court of Appeal allowed the defendant's appeal, despite the fact that he had been the one who had started the trouble and even though he had been armed with a knife and the other only had a broken glass. Watkins L J, for the Court of Appeal stated:

In view of the express wording of s3 . . . we find it impossible to accept that the mere fact that a defendant caused a reaction in others, which in turn led him to lose his self-control, should result in the issue of provocation being kept outside a jury's consideration.

In **Baillie 1995**, a similar appeal was successful. The defendant went to the house of a drug dealer armed with a sawn-off shotgun and a cut-throat razor, after serious threats were made by the dealer to the defendant's three drug addicted sons. The father seriously injured the drug dealer with the razor and, when the latter tried to escape, the defendant fired the shotgun after him. The drug dealer was killed by particles of pellets blasted towards him from a wire mesh fence by the force of the shots.

The defendant tried to plead provocation, arguing that he suffered a temporary loss of control after his son told him about the threats and that this had lasted up to the time of the shooting. In the alternative, he also tried to claim that he lost his self-control when the victim tried to wrestle the gun from him, i.e. that this was self-induced provocation. The judge allowed the latter defence to be put before the jury but not the first issue, deciding that the loss of self-control must have ceased by the time the killing took place.

The appeal court decided that both issues should have been put to the jury and that failure to do so amounted to a material misdirection. The murder conviction was therefore quashed and one of manslaughter substituted.

Limitations

From the cases just discussed, it might appear that almost anything can amount to evidence of provocation. There are, however, some limitations.

- In **Acott 1997**, the defendant first claimed that his mother's death was an accident caused by a fall but, on his conviction for murder, he appealed, arguing that the defence of provocation should have been put to the jury.

  The House of Lords decided that there was no evidence of any provoking words or conduct by another party, even though the savagery of the attack on the victim might
have indicated that the perpetrator had lost his self control for some reason.

- In Miao 2003, the Court of Appeal decided that it was not a misdirection when 'a mere speculative possibility' that provocation might have existed had not been put before the jury.

- In addition, the wording of s3 states that the provocation must have been something said or something done, which would exclude naturally occurring acts. If a landowner lost control and killed his gardener after discovering that his gardens had been destroyed by a terrible storm, he would not be able to plead provocation.

4.4.2 THE DEFENDANT MUST HAVE LOST HIS SELF-CONTROL

It is not enough for the defendant to show that he has been provoked. **He must show that the provocation affected him so strongly that he then lost his self-control. This is obviously a subjective test.**

The classic definition of provocation was uttered by Lord Devlin in the case of **Duffy 1949** and, despite the changes made by **s3 Homicide Act** and later criticism of the definition, it remains, for the present, good law. It was quoted with approval by the House of Lords in **Baillie 1995,** mentioned earlier.

The definition in **Duffy** allows the defence to be used where the provoking event has caused:

a sudden and temporary loss of self-control rendering the accused so subject to passion as to make him or her, for the moment, not master of his mind.

In Richens, the Court of Appeal decided that there did not need to be a complete loss of control to the extent that the person had no knowledge at all of what he was doing. There must, however, be enough loss of control, which was not established in **Cocker 1989**. The defendant killed his incurably ill wife by suffocating her with a pillow after repeated demands from her to end her suffering. Because there was insufficient evidence that he had lost his self-control, the judge withdrew the defence from the jury and the latter reluctantly convicted him of murder. **The Court of Appeal upheld the conviction.**

A cooling-off period?

The words 'sudden and temporary loss of self control' have also caused problems in cases where the accused has waited some time before acting. The courts are less inclined to believe that a person has lost his self control if he or she has had time for a 'cooling-off' period and has then gone on to commit the offence.

This was the position in **Duffy 1949**, **Thornton 1996** and **Ahluwahlia 1992**, all cases concerning 'battered wives'.

In **Duffy 1949**, an abused wife, after a quarrel, left the room, changed her clothes and then returned with a hammer and a hatchet when her husband was in bed and killed him.

Lord Devlin gave the now famous direction and decided that the woman's actions did not fall within it. Her conviction for murder, therefore, was upheld.

In the case of **Thornton 1996**, the couple had a very stormy relationship. Both of them drank heavily and in this state, the husband sometimes became violent and assaulted his wife.

On the night in question, after a serious quarrel, Mrs Thornton went into the kitchen, allegedly to find a truncheon to protect herself, and when she could not find it, sharpened a kitchen knife instead and returned to where her drunken husband was sleeping on a sofa. She asked him to come to bed but he refused and, after a further acrimonious exchange, she slowly plunged the knife into his stomach and killed him.

The defence relied on the plea of diminished responsibility at the trial but the trial judge also introduced the possible defence of provocation.

Both pleas were unsuccessful and the jury convicted Thornton of murder. The issue of provocation was again raised on her first appeal but this, too, was unsuccessful because it was felt that her actions of obtaining a knife and sharpening it did not indicate a loss of self-control. After several years in prison, another appeal was allowed and, at this, a retrial was ordered.

At Oxford Crown Court, the defence of provocation was again dismissed but the alternative plea of diminished responsibility was accepted by the jury and a verdict of manslaughter substituted for murder. A sentence of six years' imprisonment was given, which in view of the time already served, meant that Thornton could walk free from the court.

In **Ahluwalia 1992**, the defendant, who had been subjected to an arranged marriage, had suffered serious physical abuse by her unfaithful husband over a number of years. At the time of the killing, she had been threatened with a further beating in the morning. She therefore waited until her husband was asleep and then poured petrol over the bed and set fire to it. The victim later died of his injuries. Once again, it was difficult for the defence to show a sudden loss of self control and Ahluwalia was convicted of murder. After a strenuous campaign to free her, the murder conviction was changed to one of manslaughter but only because the defence of diminished responsibility, caused by what has become known as 'battered woman syndrome', and 'learned helplessness', was accepted.

The Court of Appeal was prepared to accept that acts of provocation could take place over a period of time, a 'slow burn' effect, but Lord Taylor, the Lord Chief Justice at that time still reiterated that the actual loss of self control at the end of the period had to be a sudden one. He said that 'the longer the delay and the stronger the evidence of deliberation on the part of the defendant, the more likely it will be that the prosecution will negative provocation'.

In the case of **Duffy**, mentioned above, the

judge had followed his classic statement with the following comment:

> circumstances which induce a desire for revenge are inconsistent with provocation, since the conscious formulation of a desire for revenge means that a person has had time to think, to reflect, and that would negative a sudden temporary loss of self control, which is of the essence of provocation.

Revenge, rather than provocation, was said to be the reason for the crime in the case of **Ibrams and Gregory 1981**. The defendants had been terrorised and bullied by the victim. They and another woman involved in the case had failed to obtain satisfactory police protection so decided to take matters into their own hands. A few days later, they devised a plan for the woman to lure the man to bed, whereupon the defendants would burst in, attack him and break his arms and legs. Instead, the victim was killed and the defendants were found guilty of murder.

The Court of Appeal upheld the conviction, deciding that the formulation of a plan indicated that there was no sudden loss of self control and therefore no defence.

◄ *Comment*

These cases show that a person who has been ill-treated in some way, whether physically or mentally, but who fails to retaliate immediately, either through fear or through a delayed reaction to the events, faces great difficulty in English law. At present, the defence of provocation will not be open to such people if there has been enough time for a cooling-off period. They will have to rely on the more limited defence of diminished responsibility and show that their minds have been substantially affected by the cumulative effect of the abuse they have suffered.

4.4.3 A REASONABLE MAN MUST HAVE ACTED IN A SIMILAR WAY

This last point, which, at first sight appears to be a simple issue, has caused great difficulty. It involves examining the behaviour of the accused and assessing the extent of his reaction to the provocation and asking the jury to decide whether a reasonable man might have acted in the same way. But who is a reasonable man? Is he an adult of normal temperament and attributes? This was the position originally taken until the House of Lords' decision in **Camplin 1978. Now however, the reasonable man is said to be a reasonable person sharing similar characteristics to the accused. This means that the defendant's age, sex and all other physical and mental characteristics may be taken into account when assessing the effect of the provocation on the accused.**

The current statement of the law is to be found in the case of Smith (Morgan) 2000, discussed below. It was recently affirmed by the Court of Appeal in Weller 2003. We need to examine how this change in the law came about.

The original, more objective view of a reasonable man can be seen in the case of **Bedder 1954**. The accused had been unsuccessful in his attempts to have intercourse with a prostitute. He claimed that she had struck him and taunted him about his impotence and that these provoking acts had caused him to lose his temper and kill her.

The House of Lords dismissed his appeal against the conviction for murder, stating that a reasonable man would not have lost control in this way. No allowance was made for the special circumstances of the man's impotency.

Changes made after *Camplin*

This purely objective test of the reasonable man was modified by the House of Lords in DPP v Camplin 1978. Their Lordships felt that a better test should be: 'Would a reasonable man, or in this case, boy, with the same characteristics as the accused have acted in this way?'

In this case, a 15-year-old boy had been drinking and went with a middle-aged man to the latter's house, where the boy was forcibly subjected to a homosexual assault. When he expressed shame at what had happened, the older man was alleged to have laughed and taunted him. The boy then attacked him with a heavy chipatti pan and killed him. He was convicted of murder after a direction from the judge about the qualities of a reasonable man.

The House of Lords decided that, while certain of the boy's characteristics should not be taken into account for policy reasons, such as his drunkenness and excitability, other characteristics, such as his young age, could be. The question for the jury, therefore, was whether a reasonable youth of 15, in similar circumstances, would have acted as he did. Because this was a possibility, the appeal against the murder conviction was allowed.

Unfortunately, the use of the word 'characteristics', and the decision as to which of these may be taken into account, has inevitably led to further appeals.

In **Newell 1980**, the accused killed the victim by hitting him with a heavy ashtray, after the friend made homosexual advances to him. The defendant was an alcoholic who, at the time of the attack, was recovering from a drug overdose. He was in a bad emotional state because his girlfriend had recently left him.

The Court of Appeal held that, when looking at the characteristics of the accused, the jury should only take into account permanent ones and ones that actually relate to the provocation. Therefore the effects of his drinking and drug taking could not be considered. It was decided that alcoholism could be a permanent factor, which in some situations could be taken into account, but not in this case because it was unrelated to the actual attack. The appeal

against the murder conviction was therefore unsuccessful.

Mental characteristics

Even though **Newell's** appeal was unsuccessful, the case seemed to mark a turning point in allowing a greater range of characteristics to be attributed to the reasonable man. The Court of Appeal decided that even certain mental characteristics could be taken into account, following statements made earlier in **McGregor 1962** – a New Zealand case. This new approach can be seen in the appeal of **Humphreys 1995**, who had been convicted of murder after stabbing her lover.

The severely disturbed girl had been brought up by an alcoholic mother and stepfather and had made several suicide attempts. She became a prostitute at the age of 16 and later moved in with the deceased, a much older man. The latter was of a violent disposition and unfaithful to her.

On the night of the stabbing, the deceased had made public remarks about the possibility of a 'gang bang' later that night. Humphreys claimed that her fear that he was about to rape her, coupled with her distress over his jeering comments about a recent suicide attempt caused her '**to snap**'. Despite this plea of provocation, the jury found her guilty of murder.

After a strenuous campaign to secure her release, her case was eventually referred back to the Court of Appeal.

The court decided that the girl's characteristics of immaturity and attention-seeking could be likened to an illness like anorexia. They could be seen as part of a psychological illness and were thus sufficiently permanent characteristics to be attributed to the reasonable young woman. The court also stated that, in a complex case such as this, the jury should have been given a more detailed analysis of the possible areas of provocation and not have been left without guidance simply to make its own decision. The appeal was allowed.

As stated earlier, **Ahluwalia** and **Thornton** also benefited from this more liberal approach. While their retrials succeeded on the issue of diminished responsibility, the Court of Appeal, in an obiter statement in **Ahluwalia 1992** had stated that post traumatic stress disorder and battered woman syndrome could come under the heading of characteristics for the purposes of provocation. This view was supported in **Thornton (No 2) 1996**, even though, as in the previous case, diminished responsibility rather than provocation, was accepted as the more relevant defence.

In Dryden 1995, the Court of Appeal decided that the defendant's 'eccentric and obsessional personality traits' were mental characteristics of sufficient permanence to be attributed to the reasonable man and ones which should have been pointed out to the jury. Despite the misdirection, the appeal failed because it was felt that no jury would have believed that a reasonable man, even one possessing the qualities of the accused, would have reacted to a demolition order by killing those trying to enforce it.

In **Morhall 1995**, the defendant was taunted about his addiction to glue-sniffing several times on the day in question. He was involved in a fight with the victim, which was broken up. The deceased then followed the defendant up to his room and was stabbed seven times. Morhall was convicted of murder, a decision that was upheld by the Court of Appeal.

The House of Lords, however, reversed the decision and substituted a conviction for manslaughter.

The judges decided that a distinction had to be made between cases where the accused is taunted about an addiction he possesses, such as drug addiction, alcoholism or being a glue-sniffer, who then loses his self control, and cases where, because of his drugged state or his drunkenness, he loses that self control more readily. In the first type of situation,

provocation could be pleaded but, in the latter case, it is felt that a reasonable man, or ordinary man as the House of Lords now chose to call him, would not have been drunk or drugged.

Their Lordships approved of the reasoning in DPP v Camplin mentioned earlier, but decided that, since that case, too much emphasis had been placed on the word 'characteristic' and attempts to decide which of these could or could not be taken into account. They decided that, instead of being asked to look at various characteristics of the accused, the jury should be asked to look at 'the entire factual situation'. This could include other factors that might be relevant to the provocation, in addition to the characteristics of the accused. These could include various addictions if they had been the subject of the provocation, as was the case here.

Retraction!

A warning that the concept of the reasonable man was being widened in an unacceptable way came from the Privy Council hearing the case of **Luc Thiet Thuan 1997**, an appeal from Hong Kong.

The Privy Council decided, four to one, that factors such as mental instability which reduced the defendant's powers of self control should not be attributed to the reasonable man in a provocation case. Lord Goff argued that the Court of Appeal had taken a wrong turning in the case of Newell 1980 regarding the characteristics to be attributed to the reasonable man. It had adopted, 'without analysis', statements made in the New Zealand case of McGregor 1962. That case had allowed 'purely mental peculiarities' to be included as characteristics in the defence of provocation, which Lord Goff believed was wrong. He pointed out that New Zealand does not have a separate defence of diminished responsibility and therefore needed to take its own steps to rectify this shortcoming, as was discussed later in another New Zealand case—that of McCarthy 1992. English law, however, does have two separate defences, so he felt that such an approach should not have been adopted here.

He declared that the use of provocation in the cases of Ahluwahlia (post traumatic stress disorder or battered woman syndrome), Dryden (eccentric and obsessional personality traits), and Humphreys (abnormal immaturity and attention-seeking) would have been decided differently if the case of McCarthy had been brought to the Court of Appeal's attention. If this had been done, he argued, such mental characteristics would not have been considered.

Expansion!

Be that as it may, the Court of Appeal was not prepared to admit it was wrong. Under the doctrine of precedent, earlier decisions of the Court of Appeal are normally binding on the Court of Appeal in later cases, whereas decisions of the Privy Council are only persuasive.

In Campbell 1997, therefore, the Court of Appeal stated that it would still abide by its own earlier decisions until such time as it was ordered not to do so by the House of Lords.

Matters came to a head in the case of **Smith (Morgan) 2000**. The defendant and the victim, James McCullagh were both alcoholics and long-standing drinking partners and, during an argument over an alleged theft of his tools, Smith became increasingly furious at the other's denial of involvement. He then seized a kitchen knife and stabbed his friend to death. At his trial, he put forward the defences of both diminished responsibility and provocation. He claimed that medical evidence would show that he was suffering from a depressive illness that had damaged substantially his capacity for self control. The trial judge, however, directed the jury that, with regard to **s3** and the provocation plea, the characteristics of mental impairment could only be brought forward when deciding on the gravity of the provocation; they were not relevant to the reasonable man's loss of self control. The accused was subsequently found guilty of murder. The Court of Appeal disagreed with the Crown Court decision and substituted a verdict of manslaughter.

The House of Lords upheld (but only on a 3/2 majority) the wider view of provocation. **Their Lordships agreed that the trial judge had erred by telling the jury that the effect of the defendant's depression on his powers of self-control was not material. In answer to the certified question, i.e. 'whether characteristics other than age or sex attributable to a reasonable man for the purposes of s3 Homicide Act are relevant not only to the gravity of the provocation but also to the standard of self-control to be expected?', the House of Lords decided that the answer was 'yes'.**

While the murder conviction in this case was quashed and manslaughter substituted because of the misdirection, the Law Lords did make it clear that the mere existence of such a characteristic would not in itself excuse the defendant's behaviour. Lord Slynn went on to state: 'It is thus not enough for the accused to say "I am a depressive, therefore I cannot be expected to exercise self-control". The jury must ask whether he has exercised the degree of self-control to be exercised by someone in his situation.' Lord Hoffman, while affirming that it was wrong for a judge to tell the jury to disregard a particular characteristic, also stressed that 'The law expects people to exercise control over their emotions'. He stated that the jury should decide what amounts to a sufficient excuse by 'on the one hand making allowance for human nature and the power of emotions but, on the other hand, not allowing someone to rely on his own violent disposition'.

More radically, Lord Hoffman also suggested that if judges were 'freed from the necessity of invoking the formula of the reasonable man equipped with an array of unreasonable "eligible characteristics"', they would then be able to explain the principles of provocation in simple terms.

This point was picked up by the Court of Appeal in **Weller 2003.** The 34-year-old defendant had strangled his 18-year-old girlfriend, during a quarrel over her alleged involvement with other men. The girl had already ended their relationship because of his excessive jealousy and possessiveness and had come back to collect her belongings. Weller was convicted of murder but alleged that the judge had misdirected the jury. Unlike **Smith (Morgan),** the trial judge had not removed the characteristics of possessiveness and jealousy from consideration by the jury, and when advising them as to whether the accused had lost his self-control, she had stated that all the circumstances should be taken into account. She had not specifically mentioned the above characteristics when discussing the second element in provocation of whether the defendant should reasonably have controlled himself. The judge had, however, asked the jury to consider 'what society expected of a man like the appellant in his position'. The jury, after retiring to consider their verdict, had asked for further clarification on provocation. The judge had repeated her earlier direction to them but this time had left out the piece concerning what society expects of a man like this defendant in his position.

The Court of Appeal decided that, although 'the omission was unfortunate', it was not enough to render the appeal unsafe. When looking at the original direction and the repeat direction together, there was enough evidence that the jury had been advised both about the nature of provocation and the characteristics of the accused. They had not been told to disregard the defendant's jealous and possessive nature so these characteristics would have been in their minds when reaching their verdict. The Court of Appeal did, however, add the rider that in other cases 'it might well prove the better course to identify the particular characteristics relied upon whether or not accompanied by further guidance'.

Cases on this subject still continue to reach the Court of Appeal. In Taylor 2003, the latter court affirmed that the whole of the personality of the woman in question, including her psychiatric problems, should be taken into account. Despite this, the appeal against a murder conviction failed, however, because the court was of the opinion that this matter had been explained to the jury satisfactorily at the beginning of the judge's summing up, even though he had not returned to the matter in the final part of his speech.

Comment

There has been heated discussion over the expansion of the defence of provocation, particularly in relation to the decision that mental characteristics should be taken into account, when looking at the more objective limb of provocation.

● For example, the late Sir John Smith made it abundantly clear that he did not like the decision in **Smith.** He forcibly argued that the majority of the House of Lords had misinterpreted the statements made by their predecessors in **Camplin** and **Morhall.** He stated that in **Camplin,** the House of Lords had accepted that certain characteristics, peculiar to the defendant, could be taken into account, but argued that it was clear from the judgment that these statements were only made in relation to the **gravity** of the provocation. When assessing this, it has now been accepted that mental, as well as physical, characteristics can be taken into account. He went on to say however, that the passages in **Camplin** have nothing to say about the relevance of mental characteristics **on the powers of self-restraint,** which was the point of issue in **Smith.** He quoted Lord

Diplock's view in **Camplin** of the reasonable man as being **'an ordinary person of either sex, not exceptionally excitable or pugnacious, but possessed of such powers of self-control as everyone is entitled to expect that his fellow citizens will exercise in society as it is today'.** He then wondered how the defendant in question, whose ability to control his actions is substantially injured, who is 'disinhibited' and who loses his self-control and inflicts fatal wounds with a knife simply because his friend will not admit to an accusation of stealing his property, could possibly fit such a description.

Our leading academic lawyer approved of the Privy Council decision in **Luc Thiet Thuan,** which he stated was rightly determined under **s2,** not **s3,** and argued that the case of **Smith** is **'indistinguishable'** from this earlier one.

- Professor Ashworth and Professor Glanville Williams had also argued that the characteristics of the accused **'must relate to the provocation'.** Professors Gardner and Macklem argued in the Criminal Law Review 2001, 623, that the decision in **Smith (Morgan)** was wrong in at least nine respects and felt that all questions of individual psychological make-up should be dealt with under the defence of diminished responsibility in **s2.** With regard to the argument that defendants would prefer to plead the defence of provocation to that of diminished responsibility, they argue that the expansion of **s3** makes **'provocation itself the very defence of mental abnormality that self-respecting defendants would rather not plead'.**

- The decision of the House of Lords in **Smith** means that the lines between the defences of provocation and diminished responsibility have become increasingly blurred. The late Sir John Smith stated that, as a result of the changes made to provocation, it might now be possible for someone like **Byrne**, mentioned earlier, to argue provocation, in the form of 'a young woman flaunting her charms in sight of a sexual psychopath'. A worrying thought!

- The present state of the law on provocation has certainly made life more difficult for the trial judge. It is far from clear as to how he must now direct the jury. In addition, the jury itself now has a more difficult task. The House of Lords has clearly affirmed that the decision as to whether provocation has been established is one for that body to make. These lay personnel must now try to take into account the relevant characteristics of the accused in relation to the gravity of the provocation and also come to an opinion on the effect of these characteristics on his degree of self-control. A daunting task!

Activity

- The defence of provocation, as expanded in cases like **Smith (Morgan) 2000**, is difficult for the jury to understand and is badly in need of reform. Discuss.
- Decide whether the defence of provocation is available for Darby and Joan in the following unrelated circumstances:

Darby was often ill-treated by his domineering wife. He brooded about this for several months, but then crept into her bedroom and smothered her with a pillow.

Joan suffers from a long term depressive illness. One night, after downing several vodkas, she killed her partner by battering him with her chip pan, after he taunted her about her weight gain.

TEN KEY FACTS ON PROVOCATION

- The law is to be found under common law and in **s3 Homicide Act 1957**. The aforementioned Act extended provocation to things said as well as things done.

- The provoking words or action need not be directed at the accused (**Doughty 1986, Pearson 1992**), nor need they come from the victim (**Davies 1975**), but they do need to be something said or something done. It appears that if there is any possible evidence of provocation, the jury should be advised of this, even if it is felt that the plea would not succeed (**Doughty 1986** and **Baillie 1995**). It has also been made clear that the defendant can use the defence of provocation, even if he started the trouble, as in **Johnson 1989** and **Baillie 1995**. This is known as self-induced provocation.

- Three elements have to be established before the defence can be used: as stated, there has to be evidence of provocation, the accused must have lost his self control and the jury must be convinced that the provocation was enough to make a reasonable man act in the same way.

- When looking at whether the defendant has lost his self control, the direction in **Duffy 1949** is still approved of, although a complete loss of control is not necessary (**Richens 1993**). As the law currently stands, the loss of control can now come after a 'slow burn' (**Ahluwalia 1992**) or some delay (**Baillie 1995**), but there still must be a final 'snapping' of the self control (**Cocker 1989**). Evidence of any premeditation will normally be fatal (**Ibrams and Gregory 1981**).

- The concept of the reasonable man, first laid down in **Welsh 1869**, has now changed to that of the 'ordinary' man (**Morhall 1996**). The question of whether such an ordinary man would have acted the same way, is decided by the jury.

- In the past, a purely objective approach was used, as in **Bedder v DPP 1954**. This was changed in **DPP v Camplin** to whether a reasonable person, sharing the same characteristics of the accused would have acted in the same way. In **Morhall 1996**, it was suggested that the whole factual situation needed to be looked at.

- Drunkenness or drug taking which might accelerate a person's loss of control are not characteristics that can be taken into account, although, if the defendant is an alcoholic, drug addict or glue sniffer, taunts actually relating to such factors could be considered (**Morhall 1996**).

- The appeal courts decided to attribute certain mental characteristics to the reasonable man, such as learned helplessness caused by long-term abuse, as in **Ahluwalia 1992**, eccentric and obsessional personality traits (**Dryden 1995**), abnormal immaturity and attention-seeking, as in **Humphreys 1995**, and a severe depressive illness as in **Smith (Morgan) 1998**.

- In **Luc Thiet Thuan 1997**, the Privy Council disapproved of this extension and stated that the courts should return to the law as laid down in **DPP v Camplin 1978** and applied in **Morhall 1995**. There was therefore a conflict between this court and the Court of Appeal. In **Campbell 1997** the latter court decided that it would abide by its own earlier decisions unless the House of Lords decreed otherwise.

- This conflict was resolved by the House of Lords in **Smith (Morgan) 2000**, which approved of the direction taken by the Court of Appeal. The Law Lords, but only on a three to two majority, decided that characteristics of the accused, including mental ones, could also be taken into account, not only when considering the gravity of the provocation but also when considering the degree of self control expected of the reasonable man.

4.4.4 THE FUTURE OF PROVOCATION

In the light of the criticism regarding the extension of the defence of provocation following the case of **Smith (Morgan) 2000** and its blurring with the defence of diminished responsibility, plus other concerns that had been raised over these two defences and self-defence, the Law Commission issued a consultation paper on Partial Defences to Murder in October 2003. With regard to provocation, it noted that the law was unclear and unsatisfactory and canvassed opinions on this.

The Law Commission then produced Partial Defences to Murder, Provisional Conclusions on Consultation, Paper No 173, on 1 May 2004.

The Commissioners decided that there were three broad options when deciding on the future of provocation:

- abolition,
- retention
- reform

They did not favour abolition even if the mandatory life sentence were to be removed and noted that, in any event, the Government had indicated that it was unwilling to take such a step. They recognised that some would prefer to keep the defence in its current form if the more radical changes to murder generally could not be not effected. **The Commissioners felt strongly, however, that the defence was 'beyond cure by judicial reform' but could be improved by legislation.** They therefore suggested the following changes:

1   Unlawful homicide that would otherwise be murder should instead be manslaughter if the defendant in response to:

   a   gross provocation (meaning words or conduct or a combination of words and conduct which caused the defendant to have a justifiable sense of being seriously wronged); or

   b   fear of serious violence towards the defendant or another; or c   a combination of both a) and b); and a person of the defendant's age and of ordinary temperament, i.e. ordinary tolerance and self-restraint, in the circumstances of the defendant might have reacted in the same or a similar way.

2   In deciding whether a person of the defendant's age and of ordinary temperament in the circumstances of the defendant might have acted in the same or a similar way, the court should take into account all the circumstances of the defendant other than matters (apart from his or her age) which bear only on his or her general capacity for self-control.

3   The partial defence should not apply where:

● the provocation was incited by the defendant for the purpose of providing an excuse to use violence, or

● the defendant acted in a pre-meditated desire for revenge.

4   A person should not be treated as having acted in a pre-meditated desire for revenge if he or she acted in fear of serious violence, merely because he or she was also angry towards the deceased for the conduct which engendered that fear.

5   A judge should not be required to leave the defence to the jury unless there is evidence on which a reasonable jury, properly directed, could conclude that it might apply.

It was stressed that these provisions only identified the principles governing the proposed reform and that it was up to Parliament to draft them as it saw fit.

It can be seen that the proposed new defence is both narrower and wider than the current one. It would tighten up the defence in the following ways:

● The provocation would have to be 'gross' (the crying of a baby, as in **Doughty,** would not be sufficient).

● It must not be self-induced. (**Johnson** would be overruled).

● Matters, other than age, relating solely to the defendant's general capacity for self-control would not be taken into account (expansion of the defence resulting from **Smith (Morgan)** would be halted).

● The judge would have the discretion to decide whether the evidence was sufficient to put before a jury. (The current trend that almost anything amounting to possible provocation should be put before the jury would be reversed).

On the other hand, the defence would be widened to include the following groups of people:

● It specifically provides a partial defence for those fearing violence towards themselves or

▶ *Comment*

It is submitted that these reforms, if ever enacted, would do much to alleviate concerns expressed over the current operation of the defence of provocation and its uneasy relationship with diminished responsibility. They also deal with the shortcomings in the defence of self-defence, (discussed in Chapter 11), under which a defendant who, in the heat of the moment uses excessive force to defend himself, faces a charge of murder and a mandatory sentence of life-imprisonment.

On the downside, the length of the provisions and statements as to the various factors that should or should not be taken into account when using the defence, could well lead to further difficulties for judges as they try, in simple terms, to explain the law to the jury. The latter could also face problems when trying to interpret such directions when deliberating on the verdict.

'Loving' husband killed his sick wife

By Paul Cheston

A retired policeman who killed his terminally ill wife was described as 'a loving husband' as he walked free from the Old Bailey today.

Brian Blackburn, 62 received a nine-month suspended sentence after failing in his attempt to commit suicide.

Judge Richard Hawkins said Blackburn had done 'the last loving thing you could do for her' when his wife, former nurse Margaret, 62, asked him to cut her wrists because she had only weeks to live.

He then cut his own wrists but his blood congealed and he rang the police when he did not die. Judge Hawkins said a post-mortem examination had shown Mrs Blackburn had stomach cancer, as she had suspected. She had not sought medical help because of her work in a hospice and her abhorrence of surgery.

Mrs Blackburn had asked her husband to make sure she was dead before killing himself after she was awake all night in terrible pain.

The judge accepted that the relationship was 'thoroughly loving'.

Blackburn, a policeman with an exemplary 30-year record, wiped his eyes during the hearing. Mrs Blackburn's sons Colin and Martin Lawrence had written to the judge pleading for mercy.

The couple married in 1969 after Blackburn's first wife, Angela, died from breast cancer.

Blackburn, of Ash, Surrey pleaded guilty to manslaughter. His sentence was suspended for two years and he was made the subject of a supervision order.

The Voluntary Euthanasia Society said the case was 'desperately sad' and urged a change in the law so that people such as Mrs Blackburn could have the 'gentle, dignified' death they wanted.

Evening Standard, 14 January 2005

others (this could provide greater help for battered wives and others in similar circumstances, because it would no longer be necessary to demonstrate a sudden and temporary loss of self-control).

- It would also provide a partial defence to those who use excessive force in alleged self-defence (this could cover the police dealing with dangerous suspects or homeowners confronting armed burglars).

4.5 THE SURVIVOR OF A SUICIDE PACT

Until the **Suicide Act 1961** was passed, suicide was a crime and the person faced prosecution if he survived. In addition, if another was involved in a plan to commit suicide and he survived and the other did not, he would be charged with murder. **Suicide is no longer a crime and the law has decided that aiders and abettors in suicide pacts should be treated more leniently if they do not die along with the other.**

Under **s4(1) Homicide Act 1957, should two or more people enter into a suicide pact and one of them survive, that survivor would be charged with manslaughter, not murder**. The burden of proving such a pact, should the accused have originally been charged with murder, will be on the defendant, **s4(2)**. Under **s4(3)** of the Act, a suicide pact is defined as:

an agreement between two or more persons which has as its objects the death of all parties to it.

The defendant therefore must have had a settled intention of dying. Such an intention saved **Blackburn 2005** from facing a charge of murder, rather than manslaughter, as seen in the newspaper article on the previous page.

4.6 INFANTICIDE (JWEC ONLY)

The law on this subject is in **s1(1) Infanticide Act 1938**, which provides a partial excuse for a woman who '**by any wilful act or omission**' causes the death of a child of hers under the age of 12 months but does so because she has not fully recovered from the effect of giving birth or from breast feeding the baby. In appropriate circumstances, the woman would be charged under this Act rather than with murder or manslaughter and, normally, dealt with more leniently.

Self-assessment questions on Chapter 4

1 Define voluntary manslaughter and state where the law is to be found.
2 What is meant by the term 'diminished responsibility'?
3 Why were the defendants in **Borthwick** and **Martin** allowed to bring up the defence of diminished responsibility in their appeals?
4 Giving clear explanations and case examples to illustrate your answer, describe the three elements of the defence of diminished responsibility.
5 Give three criticisms that have been made of this defence. What is the current view of the Law Commission?
6 Why did the appeals concerning provocation succeed in the cases of **Doughty**, **Baillie** and **Johnson**?
7 Describe the definition laid down in **Duffy** and state why this caused problems in the cases of **Cocker, Ibrams, Ahluwalia** and **Thornton**? How were the last two cases eventually decided?
8 Why were the cases of **Camplin** and **Morhall** important in the law on provocation?
9 Which conflict did the House of Lords eventually resolve in **Smith (Morgan)**? Explain why this decision and other aspects of the defence of provocation have been criticised and describe the reforms suggested by the Law Commission in May 2004.
10 What defence exists by virtue of **s4(1) Homicide Act**? Why would this defence as it stands, be of no avail in some mercy killings?

Chapter 5

UNLAWFUL KILLING III: INVOLUNTARY MANSLAUGHTER AND CORPORATE KILLINGS

5.1 INTRODUCTION

With both murder and voluntary manslaughter, an intention to kill or cause grievous bodily harm has to be proved. **With involuntary manslaughter, no such intention is necessary. It is enough that the defendant has committed an unlawful and dangerous act and from that act a death has resulted, or that the accused has been so grossly negligent that someone has died.**

The following diagram illustrates this.

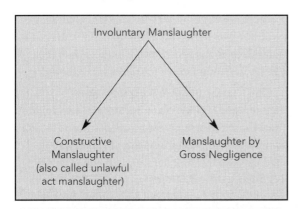

Figure 5.1 Types of involuntary manslaughter

A third category of involuntary manslaughter has also been recognised over the years, that of reckless manslaughter, but at the present time this type of manslaughter has been merged with killings as a result of gross negligence. The rise and fall of reckless manslaughter will therefore be investigated. In addition, towards the end of the chapter, the subject of deaths caused by the alleged negligence of business organisations will be examined.

These matters are dealt with in the following order:

✔ **Constructive manslaughter**
✔ **Manslaughter by gross negligence and the demise of reckless manslaughter**
✔ **Reform of involuntary manslaughter**
✔ **Corporate killings.**

5.2 CONSTRUCTIVE MANSLAUGHTER

This is also known as unlawful act manslaughter because it is committed where the defendant has caused the death of a person by an unlawful and dangerous act. The distinction between this type of manslaughter and that of gross negligence manslaughter was clearly stated by Humphreys J in the case of Larkin 1943.

If a person is engaged in doing a lawful act, and in the course of doing that lawful act behaves so negligently as to cause the death of some other person, then it is for the jury to say, upon a consideration of the whole of the facts of the case, whether the negligence proved against the accused person amounts to manslaughter, and it is the duty of the presiding judge to tell them that it will not amount to manslaughter unless the negligence is of a very high degree [. . .] That is where the act is lawful. Where the act which a person is engaged in performing is unlawful, then if at the same time it is a dangerous act, that is an act which is likely to injure another person, and quite inadvertently he causes the death of that other person by that act, then he is guilty of manslaughter.

From the above, it can be noted that three elements have to be established before a person is liable for constructive manslaughter.

- There must have been an unlawful act.
- This act must have caused the death.
- The unlawful act must have been a dangerous one.

5.2.1 THERE MUST BE AN UNLAWFUL ACT

It was held in earlier times that the unlawful act causing the death could be a civil wrong in addition to a criminal act.

In **Fenton 1830**, it was held that a person could be liable for unlawful act manslaughter when he committed the tort of trespass. The accused had thrown stones down a mineshaft and this act had caused the scaffolding to collapse, which resulted in the death of miners in the shaft.

In the later case of **Franklin 1883**, however, this view was not sustained. The defendant had thrown a box belonging to a stall holder in Brighton, into the sea, where it had struck a swimmer and caused his death.

The judge, Field J stated: '. . . the mere fact of a civil wrong committed by one person against another ought not to be used as an incident which is a necessary step in a criminal case.'

Such a defendant could, of course, be convicted on the grounds of manslaughter by gross negligence if it was felt that the degree of negligence was very high and, in the event, this is what happened.

When a person is charged with constructive manslaughter, the unlawful act often consists of an assault. It will not be a viable defence for the defendant to argue that he did not intend to injure the person who was actually harmed, provided that the assault itself has been established and he had been reckless in his conduct.

In the case of **Larkin**, the accused had discovered his mistress in the company of another man, had brooded about this for a while and had returned with an open razor. He alleged that he had only meant to frighten the man but that his mistress, who had been drinking, staggered into the path of the razor and cut her throat on it.

Despite this claim, the conviction for unlawful act manslaughter was upheld because an assault had been committed and this assault had caused the death in question.

Difficulties in finding an unlawful act

For liability to arise, the prosecution has the task of establishing that an unlawful act has taken place. This was not proved in the following two cases.

In **Lamb 1967**, the accused and his friend had been playing with a revolver. This had two bullets in it, neither of which was opposite the barrel. Believing that this meant that the gun was safe, the defendant pointed it at his friend and pulled the trigger. It was established that he did not intend to harm the friend and the latter was not in fear of his acts. Unfortunately, the gun fired a live bullet and the friend was killed.

The Court of Appeal quashed the manslaughter conviction because it was decided that there had not been an unlawful act. It will be noted later, when looking at non-fatal offences against the person, that the crime of assault requires the victim to be put in fear that a battery will be inflicted upon him. In this case, no such fear existed.

In **Ariobeke 1988**, there was certainly fear on the victim's part but the actions of the defendant did not amount to criminal acts. There had been evidence of bad relations between the two men and the accused had been peering into the carriages of a train apparently looking for the victim. The latter appeared to have panicked and ran across the railway lines trying to escape. He was then electrocuted when he stepped on a live rail.

Ariobeke was convicted of manslaughter but the Court of Appeal quashed the conviction on

the grounds that an assault had not been established.

A similar approach was taken in **Scarlett 1993**. A publican ejected a drunken customer and the latter fell, hit his head and died.

The Court of Appeal quashed the conviction, deciding that an unlawful act had not been clearly established. There was insufficient evidence that the publican had intentionally or recklessly used excessive force to remove the victim.

Stretching the rules

In **DPP v Newbury and Jones 1977** two young boys had thrown a slab of paving stone from a bridge into the path of a passing train. This entered the window of the cab and killed the guard. The *mens rea* of assault requires that the accused must have foreseen that his act would cause harm and the boys claimed that they had not foreseen the possibility that anyone would have been injured by their actions.

Despite this allegation, the House of Lords upheld the conviction for unlawful act manslaughter without further investigation into the unlawfulness of the act, a decision that has been questioned by legal writers. Their Lordships merely accepted that an unlawful act had been committed and proceeded to answer the point of law put forward on that basis.

◀ *Comment*_____

While it might have been difficult to establish an assault against the guard, because of a lack of intention or subjective recklessness on the part of the defendants, it has been argued that an unlawful act would still have arisen, either in the form of criminal damage or by endangering passengers contrary to **s34 Offences Against the Person Act 1861**. It is, however, unfortunate that the matter was not clarified by their Lordships.

Similar claims that no unlawful act has been established have arisen in relation to dealers or friends of drug addicts who have helped the latter to take drugs and have been prosecuted when a death occurred. In **Cato 1976,** the defendant and the person who died agreed to give each other their 'fixes'. The defendant injected the other man several times during the night with a mixture of heroin and water, previously prepared by the victim. The amount taken proved to be fatal and the defendant was charged with administering a noxious thing, contrary to the **Offences Against the Person Act 1861,** and with manslaughter. The jury found him guilty on both counts. Cato then appealed. He tried to argue that while it is an offence to possess or supply heroin under the **Misuse of Drugs Act 1971**, it is not an offence under that act merely to take a mixture, already prepared by another person and then just give it to him. He therefore argued that his conduct was not unlawful.

The Court of Appeal decided that the unlawfulness had been established by the fact that the defendant had administered a noxious thing contrary to the Offences Against the Person Act 1861, and as a death had resulted, he was rightly guilty of involuntary manslaughter. Lord Widgery CJ also chose to deal with the point raised by the defence. He decided that even if it had not been possible to rely on the above charge, there would still have been an unlawful act due to the fact that the defendant had unlawfully taken drugs into his possession and then injected the deceased with them.

In **Kennedy 1998**, the reasoning appeared even more strained. The defendant was held to have assisted in an unlawful activity when he handed a loaded syringe to the victim, who then injected himself and later died. In fact, the latter action is not, in itself, unlawful, and as will be seen later when dealing with parties to a crime, a person should not be found guilty of being an accessory to a crime if, in fact, no crime has been committed. Nevertheless, the Court of Appeal upheld the manslaughter conviction.

This decision was criticised by the late Sir John Smith and was distinguished in the case of **Dias 2002**. In **Rogers 2003**, Smith's criticisms and the case of **Dias** were both reviewed by the Court of Appeal and this time a different approach was taken. The court decided that it was immaterial whether the **deceased** had been committing an unlawful act at the time. The point to establish was whether the **defendant** had committed an unlawful act.

The Court of Appeal decided that if a third party applied and held a tourniquet on the arm of a drug addict while the latter injected himself with heroin, the former person was playing a part in the mechanics of the injection. This was an unlawful act on his part, because he was administering poison so as to endanger life, contrary to s23 Offences Against the Person Act 1861. If a death subsequently resulted, the defendant would also be guilty of manslaughter.

5.2.2 THE UNLAWFUL ACT MUST HAVE CAUSED THE DEATH

As noted in Chapter 3, when looking at the subject of causation, the unlawful act of the accused must be closely connected to the death that has resulted, and a *novus actus interveniens* (a new intervening act) must not have arisen to break the chain of causation. The unlawful act need not however, be the sole cause of the death, provided that it made a significant contribution to it.

It was originally decided by the courts that the unlawful act had to be directed at a human being, even if the wrong person actually died or was injured, as occurred in **Latimer**. The Court of Appeal went further than this, in the case of **Dalby 1982**, where the judges, rather surprisingly, stated that the unlawful act must be directed at the victim. The defendant and the victim were

drug users but, unlike the cases mentioned above, the defendant had obtained a drug called diconal lawfully on prescription and then given some of the tablets to his friend. They injected themselves intravenously before going to a discotheque. While they were out, the friends parted company and there was evidence that another person also injected the victim at least twice more with unspecified drugs. The latter died the following day.

Dalby was charged with supplying drugs and also with the offence of constructive manslaughter. One of the questions the jurors were asked to consider was whether the supply of the diconal was a substantial cause of the victim's death, i.e. one which was not merely trivial. The jury found him guilty of manslaughter.

The Court of Appeal quashed the manslaughter conviction, stating that:

> *The difficulty in the present case is that the act of supplying a controlled drug was not an act which caused direct harm. It was an act which made it possible, or even likely, that harm would occur subsequently, particularly if the drug was supplied to someone who was on drugs. In all the reported cases, the physical act has been one which inevitably would subject the other person to the risk of some harm from the act itself.*

The Court of Appeal then went on to state categorically that:

> *In the judgment of this court, where the charge of manslaughter is based on an unlawful and dangerous act, it must be an act directed at the victim and likely to cause immediate injury, however slight.*

The acceptance of indirect acts

Later cases have modified the strong statements made in **Dalby**. In the case of **Mitchell 1983**, it was decided that an act intended for another person could, under the doctrine of transferred malice, be classed as being directed at the victim.

In this case, the defendant had tried to 'jump the queue' in a busy post office and a 70-year-old man had remonstrated with him. The accused hit him in the mouth and then either hit him again or pushed him backwards so that he fell against others in the queue, including an even older woman who suffered a broken leg. As a result of this, she had to have an operation to have a hip joint replaced. At first she appeared to be recuperating well but then died suddenly. The defendant was convicted of manslaughter, but appealed.

The Court of Appeal had to decide whether the person at whom the act is aimed must also be the person whose death is caused. Staughton J stated:

We can see no reason of policy for holding that an act calculated to harm A cannot be manslaughter if it in fact kills B. The criminality of the doer of the act is precisely the same whether it is A or B who dies.

In **Goodfellow 1986**, the Court of Appeal went further and decided that the accused could still be liable even though he did not direct his unlawful act at a person at all.

The accused was being harassed by two other men and wanted to move from his council accommodation, but knew that his chances of a transfer were slight. He therefore decided to take matters into his own hands and set fire to his house, making it look as if it had been petrol-bombed, hoping that this would lead to him being re-housed. Unfortunately, the intensity of the fire was greater than was planned and Goodfellow's wife, son and his son's girlfriend all died in the blaze.

The Court of Appeal upheld his conviction for manslaughter even though the unlawful act of arson was not directed at the people who died. The court held that the accused could have been liable for both reckless manslaughter, which existed at that time and for unlawful act manslaughter. With regard to the latter charge, the court held that it had to be shown that the act was committed intentionally, that it was an unlawful one, that reasonable people would recognise that it was likely to cause harm and that a death had resulted. The Court of Appeal felt that all these points had been established and the conviction was upheld.

The correctness of this decision was upheld by the House of Lords in **AG's Reference (No 3 of 1994) 1998**.

5.2.3 THE ACT MUST ALSO BE DANGEROUS

For constructive manslaughter to arise, the act has to be dangerous as well as being unlawful. This means that it has to be an unlawful act that is likely to injure another. The approach of the courts can be seen in **Larkin 1943**, mentioned earlier.

Whether the act is considered a dangerous one is decided objectively, i.e. it must be an act that a sober and reasonable man would regard as dangerous.

This was affirmed in the case of **Church 1966**, where the defendant panicked after hitting a woman who had mocked his inability to satisfy her. Believing her to be dead, he threw her into a river, where she drowned. His conviction for manslaughter was upheld. The appeal court stated:

An unlawful act causing the death of another cannot, simply because it is an unlawful act, render a manslaughter verdict inevitable. For such a verdict inexorably to follow, the unlawful act must be such as all sober and reasonable people would inevitably recognise must subject the other person to, at least, the risk of some harm resulting therefrom, albeit not serious harm.

In DPP v Newbury and Jones 1977 mentioned earlier, the House of Lords specifically approved of the dicta in Church and decided that an act of throwing a paving slab in front of a passing train was one which all reasonable people would look upon as dangerous.

Similarly, in **Ball 1989**, the defendant's argument that he believed that the cartridge in his gun was merely a blank, and so should not be liable, was rejected by the Court of Appeal.

The court stated:

> . . . the question whether the act is a dangerous one is to be judged not by the appellant's appreciation but by that of the sober and reasonable man, and it is impossible to impute into his appreciation the mistaken belief of the appellant that what he was doing was not dangerous because he thought he had a blank cartridge in the chamber. At that stage the appellant's intention, foresight or knowledge is irrelevant.

FIVE KEY FACTS ON CONSTRUCTIVE MANSLAUGHTER

- Constructive manslaughter occurs where there is an unlawful and dangerous act and, as a result the victim dies; it is also known as unlawful act manslaughter.

- The *actus reus* is the death resulting from the unlawful act. The *mens rea* will be that which is required by the unlawful act.

  In the case of assault and battery, an intention to commit the assault or battery will need to be proved or **Cunningham**-style recklessness, i.e. subjective recklessness. There is no requirement to prove an intention to cause the death of the victim, nor to prove recklessness that such a death might occur.

- Three elements have to be established for constructive manslaughter: an unlawful act, which is also dangerous, which has brought about the death of the victim.

- The unlawful act must be a criminal wrong, not merely a civil one (**Franklin 1883**), and must be clearly established. In **Lamb 1967**, **Ariobeke 1988** and **Scarlett 1993**, it was decided, on appeal, that the alleged assaults had not been proved. In **DPP v Newbury and Jones 1977**, **Cato 1976** and **Kennedy 1998**, the unlawfulness of the acts was upheld, perhaps for reasons of public policy. The case of **Rogers 2003** has helped to clarify the law relating to those who assist drug addicts, but does not absolve them from liability. The unlawful act must have been a substantial cause of the victim's death, although it need not be the only cause. Despite the dicta of the Court of Appeal in **Dalby 1982**, it now appears that the unlawful act need not be directed at the victim nor, indeed, at a human being at all (**Mitchell 1983** and **Goodfellow 1986**).

- A dangerous act is one which carries with it the risk of some harm resulting, although not necessarily serious harm (**Church 1966**). Whether the act is dangerous is to be assessed objectively, i.e. by the view of a sober and reasonable person (**Larkin 1943** and **Church 1966**). When deciding whether the act is dangerous, these sober and reasonable people will look at the situation encountered by the defendant (**Dawson 1985**), but may not accept his claim that his mistaken belief frees him from liability (**Ball 1989**). They may also expect him to become aware of the vulnerability of his victim (**Watson 1989**).

Ball's counsel had tried to use the earlier case of **Dawson 1985** to support his argument, where the defendant had been luckier and his appeal allowed. Dawson and masked accomplices had attempted to rob a garage. They threatened the 60-year-old garage attendant with a pickaxe and an imitation gun. After he pressed the alarm, however, they fled empty-handed. The attendant, who suffered from a heart disease, had a fatal heart attack shortly after the police arrived on the scene. Dawson was convicted of unlawful act manslaughter.

The Court of Appeal decided that the conviction should be quashed because the trial judge had told the jurors that they must decide whether the act of the robbers was a dangerous one and that they should approach this from the point of view of a reasonable man 'who knew the facts that you know'. The jury, however, had knowledge of the victim's heart condition, whereas a reasonable man, at the time of the attack, would not have known this fact. He therefore might not have assumed that the acts of the defendant might cause the victim injury: fear, perhaps but not physical harm.

Dawson was distinguished in the case of **Watson 1989**. The latter and an accomplice threw a brick through the window of the victim's house and disturbed the 87-year-old resident. They then fled without taking anything. The elderly man died shortly afterwards from a heart attack.

The Court of Appeal held that the defendant should have become aware of the great age and frailty of the victim during the course of the burglary.

In the event, the defendant's conviction was quashed because it could not be satisfactorily established whether the burglary had caused the attack or the entry of the police workmen afterwards. The dicta of the Court of Appeal, however, could ensure that liability might arise in future.

Activity

While waiting on the edge of the platform for a train to take them to college, Bill and Ben started to argue loudly about the merits of two pop groups currently in the charts. Their heated discussion turned into anger and they began to throw punches at each other. Bill's second punch sent Ben reeling. He was pushed against Daisy, who fell in front of the incoming train and was killed.

Advise Bill, who has been charged with the manslaughter of Daisy.

5.3 MANSLAUGHTER BY GROSS NEGLIGENCE

In the preceding paragraphs, we have been looking at defendants who have committed criminal acts that have resulted in a death. There may also be other situations in which it is felt that the defendant should face a manslaughter charge, even though he may not have been involved in any criminal activity. Under this second form of involuntary manslaughter he may be charged with this offence because his behaviour has been so grossly negligent that it has brought about the death of another person.

In **Adomako 1995**, Lord Mackay decided that liability for this type of manslaughter will arise where the jury decides that:

having regard to the risk of death involved, the conduct of the defendant was so bad in all the circumstances as to amount in their judgment to a criminal act or omission.

- The *actus reus* of the offence is the death which has resulted from the negligent act.
- The *mens rea* of the offence appears to be the defendant's grossly negligent behaviour.

Manslaughter by gross negligence has had a chequered history and, before the above case, it seemed to have virtually disappeared and to have been overtaken by reckless manslaughter. The position now appears to have come full circle and there is serious doubt as to whether reckless manslaughter continues to exist. **In Adomako, it was firmly decided by the House of Lords that the gross negligence test is the correct one to use in all cases where a duty of care has been broken.**

This mixing of the principles of civil law and criminal law has caused problems, as can be seen in the horrific case of **Wacker 2003.**

This case hit the headlines when the bodies of 58 illegal immigrants and two survivors were found in a container loaded onto the trailer of a lorry. The driver had been stopped after disembarking at Dover. The container had been adapted by a partition, behind which the unfortunate human cargo had been herded. The front part had been filled with tomatoes in order to conceal them. The deaths arose because the container was then sealed from the outside and the only air vent was closed for too long a period.

The defendant was convicted of 58 offences of manslaughter by gross negligence but appealed. He tried to argue that, because the illegal immigrants had shared the same illegal purpose as him, i.e. the attempt to gain illegal entry to the UK, he did not, according to principles established in civil law cases, owe them a duty of care. One of these principles is that no action will arise from a base cause, expressed in Latin as '*ex turpi causa non oritur actio*'.

The Court of Appeal rejected this argument. It decided that the public policy issues relating to criminal law were different to those of civil law and that even where there was an underlying illegal purpose in the arrangement, this did not prevent criminal liability arising. The conviction was upheld.

5.3.1 THE DEVELOPMENT OF GROSS NEGLIGENCE MANSLAUGHTER

The leading cases on gross negligence manslaughter are **Bateman 1925, Andrews 1934** and **Adomako 1995.**

In **Bateman 1925,** the accused took away part of a woman's uterus during childbirth and did not remove her to hospital until five days later, where she subsequently died. Bateman's conviction for manslaughter was quashed because it was felt that he had been carrying out normal procedures which were approved by the medical profession. The procedure itself had been at fault.

The Court of Appeal stated that manslaughter by gross negligence should not be found lightly. It would only arise where in the opinion of the jury, the negligence of the accused went beyond a mere matter of compensation between subjects and showed such disregard for the life and safety of others as to amount to a crime against the State and conduct deserving punishment.

In **Andrews v DPP 1937** the defendant was charged with manslaughter after a pedestrian was killed by his dangerous driving. Andrews was sent by his employers to deal with a broken-down bus. On his way to the scene, he drove above the speed limit, overtook a car and was well over the wrong side of the road, when he struck a pedestrian. The victim was carried along the road on the bonnet of the defendant's van, then thrown from this and run over. The defendant did not stop. He was later convicted of manslaughter but appealed.

The House of Lords stated that manslaughter caused by bad driving was to be treated in the

same way as other cases of homicide caused by the defendant's negligence, and went on to state that a person would only be criminally liable if his behaviour was very bad. Their Lordships laid down the following test:

> *Simple lack of care which will constitute civil liability is not enough. For the purposes of the criminal law there are degrees of negligence and a very high degree of negligence is required to be proved.*

5.3.2 THE RISE OF RECKLESS MANSLAUGHTER

The development of gross negligence manslaughter came to a halt for a while after the case of **Seymour 1983**. In this case, the House of Lords followed the cases of **Caldwell** and **Lawrence**, mentioned in Chapter 2 and decided that this type of involuntary manslaughter should be redefined as reckless manslaughter. Their Lordships obviously desired to simplify the law in this area by adopting a similar test for all types of involuntary manslaughter on the lines of **Caldwell** recklessness.

The defendant and his woman friend quarrelled and her car and his lorry were involved in a collision. The woman got out of her car and went towards the accused. The latter then drove his lorry at the car. He later claimed that he only intended to push it away but the woman was crushed between the lorry and her own vehicle. She died later of her injuries and the defendant was found guilty of manslaughter.

The House of Lords stated that the ingredients for causing death by reckless driving (now replaced by dangerous driving), and the type of involuntary manslaughter which did not come within the definition of constructive manslaughter, were identical. From this case, and later cases modifying the principle to some extent, it appeared that criminal liability would arise if the defendant's conduct caused an obvious and serious risk of some personal injury and, as a result, someone died.

The Privy Council supported this approach in the case of Kong Cheuk Kwan 1985, a case concerning the collision of two hydrofoils near Hong Kong, and denied that a separate category of manslaughter by gross negligence was still appropriate.

By 1993, therefore, it appeared that the concept of gross negligence manslaughter had given way to **Caldwell**-style reckless manslaughter. Enough doubts remained, however, to make it inevitable that the matter would be reopened.

5.3.3 THE RE-EMERGENCE OF GROSS NEGLIGENCE MANSLAUGHTER

This occurred in the case of Prentice and Others 1994, when the Court of Appeal resurrected manslaughter by gross negligence for cases where there was a breach of a duty of care by the defendant.

In **Prentice and Others**, three separate appeals were heard together by the Court of Appeal to decide on the correct test to be used in involuntary manslaughter cases, other than those of constructive manslaughter. These three appeals concerned the cases of **Prentice and Sullman, Holloway** and **Adomako**, and only in the last case was the conviction upheld.

The case of **Prentice and Sullman** concerned two junior hospital doctors. Prentice, the least experienced, had wrongly injected a drug directly into the spine of a patient suffering from leukaemia. This very serious error was compounded by the wrong action being taken when the mistake was discovered. The result was damage to the patient's brain and spinal cord which ultimately caused his death.

Prentice had been supervised by Sullman and had assumed that the latter was approving of the whole procedure. Sullman, on the other hand, believed that he was only supervising the actual injection.

The trial judge had felt bound by the case of **Seymour** and had therefore directed the jury on the lines of **Caldwell**-style recklessness. There was an obvious and serious risk of harm and the patient had died, so the defendants were originally found guilty.

In **Holloway**, a qualified and experienced electrician had installed a new domestic central heating system and afterwards family members began to get electric shocks. The electrician checked his work and found no faults in the wiring but, when the trouble continued, he made arrangements to replace the heating programmer. Before this new part could be obtained, a member of the family received a fatal electric shock.

It was discovered that some of the wires were 'live' and that the circuit breaker, which should have afforded protection, was ineffective. The electrician was charged with manslaughter and found guilty after the judge, as in **Prentice**, directed the jury on the lines of reckless manslaughter.

In both cases, the Court of Appeal quashed the convictions, stating that the correct test to use in these cases, where a duty of care was owed to the victim, was not that of recklessness but that of gross negligence manslaughter.

In Adomako 1995, the last of the three cases, the manslaughter conviction was upheld. The defendant was an anaesthetist in a hospital who had been left in sole charge after the senior anaesthetist was called away. Adomako had failed to notice that a tube leading from the patient to the ventilator had become disconnected. When the alarm sounded, his first thought was that the machine itself was faulty and he therefore took the wrong action. By the time the mistake was discovered, the patient had died.

Rather surprisingly in this case, the jury had been directed on the issue of gross negligence, rather than recklessness, despite the fact that gross negligence manslaughter was then in decline. The defendant was convicted by a majority of ten to one. Adomako based his appeal on the issue that the jury should have been directed with regard to recklessness.

The Court of Appeal was satisfied that the jury had, in fact, been properly directed and upheld the conviction for manslaughter. A duty of care had been owed (in this case by the anaesthetist to the patient), and this duty had been broken by the high degree of negligence of the defendant.

The new test of gross negligence manslaughter

As stated earlier, the Court of Appeal looked at these three appeals together to decide on the correct test to use in such cases. **Lord Taylor, the former Lord Chief Justice, decided that manslaughter by gross negligence should be revived and should be classed as the proper test to use in all cases where a breach of duty had arisen.** He decided that only cases of motor manslaughter should be treated differently, where the test of reckless manslaughter (**Caldwell**-style) should be retained. (The Court of Appeal felt obliged to make this distinction because in motor manslaughter cases it was bound by the House of Lords' decision in **Seymour**.)

There was a further appeal in the **Adomako** case to the House of Lords. **Their Lordships agreed with the revival of the gross negligence test set out by the Court of Appeal with regard to criminal negligence involving a breach of duty and approved of the cases of Bateman and Andrews, cited in that court. Lord Mackay stressed that it was no longer appropriate to refer to the detailed definition of recklessness stated in Lawrence and said that the test in cases such as this should be one which is clear to an ordinary member of the jury with no particular knowledge** of the law. He felt that complicated definitions that the jury could not later remember, gave 'no service to the cause of justice'. He did, however, agree that, in some circumstances, it would not be a misdirection for a judge to use the word 'reckless' in its ordinary sense, if this was felt to be necessary to indicate the seriousness of the behaviour, a statement that was utilised by the Court of Appeal in Lidar 2000.

In addition to agreeing with the Court of Appeal's new direction in Prentice and Others, their Lordships went further and stated that motor manslaughter should not be put into a separate category. It was clearly stated that the gross negligence test was the one to be used in all forms of involuntary manslaughter where no unlawful act was found.

When deciding whether a person is criminally liable, therefore, the House of Lords agreed with the Court of Appeal that ordinary principles of negligence should be adopted to see if the defendant had broken a duty of care to the victim and this breach had caused his death. If the answer was in the affirmative, then the jury should be given the task of deciding whether the negligence was so gross that it should be considered to be a crime. Lord Mackay put it succinctly:

> The essence of the matter, which is supremely a jury question, is whether, having regard to the risk of death involved, the conduct of the defendant was so bad in all the circumstances as to amount in their judgment to a criminal act or omission.

The very vagueness of this test is bound to cause further discussion and possible appeals.

Recent cases on gross negligent manslaughter

In Kite 1996, the Court of Appeal rejected the defendant's appeal against his conviction for gross negligence manslaughter. He was the managing director of the St Albans Activities Centre and had allowed an 'ill-conceived and poorly executed' canoe trip in adverse weather conditions to take place. What was meant to be a mere two-hour paddle by students and their teachers to Charmouth in Dorset, ended with the canoes being swamped and the occupants being forced into the water for hours. This led to the deaths of four of the sixth-formers and Kite's subsequent conviction.

This case is revisited later in this chapter in relation to the punishment for gross negligence manslaughter and also in relation to corporate killing.

In **Litchfield 1997**, the Court of Appeal also upheld the conviction of the owner and captain of a square-rigged schooner, which had foundered on the rocks off the Cornish coast. He had steered too closely to the shore and had also used contaminated fuel, causing the engines to fail. Three members of the crew of 14 had died.

The court decided that the principles laid down in Adomako had been correctly applied and the defendant had been rightly convicted of being grossly negligent.

The tragic consequences of gross negligence can be seen in **Edwards 2001**. Gareth Edwards and his wife Amanda were found guilty of this form of manslaughter after failing to prevent their children and two of their friends playing on a railway line while they sat looking at the sea. The two boys managed to jump to safety when a train suddenly appeared but the two girls, the couple's daughter and her eight-year-old friend were mown down and killed.

It should be remembered however, that the negligence has to be gross. The jury did not believe that this had been established in the case of **Warren 2004**, as shown in the newspaper article overleaf.

The punishment for gross negligence manslaughter

As with all other types of manslaughter, there is a maximum sentence of life imprisonment for this

Beach racer cleared over crash that killed mother

By Paul Stokes

An international sand yacht racer who ploughed into a woman at 45mph as she strolled on a beach with her two sons, was cleared of manslaughter yesterday.

Adrian Warren, 49, had broken down in tears as he told the jury that he blamed himself for the 'terrible and tragic accident'.

Carole Cruz, 38, a teaching assistant, had been enjoying a family picnic on St Annes beach, Lytham St Annes, Lancs, when she was killed in August 2002.

Her back was broken and her legs virtually severed when she was hit and dragged for 100 yards by the three-wheeled craft.

The prosecution at Preston Crown Court claimed that Mr Warren had been criminally negligent while taking part in his second race of the day organised by Fylde International Sand Yacht Club.

Mrs Cruz's Sons Jason, now 16, and Steffan, 14, from Buruley, Lancs, gave harrowing accounts of how they tried to comfort their mother as she lay dying.

After the acquittal at the end of a week-long trial, Mrs Cruz's family said that they had never believed Mr Warren was solely to blame for the death.

Aramis Salter, who was on the picnic with Mrs Cruz's sister, Julie Christian, his girlfriend, said: 'We have lost a beautiful, devoted and caring person. But no one has suffered as much as the two boys.'

Mr Salter said he hoped something would be done to improve the safety regulations of sand yachting. 'Another tragedy like this simply must not happen again,' he added.

Mr Warren, a lorry driver, from Doncaster, South Yorks, has sailed sand yachts since he was 10 and has represented Great Britain 12 times.

He was too emotional to speak outside the court, but said in a statement read by his solicitor Peter Turner: 'I do not regard my acquittal as a triumph of any sort.

'I did not believe that my actions in those two fatal seconds were criminal and the jury agreed. I have been living with the unbearable knowledge that I was the pilot of that sand yacht for over two years and I will continue to live with that knowledge for the rest of my life.

'My pain can't be measured against the loss and pain felt by Carole Cruz's family. I can only hope that at some time in the future they will come to forgive me.'

Mrs Cruz and the boys were walking back along the beach towards sand dunes when she was hit by the sail-powered, almost silent craft.

Mr Warren told the jury he had gone through the incident his mind every night and every morning since it had happened.

He said: 'I cannot understand where she came from. I blame myself. I can't say it's not my fault. I was racing. I didn't see anybody. I was concentrating on the yacht in front of me.

'I was looking to the front and to the left. It affected my peripheral vision. I just didn't see the girl. I don't know where she came from.'

Mr Warren accepted that his actions were a significant cause of Mrs Cruz's death, but said that as a competitor he was not responsible for safety measures and relied on the marshal and the sailing master to do a proper job.

Daily Telegraph, 25 September 2004

FIVE KEY FACTS ON GROSS NEGLIGENCE MANSLAUGHTER

- This form of manslaughter is to be used in all cases where there is no unlawful act but where a death has arisen because of the high degree of negligence of the defendant (**Adomako 1995**). Reckless manslaughter, in the form of the detailed direction in **Lawrence 1982**, seems to have disappeared and should no longer be used.

- The cases of **Bateman 1925** and **Andrews 1937** on gross negligent manslaughter have been specifically approved by the House of Lords.

- The *actus reus* of gross negligence manslaughter is a death arising from the negligent act of the accused. The *mens rea* appears to be the gross negligence of the accused.

- The jury will decide this, after considering whether, having regard to the risk of death involved, the defendant's conduct was so bad that it should be classed as criminal. In **Warren 2004**, the jury decided against this.

- At present, the maximum punishment for this type of involuntary manslaughter is life imprisonment, although such a sentence is extremely unlikely. There is no minimum, allowing the particular circustances to be examined.

offence but no minimum. Because the circumstances are often so varied, such discretion is felt to be very necessary. Despite this freedom, the judges often come under fire. If they are too lenient, the relatives of the victims are rightly outraged. If they sentence too harshly, this could lead to a costly appeal, as seen in the case of **Kite 1996**, mentioned above. **While Kite was unsuccessful in getting the verdict changed, he did get his prison sentence reduced from three years to two.** Kite's counsel had argued that the longest prison sentence passed for a similar offence had been 21 months. Inevitably, the relatives of the victims were angered. One declared: **'My daughter was sentenced to death. Why couldn't Kite behave like a man and serve the rest of his sentence.'**

In some cases, the defendants may not face prison at all, as shown in the case of **Edwards**. The judge took the view that the couple's surviving children would be the ones to suffer most if their parents were sent to jail. **Their sentences of 12 months' imprisonment were suspended.**

Activity

- In **Adomako**, Lord Mackay made the following comment: 'I entirely agree with the view that the circumstances to which a charge of involuntary manslaughter may apply are so various that it is unwise to attempt to categorise or detail specimen directions'.

In group discussion or in essay form, discuss whether this is the correct approach for the law to take in cases of involuntary manslaughter where there is no unlawful act, or whether you feel that it puts too much responsibility onto the jury.

5.4 REFORM OF INVOLUNTARY MANSLAUGHTER

The state of the law on involuntary manslaughter has been widely criticised over the years. Some have argued that constructive manslaughter is unfair to the accused and should be reformed or abolished altogether; the late Sir John Smith, for example, declared in the *Criminal Law Review* in 1986, when discussing the case of **Goodfellow**, that the law in this area was in 'a discreditable state of uncertainty'. Other commentators have disapproved of the constant changes regarding reckless and gross negligence manslaughter.

The Law Commission considered the matter and published a report on the subject *(Law Com No 237, Involuntary Manslaughter 1996)*. It recommended the abolition of constructive manslaughter in its present form and suggested modifications to the law on gross negligence manslaughter.

In more detail, the Commission suggested the creation of two new offences, that of reckless killing and killing by gross carelessness.

- Reckless killing would be committed where the accused is aware of a risk that his conduct will cause death or serious injury and it is considered unreasonable for him to have taken that risk. When considering the latter, all the circumstances known or believed by him to exist will be taken into account.

The maximum sentence for this would be life imprisonment.

- The second new offence would be killing by gross carelessness. The offence will be committed where a person's careless conduct has caused a death and it would have been obvious to a reasonable person in the defendant's position that this would happen. The defendant will only be liable if he was capable of appreciating such a risk and it is established either that his conduct had fallen far below the standard expected or that he had intended by his conduct to cause injury or was aware of the risk that this might occur.

This offence is not considered so blameworthy as that of reckless killing and this is reflected in a maximum sentence of ten years.

In May 2000, the Home Office published its own Consultation Paper, 'Reforming the Law on Involuntary Manslaughter: the Government's Proposals'. This accepted the Law Commission's recommendations for the two new offences of reckless killing and killing by gross carelessness but also sought views on whether an additional offence was needed to cover the situation:

- where a death was unforeseeable
- a person had caused this by his conduct
- he had intended or was reckless as to whether some injury was caused and
- the conduct causing, or intended to cause the injury, constituted an offence.

The Home Office obviously had concerns that some offenders would escape liability altogether if constructive manslaughter were to be abolished and nothing comparable put it in its place. This proposed new offence would be narrower than the former one but would still cover the **Mitchell** type of situation.

◀ *Comment*

The proposed abolition of unlawful act manslaughter by the Law Commission came as no surprise and many would argue that it is a logical step forward. In earlier times, any unlawful act causing death would have resulted in a **murder** charge. This was then perceived as unjust where there was obviously no intention to kill or cause serious injury to the victim. Taken further, it could be argued that, in similar circumstances, a person should not face a manslaughter charge either. The Home Office however, has reservations about this, hence its suggestion that an additional offence is necessary.

In relation to the other proposed offences, reckless killing would cover the situation where the unlawful act is considered a manifestly reckless way to act. It should be remembered, however, that a more subjective approach is taken here when establishing possible liability so there would be those who would not be found guilty under reckless killing who would have faced liability for constructive manslaughter.

With regard to the second offence, the change from the word 'negligence' to that of 'carelessness' showed an intention to move away from civil law concepts of liability which, some have argued, have no place in criminal law. It would also solve the problem of having to establish whether a duty of care exists. Under the new offence, the defendant would be liable if the conduct causing the death fell far below that which was expected and he appreciated this fact.

5.5 CORPORATE KILLING

A corporation is a legal body, an artificially created organisation with directors managing the business and, in theory at least, the shareholders controlling it. The most common example is the private or public limited company, first recognised in the middle of the nineteenth century. These businesses vary from very small organisations to vast corporations employing thousands of people. We need to investigate whether such a body can ever be criminally liable.

Originally, the courts decided against this on the grounds that a personal appearance was needed in court. That problem was solved by using a complicated procedure which enabled an attorney to appear on the corporation's behalf in the Court of King's Bench but this became unnecessary with the passing of the **Criminal Justice Act 1925**. A corporation may now appear in court through a representative and we need to examine the circumstances under which it could become liable. This could be in one of three ways:

● **When the principle of vicarious liability is invoked**
In limited circumstances, a company might be held vicariously liable for the criminal acts of its employees. For example, in the case of **Mousell Ltd v London and North Western Railway Co 1917** the company was held liable for evading freight charges and in **National Rivers Authority v Alfred McAlpine Homes East Ltd 1994**, the company was convicted of being involved in the pollution of a river.

● **Where a statute expressly makes a corporation liable**
Some statutes expressly create such liability and often this will be absolute, thus evading the need to establish *mens rea*. It should also be noted that the word 'corporation' or 'company' does not always have to be expressly stated. The **Interpretation Act 1978** states that the word 'person' includes a body of persons corporate or unincorporate, which includes companies and partnerships, unless otherwise stated.

● **Where the doctrine of identification is used**
The general rule is that a company cannot be convicted of a crime for which it cannot be sentenced, so it can only be convicted of an offence where a fine can be imposed. It could not therefore face liability for murder. Over the years, the courts have also added the crimes of incest, perjury and rape as ones for which a company cannot be liable.

Liability for manslaughter

In an important ruling in P & O European Ferries Ltd 1991, it was decided that a company could be held liable for manslaughter. The defendants had tried to argue on an old common law premise that a killing had to be 'of a human being by a human being'. Therefore, it was argued, a company could not be liable. Turner J disagreed, but made it clear that liability will not be easy to establish. **He stated:**

> *A company may be vicariously liable for the negligent acts or omissions of its servants and agents, but for a company to be criminally liable for manslaughter – on the assumption I am making that such a crime exists – it is required that the* **mens rea** *and* **actus reus** *of manslaughter should be established not only against those who acted for or in the name of the company but against those who were identified as the embodiment of the company itself.*

Where an offence requires *mens rea*, therefore, there has to be some way of finding this within a company structure, because an inanimate body obviously has no mind. In relation to lesser crimes, the courts have addressed this problem by developing the doctrine of identification. This is done by looking for personnel in the company who are said to be "the directing mind and will" of the organisation, a phrase first used back in 1915 in **Lennard's Carrying Co Ltd v Asiatic Petroleum 1915.**

Gradually, the identification principle was taken further. **In DPP v Kent and Sussex Contractors Ltd 1944**, it was held that the intention and belief of a responsible agent of the company could be imputed to the company itself. In **Millar 1970**, the appeal court upheld the conviction of the managing director of a company for counselling and procuring causing death by dangerous driving. He had allowed a heavy lorry and trailer to be taken out on the road, laden with 18 tons of bricks, knowing that the front offside tyre was badly worn.

The difference between the brains and the hands of a company

In **H L Bolton (Engineering) Co Ltd v T J Graham and Sons Ltd 1957**, Lord Denning delivered his interpretation of the doctrine of identification in his own inimitable style. He likened a company to a human body and went on to say

> *It has a brain and nerve centre which controls what it does. It also has hands which hold the tools and act in accordance with directions from the centre. Some of the people in the company are mere servants and agents who are nothing more than hands to do the work and cannot be said to represent the mind or will. Others are directors and managers who represent the directing mind and will of the company and control what it does. The state of mind of these managers is the state of mind of the company and is treated by the law as such.*

This statement was quoted with approval by the House of Lords in **Tesco Ltd v Nattrass 1972** but it allowed Tesco to escape liability. An old age pensioner tried to buy a packet of washing powder at a price shown in advertisements and Tesco's shop window but was told that the only packets left were at the normal price. The company was susequently prosecuted under the **Trade Descriptions Act 1968**. Tesco relied on a defence of 'due diligence' provided in the Act. This states that liability will not arise if the person charged can prove that he has taken all reasonable precautions and exercised all due diligence to avoid the commission of the offence and shows that the offence was committed by 'another person'. The branch manager was duly named as that other person. Despite this, the magistrates decided that he was an integral part of the company and convicted Tesco.

The House of Lords disagreed, deciding that the branch manager was too far down in the scale of command to be part of the 'directing

mind or will' of the company. To be in such a position, Lord Reid felt that the company member needed to be part of the board of directors, the managing director or perhaps be one of the other superior officers. Viscount Dilhorne included a person in actual control of the operations of a company and who is not answerable to anyone else.

In **Boal 1992**, an assistant general manager at a large bookstore was not held to be in such a position, therefore no liability was incurred under the Fire Precautions Act 1971 for the company's breaches of its fire certificate. In **Seaboard Offshore v Secretary of State for Transport 1994**, one of the owner's ships had been put to sea within three hours of a new chief engineer joining it. This employee had been given no time to study the workings of the ship and, as a result, had succeeded in flooding the engines.

The House of Lords quashed the conviction under the Merchant Shipping Act 1988. This imposed a duty to ensure that the ship operated in a safe manner but the owner could discharge this by showing that he had taken reasonable steps to comply with the provisions.

These decisions show that it is not easy to gain a conviction under the identification principle but there has been some small movement on this issue. **In Redfern 1993, the Court of Appeal stressed that the person committing the offence must possess true powers of management. In two civil cases in 1995, the Privy Council and the House of Lords respectively were prepared to widen the principle to enable it to cover personnel other than directors. For example, a financial investment manager was held liable.**

Problems in establishing liability in manslaughter cases

In more serious criminal cases, use of the identification principle has proved problematic. This was highlighted after the sinking of the Herald of Free Enterprise, a roll-on, roll-off ferry,

just outside Zeebrugge harbour in March 1987. The ferry had left the port with its bow doors left open and the ship capsized, causing the death of nearly two hundred passengers. It was the job of the assistant bosun to ensure that the doors were shut but he was asleep at the time. The captain was responsible for the ship setting sail safely but had no way of confirming whether or not the doors were shut. In **P & O European Ferries (Dover) Ltd 1991**, these two employees were charged with manslaughter, along with directors of the company and the company itself, but the case against all seven parties collapsed. While it was established that a high degree of mismanagement within the company existed, this was not held to be enough for a successful prosecution.

The test at that time was for reckless manslaughter and the judge came to the conclusion that it could not be established that there was an obvious and serious risk of death or serious harm occurring by operating the ship in this manner. The system in use was said to have operated for over 60,000 crossings without previous trouble and was also adopted by other ferry operators. No outside bodies, such as the insurers and the Department of Trade, had attempted to impose higher standards.

The Sheen Report in 1987 came to the conclusion that the company was 'infected with the disease of sloppiness' but, because of the state of the law at that time, several separate errors could not be combined, under what was called the 'aggregation principle' to make the company liable for reckless manslaughter. As mentioned earlier, the case collapsed. The only positive point to come from the whole sorry mess was the affirmation by Turner J that it was possible, as a matter of principle, for a manslaughter charge to be brought against a company in its own right.

There are signs of slow progress. In **R v DPP ex p Jones (Timothy) 2000**, a brother of a victim who had been decapitated on his first day at the company in question, successfully challenged a decision of the DPP not to pursue a manslaughter charge against it. Manslaughter charges have also been taken successfully against smaller companies, where it is easier to establish liability under the identification doctrine.

In **Kite and OLL Ltd 1996, discussed earlier, both the managing director of the outdoors activity centre in question, and the company itself, were found to be liable for gross negligence manslaughter. The company was fined and Kite was jailed for three years, although, as already noted, the sentence was later reduced.**

Difficulties in relation to larger companies

There has been a conspicuous lack of success in this repect. No manslaughter charges were upheld after the Kings Cross fire, the P & O ferry case, as noted above, the Clapham rail crash or the Southall train disaster in West London. In the latter case, a high-speed train from Swansea had crashed into a freight train at Southall, killing seven people and injuring many others. The operator, Great Western Trains, was charged later with gross negligence manslaughter but the trial judge stopped the trial. He stated that it was necessary in this type of manslaughter to prove a guilty mind. Where a non-human defendant was prosecuted, therefore, that body could only be convicted via the guilt of a human being with whom it could be identified. Because this could not be established, the company was only found liable for breaches of the **Health & Safety at Work etc Act 1974.** There was, however, some consolation in the fact that the company was fined the exceptionally large sum of £1,500,000. In addition, the collapse of the manslaughter case led to an **Attorney-General's Reference (No 2 of 1999) 2000.**

The Attorney General asked two questions of the Court of Appeal:

1   **Can a defendant be convicted of gross negligence manslaughter in the absence of** evidence as to the defendant's state of mind?

2   **Can a non-human defendant be convicted of the crime of gross negligence manslaughter in the absence of any evidence establishing the guilt of an identified human being for the same crime?**

The Court of Appeal answered 'yes' to the first question and 'no' to the second. The affirmative answer to question 1 means that the

▶ *Comment*

This part of the Reference makes it very clear that, at the present time, the identification principle is the only way to establish liability for gross negligence manslaughter against a company. The Court of Appeal rejected the opportunity to recognise the 'aggregation principle', allowing several individual failures to be added together to illustrate the grossly negligent behaviour. It was true that this had been rejected in the P & O case but, at that time, subjective recklessness had to be proved. Now that the standard is one of gross negligence and the test is more objective, the case for a change of approach could be made out. The late Sir John Smith was strongly critical of the court's failure to accept this.

Other commentators have argued that a change in the law is urgently required. The Law Commission recognised this concern and put forward proposals for reform in 1996 but little happened. In 2000, however, the Home Office decided to produce its own proposals for reform, which are noted below. There is still criticism that the Government is dragging its heels on these, as was noted back in 2001 by Professor Gary Slapper in his Times' article 'A law long overdue'.

A law long overdue

Companies should face charges of 'corporate killings', says Gary Slapper

Glanville Evans was killed when the bridge he was working on collapsed and he fell into the River Wye. The company that employed him had clearly been reckless but an attempt to convict it for manslaughter failed. That was in February 1965.

Since then more than 31,000 people have been killed at work or through commercially related disasters like train crashes. Safety reports have shown that management failures are responsible in most cases but the number of prosecutions for manslaughter since the death of Evans has been 12 and the number of companies convicted has been three. Each year, however, the law has no difficulty in convicting more than 200 ordinary people for killing through carelessness while engaged in antics of various sorts.

Last week the police, the TUC and the Director of Public Prosecutions all called for a new law on corporate manslaughter. The families of four men killed in horrifying circumstances while repairing Avonmouth Bridge released a statement after the company had been convicted of regulatory safety offences and fined. They said: "Considering the gross and appalling failures of the companies and the assets of the companies, we do not feel this fine will have the deterrent effect necessary to force companies to ensure that safety is paramount above profit and to ensure that such an accident could not happen again." In the same week Euromin Ltd, the company responsible for the death of Simon Jones, decapitated on his first day at work in Shoreham Docks, was also convicted of serious safety law violations but not one that

has "killing" as a part of the offence.

There are now more than one million companies in England and Wales and their activities permeate every pore of social life. It is a reasonable expectation that the considerable body of people and rules used to protect customers, investors and rival businesses from financial irregularity will be matched by laws to protect life and limb. For the early part of its history, the company lay outside the criminal law. "It had no soul to damn, and no body to kick," observed Lord Thurlow, the 18th-century Lord Chancellor. Certainly, the practice of excommunicating corporations had been pronounced contrary to canon law by Pope Innocent IV at the Council of Lyons in 1245.

The main difficulty in using the current law of manslaughter to proceed against corporate bodies is that the rules were evolved in relation to individuals. This means that they are concerned with things like evaluating the state of mind of the defendant, and companies do not have easily identifiable "minds". For a while in the Middle Ages, certain clerics could escape liability for serious crimes by pleading "benefit of clergy". They were effectively outside the normal law. Today we see that as unjustifiable and rather bizarre, and it is likely that today's legally privileged status afforded to companies will, in future, be regarded in the same way.

Under current law, the courts must look at the conduct of senior company officers who are taken to personify the company. These are what Lord Denning once referred to in a renowned anthropomorphic metaphor as people who act as the "brain and nerve centre" of the company. There must, however, be at least one fully culpable officer; a company will be acquitted if, through a diffuse management or chaos, various directors each knew only part of the full picture.

In its report *Legislating the Criminal Code: Involuntary Manslaughter* (1996), the Law Commission recommended a new offence of "corporate killing". It said it saw no reason for companies effectively to remain exempt from the law of manslaughter and recommended that there should be a specific offence of "corporate killing" broadly comparable to "killing by gross negligence" on the part of an individual. A company would become liable for prosecution if a "management failure" by the corporation resulted in death, and the failure constituted conduct falling "far below what can reasonably be expected of the corporation in the circumstances". The corporation would be judged simply by the results of its collective efforts.

Innovation is often an agonisingly gradual process in law. The Law Commission's 1996 report was ignored, causing Mr Justice Scott Baker, the trial judge in the manslaughter prosecution of Great Western Trains in 1999, following the Paddington crash, to ask why the report had been permitted "to lie for years on a shelf gathering dust". New legislation on corporate killing has been intermittently promised as due "in the near future" for more than ten years. The Government produced a draft law in May last year but a Bill again failed to appear in this year's Queen's Speech.

The 1965 death of Glanville Evans and those of the Avonmouth workers in 1999 are bridged by a long curve of law that conspicuously failed to protect many of the 30,000 victims of commercial incidents who died in that span. A much better legal bridge to the future has been designed. It remains to be seen whether there is the political will to build it.

The Times, 11 December 2001

fact that a company does not possess a mind of its own is not fatal to a successful prosecution, provided that, under the identification principle, a human being can also be identified on whom to fix liability. The Court of Appeal's clear affirmation of this point may result in a few more convictions, while more radical reform from Parliament is awaited. The negative answer to the second point, however, means that many prosecutions will still be doomed to failure.

5.5.1 POSSIBLE REFORM OF CORPORATE LIABILITY

As noted above, the Law Commission specifically addressed this issue after heeding the depth of feeling on the subject and in Law Com No. 237, part VIII, recommended the creation of a new offence of corporate killing. It was proposed that this would arise where a management failure of the company was the cause, or one of the causes of the person's death and the failure constituted conduct falling far below what could reasonably be expected of the corporation in the circumstances.

It took two further rail disasters before there was any action. This came in 2000, when the Home Office published a consultation paper 'Reforming the Law on Involuntary Manslaughter: The Government's Proposals'. Rather surprisingly, these go further than was suggested by the Law Commission. A new offence of corporate killing is recommended but the Home Office has also suggested that liability should extend to non-corporate businesses, such as partnerships and sole traders.

The new offence of corporate killing

The Home Office proposals adopt the terminology of the Law Commission for the actual offence. A corporation would therefore be guilty of corporate killing if:

a a management failure by the corporation is the cause or one of the causes of the person's death; and

b that failure constitutes conduct falling far below what can reasonably be expected of the corporation in the circumstances

Such failure on the part of a company would arise:

a If the way in which its activities are managed or organised fail to ensure the health and safety of persons employed in or affected by those activities: and

b such a failure may be regarded as a cause of a person's death notwithstanding that the immediate cause is the act or omission of an individual.

It will be noted that the offence is carefully worded to try to ensure that the company cannot pass the liability on to another. The new offence is designed to run parallel to the existing offence of gross negligence manslaughter and would also co-exist with the proposed new offence of manslaughter by reckless killing, should this change be effected by Parliament. Unlike these two offences, however, it is not necessary to find that the conduct of one particular individual has caused the death. Liability can be imposed where the standards as a whole fall far below that what is expected. The offence would be an indictable one and the sanctions would be an unlimited fine and/or a remedial order.

Other changes recommended by the Home Office

● A proposal to extend liability from corporations alone to other undertakings (these would include schools, hospital trusts and charities which are not incorporated, plus partnerships and sole traders, i.e. 'any trade or business or other activity providing employment').

● The creation of another new offence of 'substantially contributing to a corporate killing'. This could be used against individuals connected to the organisation and the corporate killing, where it is not possible to secure a conviction for reckless or careless killing.

It was believed that the conclusions reached in response to these proposals and the others relating to involuntary manslaughter would be published in late 2003 but, as yet, there has been no move on this.

Comment

In his well-reasoned article 'Corporate Killing – Some Government Proposals', Criminal Law Review 2001, p31, Bob Sullivan, Professor of Law at Durham University, stated that 'the Government has grasped a major truth. Deterrent incentives to promote greater safety will have the most immediate and direct impact if they are targeted at individual managers who have or should have assumed responsibility for safety matters'. He did, however, express concern over the extension of liability to small businesses with unlimited liability. A partner, for example, could find his personal assets at risk if there was a big fine to pay. It could lead to the partnership breaking up and jobs being lost.

Despite such reservations, which, hopefully, would be debated by Parliament if not dealt with before this, it is submitted that the creation of a new offence of corporate killing is one that the public would welcome, given the present difficulties in securing convictions against grossly negligent companies.

FIVE KEY FACTS ON CORPORATE LIABILITY

- A corporation may be vicariously liable for certain criminal offences committed by their employees (**Mousell Bros v London and North West Railway 1917, National Rivers Authority v Alfred McAlpine Homes East 1994**). It may also be liable on its own account when a statute expressly imposes such liability or when the doctrine of identification is used successfully.

- This doctrine could apply if those with the 'directing mind and will of the company' have committed the offence **(Lennards Carrying Co v Asiatic Petroleum 1915)**.

- Lord Denning talked of those at the brain and nerve centre, for whose actions the company would be liable and the mere 'hands' of the business, where the company was not liable **(HL Bolton v TJ Graham 1957)**. The Court of Appeal found the company liable where the employee had 'true powers of management', **(Redfern 1993)**, but the employees were not held to be part of the 'directing mind and will' in **Tesco v Nattrass 1972**, nor **Boal 1992**.

- A company may be liable for most offences, except murder, bigamy, rape and incest. It can be liable for manslaughter **(P & O European Ferries 1991)**, but convictions are rare in the case of large companies. There has been limited success in relation to smaller companies where the doctrine of identification can be used to find the 'directing mind', **(Kite v OLL 1994, Litchfield 1997)**.

- The courts are not yet prepared to use the 'aggregation principle' to impose liability on a company even though the test has changed from recklessness to gross negligence and several errors could amount to this **(P & O European Ferries 1991, Great Western Trains)**.

Activity

- The deficiencies in the present state of the law in relation to the liability of companies, indicate a pressing need for the proposed offence of corporate killing to be introduced as soon as possible. Discuss.

- Rachel was the director of a company running weekend adventure courses in Snowdonia. She was left short-staffed when two of her experienced guides left to take up positions elsewhere, after criticising the lack of instruction being given on basic safety procedures. Rachel then engaged two teenagers on a part-time basis, hoping that they would gain experience as they went along.

Joey was among those attending a course on a very cold weekend in December. Without further instruction, he was sent off to climb Mount Snowdon, in the company of Monica, one of the new part-timers. Rachel had received reports of imminent adverse weather conditions but decided to ignore them, as a cancellation of the course would result in heavy losses for her. The temperature dropped sharply and it started to snow. Joey, who was only wearing ordinary trainers and a thin sweater, slipped and fell down a crevasse. The part-time instructor did not have enough skill to effect a rescue herself and Joey died before more expert help arrived.

Discuss the possible liability of Rachel and Monica.

Self-assessment questions on Chapter 5

1 State the other name for unlawful act manslaughter.
2 Describe the three elements that have to be proved for this offence.
3 Why was the crime established in **Larkin** but not in **Lamb** and **Ariobeke**?
4 Why have the cases of **Cato** and **Newbury & Jones** caused problems for the courts and how were these difficulties resolved?
5 Why were the convictions quashed in the cases of **Dalby** and **Dawson** but upheld in **Mitchell** and **Goodfellow**?
6 With regard to unlawful act manslaughter, what is the definition of a dangerous act and where is the law?
7 Why was the conviction for gross negligence manslaughter confirmed in the case of **Andrews** but quashed in **Bateman**?
8 Why were the convictions quashed in **Prentice** and **Holloway** but not in **Adomako**? What test was laid down by the House of Lords in the latter case?
9 Define the term 'corporate liability', and explain why it is so difficult to secure a conviction for manslaughter against a large organisation.
10 How does the Government propose to deal with this problem?

Chapter 6

NON-FATAL OFFENCES AGAINST THE PERSON

6.1 INTRODUCTION

This chapter deals with the non-fatal offences against the person currently covered in the three A Level specifications. The following diagram shows that these offences graduate upwards in seriousness, as noted in the following diagram.

Certain preliminary points should be noted about these non-fatal offences:

● **The legal definitions of assault and battery are very different. The term 'assault', however, is often used in a wider sense to include both assaults and batteries, as will be explained in due course.**

● **The maximum punishment for actual bodily harm under s47 and grievous bodily harm under s20 is the same, i.e. five years imprisonment. In practice, the judges**

recognize the difference in the degree of seriousness of these two crimes and will take this into account when sentencing.

● **The Offences Against the Person Act (not, as one student delightfully described it, the Offensive Person's Act!) was enacted in the nineteenth century and the wording sometimes reflects this. For example, the terms 'malicious wounding' and 'grievous bodily harm' are not ones found in ordinary speech!**

It will come as no surprise, therefore, to learn that there have been strong calls for the urgent reform of this whole area of law.

Matters relating to non- fatal offences against the person are dealt with in the following order:

✔ **Assault**
✔ **Battery**
✔ **The defence of consent**
✔ **Actual bodily harm**
✔ **Malicious wounding or grievous bodily harm under s20 Offences Against the Person Act 1861**
✔ **Malicious wounding or grievous bodily harm with intent, under s18 Offences Against the Person Act 1861**
✔ **Suggested reform of offences against the person.**

6.2 ASSAULT

An assault (or common assault as it is sometimes called) is committed when the accused intentionally or recklessly causes the victim to apprehend immediate and unlawful violence.

The House of Lords recently confirmed this definition in the case of **Ireland 1998**. A battery,

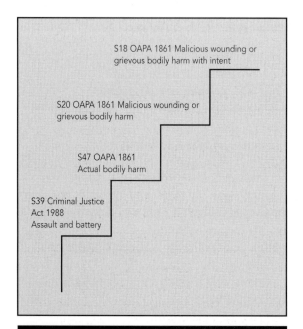

Figure 6.1 Non-fatal offences against the person

S18 OAPA 1861 Malicious wounding or grievous bodily harm with intent

S20 OAPA 1861 Malicious wounding or grievous bodily harm

S47 OAPA 1861 Actual bodily harm

S39 Criminal Justice Act 1988 Assault and battery

on the other hand, is a separate offence and concerns the actual infliction of the force.

These two separate crimes were developed under common law but were classified as indictable offences under **s47 Offences Against the Person Act 1861** (noted in future as **OAPA 1861**), which also laid down the punishment. This part of **s47** was repealed and now **s39 Criminal Justice Act 1988** decrees that the offences of common assault and battery are to be treated as summary offences. The same section also lays down a maximum sentence of six months' imprisonment and a fine not exceeding level 5.

It was generally believed that the two crimes remained as common law offences, despite the fact that certain procedural information, such as the provisions just mentioned, was put into statutory form. In **DPP v Taylor**, **DPP v Little 1992**, however, the Divisional Court stated that common assault and battery had been classed as statutory offences since the enactment of **s47 OAPA 1861**! A prosecutor, therefore, should now charge the defendant with either assault or battery under the amended law, i.e. under **s39 Criminal Justice Act 1988**.

6.2.1 THE *ACTUS REUS* OF ASSAULT

The *actus reus* of assault occurs when the defendant causes the victim to apprehend immediate and unlawful violence.

It can be seen that no force need actually be applied to constitute this offence. The victim need only anticipate anxiety or fear of personal injury. Examples might include having a fist raised against him or a gun pointed at him. Some concern about the action must, however, exist. In **Lamb 1967**, mentioned in Chapter 5, the victim at whom the gun was pointed did not fear the possible infliction of violence because neither he nor his friend believed that the gun with which they were playing would fire. No assault, therefore, had taken place. On the other hand, an

assault would have been committed if an imitation weapon had been used but the victim believed it to be real.

Can words alone constitute an assault?

It has been clearly decided that conduct causing the victim to believe that harm might be inflicted can amount to an assault. In addition, it was recently affirmed that words and conduct combined, could do this, as noted in **DPP v Santana-Bermudez 2003**. Until very recently, however, there was far less certainty as to whether words alone could do this. Earlier dicta suggested that they could not. In **Meade and Belt 1823, the judge stated that 'no words or singing are equivalent to an assault'.**

Over the years, however, the judges have changed their opinion on this. In the case of **Wilson 1955**, Lord Goddard stated, *obiter*, that the words 'get out the knives' would, on their own, be sufficient to constitute an assault. Similarly, in the civil case of **Ansell v Thomas 1974**, a verbal threat to eject the plaintiff was considered to be a civil assault. **In Constanza 1997 the Court of Appeal stated categorically that an assault could arise from words alone and held that older authorities stating otherwise rested on 'a dubious foundation'.**

In Ireland 1998, the House of Lords went further and decided that, in certain circumstances, even silence could amount to an assault, as in this case, where the defendant terrorised women with silent phone calls.

Words might prevent an assault

What was established much earlier was that words could prevent an action from being an assault. In the very early case of **Tuberville v Savage 1669**, the accused put his hand on his sword and said 'if it were not assize time I would not take such language from you'. The act of putting his hand on his sword was threatening but this had to be weighed against his words, which clearly implied that no physical action would be taken because the judges were in the vicinity!

How immediate must the threat be?

When looking at the the *actus reus* of assault, it will be seen that the victim must believe that immediate violence will be inflicted upon him. The courts, however, have adopted a liberal interpretation of the word 'immediate', in order to give justice to the victim.

It appears that, provided that the victim believes that he or she might be subjected to immediate violence, the fear need not be a completely rational one. It was stated in **Smith v Chief Superintendent of Woking Police Station**, **1983** that: **'When one is in a state of terror, one is very often unable to analyse precisely what one is frightened of as likely to happen next'.**

In this case, the victim, who was in her nightclothes, was badly frightened by the accused, who had trespassed onto private property and was staring in at her through the windows of her ground floor bedsitting room.

The Divisional Court upheld the defendant's conviction for being on enclosed premises for an unlawful purpose (i.e. an assault). The defence tried to argue that the accused could not have committed an immediate assault because the windows and doors were all locked. The appeal court held that it was enough that the woman believed that she was in danger of having immediate violence inflicted on her. Her fear did not have to be rationalised.

The issue of whether a threat needs to be an immediate one was also addressed in the case of **DPP v Ramos 2000. The Divisional Court decided that the important matter was the victim's state of mind, rather than the statistical risk of violence occurring within a short space of time. Provided therefore, that the victim believed that something nasty could happen at any time, the defendant could be convicted.**

It will be seen, when looking at cases on actual bodily harm that a similar approach was taken by the Court of Appeal in the case of **Constanza 1997**.

6.2.2 THE *MENS REA* OF ASSAULT

The *mens rea* of assault is satisfied when the **defendant intends to cause the victim to apprehend immediate physical violence or does this recklessly.**

The Court of Appeal stated in the case of Venna 1976:

We see no reason in logic or in law why a person who recklessly applies physical force to the person of another should be outside the criminal law of assault.

The need to establish Cunningham recklessness

It will be remembered that until 2003, there were two types of recklessness in English law, **Cunningham** recklessness and **Caldwell** recklessness. In **Venna**, **Cunningham**-style recklessness, i.e. subjective recklessness, was applied but after the decision in **Caldwell 1982** it was for a short while assumed that it would be sufficient to establish the more objective type of recklessness in all criminal offences where recklessness was part of the *mens rea*. **Caldwell**-style recklessness was therefore accepted by the Divisional Court in **DPP v K 1990**. As noted in Chapter 2, this change in the accepted position did not last long with regard to offences other than criminal damage. **DPP v K was overruled by the Court of Appeal in Spratt 1991 and, although that case was itself overruled on another point, this stricter approach to the *mens rea* of assault and battery was affirmed by the same court in Parmenter, also in 1991. When the latter case went to the House of Lords, this point was not directly discussed but *obiter dicta* by Lord**

Ackner appears to support the Court of Appeal's view. **Cunningham recklessness, therefore, must be established for the offences of assault and battery and, since the case of G and another, for criminal damage also.**

6.3 BATTERY

This offence is committed when the defendant intentionally or recklessly applies unlawful physical force to another person, as affirmed by the House of Lords in Ireland 1998.

The difference between assault and battery, therefore, is as follows:

- **an assault is committed where the victim believes that he is likely to be subjected to some sort of harm**
- **a battery does not take place until the force is applied.**

While the latter offence is known by the term 'battery', it is not usual to state that the defendant has battered the victim. Instead, to the great confusion of all, the word 'assault' is used in its wider layman's form.

What constitutes battery?

With regard to a battery, the law starts with the assumption that an individual has a right to be protected from molestation. Blackstone, the eminent legal writer stated:

> the law cannot draw the line between different degrees of violence and therefore totally prohibits the first and lowest stage of it; every man's person being sacred and no other having a right to meddle with it, in any the slightest manner.

In the case of Collins v Wilcock 1984, Goff L J affirmed this approach. He declared that 'The fundamental principle, plain and incontestable is that every person's body is inviolate'. He went on to quote with approval, the statement in Cole v Turner 1704, that 'the least touching of another in anger is a battery.'

The Divisional Court of the Queen's Bench Division therefore decided that a policewoman had committed an unlawful battery. She had taken hold of the arm of the defendant she believed to be soliciting, in order to detain her, but without intending to effect an arrest. Because of this unlawfulness, the court then quashed the defendant's conviction for the assault she had inflicted in return.

This decision clearly shows that the police are not permitted to grab hold of a suspect, or forcibly prevent him leaving, unless they first arrest him. The detentions were therefore unlawful in the cases of **Kenlin v Gardner 1967** and **Ludlow v Burgess 1971**.

The courts have decided that touching the clothing of a person amounts to touching the person himself, provided of course that the defendant has the necessary *mens rea* of battery. In the case of **Day 1845**, the defendant slashed the victim's clothes while in **Thomas 1985**, even though the actual offence was not made out, the rubbing of a girl's skirt was held to amount to a battery.

Lawful contact

Obviously not all touching will be unlawful. In **Collins v Wilcock,** Goff went on to note:

> most of the physical contacts of ordinary life are not actionable because they are impliedly consented to by all who move in society and so expose themselves to the risk of bodily contact. So nobody can complain of the jostling which is inevitable from his presence in, for example, a supermarket, an underground station or a busy street; nor can a person who attends a party complain if his hand is seized in friendship, or even if his back is (within reason) slapped.

In **Donnelly v Jackman 1970**, the court held that the officer in question did not commit a battery when he merely tapped on the other's shoulder to attract his attention.

A similar view was taken in **Smith v DPP 2001**. The police had been summoned via a 999 call and found the defendant outside the house, shouting and banging on the door. One of the officers took his arm, not to arrest him but to lead him away from the door so that the 999 call could be investigated. The defendant resisted this and lashed out at the officers. He was charged with assault but appealed, claiming that the policemen had exceeded their duty by taking his arm.

The Divisional Court rejected the appeal, deciding that a person interfering with a right of entry could be made to move by the use of reasonable force.

Indirect batteries

The courts have long since decided that the battery need not be directly inflicted on the victim. In **Scott v Shepherd 1773**, a civil case, the court held that the defendant had committed a battery when he threw a live squib into a market place and, after two people had picked it up and thrown it further away, it injured a third party. In **Martin 1881**, an even more serious offence was committed when the defendant placed an iron bar across an exit in a theatre, turned out the lights and shouted 'fire!' In the ensuing panic, several people were injured as they rushed out. The defendant's conviction for grievous bodily harm was upheld.

This view was supported in the case of **Fagan v MPC 1969**, mentioned in Chapter 2. A police officer had ordered the defendant to park his car close to the kerb, and Fagan had reluctantly complied. In doing so, he drove the car onto the policeman's foot. This was done accidentally but, when asked by the policeman to remove the car, he said **'F . . . you, you can wait'** and proceeded to turn off the ignition. He unsuccessfully tried to argue on appeal that no offence had been committed.

The Divisional Court disagreed, stating: 'it matters not, in our judgment, whether the battery is inflicted directly by the body of the offender or through the medium of some weapon or instrument controlled by the action of the offender . . .'

This point was taken further in **Haystead 2000** where the defendant punched a woman in the face causing her baby to fall out of her arms and hit his head on the floor.

The Divisional Court of QBD rejected his argument that his conviction was wrong because there had been no direct force against the baby.

6.3.1 THE *ACTUS REUS* OF BATTERY

This consists of the application of unlawful physical force on another, as confirmed by Ireland 1998. It will be seen, when discussing actual bodily harm, that the House of Lords decided in the latter case that the causing of psychiatric injury by silent telephone calls would not constitute a battery, though such an action may well be an assault.

6.3.2 THE *MENS REA* OF BATTERY

This is satisfied where the defendant intends to do such an act or is reckless about whether such force will be applied.

As with assault, this is **Cunningham**-style recklessness, as laid down in **Venna 1976**.

A battery may start off as an innocent, accidental act but may later become a battery during a sequence of events among which the *mens rea* of the offence is formed. In **Fagan**, mentioned above, the defendant had also argued that he did not have the necessary *mens rea* for the offence.

The Divisional Court held that 'there was an act constituting a battery which at its inception was not criminal because there was no element of intention, but which became criminal from the moment the intention was formed'.

FIVE KEY FACTS ON ASSAULT AND BATTERY

- Assault and battery are two distinct crimes, although the word 'assault' is often used as a verb to cover both types of offence. Both were created at common law but are now held to be statutory offences under **s39 Criminal Justice Act 1988, (DPP v Taylor, DPP v Little 1992)**. The maximum sentence for either offence is six months imprisonment, coupled with a fine.

- The definition of an assault is where the accused intentionally or recklessly causes the victim to apprehend immediate and unlawful violence.

- The *actus reus* of assault is causing the victim to apprehend immediate and unlawful violence **(Ireland 1998)**. The word 'apprehend' covers anxiety as well as fear. The *mens rea* of assault is satisfied where such apprehension is caused either intentionally or recklessly **(Venna 1976)**. The type of recklessness to be proved is **Cunningham** style recklessness **(Savage and Parmenter 1992)**. The Court of Appeal, in **Constanza 1997** decided that words alone could be enough to constitute an assault. The House of Lords went even further in **Ireland 1998** and held that even silent telephone calls could amount to an assault. The victim must apprehend immediate violence but the courts will not inquire too deeply into the rationality of the fear, provided that it is a genuinely held belief **(Smith 1983, Ireland 1998, Ramos 2000)**.

- A battery occurs where the defendant intentionally or recklessly applies unlawful physical force to the victim. Psychiatric injury caused by silent telephone calls will not suffice **(Ireland 1998)**. The force applied need only be minimal, provided that it is unlawful **(Cole v Turner 1704, Collins v Wilcock 1984)**. The slashing and even touching of someone's clothes could be included **(Day 1845, Thomas 1985)**, although there is implied consent to a certain amount of touching in everyday life, even by the police **(Collins v Wilcock 1984, Donnelly v Jackman 1970, Smith v DPP 2001)**. There is no requirement that the force must be directly inflicted, **(Scott v Shepherd 1773, Martin 1881, Fagan v MPC 1969, Haystead 2000)**.

- The *actus reus* of a battery is the application of physical force on the victim **(Ireland 1998)**. The *mens rea* is doing this intentionally or recklessly. Like assault, **Cunningham** recklessness must be proved **(Venna 1976)**. The *mens rea* may be formed at a later time provided that the sequence of events is continuing **(Fagan v MPC 1969)**.

6.4 THE DEFENCE OF CONSENT

General defences, which can be put forward in response to many different types of crime including offences against the person, will be discussed in Chapters 10 and 11, but the defence of consent, which is of special relevance to offences against the person, will be examined in this chapter.

The general rule

The courts have decided that if the alleged victim has given a valid consent to the crime committed against him, no offence will have been committed. The defendant, therefore, would be entitled to a full acquittal.

This position was clearly affirmed by Lord Lane, a former Lord Chief Justice, in **AGs Reference (No 6 of 1980) 1981.** He stated that as a general starting point: **'it is an essential element of an assault that the act is done contrary to the will and without the consent of the victim.'**

Restrictions placed on the defence of consent

As one would expect, strong restrictions have been put upon this general proposition. The consent must be one that the law recognises as a valid one and these circumstances are limited. It was stated in the above case: **'It is not in the public interest that people should try to cause, or should cause, each other bodily harm for no reason.'**

The defence could not therefore be used in this case where a fist fight in the street took place, even though the parties had agreed to settle their differences in this way.

This followed an early decision in **Coney 1882,** where the courts held that a prize fight conducted with bare fists was unlawful, despite the agreement of the parties. In **Leach 1969,** the defendants were unable to argue that the victim consented to his injuries, even though he had asked to be crucified on Hampstead Heath! Fortunately, in this case, the misguided victim lived.

Situations where the defence might succeed

Consent may be available in the limited circumstances described in **AG's Reference (No 6 of 1980) 1981,** i.e. for **'properly conducted games and sports, lawful chastisement or correction, reasonable surgical interference, dangerous exhibitions etc.'** In addition, practical joking and consent to minor harm in sexual activities have also been tolerated.

Properly conducted games and sports

Here there is always a risk of some bodily harm occurring. The most obvious and perhaps difficult case to justify is boxing, where, by the very nature of the sport, the participants intend to cause harm to the other. Despite this, it was clearly affirmed by the House of Lords in **Brown 1994,** that the sport of boxing is a lawful activity. 'Cudgels, foils and wrestling' were other examples which came under the heading of **'manly diversions'** which were said **'to give strength, skill and activity, and may fit people for defence, public as well as personal, in time of need'.** This early view was quoted with approval in **Donovan 1934.**

With regard to these 'manly diversions', which include related sports like football, rugby and hockey, the victim is said to consent to harm that occurs within the rules of the game, provided the

Public school boy locked up for rugby kick that broke jaw

A father lashed out today after his son was put behind bars for smashing an opponent's jaw during a rugby match at his public school.

Civil engineer Chris Calton, 50, said outside court: 'It seems to me to be ridiculous that an incident on a rugby pitch should end up in court.'

David Calton, 19, now a tourism student at Sheffield Hallam University, was given a 12-month youth custody sentence at Sheffield Crown Court for kicking another boy with such force that one spectator said the impact 'sounded like a gunshot'.

The court heard how Calton, while a pupil at Mount St Mary's Catholic College, Spinkhill, near Sheffield, was playing 'a hard fought and closely contested game' at Pocklington School, East Yorkshire, when he attacked 16-year-old Andrew Wilson late in the game. Mr Mark Bury, prosecuting, said:

'The victim was knocked out with a kick to the head which broke his jaw while he was getting up from a ruck.

'There was a crowd at the game and Pocklington headmaster David Grey said the kick was levelled with all his might.' The victim was taken to York District Hospital and underwent surgery.

The court heard how, since the incident in January, the boy had been left with throbbing pains in his jaw which makes 'cracking sounds' when he eats.

Calton told police that Wilson had been aggressive towards him during the game, which was abandoned with the score at Pocklington 12, Mount St Mary's 17. But he admitted kicking out at him.

Taken from an article in the *Evening Standard*, 28 September 1998

defendant did not intend to cause serious injury. If he did have such an intention, then it would, of course, be immaterial that he was playing within the rules. Bramwell L J made this point clear in **Bradshaw 1878**, where the victim died during a game of football. Similarly, the defence would not be available to someone who deliberately broke the rules, as the newspaper article above illustrates.

Lawful chastisement

Traditionally parents have always been allowed to use reasonable force to chastise their children and after the decision in **Watkins 2001**, it appears that teachers, too, can use reasonable force to restrain unruly pupils. Punishment, however, cannot be inflicted **'for the gratification of passion or rage or if it be immoderate or**

excessive in its nature or degree'. This view was taken in the case of **Hopley 1860** and currently, there is much less tolerance of any physical punishment. In June 2001, a man who punished his stepson so severely that he was left with permanent injuries, was jailed for two years.

Reasonable surgical interference

A person may consent to the infliction of bodily harm for good medical reasons, even where the risk is substantial, such as an operation with only a small chance of success. The matter is not so clear cut in situations where the operation or other process has little medical advantage. Generally it is believed that the act is acceptable if it has some therapeutic value to the person requesting it. The defence of consent, therefore, could normally be raised by those performing cosmetic surgery, ear-piercing or tattooing, (though not tattooing of a minor as this is forbidden by legislation). Circumcision of males, as required in some religions, has long been accepted as lawful although female circumcision is banned by statute. Sterilisation, sex change operations and organ transplants have been added more recently. In **Richardson 1999**, patients were held by the Court of Appeal to have consented to their dental treatment, despite the fact that they might have been less willing to undergo this if they had known that the woman had been struck off by the General Dental Council!

In Tabassum 2000 however, the accused who pretended that he was a qualified doctor and intimately examined several women, failed to get his convictions quashed. The Court of Appeal decided that the women involved had not given a valid consent.

Dangerous exhibitions etc.

Within the field of entertainment, the law allows a person to consent to the possibility of some harm arising, as for example, where a person allows knives to be thrown at him or a cigarette to be shot from his mouth. It is, however, uncertain just how far this licence would extend.

Horseplay

In addition to the categories mentioned in **AG's Reference (No 6 of 1980) 1981**, other limited exceptions have been recognised. For example, the courts appear to be remarkably tolerant of what they call horseplay, as seen in **Jones 1986**, where two young schoolboys were injured after being tossed in the air by the defendants.

The Court of Appeal quashed the convictions for grievous bodily harm, deciding that the boys' consent to such 'rough and undisciplined play' could have provided a defence.

In **Aitken and Others 1992**, the practical jokes engaged in by RAF officers were even more potentially dangerous. The defendants set fire to the victim's supposedly fire resistant suit but the joke backfired and the victim received severe burns.

Despite this the Court of Appeal held that it was a misdirection to state that such an activity could never be lawful and the convictions were set aside.

Consent to harmful sexual activity

This has caused problems for the courts, with different approaches being taken by different judges. A controversial early example was the case of **Clarence 1888** (now no longer good law, as noted below) where the defendant escaped liability for both assault and rape because his wife had consented to the actual act of intercourse. She unsuccessfully contended that she would not have given this consent if she had been made aware that her husband was suffering from venereal disease which was then communicated to her.

In Slingsby 1995, the charge of unlawful act manslaughter was not made out after a woman later died from blood poisoning after engaging in consensual sexual activity. Internal cuts caused by the defendant's signet ring had become infected.

No defence to serious intentional harm

The defendant may be held liable, despite the other's consent, if the harm inflicted is more than trivial and is directly and deliberately inflicted on the victim, as in **Nichol 1807**, where the defendant harmed a 13-year-old pupil. In **Donovan 1934**, a young girl of 17 was beaten on her buttocks with a cane merely to give sexual gratification to the defendant, and in **Boyea 1992**, the victim was held to have consented to the sexual intercourse but not to the harm that this had caused. In **Currier 1998**, a Canadian case, the defendant was convicted after having unprotected sex with two women, knowing he was HIV positive.

In Dica 2004, the Court of Appeal decided that if a party had consensual sex with another, knowing that he was HIV positive, he was inflicting grievous bodily harm on that person and was reckless as to whether the party might become infected. The fact that the victim had consented to the sexual intercourse was irrelevant. The latter had not consented to the possible harm from AIDS or any other serious sexual disease. The case of Clarence was overruled in this respect. In cases where a person had known of the risk of infection and still embarked on sexual activity, however, the Court of Appeal took a different approach. In such a case, it was decided that the defence of consent, raised in a charge of grievous bodily harm, might still be available to the party with the disease. The trial judge had been of the opinion that, following the case of Brown, discussed below, the defence should not be allowed in this situation either, as it had been decided that a party cannot consent to more than trivial harm. He had therefore withdrawn the issue of consent from the jury. The Court of Appeal decided that this was wrong. Judge LJ stated: 'in every case where these issues arose, the question of whether the defendant was or was not reckless, and whether the victim did or did not consent to the risk of a sexually transmitted disease was one of fact, and case specific.'

Sado-masochism — the courts' approach

While very few people would knowingly consent to the risk of contracting AIDS in the future, there is a significant minority that actively seek physical pain during the course of their sexual activities. The House of Lords had to decide on the law's attitude towards such behaviour in **Brown and Others 1994**. The case had attracted a great deal of publicity because it involved the exploits of a group of homosexual males who took part in sado-masochistic activities, apparently enjoyed by all concerned. They burnt each other with matches and metal wires, beat each other with whips and indulged in unusual and painful forms of genital torture. The instruments were sterilised and the wounds dressed so none of the men suffered permanent injury. Their activities came to light when the police found a video detailing them, which had been circulated to group members. The participants were convicted of offences under **ss47** and **20 OAPA 1861** and were sentenced to terms of imprisonment ranging from two to four and a half years. Their appeals reached the House of Lords, where their convictions were upheld by a majority of three to two.

The majority view

Lord Templeman stated that in cases where no actual bodily harm had been caused, the consent of the person affected precludes him from complaining, thereby recognising the defence of consent in relation to common assault and battery. He also added that Parliament, under the **Sexual Offences Act 1967** had permitted homosexual activities in private between consenting adults. **He refused, however, to accept the contention of the defendants that their sexual appetites could only be satisfied by the infliction of more serious harm because, as he pointed out:**

> *sado-masochism is not only concerned with sex. Sado-masochism is also concerned with violence. The evidence discloses that the practices of the appellants were unpredictably dangerous and degrading to body and mind and were developed with increasing barbarity and taught to persons whose consents were dubious or worthless.*

He ended with a very clear message, stating that 'I am not prepared to invent a defence of consent for sado-masochistic encounters which breed and glorify cruelty and result in offences under sections 47 and 20 of the Act of 1861.'

Lord Jauncey discounted the argument that there needed to be hostility, as laymen understood the word, on the part of the person inflicting the bodily harm. He decided that if the act was unlawful, it was also a hostile one under the legal meaning of the word. He went on to stress the dangers to health inherent in these activities and the possible corruption of younger participants and decided that if such acts were to be rendered lawful it was up to Parliament to do this.

Lord Lowry stated that 'Sado-masochistic homosexual activity cannot be regarded as conducive to the enhancement or enjoyment of family life or conducive to the welfare of society'.

The dissenting view

Lord Mustill, in one of the two dissenting judgments, took a more liberal view. He stated that the state should intervene **'no more than is necessary to ensure a proper balance between the special interests of the individual and the general interests of the individuals who together comprise the populace at large.'** He argued that the acts indulged in by the group were not, at that time, criminal ones and was not prepared to create a new offence to make them so. He argued that this was Parliament's role, if it was deemed to be necessary.

Summary of the current position on the defence of consent

- It can, in appropriate cases, be a defence in cases of ordinary assault and battery (Brown 1994)

- It will not normally be a viable defence in cases of actual bodily harm and grievous bodily harm (Brown 1994).

- It is not available for those who transmit sexual diseases to another even if the other has consented to the act of intercourse (Dica 2004).

- It could be available in the above type of case if the defendant has clearly accepted the risk (Dica 2004).

- It could, in limited circumstances, be a defence even for more serious non fatal offences if the situation comes within one of the recognised exceptions, including properly conducted games and sports, horseplay and reasonable surgical interference. In Wilson 1997, the Court of Appeal decided to include 'bottom branding' under the latter head.

A doctor had discovered that Wilson's wife had scars on her buttocks in the form of the initials A and W, and reported the matter to the police. They discovered that her husband, at her request, had burnt his initials onto her buttocks with a hot knife. Wilson was charged with assault occasioning actual bodily harm under **s47 OAPA 1861**. The judge decided that he was bound by the cases of **Donovan** and **Brown** and directed the jury to convict.

The Court of Appeal quashed the conviction and expressed its disquiet that the prosecuting authority should have thought it necessary to bring the proceedings, which served no useful purpose and yet involved considerable public expense. The court decided that Brown did not lay down a proposition that consent was never a defence to actual bodily harm, deliberately inflicted, as all five Law Lords had recognised that there were exceptions to the general rule. The court also decided that it was preferable for the law to develop on a case by case basis. It believed that the current case was vastly different to the cases of Donovan and Brown. It felt that the first case involved aggression on the part of the defendant and the second physical torture that carried risks of serious physical injury and blood infection. The court felt that in the current case, there was no aggression and the act was more akin to a desire for physical adornment, similar to tattooing or ear piercing. It was therefore decided that the public interest did not demand that the defendant's activities should be treated as criminal.

Comment

There are many problems concerning the defence of consent. The following are examples:

- The current position, involving as it does a possible divergence of opinion between the House of Lords and the Court of Appeal as to the extent to which consent can be a defence for the more serious cases of bodily harm leaves a lot to be desired. The House of Lords has decided that the defence of consent to actual or grievous bodily harm is not available unless it comes within one of the recognised exceptions. The Court of Appeal seems to be taking a different approach, as seen in the cases of **Wilson** and **Dica**, unless use of the defence is felt to be against public policy.

- The adoption of a 'case by case approach', as suggested by the Court of Appeal in **Wilson** and **Dica** could make the law very uncertain.

- Some would argue that the defence should not be available for 'horseplay', so that the participants in such activities would know that they could not rely on the law to help them if the joke backfired. This approach has been taken in civil law and has helped to curtail some of the more harmful practical jokes and rituals, particularly in the field of employment.

- There also appears to be a fundamental difference among the judiciary about how to treat cases of bodily harm inflicted at the request of the victim. Some argue that the prevention of such activities is an interference with the liberty of the subject and is too paternalistic in approach. Increasingly, it is considered that what consenting adults do in the privacy of their homes is their own concern and the State should not intervene.

- Critics of this view would argue that any intentional infliction of pain degrades both the aggressor and the victim and can lead to an escalation of the violence. As stated earlier, Lord Templeman subscribed to this view.

- These critics believe that, even in these more permissive days, the courts have a duty to draw the line somewhere and state the limits of what is acceptable. If the participants then wish to continue and hope that they will not be discovered, then that is their affair.

- In **Laskey and Others v United Kingdom 1997**, the European Court of Human Rights refused to uphold a complaint by the men in **Brown** that their convictions were an unjustifiable interference with their right to respect for private life. Even that famously liberal court decided that their prosecutions were necessary in a democratic society for the protection of health.

- It is also maintained that the young could be corrupted by such actions. In the case of **Brown**, the perpetrators of the violence were middle-aged but the 'victims' were young men. There was also some evidence that a youth had been initiated into what were known as 'bondage affairs' at the age of 15.

- It can be argued that, even in the less extreme situation in **Wilson**, a doctor was obviously concerned enough about the degree of harm to report the matter to the police. Why then should not the law take the matter seriously?

The law makes a distinction between actual consent and mere submission but, in practice, the two states may be confused. It was clear in **Wilson** that the wife desired to be branded but there could be other cases where a partner merely submitted to the infliction of harm, through fear, perhaps or for love of the partner. The decision in **Wilson**, which apparently sets the law's seal of approval on some violent acts, may make it more difficult for the victim to protest. To conclude, it might be beneficial for Parliament to take the initiative in this matter and lay down clear guidelines on the use of consent as a defence.

Activity

Using the cases of **Brown, Wilson and Dica** as a basis for your arguments, decide whether the defence of consent should be extended, curtailed or remain as it is.

6.5 ACTUAL BODILY HARM

This offence is found under **s47 OAPA 1861**. It concerns an aggravated assault. It was stated, rather confusingly, in **Chan-Fook 1994** that the offence **'must be an assault which besides being an assault (or assault and battery) causes to the victim some injury.'**

FIVE KEY FACTS ON CONSENT

- The general rule is that consent by the victim may be a defence to assault and battery (**Attorney General's Reference (No 6 of 1980) 1981, Brown and Others 1994**) provided that the activity comes within one of the recognised categories.

- These include properly conducted sports like boxing, football, rugby and similar games (**Bradshaw 1878, Brown 1994**).

- Consent can also be given expressly or impliedly for limited lawful chastisement, (which was not the case in **Hopley 1860**), for lawful surgical operations and other procedures if there is some benefit in the activity, for dangerous exhibitions and for horseplay which goes wrong (**Jones 1986, Aitken 1992**).

- Consent will not be a valid defence for bare knuckle fighting (**Coney 1882**) and fist fights in the street (**Donovan 1934**). It is no defence to a charge of gbh where the victim may have consented to sexual intercourse but has not been warned of the risk of AIDS or another sexual disease. The position would change where the victim was aware of the facts and voluntarily accepted the long-term risk (**Dica 2004**).

- The defence is not available where actual bodily harm is inflicted at the time of the sexual activity (**Nichol 1807, Donovan 1934, Boyea 1992** and **Brown and Others 1994**), although the Court of Appeal appears to have made an exception with regard to 'bottom branding', likening this to a mere tattoo (**Wilson 1997**).

There is no definition in the act itself as to what constitutes actual bodily harm, although case law has provided assistance, as seen below. The offence of occasioning actual bodily harm was created at common law and **s47** merely describes the penalty.

In the case of **Courtie 1984**, however, the House of Lords decided that the offence of actual bodily harm should be treated as a statutory offence, despite the fact that the section merely states:

> *whosoever shall be convicted on indictment of any assault occasioning actual bodily harm shall be liable to imprisonment for not more than five years.*

The offence has since been made a triable either way offence and the section lays down a maximum sentence of five years for when the offence is tried in the Crown Court. If the magistrates agree, however, and the defendant chooses this form of trial the offence can be dealt with summarily.

There must be an assault or battery

As mentioned earlier, actual bodily harm is a form of aggravated assault so before it is decided that the victim has suffered such harm, it is first necessary to establish that he has been subjected to either an assault or a battery. It is therefore very important to remember the constituents of these offences.

In the case of **Constanza 1997**, the defendant, a former work colleague, had subjected the victim to a sustained campaign of harassment. This included numerous telephone calls, over 800 letters, following the victim, daubing offensive words on her door and making other unsolicited visits. As a result, the woman became clinically depressed and, after receiving two further letters, of the belief that the man was going to harm her physically.

The Court of Appeal stated that there was sufficient evidence that the victim was in fear of

immediate violence because it might have occurred at any time, particularly as the defendant lived quite close. The court also decided that there was no actual rule that an assault could not be committed by words alone and disapproved of earlier authorities which stated otherwise. The court therefore upheld a conviction under s47 after deciding that the assault had caused actual bodily harm.

In **Ireland 1998**, another case concerning harassment, the House of Lords upheld the view that repeated silent telephone calls could constitute an assault. The court decided, however, that a battery could not be committed in this way, because this offence required proof that unlawful force had been applied.

6.5.1 THE DEFINITION OF ACTUAL BODILY HARM

In **Miller 1954**, the term was said to include **'any hurt or injury calculated to interfere with the health or comfort of the victim'**.

In **Chan-Fook 1994** the Court of Appeal stated that the words 'actual bodily harm':

> *are three words of the English language which require no elaboration and in the ordinary course should not receive any. The word 'harm' is a synonym for 'injury'. The word 'actual' indicates that the injury (although there is no need for it to be permanent) should not be so trivial as to be wholly insignificant . . . The body of the victim includes all parts of his body, including his organs, his nervous system and his brain. Bodily injury therefore may include injury to any of those parts of his body responsible for his mental and other faculties.*

In this case, the Court of Appeal held that the judge had misdirected the jury when he said that it was enough to amount to actual bodily harm if the victim had been put in 'a nervous, maybe hysterical condition'. She had been questioned roughly by the defendant and locked in a room, after being suspected of stealing an engagement ring.

From this it is apparent that, while actual bodily harm encompasses physical harm, psychiatric injury and other identifiable clinical conditions, it does not cover emotions like fear, distress or panic. There may well have been a common assault and even a battery if the victim was manhandled but the more serious offence under s47 would not exist.

6.5.2 THE *ACTUS REUS* OF ACTUAL BODILY HARM

This is simply an assault (with the word used in its wider sense), causing actual bodily harm. As with a battery, it appears that the bodily harm need not be directly applied. In **DPP v K (a minor) 1990**, a 15-year-old boy left his chemistry class alleging that he needed to wash acid from his hand. He took a boiling tube of concentrated sulphuric acid with him to the toilet block in order to conduct some tests of his own. While he was experimenting with the acid, he heard footsteps and, in his panic, poured the remaining acid into a hot air hand and face dryer. The footsteps then receded but the boy left the acid in the dryer and returned to class, intending to deal with the problem at a later time. Unfortunately for him and the victim, the latter went into the toilet before this and his face was permanently scarred after he turned on the dryer and the acid was ejected.

K's conviction for actual bodily harm was upheld by the Divisional Court.

6.5.3 THE *MENS REA* OF ACTUAL BODILY HARM

Originally, there was a great deal of confusion over the *mens rea* for this offence but in Savage and Parmenter 1992, the House of Lords clearly stated that the *mens rea* is the same as that required for common assault and battery. This means that all the prosecution has to show is that the accused intended or was reckless about putting the victim in the state of apprehending immediate physical violence (as an assault) or intended or was reckless about touching the victim unlawfully (as in a battery). There is no requirement to go further and prove that he intended or was reckless about causing actual bodily harm.

This restated the position laid down in the case of **Roberts 1971** where the victim had jumped out of a car travelling between 20 and 40 miles per hour, after the driver, who was giving her a lift to a party, had told her to undress and had grabbed her coat. He had claimed earlier that he had beaten up other girls who had refused his advances.

The Court of Appeal upheld his conviction for actual bodily harm because, although he had not directly inflicted the injuries, he was responsible for them. The defendant had inflicted a battery on the girl and her action of jumping out of the car was one which could reasonably have been foreseen as a consequence of this. The court stated that the matter would have been different if the girl had done something 'so "daft" . . . or so unexpected . . . that no reasonable man could be expected to foresee it'.

This view prevailed until the case of **Spratt 1991**. The Court of Appeal, without referring to **Roberts**, suddenly decided that subjective recklessness about causing, not just a battery, but actual bodily harm itself, was required. This new view of the law was later followed by the same court when looking at **Parmenter**.

By a strange and embarrassing coincidence, however, in the case of **Savage**, which reached the courts on the same day as **Spratt**, the original view of the law had been upheld by another sitting of the Court of Appeal! The defendant had thrown a glass of beer over a former girlfriend of her husband. While attacking her rival, the beer glass had also left her hand (she claimed this was an accident), and had broken and cut the victim's wrist. The conviction for grievous bodily harm was quashed but the defendant was found guilty of the lesser crime of actual bodily harm. With regard to the *mens rea* required for this latter offence, the Court of Appeal restated the position in **Roberts**, although, once again, the name of that case was not mentioned.

There were therefore two conflicting views as to the *mens rea* required for actual bodily harm so the House of Lords was called upon to decide the matter in the joint appeals of **Savage and Parmenter 1992**.

The House of Lords decided that the law was correctly decided in Roberts.

The *mens rea* for actual bodily harm therefore is the same as for common assault and battery. If actual bodily harm results as a consequence of either putting the person in fear of a battery intentionally or recklessly, or intentionally or recklessly touching the victim unlawfully, then the greater crime under s47 has been committed. There is no extra requirement to prove that the defendant intended to cause actual bodily harm itself or had been reckless about whether this would happen.

It should be remembered that, when recklessness is alleged, Cunningham-style recklessness must be proved, as was clearly affirmed by the Court of Appeal in the case of Venna 1976.

FIVE KEY FACTS ON ACTUAL BODILY HARM

- Actual bodily harm is an aggravated assault, details of which appear under **s47 OAPA 1861**. The offence is a statutory one (**Courtie 1984**), for which the maximum punishment is five years' imprisonment.

- The prosecution must first establish the existence of an assault or a battery (**Constanza 1997**). If fear of immediate harm is present, an assault may arise from harassment caused by words alone or even by silent telephone calls (**Constanza 1997, Ireland 1998**). A battery, however, cannot be committed this way; it requires unlawful force (**Ireland 1998**). Such force can, however, be inflicted indirectly, as in **DPP v K (a minor) 1990**.

- The word 'actual' means more than trivial, the word 'harm' means some injury and the words 'bodily harm', include psychiatric injury. The words do not cover mere emotions like distress, fear and panic (**Chan-Fook 1994**).

- The *actus reus* of **s47** is an assault causing actual bodily harm. The *mens rea* is the same as for an assault or a battery, i.e. the defendant has intentionally or recklessly caused the victim to apprehend that a battery might be inflicted upon him (assault) or has intentionally or recklessly unlawfully touched the victim (a battery). There is no further requirement to show that the defendant intended to cause actual bodily harm (**Roberts 1971, Savage and Parmenter 1992**) or was reckless about this.

- The recklessness must be subjectively proved (**Cunningham 1957, Venna 1976**).

6.6 MALICIOUS WOUNDING OR GRIEVOUS BODILY HARM UNDER S20 OAPA 1861

S20 states that: 'whosoever shall unlawfully and maliciously wound or inflict any grievous bodily harm upon any person, either with or without any weapon or instrument shall be guilty of an offence'.

The maximum punishment for this offence is, surprisingly, the same as for actual bodily harm, i.e. imprisonment for five years.

▶ *Comment*

The **Offences Against the Person Act 1861** was merely a consolidating act and made no attempt to rationalise the law which came from several different sources. **S20**, however, has always been thought of as the more serious offence and it appears very strange to a layman that it attracts the same maximum penalty as actual bodily harm. It is one more reason why reform in this area of law is long overdue.

It can be seen from the definition of s20 that the offence has two aspects to it, the malicious wounding of another or the malicious infliction of grievous bodily harm. It is important for the prosecution to make a correct charge, as otherwise the defendant could escape liability. This occurred in **JJC (a minor) v Eisenhower 1984**, where pellets from the defendant's air gun caused injury to the victim's eye. There was bruising under his eye and rupturing of the internal blood vessels surrounding it but, crucially, no breaking of the skin.

The Divisional Court held that no wounding had taken place. It was decided that there must be 'a break in the continuity of the whole skin'.

It was, however, pointed out that the term 'skin' may also include the skin of an internal cavity where it is continuous with the outer skin. It is also important to realise that if there is proof of a wounding, the actual injury need not be severe; any breaking of the skin will suffice.

▶ *Comment*

The latter fact has also been criticised. Many people would be puzzled to learn that the degree of harm needed for malicious wounding need not be as high as that required for the second aspect of the defence, i.e. the infliction of grievous bodily harm. To the non-legal eye, the infliction of a minor wound would equate more easily to the offence of actual bodily harm. On the other hand, the law takes the view that the use of a weapon to cause any sort of wound is a serious matter, however small the actual harm.

With regard to the second part of the offence, it has to be established that the defendant has unlawfully and maliciously inflicted grievous bodily harm upon the victim.

In the case of **DPP v Smith 1961**, the House of Lords held that the words 'grievous bodily harm' simply mean really serious harm. In **Saunders 1985**, it was also decided that it would not be a misdirection to leave out the word 'really'; the words 'serious harm' would suffice.

6.6.1 THE *ACTUS REUS* OF S20

This consists of an unlawful wounding or the unlawful infliction of grievous bodily harm.

The word 'inflict' in **s20** has caused problems. In **s18 OAPA**, where the offence of grievous bodily harm with intent is laid down, the word 'caused' is used, rather than 'inflict'. The courts had to decide whether these two words have the same meaning. If the words were given different meanings, it then had to be decided whether the word 'inflict' in **s20** meant that the harm done to the victim has to be directly inflicted upon him. Until the House of Lords' decision in **Ireland** and **Burstow 1998**, there seemed to be conflicting authorities on this. One strain of cases suggested that the word 'inflict' should be interpreted narrowly and only apply if the defendant had caused direct harm. As noted, this view prevailed in **Clarence 1888**. The defendant was not held to have inflicted grievous bodily harm on his wife by infecting her with venereal disease because he had not made a direct assault upon her. She had consented to the sexual intercourse, even though she would not have done so if she had known the full facts.

Indirect harm included

The other line of cases treated the word 'inflict' in the same way as the word 'cause'. The judges took the view that the defendant could be convicted if the harm was caused in a more indirect way. In the case of **Martin 1881**, mentioned earlier, the defendant was convicted under **s20** when he placed a wire across the gangway in a theatre, because he had indirectly caused the injuries. Similarly, in **Halliday 1889**, a man was convicted of grievous bodily harm when he so frightened the victim that the latter jumped through a window and sustained serious injuries. In **Lewis 1970**, a husband was equally liable when his wife broke her legs in her efforts to escape him.

In Wilson 1984, the House of Lords clearly decided that they preferred the latter approach. Their Lordships relied on an Australian case, that of **Salisbury 1976,** to support their contention, although certain exceptions had been detailed in that case.

In Ireland and Burstow 1998, Burstow had subjected the victim to a campaign of harassment. He sent letters and photographs, made telephone calls, followed the woman, stole her washing and planted offensive items in her garden. He refused to stop his campaign even after prosecution and imprisonment. As a result, the woman suffered a severe depressive illness.

The House of Lords ignored the limitations on which type of harm could result in liability, imposed in the case of Salisbury, and stated that there could be liability for grievous bodily harm without any direct or indirect application of physical violence.

The Court of Appeal reinforced this view of the law in Dica 2004. The decision in Clarence was held to have 'no continuing relevance'.

◀ *Comment*

Many would agree with the courts' decision to include more indirect harm in this offence. The ruling in Dica, opening up the possibility of a later prosecution if the party fails to warn others about a sexually transmitted disease, might help prevent the spread of AIDS in this country.

The earlier decisions in **Constanza and Ireland and Burstow** showed a welcome willingness on the part of the judges to take a liberal approach to the wording of the ancient **OAPA**. This helped to ensure convictions at a time when cases on stalking were on the increase and there was no specific legislation to deal with this problem. The position was rectified to some extent by the **Protection from Harassment Act 1997**, which created two new offences.

● The less serious summary offence is committed where the defendant pursues a course of conduct that amounts to harassment of the victim. It requires harassment on at least two occasions. It is specifically laid down in **s7** that the word 'conduct' can include words alone. The maximum punishment is six months' imprisonment and a fine.

- The more serious offence, of putting a person in fear of violence, appears in **s4**. Once again, there must be conduct causing such fear on at least two occasions and the defendant must have known or should have been aware that his conduct would cause such fear.

This is a triable either way offence and, if tried on indictment, the maximum punishment is five years' imprisonment.

The creation of these new offences means that the judges will no longer have to strain the meaning of existing words in the **OAPA**. It also gives out a clear statement that the State is not prepared to tolerate stalking and other obsessive behaviour.

Unfortunately, this very necessary act is attracting a large number of appeals due to its deficient drafting, particularly in relation to what constitutes a course of conduct, and what is meant by the word 'violence' in relation to the more serious offence in **s4**. There have been instances where the obviously guilty have exploited these weaknesses. The defendants in **C (Sean Peter) 2001** and **R (A child) v DPP 2001** were not so fortunate. The first defendant, unsuccessfully, tried to argue that he had only committed the offences because of his schizophrenia and that, taking this into account, his behaviour had been reasonable! The second defendant argued that the requisite two threats against the victim had not been made out because while the first had been made against the woman, the second threat of violence was made against her dog! Once again, the appeal was dismissed.

6.6.2 THE *MENS REA* OF S20

It can be seen from the definition of the offence, that the wounding or infliction of grievous bodily harm must be done 'maliciously'. This word requires explanation. There is no necessity for active hostility or ill-will. In Cunningham 1957, the Court of Appeal stated that what was necessary was to establish that the defendant had intended to inflict harm or have been subjectively reckless as to whether this would occur.

Originally, it was decided that the accused would only be liable if he had foreseen that his actions would cause **grievous** bodily harm, i.e. really serious harm, or been reckless about this.

It was decided by the Court of Appeal in Mowatt 1968, however, that foresight of such a high degree of harm need not be proved. It is enough for the prosecution to show that the accused must have foreseen that some harm would result. The House of Lords, in Savage and Parmenter 1992, approved of this diluting of the *mens rea* for grievous bodily harm under s20.

In **DPP v A 2000**, the magistrates originally dismissed a charge of malicious wounding under s20. The defendant and his friend had been playing a game with air pistols, aiming to shoot each other below the knees. Somehow, the defendant had managed to shoot his friend in the eye instead! There was no suggestion that the defendant had intended to do this and the magistrates dismissed the charge of malicious wounding under **s20**. The prosecution appealed by way of case stated, arguing that the magistrates had applied the wrong meaning to the word 'maliciously'.

The Divisional Court agreed, stating that the correct test to apply when judging the extent of foresight necessary for a conviction was merely whether the defendant had foreseen that harm might be done and had then gone on to take the risk. The appeal therefore was allowed.

Conviction for a lesser offence

In **Savage and Parmenter**, mentioned above, the House of Lords also affirmed that it is possible for a defendant charged under **s20** to be convicted, instead, of actual bodily harm, provided that the jury has been properly directed about this.

6.7 MALICIOUS WOUNDING OR GRIEVOUS BODILY HARM UNDER S18

S18 OAPA 1861, as amended by the **Criminal Law Act 1967**, states:

TEN KEY FACTS ON GRIEVOUS BODILY HARM

- There are two offences describing these crimes laid down in **s18** and **s20 OAPA 1861**. Both offences have two aspects to the *actus reus*, malicious wounding and grievous bodily harm.

- To constitute a wounding, there must be a breaking of the whole skin (**JJC (a minor) v Eisenhower 1984**), but the injury itself need not be a severe one.

- The word 'inflict' in **s20** is to be interpreted in the same way as the word 'cause' in **s18** (**Wilson 1984, Ireland and Burstow 1998**). This approach enables a conviction to be obtained in cases of psychiatric harm caused by stalking, etc. (**Constanza 1997, Ireland and Burstow 1998**), although the **Protection From Harassment Act 1997** will lessen the need for this. It also allows a conviction to be obtained when those suffering from sexual diseases transmit these to others that are unaware of the condition, even though the latter consented to the sexual activity (**Dica 2004**). **Clarence 1888** is no longer good law.

- To decide on the *mens rea* of **s20**, the word 'malicious' needs to be examined. It now means intending to wound or inflict some harm on the victim or being reckless about this. The earlier requirement that the defendant must have intended to inflict serious harm has been changed (**Mowatt 1968, Savage and Parmenter 1992**). **Cunningham**-style recklessness is required.

- It is possible for the defendant to be convicted of the lesser offence under **s47**, if a **s20** offence cannot be proved (**Savage and Parmenter 1992**).

- The offence under **s18 OAPA** is, apart from rape, the most serious of the non-fatal offences against the person. The maximum sentence is life imprisonment.

- The *actus reus* occurs where the defendant wounds or causes grievous bodily harm by any means whatsoever. *Prima facie*, it is therefore wider than **s20**.

- The *mens rea* will only be established if it can be proved that the defendant intended to cause grievous bodily harm or intended to resist or prevent an arrest.

- The word 'intention' has the same meaning as for murder. The prosecution must, as a minimum, show that the defendant foresaw as a virtually certain consequence that his actions would cause serious harm.

- If this cannot be proved, the word 'cause' has been held to be wide enough to allow, in the alternative, a conviction under **s20**.

Whosoever shall unlawfully and maliciously by any means whatsoever wound or cause any grievous bodily harm to any person . . . with intent to do some grievous bodily harm . . . or with the intent to resist or prevent the lawful apprehension or detainer of any person, shall be guilty of an offence.

At first glance, this seems to be very similar to the offence under **s20** and the words 'wounding' and 'grievous bodily harm' have similar meanings. There are, however, important distinctions to be made between the offences.

- The maximum sentence for a s18 offence is life imprisonment.
- The s18 offence cannot be committed recklessly. There must be an intention to cause grievous bodily harm.
- An intention to cause lesser harm than grievous bodily harm will not suffice for the s18 offence.
- The s18 offence is committed when the accused 'causes' grievous bodily harm, which some judges believed had a wider meaning than the word 'inflict' under s20. S18 also uses the words 'by any means whatsoever' which appears to reinforce this.

Alternative verdicts

In Morrison 2003, the Court of Appeal decided that where a defendant had been charged on a single count of attempted murder, it was acceptable for the jury to convict, instead, of causing grievous bodily harm with intent. The court decided that no intent to kill a person could exist without also an intention to cause that person grievous bodily harm.

In Mandair 1995, the House of Lords decided that a charge of grievous bodily harm under s18 is wide enough to cover an allegation of 'inflicting' grievous bodily harm under s20

where the full requirements of the s18 offence cannot be made out.

These decisions ensure that the accused can, in these circumstances, be convicted of a lesser offence, even if he has not been charged with it.

6.7.1 THE *ACTUS REUS* OF S18

This is committed when the accused unlawfully and maliciously wounds another or causes him grievous bodily harm by any means whatsoever.

6.7.2 THE *MENS REA* OF S18

Under s18, the wounding or grievous bodily harm must be done maliciously (which has the same meaning as in s20) but also with a further intention either to cause grievous bodily harm or with intention to resist or prevent a lawful arrest or detention.

The word 'intention' has the same meaning as required for the crime of murder. The prosecution must therefore prove that it was the defendant's purpose to cause grievous bodily harm or to resist arrest or that he foresaw this as a virtually certain consequence of his actions.

Activity

- Evaluate the following statement:

'The state of the law concerning non-fatal offences against the person is uncertain, unjust and badly in need of reform.'

- Describe the offences which might, (or might not), have been committed in the following scenario:

Tony Corleone and Michael Soprano are the leaders of two notorious London gangs, the Jets and the Comets. They agreed to merge the two gangs and to have a fist fight to decide who should be in overall charge. During the fight, Tony's eye was badly bruised by the knuckle-duster used by Michael and there were signs of internal bleeding. Tony then landed a heavy punch on Michael, which broke the latter's collarbone. While trying to deflect further blows from Tony, Michael was outraged to hear the abuse being heaped upon him by Al, a member of the opposing gang. Michael shouted, menacingly, 'If I were not so busy right now, I would not take such language from you!'

Mrs Malone, a bystander, was jeered at as she tried to pass by and, although she wasn't hurt, she was jostled and pushed by a member of the gang and her skirt was grabbed.

Meanwhile, Moll, Tony's ex-girlfriend has complained to the police about his obsessive behaviour. She said that he is refusing to accept that their relationship is over, is following her everywhere and has made so many silent telephone calls to her that she is in a state of mental collapse.

Al's partner is even more distraught. She has just discovered that Al is HIV positive and has infected her. She is seeking revenge.

6.8 POSSIBLE REFORM OF NON-FATAL OFFENCES AGAINST THE PERSON

A Draft Bill from the Law Commission in 1993 attached to the Report (Law Com No 218), *Legislating the Criminal Code: Offences Against the Person and General Principles*, sought to sweep away the old-fashioned wording of these offences and provide more modern and sensible definitions.

This Bill was never brought to Parliament's attention, an omission attracting much criticism. In 1998 therefore, the Home Office produced a consultation document on the same subject, accompanied by a Draft Bill incorporating the changes suggested by the Law Commission. Under the Offences Against the Person Bill, the offences of assault and battery, actual bodily harm under **s47**, grievous bodily harm under **s20** and grievous bodily harm under **s18** would be changed to the following:

- Assault
- Intentional or reckless injury
- Reckless serious injury
- Intentional serious injury

It can be seen that assault or battery would be combined into one new offence simply called 'assault'. This would be committed if a person intentionally or recklessly applied force to or caused an impact on the body of another without his consent or, where the act was intended to cause injury, with or without the consent of the other. It would also be committed where the defendant intentionally or recklessly, without the consent of the other, caused the victim to believe that any such force or impact was imminent.

Clause 4(2) states that no offence would be committed if the assault merely comprises the touchings experienced in the normal course of daily life if the defendant does not appreciate that such an action is unacceptable to the other party.

With regard to the more serious offences, the current word 'harm' would be changed to the word 'injury'. This would include both physical and mental injury.

- Actual bodily harm would be replaced by the offence of intentional or reckless injury, with a maximum of 5 years' imprisonment.

- Reckless serious injury would be implemented in place of **s20 OAPA**, with a maximum sentence of 7 years,
- Intentional serious injury would replace **s18 OAPA**. The maximum would remain as life imprisonment.

The words 'serious injury' are not defined and would be left to the jury.

◀ *Comment*

The creation of these new offences would be a vast improvement on the present position. One can only hope therefore, that the Bill will be given the chance to become law in the not too distant future.

The combining of the offences of assault and battery is a good move, doing away with the confusion that currently exists. The sensible, ordinary wording of the more serious offences is also to be welcomed. The phrases 'malicious wounding' and 'grievous bodily harm' can then be consigned to the history books where they rightly belong.

Self-assessment questions on Chapter 6

1   Where is the law to be found on assault and battery? Define the *actus reus* and the *mens rea* of these offences.
2   Giving cases to support your findings decide whether words can ever constitute an assault. Why was no assault found in the case of **Tuberville v Savage**?
3   How did the courts decide that the threat of assault was an immediate one in **Smith, Constanza** and **Ramos**?
4   Illustrating your answer with decided cases, decide whether a battery can be inflicted indirectly.
5   Why were the police held to be acting unlawfully in **Collins v Wilcock** and **Kenlin v Gardner** but lawfully in **Donnelly v Jackman** and **Smith v DPP**?
6   Describe four situations where the defendant can consent to being harmed and two instances when he cannot.
7   Describe the *actus reus* and *mens rea* of actual bodily harm, giving cases to back up the points made and state where the law is to be found.
8   Apart from the difference in the *mens rea*, state three other differences between the offences under **s20** and **s18 OAPA 1861**.
9   Why was the conviction for malicious wounding quashed in **JJC (a minor) v Eisenhower**?
10 State the *mens rea* required for a) **s20** and b) **s18**.

Chapter 7

PROPERTY OFFENCES I: THEFT AND RELATED OFFENCES

7.1 INTRODUCTION

This chapter deals with the following offences:

✔ **Theft under s1 Theft Act 1968**

✔ **Robbery under s8 Theft Act 1968**

✔ **Burglary under s9 Theft Act 1968**

✔ **Aggravated burglary under s10 Theft Act 1968.**

7.2 THEFT

Stealing from others has always been considered a reprehensible crime and nearly every jurisdiction has some sort of sanction against it. It can be committed in a variety of different ways, as the article below shows.

In our jurisdiction, the law is to be found in the **Theft Act 1968**. This Act was passed after the Criminal Law Revision Committee looked at this topic and decided that the time was right for **'a new law of theft and related offences… embodied in a modern statute.'** The idea was to replace old-fashioned terms like larceny and, instead, to try to make the law more understandable and more easily accessible.

Theft is a triable either way offence. Originally, the maximum penalty was ten years' imprisonment

First-class train gang

Dressed in smart suits, the thieves who prey on business commuters

By Justin Davenport

Police have dubbed them the 'first-class train gang'.

A group of about 12 thieves have been targeting commuters and businessmen in the first-class areas of trains leaving London's mainline stations.

They work by dressing smartly in suits and ties and picking on passengers who have taken off their jackets.

The thieves sit close to them in the carriage and hang their own coats alongside those of their victims. Just as the train is about to pull out they make an excuse and leave the carriage, pickpocketing the victim's wallets as

they retrieve their coats.

The thieves prefer to target trains travelling long distances to keep the crime from being detected for as long as possible. This allows the culprits several hours to plunder people's bank accounts and rack up thousands of pounds on credit cards.

One of the gang, Charles Stewart, 42, is starting a three-and-a-half year jail sentence today after being convicted of stealing from commuters at Paddington station. He was caught only months after failing to turn up for a drug treatment course imposed by a judge for a series of 14 similar offences.

Ironically he went on the run after being given a rail warrant by the court to travel from Paddington station – where he had committed most of his offences.

Stewart was also given an antisocial

behaviour order banning him from entering any London mainline station or travelling on trains without permission for five years.

Detectives for British Transport Police say the 12 thieves, all of them crack or heroin addicts, have targeted trains at Euston, King's Cross, Waterloo and Paddington in recent years.

A special squad was set up to catch the offenders, although it has now been disbanded. Many of the gang have been jailed but at least one is still operating.

Police believe the group have racked up profits of hundreds of thousands of pounds over the years, the vast majority most of it going to fund drug habits.

Detective Constable Vicki Butler of Euston CID said the victims were often unaware their wallets had been stolen until they arrived at their destination much later.

She said: "People should be more aware and remember there are thieves who go

through trains looking for opportunities.

'The simple advice is not to leave your wallet in your jacket – keep it on you.'

■ **Businessman Jim Konig was sitting in first class on a Paddington train in October last year when he fell victim to Stewart,** *writes Justin Davenport*. **Mr Korig, 46, managing director of City company Opus Consulting, said his jacket was hanging next to Stewart's. As the train was about to leave, Stewart stood up and got off.**

'I felt my jacket move and checked my wallet and found it had gone,' said Mr Konig.

'Stewart was using my cards as I cancelled them. Within 20 minutes he had got £50 cashback at Safeway, bought 1,000 euros and two laptops worth £3,000.

'People should be made aware that this is going on.'

Evening Standard, 7 October 2003

if tried on indictment. Now, under s7, as amended by the Criminal Justice Act 1991, the maximum sentence has been reduced to seven years.

Other proposals have proved more controversial, such as the decision to allow on the spot fines for minor shoplifting offences.

The law on theft

The first point to grasp is that the whole of the law of theft is to be found in just seven sections of the Theft Act 1968. S1 contains the complete definition of theft, and ss2–6 give further

information on this. It will be seen in the table below that s2 and s6 contain further detail on the *mens rea* of theft and that ss3, 4 and 5 elaborate on the *actus reus*. As noted above, s7 lays down the punishment.

The definition, under s1 Theft Act 1968, states that a person is guilty of theft if he 'dishonestly appropriates property belonging to another with the intention of permanently depriving the other of it'.

Sections 1 to 6 can be seen more easily in Figure 7.1.

Section No	Word or phrase	Actus reus or mens rea?
1	whole definition	both
2	dishonestly	mens rea
3	appropriates	actus reus
4	property	actus reus
5	belonging to another	actus reus
6	with the intention of permanently depriving the other of it	mens rea

Figure 7.1 The elements of theft

7.2.1 THE *ACTUS REUS* OF THEFT

This is appropriating property belonging to another.

These words need to be looked at more fully.

Appropriates (s3)

This part of the definition of theft has caused the greatest problems for the courts. The word is described in **s3** of the Act and the current major authorities on its interpretation are found in the cases of **Lawrence 1972, Gomez 1993, Hinks 2000** and **Briggs 2003**.

S3 Theft Act states:

any assumption by a person of the rights of an owner amounts to be an appropriation, and this includes, where he has come by the property (innocently or not) without stealing it, any later assumption of a right to it by keeping or dealing with it as owner.

A person appropriates property, therefore, when he assumes the rights of the true owner.

In the case of Pitham and Hehl 1977, the Court of Appeal decided that a man who invited the two defendants into his friend's house while the latter was in prison and then sold them some of his furniture, had been assuming the rights of the owner.

In Williams 2000, the Court of Appeal decided that the accused had appropriated property belonging to another when he presented certain cheques for payment after defrauding the victims. When the cheques were honoured, this caused a diminution of their credit balances and the assumption by Williams of their rights.

The meaning of 'appropriation' therefore, appears to be straightforward but, unfortunately for the law student, various difficulties have arisen, as seen in the following situations.

Must all of the rights of the owner be assumed?

This question was addressed by the House of Lords, in **Morris; Anderton v Burnside 1984.** In the case of **Morris**, the defendant had taken some goods from a supermarket shelf and substituted lower price labels. He then went to the checkout desk, paid the lower price and was subsequently arrested.

In **Anderton**, a shopper had removed the price label from a joint of pork and replaced it with a much lower price from another item. He reached the checkout but was arrested before he attempted to pay for the goods.

Both offenders were appealing against their convictions for theft. Their contention was that they had not appropriated property belonging to another, because they had not assumed all the rights of the real owner. Both appeals were dismissed.

The House of Lords decided that they had assumed at least one of the rights of the real owners of the store by switching the labels on the goods and this action was sufficient to amount to an appropriation.

At what time does the appropriation take place?

In **Gomez 1993**, discussed later, Lord Keith refused to follow another statement by Lord Roskill that the appropriation only occurred when the labels were switched and the goods were placed into a supermarket basket. Lord Keith decided that the appropriation took place earlier than this. He stated that:

the switching of the price labels on the article is in itself an assumption of one of the rights of the owner, whether or not it is accompanied by some other act such as removing the article from the shelf and placing it in a basket or trolley. No one but the owner has the right to remove the price label from an article or to place a price label on it.

He dealt with the possible problem of a practical joker being convicted of theft by arguing that such a person would not have the *mens rea* for the offence because he would not be dishonest and would not have intended to permanently deprive the owner of the goods.

It can be seen, therefore, that the House of Lords has decided that an appropriation takes place the moment that the offender assumes any of the rights of the real owner. Cases such as **Skipp 1975** and **Fritschy 1985**, where the courts had decided that an appropriation did not take place until the defendant had done something that he had not been authorised to do, were overruled.

Difficulties

This new view of the law meant that the convictions of the defendants in **Atakpu and Abrahams 1994** could not be sustained. The offenders had devised a plan to hire expensive cars abroad and then to bring them to England to sell them. Suspicions were aroused when the men reached Dover and they were arrested. The case came to trial before the decision in **Gomez** and it was decided at first instance that the men were guilty of conspiracy to steal. The state of the law at that time decreed that the theft would have taken place in England, i.e. when the cars had been retained after the hire period had expired. By the time the case reached the Court of Appeal, however, **Gomez** had been heard by the House of Lords and it was reluctantly decided that the offenders had, instead, appropriated the property when they had, with dishonest intent, hired the cars in Brussels and Frankfurt. The men, therefore, could not be said to have been conspiring to steal in England and the convictions had to be quashed. The Court of Appeal was prepared to recognise that an appropriation could be a continuing act while the act of stealing was taking place, but would not stretch this to include actions taken days after the cars had been obtained.

Can an appropriation still exist after consent has been obtained?

This is a very popular area for examination questions. Students should note carefully that the answer to this question is now a definite 'yes'. Lord Roskill, in **Morris**, had believed that, for an appropriation to occur, there had to be an adverse interference or a usurpation of the rights of the real owner. This statement seemed to contradict an earlier House of Lords' decision, made in **Lawrence v MPC 1972**. In that case it had been decided that an appropriation had taken place, and a theft committed, even though the real owner had apparently agreed to the taking of the money.

An Italian student had arrived at Victoria Station in London on his first visit to England. Mr Occhi spoke little English but showed a taxi driver a piece of paper on which was written an address in Ladbroke Grove. The taxi driver falsely indicated that the journey was a long and expensive one and, when offered a £1 note, took a further £6 from the student's open wallet. The driver was convicted of the theft of the £6 but appealed on the grounds that the owner had consented to the taking.

The case eventually reached the House of Lords, where their Lordships decided that there could be an appropriation 'even though the owner has permitted or consented to the property being taken'.

Until the case of **Gomez 1993**, therefore, there were two conflicting House of Lords' decisions on this subject. In the civil case of **Dobson v General Accident Fire and Life Assurance Corp 1990**, the Court of Appeal made it clear that it preferred the decision in **Lawrence**. The court stated that 'whatever R v Morris did decide it cannot be regarded as having overruled the very plain decision in Lawrence's case that appropriation can occur even if the owner consents . . .'

The House of Lords upheld this view of the law in the case of Gomez 1993. The defendant

was employed as assistant manager at a store selling electrical goods and agreed with an acquaintance to supply goods to him in return for two stolen, unsigned building society cheques, amounting to £17,200.

The manager of the shop was presented with a list of goods to the value of the first of the stolen cheques, told that it was a genuine order and asked for his authorisation for the payment to be made by cheque. He requested that the bank be contacted to confirm that the cheque was a valid one. The defendant pretended that he had taken this step and declared that he had been informed that the cheque was 'as good as cash'.

The goods were duly delivered to the accomplice, with the defendant helping to load up his van.

A similar procedure was taken with regard to the second cheque (although one of the items ordered was not delivered) and this time the manager merely accepted the position. Some time later, the cheques were returned bearing the words 'Orders not to pay. Stolen cheque'. Gomez, together with others was arrested and subsequently sentenced to two years' imprisonment. He claimed that he could not be said to have appropriated the property in question because the manager had authorised the sale. The Court of Appeal accepted this defence and quashed the conviction.

A point of law of general public importance was, however, certified for the attention of the House of Lords. This took the following form:

> *when theft is alleged and that which is alleged to be stolen passes to the defendant with the consent of the owner, but that consent has been obtained by a false representation, has (a) an appropriation within the meaning of s1(1) of the Theft Act 1968 taken place, or (b) must such a passing of property necessarily involve an element of adverse interference with or usurpation of some right of the owner?*

Lord Keith gave the main judgment. He decided that Lawrence was right and Morris was wrong and was, in addition, only *obiter dicta*. He stated that:

> *The decision in Lawrence was a clear decision of this House upon the construction of the word 'appropriates' in s1(1) of the 1968 Act, which has stood for 12 years when doubt was thrown upon it by the obiter dicta in Morris. Lawrence must be regarded as authoritative and correct, and there is no question of it now being right to depart from it.*

The conviction for theft was reinstated.

It is now clearly the law, therefore, that there may still be an appropriation of property even if the owner appears to have consented to the

taking. **The House of Lords clearly affirmed this in Hinks 2000, discussed below.**

In **Gomez**, Lord Lowry made a powerful dissenting speech and stated firmly that cases such as **Gomez** should be dealt with under **s15** of the **Theft Act**, i.e. by charging the offender with obtaining property by deception, not with theft. He was the only judge to refer back to the Eighth Report of the Criminal Law Revision Committee that preceded the **Theft Act**. (Lord Keith had decided that this would serve no useful purpose!) This Report had clearly stated that, while it was possible for some cases of deception to also come within the definition of theft, it would not be theft where the owner obtained ownership of the goods.

◀ *Comment*

> The actual point of law in Gomez was quite a narrow one, concerning as it did a case where the consent was only given after a false representation had been made. The judges of the House of Lords, however, did not confine their reasoning solely to this situation, so therefore the implications of the decision are far wider. Smith and Hogan state that **'the effect is to create an extraordinarily wide offence, embracing many acts which would more naturally be regarded as merely preparatory acts'**. It also means that every case of obtaining property by deception under s15 (to be discussed in the next chapter) will also be theft.

Does there have to be a taking to constitute an appropriation?

We have seen that the House of Lords, in **Gomez**, implied that the answer to this question was 'no' because it decided that an appropriation occurs the moment that the defendant assumes any of the rights of the owner, whether or not he goes on to take the property. (It would, of course, be more difficult to establish the *mens rea* of theft at such a point because it would have to be shown that the defendant was acting dishonestly and had an intention to permanently deprive the owner of the goods.)

Despite this the Court of Appeal appeared to come to a different decision in **Gallasso 1993**, decided on the same day as **Gomez**. The accused was a nurse in charge of a house for people with severe learning difficulties and was authorised to deposit and withdraw money from the patients' accounts to meet their daily needs.

One of the residents received three cheques, one for £4,250, another for £4,000 and the third for £1,800.32 but, instead of depositing the money in the existing account, Gallasso opened other accounts in the patient's name and withdrew some of this money for her own use. She was charged with various counts of theft but disputed that a theft had occurred by the opening of the separate accounts in the resident's name.

The Court of Appeal quashed the conviction for theft on this count and decided that, although Gomez had laid down that an appropriation could take place even though the real owner appears to have given his consent, it was still necessary to have a taking. In this situation, while the nurse had obviously intended to commit criminal acts, it was felt that, at this stage, there had not been any appropriation of the resident's property.

This decision does not sit easily with the case of **Gomez** and is felt by many to be wrongly decided. The defendant was certainly assuming some of the rights of the owner by the opening of other accounts and **Gomez** has decided that this is enough to amount to appropriation.

What if civil law and criminal law principles conflict?

This matter came to the attention of the Court of Appeal in the case of **Mazo 1997**. A maid was appealing against a conviction for the theft of large sums of money from her employer, an 89-year-old woman whose mental faculties were weakening. The maid alleged that the money was a gift from a grateful employer and this point seemed to be made out because the employer had authorised the cashing of the cheques after the bank had made inquiries about them.

The Court of Appeal decided, therefore, that a valid gift of the money might well have been made and held that, in such a situation, there could not be a conviction for theft. The judges did pay lip service to the decision in Gomez, by stating that the act would have been theft, even though the owner had apparently consented to the taking, *if that consent had been secured by deception.* **The court, therefore, was recognising the narrowest ratio of the House of Lords in Gomez. In the present case, the judges felt that no such deception existed, the jury had been misdirected on the issues and therefore the defendant should be given the benefit of the doubt.**

It was argued that this result also conflicted with the judgment in **Gomez**. Those in favour of it pointed out that it appeared that the defendant had acquired **'an absolute, indefeasible right to the property'** and that any conviction for theft would therefore conflict with established civil law principles. **In the case of Hinks 2000, the House of Lords showed scant respect for this line of reasoning; instead their Lordships actually extended the principles in Gomez.**

Hinks had befriended a 53-year-old man of limited intelligence and between April and November 1996 had persuaded him to give her a television set and, much more seriously, to withdraw sums of money amounting to £60,000 from his building society, which were then deposited in the defendant's account. Hinks argued that the money and goods were either loans or gifts and therefore had not been appropriated by her but despite this, was convicted.

The Court of Appeal upheld the conviction but

allowed an appeal to the House of Lords on the question of whether the acquisition of an indefeasible title to property could still be classed as amounting to an appropriation of property belonging to another.

On a three-to-two decision, the House of Lords decided that it could. The court decided that the word 'appropriation' was not to be construed too narrowly; it was a natural word which comprehended any assumption of the owner's rights. Therefore, the acquisition of an indefeasible title to property by accepting a gift from a vulnerable and trusting person was capable of amounting to an appropriation under the Theft Act 1968. There had been a very strong prosecution case, which had been accepted by the jury after a fair and balanced summing up. The conviction was therefore declared safe, the precedents in Lawrence and Gomez upheld and the law on appropriation widened still further.

Have the limits been reached?

In **Briggs 2003**, the defendant had handled the purchase of a house called Welwynd Lodge, supposedly for her elderly relatives, who were in their nineties and eighties respectively. She had enclosed a letter of authority signed by them, instructing the licensed conveyancers involved in the sale of the couple's existing property, to send £49,950 of the sale proceeds to the solicitors acting in the sale of Welwynd Lodge and to send the remainder to the relatives' bank account. Welwynd Lodge subsequently was registered in the names of the defendant and her father.

The prosecution alleged that the consent of the old couple was induced by fraud as they believed that the property was being purchased on their behalf. The defendant was convicted of one count of theft, two counts of forgery, two counts of dishonestly obtaining social security benefits and one count of obtaining property by deception. Briggs was then given leave to appeal on the charge of theft only. In relation to the latter, the prosecution claimed that the defendant had appropriated the credit balance of £49,950 when she caused the licensed conveyancers to transfer the proceeds of sale to the solicitors involved in selling Welwynd Lodge, for her own benefit. Her counsel argued that a payment transferred in this fashion could not amount to an appropriation within the meaning of **s3** and quoted the case of **Naviede 1997** in support (which had been noted with approval by the late Sir John Smith).

The Court of Appeal agreed with this line of reasoning and quashed the conviction for theft. The judges decided that the word 'appropriation' required a physical act. In this case, there was only a remote act triggering the payment and this, they decided, was insufficient. They declined to substitute a verdict of obtaining property by deception, as it was unclear whether such a charge would have succeeded in the lower court. The prosecution had chosen to bring a charge of theft, because of the difficulties of bringing the elderly relatives to court as witnesses.

The current state of the law on appropriation

After the decisions in **Lawrence, Morris, Gomez, Hinks and Briggs**, the law on appropriation can be summarised in the following way:

- an appropriation will take place when just one of the rights of the owner is assumed (**Morris**).

- an appropriation can occur even though the owner apparently consents to the taking (**Lawrence, Gomez**).

- an appropriation may still take place where the defendant appears to have acquired legal ownership of the property (**Hinks**).

- This interpretation of the law now ensures that every case of obtaining property by deception under s15 Theft Act 1968 will also be theft under s1.

- An appropriation will not however take place where the act is not a physical one and is considered too remote (**Briggs**).

Before leaving the subject of appropriation, it should be noted that a person who obtains property in good faith, which later turns out to have been stolen, would not be guilty of theft for assuming the rights of the true owner. This is stated in s3(2).

◀ *Comment*

- **Hinks** is yet another example of a lack of agreement among the Law Lords in relation to an important issue in criminal law. Lord Hobhouse and Lord Hutton gave dissenting judgments, which obviously weaken the authority.

- The late Sir John Smith strongly disapproved of the decisions in **Gomez** and **Hinks**. In his commentary on **Hinks**, he stated: 'No reader of these commentaries over the years is likely to expect the decision of the majority to receive a warm welcome here'. He added wearily that 'those who make the decisions seem to turn a blind eye and a deaf ear' to any criticisms. He believed that the House of Lords went astray in the case of **Lawrence** concerning consent, and in **Morris**, when deciding that the words 'any assumption by a person of the rights of an owner' also included the assumption of just one of those rights. He argued that the decision in **Hinks** is against common sense because it allows a person to be convicted of stealing something that is his already and also creates a conflict with civil law principles. He strongly asserts that the criminal courts should take the law '– all of it – as they find it'.

- Other academics also condemned the latter decision, including Professor

Glanville Williams. Simester & Sullivan in *Criminal Law Theory and Doctrine* stated forcefully that '**Hinks** must be undone ...This decision is both impossible and absurd'. Michael Allen in his textbook on Criminal Law called the decision 'incredible'.

- The Court of Appeal, while obviously bound by decisions of the House of Lords, nevertheless appears uneasy about the width of the decisions in **Gomez** and **Hinks** and in cases such as **Gallasso**, **Mazo** and **Briggs** appear to be trying to curtail it.

- On the other hand, Stephen Shute, Professor of Criminal Law and Criminal Justice at University of Birmingham, in his article 'Appropriation and the Law of Theft', Criminal Law Review 2002 p445, concluded 'A range of arguments can be pitted against the decision in **Hinks**, but when examined in detail, none seems particularly strong'. He believed that the fault, if any, lay with **Gomez**.

Activity

Read the preceding information on appropriation and assess whether the judgments of the House of Lords in **Lawrence**, **Gomez** and **Hinks** have widened the law of theft in an unacceptable way.

Property (s4)

The word 'property' is widely defined in s4(1) to include:

money and all other property, real and personal, including things in action and other intangible property.

It can be seen, therefore, that nearly every type of property may be stolen. The definition includes both real and personal property, although, under **s4(2)**, this is qualified to some extent. This section states that a person cannot steal land, or things forming part of the land, except in the circumstances specified. These include situations where a trustee or personal representative disposes of the land under his control in an unauthorised way, where a person not in possession of the land severs something from it or where a tenant misappropriates fixtures which should have remained attached to the land.

Blood and urine samples can be classed as property, allowing the defendant in **Welsh 1974** to be convicted when he removed the urine sample he had provided for analysis by the police! Similarly, body parts preserved for scientific examination can also be stolen, as confirmed in **Kelly and Lindsey 1999**.

'Things in action'

These are known in civil law as choses in action, and consist of intangible property like patents, copyrights, shares, debts and insurance policies. The courts have had to decide how far this term 'things in action and other intangible property' extends.

In **Oxford v Moss 1978**, an engineering student at Liverpool University acquired the proof of an examination paper, intending to read its contents and then return it. He was obviously intending to cheat but what had to be decided was whether his actions amounted to theft.

The student had no intention to steal the actual paper, which was obviously the property of the university. The point of law the Divisional Court had to decide upon, therefore, was whether the information contained in the examination paper could amount to property within the meaning of **s4 Theft Act 1968**.

The Court decided that the right to confidential information was not in the category of intangible property laid down in **s4(1)** of the Act. The student, therefore, could not be convicted of theft.

'Other intangible property'

This widens the definition of property and enabled the director of a company in **AG of Hong Kong v Chang Nai-Keung 1987** to be convicted of stealing his company's property when, without authorisation, he sold his company's excess quota for a grossly reduced price to another company in which he had an interest.

'Other intangible property' includes things like gas stored in a container, but, owing to difficulties under the previous law, the dishonest abstraction of electricity was made a separate offence under **s13 Theft Act 1968**, punishable by a maximum term of imprisonment of five years.

Sections 4(3) and 4(4)

These sections deal with wild flowers, plants and animals.

Under **s4(3)** no offence is committed if a person picks mushrooms which are growing wild, or wild flowers, fruit or foliage, provided that this is not done for a commercial purpose.

S4(4) lays down that a person will not commit theft if he captures a wild animal which has not been tamed or reduced to captivity.

Activity

Decide whether the following people have stolen property as defined in **s4**. Give clear authority for your answers:

- Anthony took the manuscript of Joanna's new novel and published it under his own name.

- Jane picked a quantity of bluebells from Austen Wood and sold the blooms in her local market.

- Charlotte, a student at Bronte University, discovered the whereabouts of the English examination paper, memorised the questions and returned it to the filing cabinet.

- Anna captured a wild pony on Sewell Moor, tamed it and kept it for her own use.

- William was given notice to quit Hathaway Cottage and, in a fit of temper, dismantled and took with him all the fitted bookcases.

Belonging to another (s5)

These words are given a wide meaning under **s5(1)**, which states:

> property shall be regarded as belonging to any person having possession or control of it, or having in it any proprietary right or interest . . .

People in possession or control

It can be seen, therefore, that the property can belong, not only to the actual owners of it, but also to those who are currently in possession of it or have some sort of right over it.

This can mean that it is possible, in certain circumstances, for a person to be convicted of stealing his own property, if others have gained rights over it.

This point is illustrated in the case of **Turner (No 2) 1971**. The defendant put in his car for repairs but then returned after they had been carried out and took away the car from the road in which it had been put without informing the garage owner and without paying for the repairs.

His conviction for theft was upheld. Lord Parker stated that:

> This court is quite satisfied that there is no ground whatever for qualifying the words 'possession or control' in any way. It is sufficient if it is found that the person from whom the property is taken, or to use the words of the Act, appropriated, was at the time in fact in possession or control.

In **Meredith 1973**, however, it was decided that the police did not have sufficient control over the defendant's car to warrant a charge of theft when the owner took it back, only the right to enforce the statutory charge. The car had been impounded for causing an obstruction while the owner was at a football match.

People with a proprietary interest in the property

When looking at the term 'proprietary interest', it should be noted that the Crown has such an interest when 'treasure', is discovered on land. The **Treasure Act 1996**, and later **Regulations** have extended the definition of 'treasure' to include items of gold or silver and other precious metals, where the true owner is unknown. In **Hancock 1990**, the defendant had been charged with stealing from the Crown some Celtic silver coins, which he had discovered with the aid of a metal detector and had not disclosed to the authorities.

The Court of Appeal decided that the mere fact that an item might later be classed as treasure would not, at that point in time, be an established proprietary interest. It was therefore necessary to establish this point first.

Waverley Borough Council v Fletcher 1995, a civil case, established that if an item is not classed as 'treasure', the owner of the land will have a better claim to the article than the finder, provided that the article is attached to the land or found within it. If the find is not attached to the land, the owner will only have a better right if

he has exercised some clear form of control over the land and what is on it. In the early civil case of **Bridges v Hawksworth 1851**, the finder of some bank notes on the floor of a shop was held to have a better title than the shopkeeper.

Ss **5(2)** and **(3)** deal with situations where the defendant has acquired ownership or control of property, so that in law, it would normally be taken as belonging to him, but special circumstances exist to prevent him doing as he likes with the property.

S5(2) Trust property

With the vast majority of trusts, there are identifiable beneficiaries and if their interests are adversely affected they can take action under s5(1) as being the holders of a proprietary interest. **S5(2)** plugs a possible loophole where there are no ascertainable beneficiaries. It states that where the property in question is the subject of a trust, the property shall be taken as belonging to any of the people who have rights under it. Accordingly, if the person is in charge of a charitable trust which, as yet, has no ascertainable beneficiaries, and absconds with the proceeds, action can be taken against him.

S5(3) People holding money for a particular purpose

This section covers situations where a person receives property under the obligation to deal with it or the proceeds of the property in a special way. Once again, the property will be held to 'belong to another' if he does anything unauthorised with it.

An illustration of this is the case of **Davidge v Bennett 1984**, where the defendant was given money by her fellow flat-sharers to pay the communal gas bill.

When she spent the money on Christmas presents instead, she was held to be guilty of theft.

The facts were somewhat similar in the case of **Floyd v DPP 2000**, but in this case a third party was taking action against the wrongdoer. The defendant had collected weekly premiums from her colleagues at work, in order to purchase food hampers. She failed to pass all of the money on to the supplier but then tried to correct the deficit by giving the company various cheques. These cheques were dishonoured and the defendant was convicted of theft. She claimed that the cash belonged to her colleagues, not to the hamper company and that no obligation to pay the company existed until all the goods had been delivered. The appeal reached the Divisional Court.

This court decided that, under s5(3) Theft Act 1968 the defendant was under an obligation to hand over the money collected to Home Farm Hampers.

◀ *Comment*

It has been suggested that the reasoning in this case was wrong, although there could well have been a conviction using other arguments. The agreement to look after the money for the purchase of the hampers was made between the defendant and her fellow workers, not between Floyd and the company and it was therefore these colleagues that were the victims of theft, not the company. The court could have used the arguments put forward in **Wain** (see below), i.e. that a trust had been created and that Floyd therefore was also under an obligation to the company, as **Wain** had been to the charity in question.

There can be other difficulties with this subsection. It was stated in **Hall 1973**, that 'each case turns on its own facts'. One example, where the holder of money must deal with property in a particular way, is where the public puts money into special collecting tins; the collector cannot use the money for his own purposes. Another

such example is where a builder is given money specifically to purchase supplies; he, too, cannot use the money advanced for other purposes. Other situations where most laymen would assume that the subsection would apply, do not appear to be covered. In **Hall 1973**, a travel agent took deposits from customers, among them teachers paying a lump sum on behalf of their pupils for air trips to America, and placed the money in the firm's general trading account. The firm subsequently foundered and the flights never materialised. Nor were any of the deposits returned. At first instance, Hall was convicted of theft. **The Court of Appeal reluctantly decided that the partner was not, in these circumstances, under an obligation to deal with the customers' money in a particular way. While the defendant was undoubtedly dishonest in his dealings and his conduct was held to be 'scandalous', he was not appropriating property belonging to another.**

The question appears to turn on whether there is a clearly agreed obligation to deal with the money or proceeds in a particular way. Usually, this will arise where there is a stipulation that the money or proceeds should be kept in a separate fund but, in special circumstances, liability might continue later as in **Wain 1995**.

The defendant had raised over £2,000 for charity in a 'telethon' organised by Yorkshire Television and paid it into a separate bank account. He made several excuses for not sending it to the television company and was eventually allowed to pay the money into his own account and to send a cheque drawn on that account. The cheque was subsequently dishonoured and Wain was convicted of theft. His appeal against this was rejected. McCowan L J stated:

It seems to us that by virtue of s5(3), the appellant was plainly under an obligation to retain, if not the actual notes and coins, at least their proceeds, that is to say the money credited in the bank account which he opened for the trust with the actual property. When he took the money credited to that account and moved it over to his own bank account, it was still the proceeds of the notes and coins donated which he proceeded to use for his own purposes, thereby appropriating them . . .

In **Klineberg 1998**, although the appeal succeeded in part, the Court of Appeal affirmed that where a party (in this case buying a time-sharing property) is induced to contract on the understanding that his money would be protected by a trusteeship, there was a legal obligation under **s5(3)** to deal with the money in a particular way. A similar approach was taken in **Re Kumar 1999.**

The Divisional Court of Queen's Bench Division stated that from the time that a trustee holds money on behalf of a beneficiary he is not, without more, entitled to treat the money as his own. For the purposes of the law of theft, it is only necessary to have regard to s5(3). In the case in question, the terms on which the parties dealt were sufficiently expressed to include the requirement to 'deal with the property in a particular way', i.e. by retaining enough money in the bank account to meet the direct debit payments and this had not been done.

It is, however, very important to frame the charge correctly, as seen in the case **Dyke and Munro 2001,** where the well-deserved convictions of the defendants were overturned. They were trustees of a children's cancer charity and had been accused of stealing substantial sums of money from it. The indictment alleged that they had stolen monies 'belonging to a person or persons unknown', intending that these unknown people were the members of the public that had donated the money. The defendants appealed contending that the money stolen actually belonged to the charity concerned, rather than to the donors of the money.

The Court of Appeal allowed the appeal. The judges affirmed that when a person collected money for a charity, he was subject to an obligation to treat this money in a special way. A trust, therefore, came into existence, which meant that the money was stolen from the beneficiaries of the charity, not from the members of the public, donating the money. Ownership of the money had passed from the latter to the charity when the money was put in the collecting tin.

S5(4)

This deals with circumstances where a person receives property by mistake. **In such a case, he is under an obligation to restore the property to its rightful owner. If he fails to do this, he will be classed as intending to deprive the other of it.**

As under s5(3), the obligation imposed on the current owner of the property is felt to be a legal, rather than merely a moral obligation. It might well be argued, therefore, that an overpayment of a gambling win would not be recoverable, as any agreements relating to wagering or gaming are generally unenforceable in law. The court would have to use other means to gain a conviction.

In **Gilks 1972**, the defendant had visited one of Ladbrokes' betting shops and bet on a horse called Fighting Scot. This horse was not placed but, by a strange coincidence, another horse called Fighting Taffy won! By mistake, the defendant was paid out a sum of over £100 as if he had won on this latter horse. He was convicted of theft when he failed to disclose the mistake.

To achieve this result, the trial judge relied on the case of **Middleton 1873,** an ancient and rather dubious authority under the old law of larceny. He decided that the betting shop would not have paid out the money if aware of the mistake, therefore ownership of the money had never passed to the defendant.

The Court of Appeal accepted this very questionable decision, but did take the opportunity to declare that, if using s5 (4) Theft

Act 1968, the obligation had to be a legal, rather than a moral, obligation.

S5(4) is often invoked where employees have been overpaid and have failed to return the money. The following point of law came to the attention of the Court of Appeal in **AG's Reference (No 1 of 1983) 1985:**

whether a person who receives an overpayment of a debt due to him . . . by way of a credit to his bank account through the 'direct debit' system . . . and who knowing of that overpayment intentionally fails to repay the amount . . . may be guilty of theft.

In this case, a policewoman had been paid an additional sum of £74.74, had discovered this fact but had failed to inform her employer. The trial judge had ordered an acquittal.

The Court of Appeal decided in the Reference that, on the wording of s5(4), a person should be found guilty of theft even though he had not touched the money and had merely left it in an account.

It would of course, be a different matter if the employee really believed that he was entitled to the money or was genuinely unaware of the overpayment.

Activity

Decide whether the defendants in the following circumstances have appropriated property **'belonging to another'**. Give full legal reasons for your answers:

- Del booked a holiday in the Carribean with Peckham Travel and forwarded a large deposit. The travel agent, Rodney, used Del's money on other ventures and did not arrange the holiday, as promised. The firm then went into liquidation and Rodney was arrested.

- Edina obtained sponsorship money of £5,000 for abseiling down the White Cliffs of Dover. The money was given to help a children's charity but Edina spent it instead on new clothes from Paris.

- Patsy put her grandfather clock into the local antique shop for repair and, after the work had been effected, she entered the shop while the owner was unloading his van and removed the clock without his knowledge.

- Basil, a traffic warden, discovered that he had been credited twice with his monthly salary. He decided to keep silent about this.

- Manuel was paid an amount of £2,000 because of a mistake made by his local bookmaker. The correct amount should have been £200 but Manuel decided to keep the money in the belief that the bookmaker could afford the loss!

7.2.2 THE *MENS REA* OF THEFT

As stated earlier, the *mens rea* of theft requires that the accused should 'dishonestly' appropriate property 'with the intention of permanently depriving the other of it'. These two terms need to be examined.

Dishonestly (s2)

The drafters of the **Theft Act** preferred to use the word 'dishonestly' to the word 'fraudulently' which was used in the old law on larceny, because it was believed that a jury would find it easier to understand this new word. **There is no actual definition of dishonesty under s2 of the Act and it is the jury that has to decide the matter. What the Act does, instead, is to describe three situations in s2(1) where a person is not to be classed as dishonest and two situations in s1(2) and s2(2) where he would be.**

No dishonesty under s2(1)(a)

This states that a person will not be regarded as dishonest if he appropriates property, for himself or a third party, believing that he has a right in law to deprive the other of it. It appears from the case of **Holden 1991**, that it is not necessary for the accused to prove that his belief is a reasonable one, providing that it is genuinely held.

The defendant had been accused of stealing scrap tyres from Kwik-Fit, a previous employer. His defence was that he knew that others had taken the tyres with the permission of a supervisor. On the other hand, the depot manager gave evidence that the taking of the tyres was a disciplinary offence, meriting dismissal. The jury was directed that the question to be asked was whether the defendant had a reasonable belief that he had a right to take the tyres.

This was held to be a misdirection. The defendant only needed to establish an honest belief that he had a right to take the property.

Obviously, however, if the belief is a very unreasonably held one, the jury is less likely to believe that it is an honest one.

No dishonesty under s2(1)(b)

A person will not be considered dishonest if he takes property believing that the other would consent to this course of action if he knew about it. An example would be borrowing a fellow student's law books while that person was away, in the belief that he would approve of this course of action.

No dishonesty under s2(1)(c)

The last exception is more controversial. **Under s2(1)(c) a person will not be dishonest if he appropriates property belonging to another believing that the person to whom it belongs cannot be discovered by taking reasonable steps.** This section helps to protect a finder of property from a conviction for theft, who would otherwise satisfy the *actus reus* of the offence.

In **Small 1988**, the defendant claimed that a car he had appropriated had been abandoned by its owner. It had been left in one place for over a week with the keys in the ignition. The jury obviously did not believe his story and convicted him of theft.

The Court of Appeal decided that his conviction ought to be quashed if he had honestly believed that this was the case.

The sub-section specifically excludes trustees and personal representatives, so they may well be dishonest in the circumstances laid down. It is believed that such people should not become entitled to the property of others in such a way because, if the beneficiaries could not be found, the property should revert to the Crown.

Dishonesty under ss1(2) and 2(2)

The paragraphs mentioned above provide defences to a charge of theft. **Conversely, s1(2) decides that a person may still be convicted of theft despite the fact that his appropriation of property is not made with a view to gain, or for his own benefit and s2(2) states that he may still be classed as dishonest even if he is willing to pay for the property.**

It will still be theft, therefore, for a Robin Hood type figure to steal from the rich and give to the poor. It is also theft if property is merely removed for spite and is just destroyed or thrown away.

The basic test for dishonesty

This has changed over the years. There were differing opinions as to whether the test for dishonesty ought to be decided in an objective way or according to the defendant's own belief, i.e. subjectively. In **McIvor 1982**, the Court of Appeal sought to reconcile these differences, deciding, rather strangely, that a subjective approach should be taken where the charge was conspiracy to defraud, but that the question of dishonesty in theft should be decided objectively. A little later, in the case of **Ghosh 1982**, the Court of Appeal re-thought the matter and rejected this distinction. **Currently, therefore, the same test is to be used for both these offences and for the crime of obtaining property by deception, contrary to s15 Theft Act 1968.** The test itself, however, has been altered and is now a mixture of an objective and subjective approach. **This rather complicated twofold test asks the jury to decide upon the following matters:**

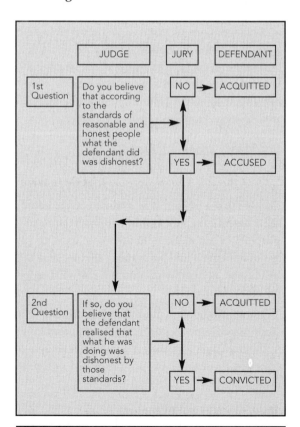

Figure 7.2 Ghosh test for jury

As noted the accused can only be convicted if the answer to both questions is 'yes', but in Price 1989 Lord Lane stated that there was no requirement for the judge to give the Ghosh direction in the vast majority of cases. It was only necessary in cases where the defendant appeared to believe that his actions were not dishonest but there was some doubt about whether he really thought that others would share this view.

For example, the test would be applicable where the defendant was accused of stealing from the rich to give to the poor and argued that he honestly believed that ordinary reasonable people would not think he was doing wrong. In such a case, using the **Ghosh** test, he could not be said to be acting dishonestly.

If, however, the accused merely liked to think of himself as a latter-day Robin Hood but knew that others would think that he was acting wrongly, he would be considered dishonest.

◀ *Comment*

The **Ghosh** test is not an easy one for juries, and indeed students, to understand. It has been subjected to a great deal of criticism, with some opponents of it calling, instead, for a statutory definition of dishonesty. In the earlier Australian case of **Salvo 1980**, the judge felt that it was not always the case that a citizen 'knows dishonesty if he sees it', and that further help was needed in some cases.

With the intention of permanently depriving the other of it (s6)

As stated by Edmund Davies L J in **Warner 1970** there is no definition of the phrase 'intention of permanently depriving the other of it' in the **Theft Act 1968**. The Criminal Law Revision

Committee had believed that the term required no further explanation but emphasised that mere borrowing, even dishonest borrowing, was not normally meant to be included. **S6**, however, was added later and, while said by J R Spencer in the *Criminal Law Review* in 1977 to sprout 'obscurities at every phrase', gives extra illustrations of where such an intention to permanently deprive can be assumed even when it is argued that there is no such intention.

Summarising these instances, s6(1) provides that a person will be taken as permanently depriving the other of property if he intends to treat the property as his own to dispose of regardless of the real owner's rights and states that this may sometimes occur even in cases where the offender is claiming that he has only borrowed the goods.

The full, rather obscure wording of **s6(1)** is as follows:

A person appropriating property belonging to another without meaning the other permanently to lose the thing itself is nevertheless to be regarded as having the intention of permanently depriving the other of it if his intention is to treat the thing as his own to dispose of regardless of the other's rights; and a borrowing or lending of it may amount to so treating it if, but only if, the borrowing or lending is for a period and in circumstances making it equivalent to an outright taking or disposal.

Borrowings

This would cover situations where a person borrows property without intending to return it or takes the property of another intending to sell or otherwise dispose of it.

In Downes 1983, the Court of Appeal upheld a conviction for theft when the defendant sold some tax vouchers, made out to him but belonging to the Inland Revenue, to others so that they could obtain tax advantages.

The same court felt that that there was also an intention to treat the employer's property as the defendant's own to dispose of in the case of **Velumyl 1989**. The defendant took over £1,000 from his employer's safe in breach of company rules and was convicted of theft. He was unsuccessful in his allegation that he had not committed the crime because he had intended to repay the money after the weekend break and, therefore, had no intention permanently to deprive the employer of his property.

The Court of Appeal showed scant sympathy for this argument and upheld the conviction on the grounds that he could not have intended to pay back the exact notes and coins he had taken.

In the earlier case of **Lloyd, Bhuee and Ali 1985**, the defendants had been luckier. Lloyd was chief projectionist at the Odeon Cinema in Barking and over a period of months had temporarily removed films from the cinema in order that his accomplices could take illegal copies of them and sell the pirate videos at a substantial profit. The films were only taken for a few hours and then returned but the defendants had been caught red-handed while making a copy. It had to be decided whether the defendants had committed the offence of theft.

The Court of Appeal decided that there were circumstances where there could be an intention to permanently deprive even though the goods were actually returned, but stated that this would be in cases where the value of the item stolen was affected. Here, it was decided that 'the goodness, the virtue, the practical value of the films to the owners has not gone out of the article . . . The borrowing, it seems to us, was not for a period, or in such circumstances, as to make it equivalent to an outright taking or disposal'.

In Bagshaw 1988, the defendant had been charged with the theft of some glass cylinders but alleged that he had only borrowed them. The trial judge had failed to explain to the jury that he could only be convicted in such a case if he had intended to keep the cylinders until all the 'goodness' in them had been utilised.

His appeal against his conviction on the grounds of this misdirection was therefore upheld.

From these decisions it can be seen that a person would be permanently depriving the other of property if he took an article like a season ticket, used it until it had expired and then returned it. The value (or goodness or virtue) in the article would have been removed. A person would also be guilty if he took the property and then put conditions on its return. Here, it may be safely assumed that if the conditions were not met, the property would not go back to the rightful owner. Lord Lane has quoted the example of an offender taking a valuable painting and refusing to return it until a large sum of money had been paid.

An examination of the cases shows that people steal the oddest things. In **DPP v Lavender 1994,** the alleged theft concerned two doors! The defendant had removed these from property being renovated by the local council and used them to replace two damaged doors in his girlfriend's residence.

Despite the difficulties caused by the fact that this property, too, was owned by the local authority, the defendant was classed by the Divisional Court as treating the doors as his own to dispose of and this, it was felt, was enough.

This appears to widen the law and sits uneasily with the view of the Court of Appeal in **Cahill 1993,** that there had to be more than a mere intention to use the thing as one's own because of the inclusion of the words 'to dispose of'. Hopefully, there will be a further discussion of this issue in the future.

Unsuccessful thefts

A last point regarding **s6(1)** which needs examination is whether an offender can be classed as permanently depriving the other of goods, and so be guilty of attempted theft, when he is trying to assess whether there is anything worth stealing. An example would be where he breaks into a car in order to see if it contains a radio or, as in **Easom 1971**, rifles through a handbag to see if the contents are worth stealing and then returns it when nothing of value is found. In this case, the handbag had been attached, by a string, to the wrist of a policewoman and, despite the fact that the bag had been returned to her, the defendant was convicted of the theft of the bag and its contents.

The Court of Appeal quashed the conviction stating that 'a conditional appropriation will not do' and this view of the law was upheld in Husseyn 1978. In AG's References (Nos 1 and 2 of 1979) 1980, however, the Court of Appeal decided that this would only be a problem in cases where the indictment specifically mentioned a particular article. In other cases, there could be a conviction for theft.

S6(2)

This states that person may be regarded as treating the property of another as his own in cases where he parts with possession of it 'under a condition as to its return which he may not be able to perform'. An example would be where he pawned the goods in question, knowing that it might not be possible to redeem them.

Now that all the elements making up the offence of theft are known, it is appropriate to look at two other offences closely connected to this crime. These are robbery and burglary.

7.3 ROBBERY

S8 Theft Act 1968 defines this. It states:

A person is guilty of robbery if he steals and immediately before or at the time of doing so and in order to do so, he uses force on any person or seeks to put them in fear of being then and there subjected to force.

TEN KEY FACTS ON THEFT

- The law on theft is to be found in **ss1–7 Theft Act 1968**. The full definition is laid down in **s1**, which states that a person is guilty of theft if 'he dishonestly appropriates property belonging to another with the intention of permanently depriving the other of it'. **Ss2–6** give further detail of the words in the definition and **s7** lays down the maximum punishment of seven years.

- The *mens rea* of theft is appropriating property 'dishonestly', as seen in **s2** and with 'the intention to permanently deprive the other of it' **(s6)**.

- There is no definition in the Act of what is meant by the word 'dishonesty' and it will be up to the jury to decide this. Normally no direction on this will be needed (**Price 1989**), but in cases where the defendant is disputing the claim of dishonesty, the **Ghosh** direction should be given. This states that the jury should first decide whether according to the standards of reasonable and honest people what was done was dishonest and, if so, whether the defendant realised this (**Ghosh 1982**).

- **S1(2)** and **s2(2)** give two examples where the defendant will still be acting dishonestly. The first will arise when he argues that he has not appropriated the goods for gain or for his own benefit and the second when he alleges that he intended to pay for the property. On the other hand, **s2(1)** lays down three special circumstances where a person will not be classed as dishonest. The first is where he believes that he has a right in law to the goods, even if this belief is not reasonably held, as in **Holden 1991**. The second instance is where he believes that the victim would have consented to the taking and the third is where he believes that the real owner cannot be discovered by the taking of reasonable steps to do this.

- There is no clear definition of the phrase 'intending to permanently deprive the other of the property' (**Warner 1970**), but **s6** states that this will occur when the defendant treats the property as his own to dispose of. **S6** also describes situations where this state of mind will be presumed, as noted in cases like **Downes 1983, Velumyl 1989 and Lavender 1994**. If the accused uses the property of another but then returns it, he will only be permanently depriving the other of it if the value in the property has been used up (**Lloyd 1985, Bagshaw 1988**). Conversely, provided that the indictment is correctly worded, the defendant can be found guilty of attempted theft where he searches property to see if there is anything worth stealing and then discards the item, as noted in **AG's References (Nos 1 & 2 of 1979) 1980**.

- The *actus reus* of theft arises where the defendant 'appropriates property belonging to another'. Explanations and further detail on these terms are found in **ss3, 4** and **5**.

- The word 'appropriates' means to assume the rights of the owner (**s3**). The House of Lords decided in **Morris 1984** that the definition will be satisfied if just one of the rights of the owner is assumed. This court also decided in **Gomez 1993** that such an appropriation takes place the first time any of the rights of the owner are assumed.

- The cases of **Lawrence 1972, Gomez 1993 and Hinks 2000**, all House of Lords' decisions, have firmly established that there can be an appropriation of property even though the victim appears to be consenting to the taking. **Gomez** also decided that there is no necessity for an actual taking. The Court of Appeal decision in **Gallasso 1993** appears to be wrongly decided. In **Hinks 2000**, the House of Lords decided that the word 'appropriation' was not to be construed too narrowly. On a three-to-two majority, their Lordships decided that there could even be an appropriation of property belonging to another in a case where the defendant had acquired ownership of the goods under civil law rules, if such a gift had come from a vulnerable and trusting person and the evidence of wrongdoing appeared to be strong. There must however be a physical act of appropriation, as noted by the Court of Appeal in **Briggs 2003**.

- The word 'property' is widely defined in s4 to include most types of tangible and intangible property. It does not however include confidential information, if the papers on which this is contained are returned (**Oxford v Moss 1978**), nor land, unless something is severed from it, a trust is involved or a fixture removed from it. Wild animals, fungi, fruit, flowers and foliage also cannot be stolen unless taken for profit but 'treasure' belongs to the Crown. Other finds belong to the owner of the land, if attached to it or under the owner's control, but to the finder in other cases.

- The property stolen must, under **s5**, belong to another but it can be taken as belonging to another if that other has temporary possession or control of it, as in **Turner (No 2) 1971** or where it is given to the defendant to deal with in a particular way (**s5(3), Davidge v Bennett 1984, Wain 1995, Floyd v DPP 2000** and **Re Kumar 1999**). No such obligation was found in **Hall 1973**. The prosecution must be careful to frame the correct charge or wrongdoers could escape liability (**Dyke and Munro 2001**). Under **s5(4)**, the defendant will be liable if he obtains property by mistake and fails to return it when there is a legal obligation for him to do so (**AG's Reference (No 1 of 1983) 1985**.

Activity

Decide whether Dennis has the *mens rea* for theft in the following situations:

- He removed several mattresses from a large furniture store without paying for them, in order to distribute them to people 'sleeping rough' in London doorways.
- He borrowed a book from the library and gave it to his cousin for a Christmas present.

- He saw a bicycle resting against the railings in the town centre, which was identical to the one he had lost in that same place the previous week, and took it home. In fact, the bicycle belonged to the local postman.
- He was suddenly invited to a 'black tie' event at a local hotel, so decided to wear a dinner jacket belonging to his absent flatmate. The friends often 'swapped' clothes. Would your answer be different if Dennis had taken £30 from the till of

his employer in order to pay for the hire of such a jacket, with the intention of returning the money after the weekend?

- On the dance floor at the hotel, he found two expensive tickets for the new musical 'Washington' and pocketed them. He took his girlfriend to see the show a few days later and then returned the ticket stubs to the hotel.

S8(2) Theft Act 1968 provides that the maximum sentence is life imprisonment.

It can be seen by the definition that robbery is aggravated theft, so it is very important to realise that theft, with all the elements discussed earlier in this chapter, must be established first. The following diagram illustrates this:

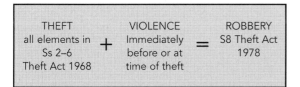

Figure 7.3 Elements of robbery

Cases on robbery

The elements of theft were not established in the case of **Robinson 1977**. The defendant ran a clothing club and was owed money by the victim's wife. A fight took place and in the course of this a £5 note fell from the victim's pocket which the defendant appropriated. He further claimed that he was still owed £2.

The Court of Appeal quashed the conviction for robbery. The defendant had an honest belief that he was entitled to the money so could not be held to have stolen it. He could, of course, have been charged with other crimes, such as actual bodily harm but should

not have been convicted of burglary.

The additional elements required before a robbery is committed would also not be made out in cases where the force is used first and then the wrongdoer decides to steal. This could occur, for example, where the offender attacked another who made derogatory comments about him and when his victim was lying unconscious, stole his wallet. It would also not be robbery where a theft took place and violence was used when the getaway was prevented. In these situations, the force is not being used or threatened **'in order to'** steal and is not taking place **'before or at the time of'** the theft.

A continuing act

The courts have taken a pragmatic approach to the words noted above, as seen in **Hale 1978**.

The defendant and an accomplice, wearing stocking masks, forced their way into the victim's house, put a hand over her mouth to stop her screaming and later tied her up. Before the latter act occurred, the accomplice had stolen a jewellery box from a room upstairs. The defendant was convicted of robbery. On appeal, he tried to argue that, because the theft had been concluded before the woman had been tied up and gagged, the definition of robbery had not been established.

The Court of Appeal refused to accept this claiming that 'the act of appropriation does not suddenly cease. It is a continuous act and it is a matter for the jury to decide whether or not the act of appropriation has finished.' The court was also prepared, in the alternative, to accept that the act of putting a hand over the victim's mouth was also using force and this, too, was done to facilitate the theft.

Interpretation of the word 'force'

The Criminal Law Revision Committee, when devising this section, had made it clear that there needed to be more than a mere snatching of property from an unresisting owner before it could be held to be a robbery. The courts, however, have decided that the definition is satisfied provided that some resistance to the taking has been shown.

In **Dawson 1976,** the jury had taken the view that jostling the victim so that he had difficulty in keeping his balance, was sufficient to amount to force and the appeal court supported this decision.

Similarly, in Clouden 1987, the defendant's conviction for robbery was upheld after he had used both hands to wrench a shopping bag from the victim and then ran off with it.

Lawton LJ stated that 'Force is a word in ordinary use. It is a word which juries understand'. He decided, therefore, that the jurors 'were entitled to the view that force was used'.

In **Corcoran v Anderton 1980**, it was held to be immaterial that the robbery had not been effected. This case concerned another bag-snatching attempt. The attack had been planned and the victim was pushed from behind and her handbag snatched from her. She then screamed and fell and the two youths ran away without taking the bag. The Divisional Court was asked to decide whether 'the tugging at the handbag, accompanied by force, amounted to robbery, notwithstanding the fact that the co-accused did not have sole control of the bag at any time.'

The Divisional Court stated: 'there cannot possibly be, save for the instance where a handbag is carried away from the scene … a clearer instance of robbery than that which these justices found was committed.' Watkins J also decided that the forcible tugging of the handbag was a sufficient exercise of control by the defendant.

Activity

Ken has borne a grudge against members of the acting profession ever since he was rejected for a part in a popular soap opera. Decide whether he has committed robbery in the following instances:

- He visited a film premiere and, as Fizz was going into the cinema, pulled one of her diamond earrings from her ear.

- He had a fight with Tod and knocked him out. While Tod was on the floor, Ken decided to steal his Rolex watch.

- He forced his way into Deirdre's house and stole the contents of her safe. He then tied her to a chair and made his escape.

- He wrestled with Rita as the latter was leaving a film set and snatched her camera. Rita then started to fight back so Ken dropped the camera and ran away.

7.4 BURGLARY

s9 Theft Act 1968 defines the offence of burglary. It is in two parts. **Under s9(1)(a) the crime is committed where:**

- **The defendant enters a building or part of one**

- **as a trespasser**

- **with the intent to steal, inflict grievous bodily harm, or do unlawful damage to the building or anything inside it.**

The crime of rape and trespass used to be included here but is now a separate offence under the **Sexual Offences Act 2003**.

Under s9(1)(b) the offence is also committed where:

- a person steals or inflicts grievous bodily harm on another
- after he has entered as a trespasser
- or attempts to do either of these things.

Differences between the sections

- Under subsection (a), the offender must intend to steal or commit the other offences laid down at the time he trespasses.
- Under subsection (b) the intent to steal can be formed after the trespass.
- S9(1)(b) only applies to theft and grievous bodily harm, but, unlike s9(1)(a), also includes attempts to do either of these things.

The maximum sentence is laid down in s9(3) and is 14 years' imprisonment when committed in respect of a building.

7.4.1 THE ELEMENTS OF BURGLARY

The words 'entry', 'trespasser' and 'building' have all caused problems and need looking at further, although all three elements appear to have been established in the report of the burglary at the house of Ozzy Osbourne, as seen below.

Entry

The first point to note is that the entry must have been effective. In earlier cases it was

Thieves grab £1m gems in raid on Osborne mansion

By Sam Jones

Veteran rocker Ozzy Osbourne spoke last night of how he struggled with a thief who stole more than £1m of jewellery from his mansion before escaping out of a window.

Two men used a ladder to get into the former Black Sabbath frontman's £5m home in Chalfont St Peter, Buckinghamshire, at about 4am yesterday. The stole the jewellery from a first-floor room, but woke Osbourne and his wife, Sharon, prompting the struggle.

Osbourne grabbed one of the burglars, and held on to him as he dangled from a window 10 metres (33ft) above the ground. 'I just looked at him, he was heavy – all I could see were his wild, red eyes,' said the 55-year-old singer. 'I thought for a mad split second, 'I could snap your neck like a straw, snap it and let you fall and then say it was an accident.' But then I just let him drop.

'I couldn't kill him. I couldn't live with that on my conscience,' he told the Sun newspaper.

Police believe the burglar injured himself in

the jump. He was described as being of large build, 5ft 10in to 5ft 11in, wearing a ski mask, light-coloured jacket and trainers. There was no description of the second man.

Officers said the men were driving a large vehicle, possibly a van, and they are keen to hear from anyone who may have seen one leaving Chalfont St Peter at speed.

Osbourne and his wife are living at the 18th century mansion while she appears in the ITV reality show The X Factor. None of their children was in the house at the time of the incident.

Police said that, although not many items of jewellery had been stolen, the total value was more than £1m. The thieves were thought to have specifically targeted the high-price gems.

One theory under consideration was that the thieves may have chosen Ms Osbourne because of her high-profile exposure during The X Factor, in which she and the other judges, Simon Cowell and Louis Walsh, pick would-be pop stars.

Guardian, 23 November 2004

decided that the entry had to be both substantial and effective, as held in **Collins 1973 but this is no longer necessary, as the cases of Brown 1985 and Ryan 1996 illustrate.**

Collins is a case known to nearly every law student because of its peculiar facts. The defendant, who was 19, had seen the girl in question when he worked near her house and after drinking a considerable amount had decided to visit the premises. He saw a light in her bedroom and fetched a ladder to reach the room. He then saw the girl naked and asleep in a bed very near the window. He descended the ladder, took off all his clothes except his socks, and then re-climbed the ladder and reached the window sill. He alleged that as he was pulling himself into the room the girl awoke. She got up, knelt by the bed, embraced him and appeared to pull him towards it. They then had sexual intercourse.

The girl argued that she had awoken at about 3.30am and seen a vague form with blond hair in the open window. She was unable to say categorically whether the person was on the outside part of the window sill or actually inside of the room. She firmly believed at that point that her boyfriend had come to make a nocturnal visit but later, during the intercourse, started to have doubts about this! She then turned on the light, discovered that her fears were justified.

Collins was later convicted of burglary. The girl, not unnaturally, argued that she would not have agreed to the intercourse if she had known that the man in question was not her boyfriend. The defendant, on the other hand, claimed that he would not have entered the room if the girl had not beckoned him in. Despite this contention, he was convicted. He later appealed on the basis that he had not entered as a trespasser.

The Court of Appeal decided that there had to be an entry into the building. Secondly, the defendant needed to have entered as a trespasser, which was far more difficult to

decide upon. Lastly, he had to have intended, at the time of entry, to commit rape.

The court believed that the judge had misdirected the jury on both of these points, particularly the second one and stated:

> *Unless the jury were entirely satisfied that the appellant made an effective and substantial entry into the bedroom without the complainant doing or saying anything to cause him to believe that that she was consenting to his entering it, he ought not to be convicted of the offence charged. The point is a narrow one, as narrow maybe as the window sill which is crucial to this case. But this is a criminal charge of gravity and, even though one may suspect that his intention was to commit the offence charged, unless the facts show with clarity that he in fact committed it he ought not to remain convicted.*

The fact that there must be a substantial and effective entry followed the earlier common law position but has since been disputed.

In Brown 1985, the Court of Appeal upheld a conviction for burglary even though the defendant argued that his entry was ineffective because a major part of his body was still on the highway. He had been caught while leaning through a broken shop window and sorting through the goods.

In **Ryan 1996**, the Court of Appeal went even further. The defendant had got stuck trying to climb through a small window of a residential property in the dead of night. Eventually, the fire brigade had rescued him. At his trial, Ryan tried to argue that he was only attempting to recover his baseball hat, which his friend had thrown through the window. The jury refused to believe such a story and **the Court of Appeal upheld his conviction for burglary, despite the fact that he was unable to go any further in his efforts to gain entry.**

acts in excess of the permission given. The court quoted with approval the civil case of Hillen and Pettigrew v ICI 1936, and particularly the comment that 'When you invite a person into your house to use the staircase you do not invite him to slide down the banisters.' The appeals, therefore, were dismissed. The court made it clear that a person is a trespasser if he enters premises of another knowing that he is entering in excess of the permission that has been given to him, or being reckless as to this fact.

Building

There is no definition of this word in the Act but s9(4) states that the word includes an inhabited vehicle and a vessel, even if they are not inhabited at the time of the offence. In the early civil case of **Stevens v Gourley 1859** it was suggested that a building was 'a structure of considerable size and intended to be permanent, or at least endure for a considerable time'. In **B and S v Leathley 1979**, there appeared to be an extension of this definition because a locked freezer container, resting on sleepers and connected to the main electricity supply, was held to be a building. In **Norfolk Constabulary v Seekings and Gould 1986**, however, the courts were not prepared to widen the definition to include two lorry trailers; these remained as mere vehicles.

Burglary will also be committed where the trespasser enters 'any building or part of a building'. This point was at issue in the case of **Walkington 1979**. The defendant went up to the first floor in Debenham's department store, went behind one of the moveable counters and looked into the open drawer of the till. He discovered that it was empty, slammed it shut and tried to leave the store. He was arrested and later convicted of burglary.

The Court of Appeal quoted from the late Sir John Smith's book, The Law of Theft, in which it is stated:

Trespasser

Usually, it will be easy to show that the wrongdoer is trespassing but occasionally there are problems, as, for example, when the defendant claims that he has a right to be there. This was the case in **Jones and Smith 1976**. The defendants removed two television sets from the home of Smith's father during the night and were convicted of burglary. At the trial, the father had tried to protect his son by arguing that he was not a trespasser because he had unreserved permission to enter the house.

The Court of Appeal was not prepared to accept this and decided that the word 'trespasser' also covered cases where a person

A licence to enter a building may extend to part of a building only. If so, the licensee will trespass if he enters some other part.

If the offender then intends to commit a crime in that other part, he will be guilty of burglary. The Court of Appeal also decided that such a person still commits the offence even if he only intends to steal on the condition that he finds something worth stealing.

7.4.2 THE *MENS REA* OF BURGLARY

The offender must know that he is a trespasser or be reckless as regards this fact and then must have the intention to commit the ulterior offence.

7.5 AGGRAVATED BURGLARY

S10 Theft Act 1968 states that:

A person will be guilty of aggravated burglary if he commits any burglary and at the time has with him any firearm or imitation firearm, any weapon of offence, or any explosive.

7.5.1 FIREARMS, IMITATION FIREARMS AND WEAPONS OF OFFENCE

S10(2) states that the term 'firearm' also includes airguns and air pistols and 'imitation firearm' means 'anything which has the appearance of being a firearm, whether capable of being discharged or not'. This obviously brings a wide range of real and imitation guns within the definition. The term 'weapon of offence' has caused problems. **It is defined as 'any article made or adapted for use for causing injury to or incapacitating a person or intended by the person having it with him for such use'.**

It can be seen from these sections that the aggravated offence is established if the defendant merely possesses any of these articles at the time of the offence; he does not have to use them or even intend to do so. In **Stones 1989**, the defendant had a household knife in his possession but claimed that this was merely for self-defence because 'some lads from Blyth' were after him. While it was accepted that this knife was not 'made or adapted for use' etc, the prosecution claimed that it was an article intended to cause injury or incapacitation.

The Court of Appeal agreed, deciding that it was not necessary to prove that the defendant intended to use the article in the burglary in question; it was enough that he had the article with him and intended to use it in any way.

In the earlier case of **O'Leary 1986**, the defendant had not been armed when he entered the house but took a knife from the kitchen upstairs with him.

His conviction under s10 was upheld as he had the weapon with him when he made the decision to steal.

TEN KEY FACTS ON ROBBERY, BURGLARY AND AGGRAVATED BURGLARY

- The crime of robbery is defined in **s8 Theft Act 1968**; the maximum sentence is life imprisonment **(s8(2)).**

- The elements of the crime of theft must first be established (**Robinson 1977**). It then has to be proved that the defendant used force, or threatened to use it, immediately before or at the time of the crime, although the courts have been prepared to find that a robbery can be a protracted affair (**Hale 1978**).

- A simple snatching of property would be theft rather than robbery but the latter may be established if the victim resists the attack (**Clouden 1987**) and maybe even where the victim has merely been jostled (**Dawson 1976**). There is no requirement that the goods have to be taken (**Corcoran v Anderton 1980**).

- Burglary is defined in **s9 Theft Act 1968** and can be committed in one of two ways. Both require a trespass by the defendant. Most trespasses will be obvious but a person will also be a trespasser if he acts in excess of any permission given to him (**Jones and Smith 1971**).

- **Under s9(1)(a)** a burglary is committed where the defendant enters a building or part of one intending to steal, to inflict grievous bodily harm, or to cause criminal damage.

- It will also be burglary where the defendant steals or inflicts gbh after having entered as a trespasser **(s9(1)(b)).**

- The entry must be considered to be an effective one but the courts now take a broader view of this. There is no longer a requirement that the entry should be substantial (**Collins 1973, Brown 1985 and Ryan 1996**).

- A building is not defined in the Act but will include a vehicle or vessel which is inhabited. The courts have also included a freezer container with mains electricity attached in this category (**B and S v Leathley 1979**) but were not prepared to recognize two stationary lorry containers as such (**Norfolk Constabulary v Seekings and Gould 1986**).

- A person will become a trespasser if he enters a prohibited part of a building and commits one of the prescribed crimes there (**Walkington1973**).

- Aggravated burglary is defined in **s10** and takes place where the burglar has a real or imitation firearm, other weapon or explosive with him at the time he commits the offence. He does not have to bring the weapon with him so long as he possesses it at the time of the crime (**O'Leary 1986**). The term 'other weapon' includes things made or adapted to cause injury or incapacitation **(s10(2))** and it is immaterial that the burglar does not intend to use the article during the commission of the crime (**Stones 1989**).

Activity

Decide whether the following people have committed any offences under **ss9** and **10** of the **Theft Act 1968**:

● Jack fell asleep at the end of a working day. He awoke to find the building empty so decided to steal one of the computers from the office of his boss.

● Jill was desperate for money and planned to steal the silver candlesticks in her local church. She had just put her head through the window when the parish priest discovered her.

● Mary broke into a department store and then stole a knife from the kitchen department. She used this to force the security officer to give her the contents of the safe.

● Simon, a chocoholic, was waiting to be served in a sweet shop. Overcome with a longing for a Toblerone bar, he vaulted across the counter and snatched one from the shelf. He later claimed that he had every intention to pay for the goods.

Self-assessment questions on Chapter 7

1. Define theft and state where the law is to be found. Decide which parts of the definition comprise the *actus reus* of the offence and which part the *mens rea*.

2. What is meant by the term 'appropriation' in **s3**? Explain why this word caused problems for the courts in the cases of **Morris, Lawrence, Gomez, Briggs and Hinks** and describe how these issues were resolved.

3. Define the word 'property' under **s4** and explain why this caused difficulties in the case of **Oxford v Moss**.

4. Why were the defendants, in **Turner (No 2)**, **Davidge**, **Floyd**, **Wain** and **Kumar** held to have property 'belonging to another' but not **Hall**?

5. When will theft be committed under **s5(4)**?

6. Giving section numbers and cases to support your answer, decide how the issue of dishonesty is settled.

7. What is meant by the phrase 'with the intention of permanently depriving the other of it'? Why were the convictions in **Downes**, **Velumyl** and **Lavender** upheld but not those in **Lloyd** and **Bagshaw**?

8. Define the crime of robbery. Explain why the offence was not made out in **Robinson** but the convictions upheld in **Hale**, **Clouden** and **Corcoran**.

9. Describe the two different ways that burglary can be committed under **s9(1)(a)** and **s9(1)(b)** of the **Theft Act**. State why the conviction in **Collins** was quashed but the crime of burglary established in the cases of **Brown**, **Ryan**, **Jones and Smith** and **Walkington**.

10. What is meant by the term 'aggravated burglary'? Describe the effect of **s10(2)**.

Chapter 8

PROPERTY OFFENCES II: MAKING OFF WITHOUT PAYMENT AND DECEPTION OFFENCES

8.1 INTRODUCTION

In this chapter, the first crime to be looked at is that of making off without payment. All students apart from those taking the WJEC course are required to study this offence. After that, five offences involving deception will be examined, knowledge of which is required for those taking AQA A Level Law, ILEX examinations and other post A Level courses. These six offences are discussed in the following order:

✔ **Making off without payment under s3 Theft Act 1978**

✔ **Obtaining property by deception under s15 Theft Act 1968**

✔ **Obtaining a money transfer by deception under s15A Theft Act 1968**

✔ **Obtaining a pecuniary advantage by deception under s16 Theft Act 1968**

✔ **Obtaining services by deception under s1 Theft Act 1978**

✔ **Evasion of liability by deception under s2 Theft Act 1978.**

8.2 MAKING OFF WITHOUT PAYMENT

This offence is described in **s3 Theft Act 1978**. It was created to plug a loophole in the **Theft Act 1968** that arose where people obtained goods without at that time deceiving the other party but later refused to pay for them. An example of this type of behaviour was shown in the case of **DPP v Ray 1974**, where a diner in a restaurant made off without paying for his meal and the courts had to strain to find liability (see later). It was also intended to cover the passenger in a taxi who fails to pay the fare and the motorist who drives off after filling his tank with petrol.

S3 Theft Act 1978 states that:

> *. . . a person who, knowing that payment on the spot for any goods supplied or service done is required or expected from him, dishonestly makes off without having paid as required or expected and with intent to avoid payment of the amount shall be guilty of an offence.*

8.2.1 THE *ACTUS REUS* OF MAKING OFF WITHOUT PAYMENT

This arises in cases where the accused makes off without paying for the goods purchased or a service supplied.

'Makes off'

JR Spencer, in the Criminal Law Review in 1983, put forward the view that the term **'making off'** means **'disappearing: leaving in a way that makes it difficult for the debtor to be traced'.** The Oxford English Dictionary states that it means **'to depart suddenly'.** Others would argue that the term merely means **'to leave'.** In **Aziz 1993**, two men asked a taxi driver to take them to a night-club, refused to pay the £15 requested when they arrived there and offered £4 instead.

The taxi driver decided to drive them to a police station but on the journey, the men started to damage the taxi. The driver then went into a garage and asked for the police to be called. The two men ran off but one of them was caught and charged under **s3**.

The defendant tried to argue that he had not made off from the spot where payment was due.

The Court of Appeal held that in journeys by taxi, payment on the spot could either be in the taxi or outside it and in this case the men were still inside it when payment was requested. The court went further and stated that it was enough that the requirement to pay the money had arisen; a particular location was not necessary.

The term 'making off' suggests that the defendant must have left the premises. Should he be prevented from doing this, it was stated in **McDavitt 1981** that the correct charge should be an attempt.

'Without paying'

For liability to arise, the payment must be 'required or expected'. In the case of **Troughton v MPC 1987**, a passenger asked to be taken to Highbury by taxi. He was under the influence of drink and quarrelled with the driver, accusing him of making an unnecessary deviation. The taxi driver was unable to get an address from the passenger so made a detour to take him to a police station to try to clarify matters. The defendant was later charged and convicted under **s3**.

The Court of Appeal quashed the conviction, deciding that, as the driver had not completed the contract, the defendant could not be required or expected to pay for the journey.

In a similar vein, payment cannot be demanded if the goods supplied or the service provided is contrary to law. This is made clear in **s3(3)** of the Act. A client who refused to pay a prostitute, therefore, would not incur liability under this section. He could, however, be charged under **s1 Theft Act 1978** for obtaining services by deception because, under this section, no such limitation is imposed.

8.2.2 THE *MENS REA* OF MAKING OFF WITHOUT PAYMENT

There are three elements to the *mens rea*:

- **The defendant must know that payment on the spot is required or expected.**
- **He must then dishonestly make off without making such a payment.**
- **He must have the intention to avoid making it.**

With regard to the first two elements, the defendant would not be liable in the restaurant type of situation if he genuinely but mistakenly believed that someone else was going to pay the bill.

In Brooks and Brooks 1982, the Court of Appeal held that this point had not been made clear to the jury and the daughter's conviction for obtaining a meal without paying for it was quashed, even though she had left the restaurant early in some haste.

'Dishonestly makes off'

In Brooks the court stated: 'the words 'dishonestly makes off' are words easily understandable by any jury which, in the majority of cases, require no elaboration in a summing up'.

'With intent to avoid payment'

In **Allen 1985**, the defendant stayed for nearly a month at an hotel but then left without paying his bill. He contacted the hotel a few days later, explained that he was in financial difficulties but stated that he would leave his passport as security for the debt when he came to collect his belongings. Instead, the police were called and he was later convicted under **s3**.

The House of Lords quashed his conviction. Lord Hailsham agreed with the Court of Appeal that the words 'with intent to avoid payment' meant an intention to evade payment altogether, not just an intention to defer or delay payment. In this case, it was felt that the accused should be given the benefit of the doubt.

The defendant in **Vincent 2001** also had his conviction quashed in somewhat similar circumstances. He had stayed at two different hotels in Windsor and left one without paying the bill at all and only part paying the other. When charged under **s3**, his defence was that he had made arrangements with the hoteliers to pay when he could and that therefore payment on the spot was not expected. He also claimed that he was not acting dishonestly and had no intention of avoiding the debts.

The Court of Appeal decided that the trial judge had misdirected the jury on the elements to be proved for s3 and quashed the conviction. The offence was said to be a straightforward one without any deception element.

Activity

Decide if liability under **s3 Theft Act 1978** exists in the following situations:

- Jamie went into Ainsley's restaurant and ordered the five-course set dinner. Jamie became annoyed about the large tips being left by some of the City workers so took the view that the owner had made enough money. He therefore ran out of the restaurant after completing his meal while his waiter, Gordon, was serving another customer.

- Would your answer be any different if Jamie merely left early in the belief that his companion Anthony would pay the bill?

FIVE KEY FACTS ON MAKING OFF WITHOUT PAYMENT

- This offence is found in **s3 Theft Act 1978** and the maximum sentence is two years' imprisonment (**s4**).

- The term 'making off' is not defined; it could mean merely 'to leave', or 'to depart suddenly' or, more precisely, 'to leave in a way that makes it difficult for the debtor to be found'.

- The *actus reus* exists when the defendant makes off without having paid as required or expected (**Aziz 1993**; contrast with **Troughton 1987**, where no liability was incurred).

- Should the offender be apprehended before he leaves the place where payment is due, the correct charge would be attempting to make off without payment (**McDavitt 1981**).

- The *mens rea* of **s3** consists of having knowledge that payment on the spot is required, being dishonest within the ordinary meaning of the word or under the **Ghosh** test, and having an intention to evade payment altogether (**Allen 1985**).

● Nigella hailed a taxi to take her to the television studios, five miles away. After travelling for a few hundred yards, she noted that there was a solid traffic jam as far ahead as the eye could see. Fearful of being late, she suddenly jumped out of the taxi and finished her journey via the underground.

8.3 OBTAINING PROPERTY BY DECEPTION

This offence is found in **s15 Theft Act 1968**. **S15(1)** lays down both the definition and the maximum sentence. It states:

A person who by any deception dishonestly obtains property belonging to another, with the intention of permanently depriving the other of it shall on conviction on indictment be liable to imprisonment for a term not exceeding ten years.

● The *actus reus* of s15 is satisfied where the defendant by any deception obtains property belonging to another.

● The *mens rea* exists when the accused does this dishonestly and with the intention of permanently depriving the other of it.

It can be seen that the definition of this offence is very similar to that of theft, under **s1**. It should also be remembered that, since the case of Gomez, every time an offender satisfies the definition of obtaining property by deception, he also satisfies the definition of theft under s1 and could be charged with this offence. In certain situations, this could make it easier for the prosecution to prove its case. There are, however, some important differences between the two crimes.

● Under s15, a deception has to be practised, so not everyone charged with theft would also be guilty of obtaining property by deception.

● Under s15, the word 'obtains' is used, rather than the word 'appropriates' in theft.

● The maximum sentence for obtaining property by deception is 10 years' imprisonment whereas the maximum for theft has been shortened to seven years.

8.3.1 THE *ACTUS REUS* OF OBTAINING PROPERTY BY DECEPTION

The various components of the *actus reus* now need to be studied.

By any deception

This phrase is the key element of this offence. There can be no liability under **s15** if the victim has not been deceived. **It was stated in Re London and Globe Finance Corporation 1903 that to deceive is 'to induce a man to believe that a thing is true which is false and which the person practising the deceit knows or believes to be false'.**

It can be seen from this that a person must be involved. There would be no liability under s15, therefore, if an offender put worthless tokens in a machine to obtain something of value from it. Likewise, a deception would not operate where the buyer makes it clear that he was not influenced by the words or conduct of the other party. In **Laverty 1970**, the defendant had changed the registration and chassis number plates on a car and then sold it. **His conviction under s15 was quashed on appeal, as the court was not convinced that the buyer had bought the car solely as a result of this action.**

S15(4) helps to clarify the word 'deception' by stating that it includes deliberate and reckless deception by either words or conduct.

In addition, the courts have decided that the deception can be either expressed or implied. There could, therefore, be liability where goods were paid for by cheque in circumstances where the drawer of the cheque knows that the bank would not honour it, provided that it can be shown that someone had been deceived. This could cause problems where a guarantee card accompanies the cheque because, in such circumstances, the retailer is relying upon the card and knows that the cheque will be honoured. It could be argued that he is not therefore concerned about the fact that there are no funds to meet it. The courts originally took a robust attitude towards the word 'deception' to ensure that cases like this were covered and the offender did not escape liability. This approach can be seen in the case of **MPC v Charles 1977**, a case which will be discussed more fully later.

The House of Lords decided that the defendant's cheques had only been accepted because of the belief that he was acting properly. It followed, therefore, said Lord Edmund-Davies, that the victim was being deceived, even though he may not have been concerned about the deception and may not have incurred any loss.

A similar approach was also taken in **Lambie 1982**, regarding the misuse of a credit card. The defendant used her Barclaycard over 60 times after her credit limit had been exceeded, including a transaction at Mothercare. Lambie had been convicted of obtaining a pecuniary advantage by deception but, on appeal, the conviction had been quashed.

The House of Lords then restored the conviction. Their Lordships decided that she had made a representation that she had actual authority to make a contract with Mothercare on the bank's behalf that the bank would honour the voucher on presentation. Lord Roskill also queried why the charge of obtaining property by deception had been rejected and decided that it would have been made out. He rejected

the contention that it was necessary in every case to call the person on whom the fraud was first perpetrated, arguing that if this were so, the guilty would often go free.

In **Nabina 2000**, the defendant was luckier. At first instance he was convicted on 14 counts of obtaining property by deception. He then appealed, arguing that the judge had misdirected the jury. He admitted obtaining a number of credit cards by giving false information about his personal circumstances. He also agreed that he had later used those cards to obtain goods and, on one occasion travellers' cheques, from several different outlets but denied that he had done this dishonestly or by falsely representing that he was the legitimate holder of the cards.

The Court of Appeal quashed the conviction, doubting that a properly directed jury would have decided that deception of the outlets was a necessary inference from the facts. In these transactions there was nothing to suggest that the money would not be forthcoming. It appeared that the defendant did have actual authority to warrant that the transactions would be honoured by the issuers, and even if the issuers would have been entitled to revoke that authority because of the fraudulent claims, they had not done so. The facts therefore, differed from those in Charles and Lambie where no such authority existed because the respective credit limits of the card users had been exceeded.

Comment

The late Sir John Smith argued that, in such circumstances, there would be a greater chance of a conviction if such a defendant were charged with theft.

A deception was found in the case of **DPP v Stonehouse** 1978, where the extraordinary conduct of the MP John Stonehouse hit the headlines all over the world. His financial affairs were in chaos so he decided to fake his death while on a business trip to Miami. He gave the impression that he had drowned by leaving his clothes on the beach, and fled to Australia to start a new life with his mistress. He had earlier transferred his money to Australia so that his estate would be insolvent but, to provide for his wife after his 'death', had taken out insurance policies in her favour. Suspicions were aroused and he was later discovered alive and well in Australia. The press, of course, had a field day and the MP subsequently returned to this country to face charges of attempting to obtain property by deception.

The Court of Appeal upheld his conviction, deciding that 'the accused . . . had done all the physical acts lying within his power that were needed to enable Mrs Stonehouse to obtain the policy moneys if all had gone as he intended'.

In **King and Stockwell 1987** the defendants pretended that they were from a reputable firm of tree surgeons and falsely told the elderly victim that many of the trees in her garden were dangerous and needed to be removed. They then offered to do the work immediately for the sum of £470, if paid in cash. Their deception came to light when a sympathetic building society cashier noted the woman's distress as she attempted to withdraw the money for the work, and called the police.

The Court of Appeal upheld the convictions stating: 'there was ample evidence on which the jury could come to the conclusion that had the attempt succeeded the money would have been paid over by the victim as a result of the lies told to her by the appellants'.

Obtains

The word 'obtains' is explained under **s15(2)**, which states that a person is treated as obtaining property **'if he obtains ownership, possession or control of it'**. This might happen without the real

owner being aware of this, as in the case of credit and debit card fraud, which is escalating in an alarming way. The newspaper article opposite gives advice on how to avoid this in relation to withdrawing money from cash machines.

A gap in the law was disclosed in cases like **Collis-Smith 1971**, where the defendant obtained the property first and then practised a deception on the other party. Collis-Smith had filled up his car with petrol; therefore, at that moment, ownership in the property had passed to him. He then falsely indicated that his company would pay for it. The conviction under **s15** was quashed because the property had not been obtained by the deception. Ownership had come earlier. It will be seen later in this chapter that this gap has been closed by the passing of the **Theft Act 1978** and that the defendant could now be charged with evading a liability by deception under **s2**.

Property

The word 'property' is not defined in **s15** but **s34** states that the definition of property in **s4(1)** will apply to all sections of the Act. The word therefore includes **'money and all other property, real or personal, including things in action and other intangible property'**. The limitations under **s4(2)**, however, imposed with regard to the offence of theft, do not apply to **s15**. It would appear, therefore, that almost anything might be obtained by deception, including land. An example of this would be where an impostor claimed the estate of a deceased person.

Belonging to another

Under **s34**, this phrase, too, will be taken to have the same meaning as in theft. It is possible, therefore, to obtain by deception property that belongs to the offender but is in the temporary control of another.

Precautions when using a cash machine

Choosing a cash machine
● Put your personal safety first
● Be aware of others around you. If someone is behaving suspiciously or makes you feel uncomfortable, choose a different machine
● If you spot anything unusual about the cash machine, or there are signs of tampering, do not use the machine and report it to the bank immediately

Using a cash machine
● Give other users space to enter their personal identity number (PIN) in private. We recommend standing about two metres away from the user in front of you until the person has completed their transaction. Some cash machines may have a safety zone marking out this area on the ground around the machine
● Be alert. If someone is crowding or watching you, cancel the transaction and go to another machine

● Do not accept help from seemingly well-meaning strangers and never allow yourself to be distracted
● Stand close to the cash machine. Always shield the keypad with your spare hand and your body to avoid anyone seeing you enter your PIN

Leaving a cash machine
● Once you have completed a transaction put your money and card away before leaving the cash machine
● If the cash machine does not return your card, report its loss immediately to your bank
● Tear up or preferably shred your cash machine receipt, mini-statement or balance enquiry when you dispose of them.

Source: Apacs

8.3.2 THE *MENS REA* OF OBTAINING PROPERTY BY DECEPTION

It will be remembered that the *mens rea* of this offence will be present when the defendant obtains the property **'dishonestly'** and **'with the intention of permanently depriving the other of it'. In addition, he must have made the deception, discussed above, deliberately or recklessly.** These points require further examination.

Dishonestly

It is very important to realise that, in addition to any deception, it is also necessary to prove a dishonest intent. This was clearly stated by the Criminal Law Revision Committee when the Bill was being drafted and is also obvious from the definition.

To clinch matters, the Court of Appeal affirmed this position in Feeny 1991, when it was said that the offence could not be committed 'unless dishonesty is established as a separate and essential ingredient'.

When deciding whether the defendant is dishonest, the **Ghosh** test, mentioned under theft, will be used. The jury needs to be convinced of two things,

● **that the defendant's behaviour was dishonest when judged against the standards of reasonable and honest people**
● **that the defendant himself realised that he was doing wrong by those standards.**

The case of **Price 1989** established that where these facts are patently obvious, the **Ghosh** direction need not be given.

In **Lightfoot 1992**, the defendant had obtained

a Barclaycard issued in the name of Plummer, a fellow firefighter. Lightfoot had used the card to purchase goods to the value of £3,000. There was some doubt as to whether he had done this with the consent of the named person and Plummer strongly denied this. The direction of the trial judge did not follow exactly the words laid down in the **Ghosh** test but they were similar.

The Court of Appeal decided that this was good enough.

With regard to dishonesty in theft, **s2(1)** lays down situations where a person is not classed as being dishonest; **it is important to realise that there is no corresponding section with regard to obtaining property by deception**.

With the intention of permanently depriving the other of it

S15(3) states that the extended definition of this phrase, laid down in **s6** concerning theft, also applies to **s15**. A person will commit the offence, therefore, if he treats the property as his own to dispose of, provided, of course, that the other elements of obtaining property by deception are present.

Whether deliberate or reckless

In addition to the two phrases within the definition of **s15(1)**, **s15(4)** also states, indirectly, that the deception must be practised deliberately or recklessly.

In Staines 1974, the Court of Appeal held that the term 'recklessness' meant more than mere carelessness or negligence on the part of the defendant. It is also made clear by the cases that in all the deception offences, Cunningham-type recklessness must be proved.

Greenstein 1975 can be cited as a rare example of a reckless deception. The case concerned the very questionable practice of 'stagging', under which large blocks of shares were applied for by the defendant, 'paid for' with a cheque for which funds were not available. This was done in the knowledge that the shares would be over-subscribed and only a proportion of the shares applied for would be issued. By using this method, the applicants would receive a higher allocation of shares than if they had only applied for shares to the amount that they could afford and had then been given a proportional allocation of this quantity. The practice of stagging was considered to be highly irregular and to try to combat it, the issuers of the shares would sometimes ask applicants to give an assurance that the cheque would be met on its first presentation. This was the position in this case and the defendants were charged with obtaining the shares by deception, when such a declaration was held to be a false one. The defendants tried to argue that they had not been dishonest because in the vast majority of cases where such a practice had been employed in the past, the cheques had almost always been honoured.

The Court of Appeal decided that the cheques could only be met if the applicants were successful in their deception on the issuers of the shares. This deception was that their application was a genuine one. It could also be argued that the defendants were reckless because, while they hoped that their cheques would be met, there was always a chance that they would not be. They were aware that in 14 out of 136 transactions the return cheque had not been cleared in time to cover the amount needed for the first cheque.

8.4 OBTAINING A MONEY TRANSFER BY DECEPTION

The law on this is to be found in a new **s15A**, inserted into the Theft Act 1968 by the Theft (Amendment) Act 1996. The very swift change in the law followed the controversial finding of the House of Lords in **Preddy 1996**, that no existing deception offence had been committed when the defendants had obtained mortgages by giving false information. Their Lordships had come to this conclusion because no property had passed from the payer to the payee; there had merely been a transfer of money between the two accounts.

S15A states:

A person is guilty of an offence if by any deception he dishonestly obtains a money transfer for himself or another.

Such an offence occurs where money is debited from one account and credited to another and **'the credit results from the debit or the debit results from the credit' (s15A(2))**. The maximum punishment is laid down in **s15A(5)** and is ten years' imprisonment.

8.4.1 THE *ACTUS REUS* OF OBTAINING A MONEY TRANSFER BY DECEPTION

The *actus reus* of this offence is satisfied when a person by any deception obtains a money transfer for himself or another.

8.4.2 THE *MENS REA* OF OBTAINING A MONEY TRANSFER BY DECEPTION

The *mens rea* occurs when the deception is deliberate or reckless (s15B states that the word is to have the same meaning as in s15), and the obtaining is done dishonestly.

8.5 OBTAINING A PECUNIARY ADVANTAGE BY DECEPTION

The offence and the punishment for it are laid down in **s16(1) Theft Act 1968**, which states:

a person who by any deception dishonestly obtains for himself or another any pecuniary advantage shall on conviction on indictment be liable to imprisonment for a term not exceeding five years.

Under **s16(2)(b)**, a person unlawfully acquires a monetary advantage for himself if, by deception, he is permitted to become overdrawn, take out an annuity or insurance policy or to secure an improvement on the terms of any such transaction.

In **MPC v Charles 1977**, the defendant visited a gaming club and, in just one evening, used all the cheques in his book to purchase chips for gaming. Each of them was made out for the sum of £30 and covered by a cheque guarantee card so each cheque subsequently had to be honoured by the bank. The defendant tried to argue that the casino owner was not deceived, because he was unconcerned as to whether the defendant had the bank's authority to issue these cheques; he would be paid in any event.

As noted previously, however, the House of Lords took a liberal approach to the question of deception and his conviction was upheld.

S16(2)(c) states that a person also commits this offence if, by his deception:

he is given the opportunity to earn remuneration or greater remuneration in an office or employment.

Such an offence would be committed if the defendant lied about his qualifications and thereby obtained a higher paid job, as occurred in the case of **Steel 1998**.

In **Callender 1993**, the wording was held to cover self-employed people as well as employees. The defendant had been engaged to prepare the accounts for several small businesses, had received payment for the work but had not performed his side of the bargain. It was discovered that he had lied about his professional qualifications and was not, as claimed, a qualified accountant. He was therefore charged under **s16**. In his defence, Callender tried to argue that his self-employment did not come under the definition of 'an office or employment'.

The Court of Appeal decided that this term should be interpreted liberally and upheld his conviction.

The repeal of s16(2)(a)

This section was repealed after criticism of its ambiguous wording and the difficulty of obtaining convictions under it. In its place, **s2 Theft Act 1978** has created a new offence of evading a liability by deception. A case illustrating the now defunct section is that of **DPP v Ray 1974**.

The defendant, together with his three friends, ordered a meal in a restaurant. The defendant did not have enough money to pay his share but an arrangement was made that the others would lend him the money. After the meal, however, they all decided not to pay, and, later, when the waiter was out of the room, they ran out of the restaurant. The defendant was convicted of obtaining a pecuniary advantage by deception under **s16(2)(a)** but this was quashed, on appeal, by the Divisional Court. There was a further appeal to the House of Lords where, on a rather strained interpretation, the conviction was restored.

Their Lordships decided that the defendant had evaded his debt by deceiving the waiter. This deception had been practised by the defendant remaining in the restaurant after finishing the main meal thereby giving the impression that the group were 'ordinary honest customers'. In this way, they had encouraged the waiter to lower his guard and disappear into the kitchen.

8.5.1 THE *ACTUS REUS* OF OBTAINING A PECUNIARY ADVANTAGE BY DECEPTION

This takes place when a person by any deception obtains for himself or another a pecuniary advantage.

8.5.2 THE *MENS REA* OF OBTAINING A PECUNIARY ADVANTAGE BY DECEPTION

The mental element is satisfied when the deception is practised deliberately or recklessly (S16(3)), and the obtaining is done dishonestly.

Ten years after the passing of the **Theft Act 1968**, the **Theft Act 1978** came into force to help remedy some of the shortcomings found in the earlier Act. Three new offences were created, two of them dealing with deception.

8.6 OBTAINING SERVICES BY DECEPTION

This offence is found in **s1 Theft Act 1978**, which states:

A person who by any deception dishonestly obtains services from another is guilty of an offence.

S1(2) goes on to state:

It is an obtaining of services where the other is induced to confer a benefit by doing some act, or causing or permitting some act to be done, on the understanding that the benefit has been or will be paid for.

S4 states that the maximum punishment for this offence is five years' imprisonment and s5 states that deception is to have the same meaning as in s15 Theft Act 1968.

This offence could, in certain situations, overlap with obtaining property by deception under **s15 Theft Act 1968**.

The deception element

S1 Theft Act 1978 makes it clear that the deception must occur before the services are obtained. Such a deception can be effected in many different ways:

- **Paying for services with a worthless cheque**
- **Posing as a wealthy client to obtain a deferment of payment**
- **Obtaining a grant for a downstairs bathroom for use by his elderly sick mother and then failing to tell the council that she had died, as in Rai 2000.**

The obtaining of services

It has been suggested by academics that benefits concurred could include the following:

- Car repairs
- Taxi rides
- House painting
- The provision of hotel accommodation
- The provision of seats in a theatre.

Mortgage advances

There was great consternation when it was decided by the Court of Appeal in **Halai 1983**, that a mortgage advance was not a service under this section and that the correct charge should have been one under **s15. Halai** was distinguished in **Widdowson 1985**, where the Court of Appeal decided that a hire-purchase agreement was not to be treated in the same way as a mortgage advance. The same court suggested in **Teong Sun Chuah 1991** that **Halai**

was wrongly decided and overruled it in **Graham 1997**. At roughly the same time, Parliament also decided to deal with the problem. The Theft (Amendment) Act 1996 inserted a new subsection into s1 Theft Act 1978. S1(3) now makes it abundantly clear that a loan is to be treated as a service.

Bank accounts and credit cards for which no charge is made

The Court of Appeal decided that these could be included in the definition of **s1** in the complicated case of **Sofroniou 2003**. The latter was convicted of obtaining services by deception after assuming false identities in order to obtain bank loans, credit cards and overdraft facilities. It had not been established whether the defendant had opened the accounts. Nor was there clear evidence as to whether, or on what basis, the bank would charge for its services. The defendant appealed, claiming among other things, that there was insufficient evidence that he had obtained a service in the first place and that, even if a service had been provided, there was insufficient evidence that it had to be paid for.

The Court of Appeal dismissed his appeal and made the following important points:

- **There was no substantial difference in the context of this offence between dishonestly obtaining services by credit card or by the dishonest operation of a bank account once opened.**
- **Dishonestly inducing a bank or building society to provide banking or credit card services and the dishonest operation of such an account or the dishonest use of a credit card over a period of time could all come under the ambit of s1. No distinction should be made between the opening of an account and the later operation of it.**
- **The words 'on the understanding that the benefit has been or will be paid for' under 1(2), although seemimgly subjective, could also cover situations where it was clear**

from the surrounding circumstancess that the service would not be provided free. The words would not be stretched to cover the mere opening of an account or the provision of a credit card but would apply when an account became overdrawn or a loan was provided.

8.6.1 THE *ACTUS REUS* OF OBTAINING SERVICES BY DECEPTION

This occurs where a person by any deception obtains services from another.

8.6.2 THE *MENS REA* OF OBTAINING SERVICES BY DECEPTION

The required *mens rea* exists when the offender deceives the other party deliberately or recklessly and obtains the service dishonestly. S5 of the Act states that the word 'deception' is to have the same meaning as in s15 Theft Act 1968.

8.7 EVASION OF LIABILITY BY DECEPTION

This offence is to be found in **s2 Theft Act 1978**. It was designed to cover several different situations where the accused, by deception, has tried to avoid the payment of a debt so has three parts to it. There has been some criticism of this as there appears to be some overlap between them.

Section 2(1)(a)

Under this subsection a person commits an offence if, by any deception, he:

dishonestly secures the remission of the whole or part of any existing liability to make a payment, whether his own liability or another's.

This means that by deceiving the other party and by acting in a dishonest way, the defendant has managed to get all or part of his debt extinguished, or the debt of someone else extinguished.

An example would be if a person dishonestly convinced his creditor that he (the debtor) was dying and thereby persuaded him not to enforce the debt. The offence was also committed in **Jackson 1983**, when the defendant paid for petrol with a stolen credit card.

The court decided that he had an existing liability to pay for the petrol already poured into the tank of his motorbike and he had deceived the garage owner about the validity of the credit card.

The *actus reus* of this part of the offence is where the defendant secures the remission of his own or another's liability.

The *mens rea* of the offence is doing this dishonestly and by practising a deliberate or reckless deception. S5(1) states that the word 'deception' in all parts of s2 is to have the same meaning as in s15 Theft Act 1968.

Section 2(1)(b)

Here a person evades liability if:

with intent to make permanent default in whole or in part of any existing liability to make a payment, or with intent to let another do so, [he] dishonestly induces the creditor or any person claiming payment on behalf of the creditor to wait for payment . . . or to forgo payment.

A person who writes a cheque or uses a credit card knowing that he is exceeding his authorisation to do this would be liable under this subsection, because **s2(3)** specifically provides for this. A person who convinces the creditor that payment has already been made would also be liable.

TEN KEY FACTS ON DECEPTION OFFENCES

- Obtaining property by deception is an offence found under **s15 Theft Act 1968** and carries a maximum punishment of ten years. Since the case of **DPP v Gomez**, all those liable under **s15**, would also be guilty of theft under **s1**.

- The *actus reus* of **s15** is established when, by any deception, the defendant obtains property belonging to another (**DPP v Stonehouse 1978**, **Lambie 1982**, **King and Stockwell 1987**). The *mens rea* arises when the defendant does the obtaining in a dishonest way, intending to permanently deprive the other of the property and his deception is practised deliberately or recklessly (**s15(4)**, **Greenstein 1975**, **Lightfoot 1993**).

- **S15A Theft Act 1968** creates a new offence of obtaining a money transfer by deception (**Theft (Amendment) Act 1996**). The punishment for this is ten years' imprisonment (**s15A(5)**). The *actus reus* exists when a person by any deception obtains a money transfer for himself or another (**s15A(1)**). The *mens rea* is established when the obtaining is dishonest and the deception is deliberately or recklessly practised (**s15A(1)**, **s15B(2)**).

- **S16(1)** lays down the offence of obtaining a pecuniary advantage by deception and states that the maximum punishment is five years' imprisonment. **S16(2)(a)** has been repealed. **S16(2)(b)** states that the offence will occur when a person, by his deception is allowed to become overdrawn, to take out an annuity or insurance policy or to obtain an improvement on existing terms (**MPC v Charles 1977**). Under **s16(2)(c)** the offence is also committed when the offender deceives another in order to gain remuneration or a higher salary or other payment 'in an office or employment'.

- The case of **Callender 1993** decided that the term 'in an office or employment' is to be construed widely, so it will cover self-employment.

- The *mens rea* of the offence of obtaining a pecuniary advantage by deception is acting dishonestly (**s16(1)**) and deliberately or recklessly deceiving the other party (**s16(1)**, **s16(3)**).

- The **Theft Act 1978** created two additional offences, obtaining services by deception under **s1** and evading a liability by deception in **s2**. **S4** decrees that the maximum punishment for both these offences is five years' imprisonment.

- **S1(2)** states that a service is obtained when the other party 'is induced to confer a benefit by doing some act, or causing or permitting some act to be done on the understanding that the benefit has been or will be paid for'. Services provided free, therefore, will not be covered, even though a deception may have been practised. If, however, there is a common understanding that certain services will incur payment, such as where a credit card payment is not settled in full or an overdraft or bank loan is arranged, this will suffice, (**Sofroniou 2003**). Under **s1(3)**, (added by the **Theft (Amendment) Act 1996**), the provision of mortgage advances and other loans now come within the meaning of services, overruling the much-criticised decision in **Halai 1983**.

- The *actus reus* of **s1** occurs when a person by any deception obtains services from another. The *mens rea* is present when this is done dishonestly, and the deception is deliberately or recklessly practised (**s1(1), s5**).

- The offence of evading a liability by deception under **s2 Theft Act 1978** is in three parts. **S2(1)(a)** states that it will occur when the defendant, by any deception, dishonestly secures the remission of the whole or part of a debt. Payment by a stolen credit card would be an example (**Jackson 1983**). Under **s2(1)(b)**, the offence is also committed when the defendant, by any deception, dishonestly persuades the creditor to wait for payment or to forgo payment entirely with the intention never to pay. Pretending that the debt has already been paid would be covered here (**Holt and Lee 1981**). **S2(1)(c)** states that the offence will also arise where the defendant, by any deception, dishonestly gains exemption from liability (**Sibartie 1983, Firth 1990**). **S5** states that the deception must be made deliberately or recklessly. The courts have decided that it should be **Cunningham-**style recklessness.

In **Holt and Lee 1981**, the defendants were sitting in a pizza restaurant after having consumed a meal and devised a scheme that they would tell their waitress that payment had already been made to another member of staff. They then planned to leave when the coast was clear. Unbeknown to them, however, their conversation had been overheard by another diner. He was an off-duty policeman who promptly proceeded to arrest them! **The Court of Appeal upheld their convictions**.

The *actus reus* of s2(1)(b) is satisfied if the defendant by deception, somehow induces a creditor to wait for his money or to forgo payment altogether.

The *mens rea* is present if this is done in a dishonest way, with a deliberate or reckless deception and is meant to be permanent. Temporary stalling devices by the debtor in order to obtain more time to pay would not be enough to incur liability.

Section 2(1)(c)

Under this subsection, a person will incur liability if, by any deception, he:

dishonestly obtains any exemption from or abatement of liability to make a payment.

An example would be where a person deceives the Inland Revenue into giving him a lower tax assessment or wrongfully gains a rate rebate by making a false statement. It was also decided in **Sibartie 1983** that liability could arise where the defendant by deception tries to prevent a debt from arising at all, as where the defendant passed a ticket inspector and waved an invalid season ticket in his direction.

The Court of Appeal decided that he had been correctly convicted of an attempt to commit this offence. By his deception he had tried to give the impression that he was the holder of a valid season ticket and, by this means, was trying to gain an exemption. It could be argued that he was also attempting to induce the other to forgo payment under s2(1)(b).

The *actus reus* of s2(1) (c) occurs if the defendant by any deception, obtains any exemption from, or abatement of, liability to make a payment.

The *mens rea* occurs if the deception is

effected deliberately or recklessly and the exemption is obtained dishonestly.

Both these elements were established in **Firth 1990**, the defendant was a consultant gynaecologist/obstetrician who performed both National Health and private work. He failed to inform the hospital that two of his patients were private patients so was not billed for the services provided for them.

The Court of Appeal upheld the conviction because by this dishonest deception, he had thereby gained an exemption from liability.

Activity

Discuss the possible liability of Sly in the following unrelated situations:

- He visits an upmarket tailor and purchases two designer suits, using a credit card to make payment. He had acquired this card by giving false information.

- He attends a job interview with a leading firm of solicitors, pretends that he has passed his Legal Practice Course with Distinction and secures a training contract.

- He falsifies information on a mortgage application form and acquires a substantial mortgage advance in order to purchase a riverside apartment.

- He joins a health club and starts his weight training programme in the knowledge that he cannot afford the yearly subscription.

- He tells the bookseller from whom he had purchased his law books on credit, that his father will be paying the debt in the near future. In fact, his father is in prison, having embezzled company funds. The bookseller believes Sly's tale and stops his demands for payment.

Self-assessment questions on Chapter 8

1. Define the crime under **s3 Theft Act 1978** and separate the *actus reus* and *mens rea* of the offence.
2. Explain why the defendant's conviction was upheld in **Aziz** but not in **Troughton**, **Allen** and **Vincent**.
3. Where is the offence of obtaining property by deception to be found? Identify three differences between this offence and theft under **s1**.
4. Describe the *actus reus* and *mens rea* of obtaining money by deception.
5. Explain why the defendants were found guilty of this offence in **Charles** and **Lambie** but the conviction quashed in **Nabina**.
6. How is the question of dishonesty established in this offence?
7. Which new offence was created in **s15A**? Define the *actus reus* and the *mens rea*.
8. State the different elements that have to be proved under **s16(2)(b)** and **s16(2)(c)**, giving examples to support your statements.
9. Describe the *actus reus* and *mens rea* of obtaining services by deception. Explain how the conflict caused by the decision in **Halai** was resolved and why the Court of Appeal decision in **Sofroniou** is important.
10. Analyse the three different components of evading a liability by deception, under **s2 Theft Act 1978**, giving examples of each.

Chapter 9

PROPERTY OFFENCES III: CRIMINAL DAMAGE

9.1 INTRODUCTION

You will be relieved to know that this is a comparatively easy area to learn, compared with the complications concerning theft and deception, particularly as some examination boards only require knowledge of the basic offence. It is advisable, therefore, to check the requirements of your particular board.

The law on criminal damage is in the Criminal Damage Act 1971. This Act was largely the work of the Law Commission and was designed to replace the archaic **Malicious Damage Act 1861**. The **Criminal Damage Act** now contains, in a more simplified form, most offences concerning damage to property.

S1 Criminal Damage Act creates three offences. These will be dealt with in the following order:

✔ **The basic offence of criminal damage laid down in s1(1)**
✔ **Aggravated criminal damage under s1(2)**
✔ **Criminal damage by the use of fire under s1(3).**

S2 of the Act creates two other offences, that of threatening to destroy or damage property and threatening to do so in a way that is likely to endanger life. S3 makes it an offence to have possession or control of something intending to use it for either simple criminal damage or for criminal damage likely to endanger life (these offences do not need to be studied for A Level).

9.2 THE BASIC OFFENCE OF CRIMINAL DAMAGE

A person will be guilty of the basic offence if he destroys or damages property belonging to another, either intentionally or recklessly.

The precise definition is to be found in **s1(1)** of the Act, which states:

A person who without lawful excuse destroys or damages any property belonging to another intending to destroy or damage any such property or being reckless as to whether any such property would be destroyed or damaged shall be guilty of an offence.

9.2.1 THE PUNISHMENT

If the damage or destruction is above £5,000 in value, the offence comes into the category of a triable either way offence for which the maximum punishment is ten years' imprisonment.

For damage of £5,000 or less, the offence will be tried summarily as laid down in **s22 Magistrates' Courts Act 1980**, as amended by **s4 Criminal Justice and Public Order Act 1994**.

9.2.2 THE *ACTUS REUS* OF THE BASIC OFFENCE

This is committed when a person destroys or damages property belonging to another. The meaning of the following words therefore, needs to be examined:

Fury over £20,000 graffiti vandal's 'lenient' sentence

By Justin Davenport

A senior police officer today condemned a 'lenient' community service sentence handed out to a prolific graffiti vandal.

Shane Simms, 19, who uses the tag name Frame, is one of the most notorious graffiti sprayers operating in London.

He was sentenced to 160 hours of community service and served with a three-year anti-social behaviour order after admitting 106 offences and causing £20,000 damage. Today Superintendent Simon Ovens of Merton police hit out at the sentence handed down by a judge at Kingston Crown Court yesterday

Supt Ovens said: 'This young man has admitted 106 offences and has caused over £20,000 worth of damage. He has damaged a mosque, a graveyard, buses, lorries, telephone kiosks and many private and business premises.

'The police and the local authority have invested hundreds of hours in bringing the case together because we know what a blight this is on our borough and how much distress it brings to those who live and work here.

'I am appalled by the leniency of the sentence he received and feel very let down by the courts.'

Simms of Pelham Road, Wimbledon, was convicted at Wimbledon Magistrates' court earlier this month on charges of destroying property and handling stolen goods.

Supt Ovens added: 'It is a great shame that the people of Merton will have to continue to suffer this antisocial behaviour and I am fearful for the message it will send out to others who commit this appalling criminal damage.

'It will, however, not deter us from continuing to bring those who damage the fabric of our borough to justice.'

Evening Standard, 26 November 2004

- 'destroys or damages'
- 'property'
- 'belonging to another'.

'Destroys or damages'

Neither of these words is defined in the Act and the courts appear to have taken a common sense approach to their meaning.

The courts have decided that the word 'destroys' will cover rendering the property useless, in addition to total destruction.

The word 'damage' can be used where property is made imperfect or inoperative or if the harm affects its usefulness or value. A car would be damaged if an important part of it were to be uncoupled as, for example, a brake cable. **In Roper v Knott 1898, beer was held to have been damaged after water had been added to it.**

Less permanent harm

In **Samuels v Stubbs 1972,** a policeman's cap had been trampled upon.

The court decided that the word damage 'is sufficiently wide in its meaning to embrace injury, mischief or harm done to property'. It was also agreed that property would be damaged where it could no longer serve its normal purpose. A temporary cessation of its function will sometimes be sufficient, so even though the headgear could have been returned quite easily to its original state, it was still classed as damaged.

In **Hardman v Chief Constable of Avon and Somerset Constabulary 1986**, members of CND had been convicted of criminal damage. In order to mark the 40th anniversary of the dropping of the atomic bomb on Hiroshima, they had used watersoluble paint to draw silhouettes on a pavement illustrating vaporised human beings.

The defendants tried to argue that their actions did not amount to criminal damage because the harm done was only temporary. They claimed that the paintings would have been erased naturally, if left alone, by the footsteps of pedestrians and by the elements.

Despite these submissions, the convictions were upheld because the local authority had been put to the expense of employing people to wash off the paintings with pressurised water jets.

Similarly, in **Roe v Kingerlee 1986**, the defendant had smeared mud over the walls of a police cell, which cost £7 to clean off. **This was also held to amount to criminal damage, even though no lasting damage had been done.**

There is, however, a limit to liability. **In A (a juvenile) v R 1978, spitting on a police officer's raincoat was not held to amount to criminal damage because the spittle could easily be removed with a damp cloth and no lasting damage had been done**. A different decision may well have been made if the article had been stained and had needed dry cleaning.

In a similar vein, merely running over the land of another would not amount to damaging that land, as decided in **Eley v Lytle 1885**, a civil case, whereas the actual trampling down of grass could constitute liability **(Gayford v Chouler 1898).**

In **Lloyd v DPP 1992**, a person tried to turn the tables on those arguing that he was at fault by accusing the other party of effecting criminal damage to his car by wheel-clamping it.

He had parked in a prohibited place and then refused to pay the amount demanded for the release of the clamp. Instead, he had used a disc cutter to prise it off. He was later charged with effecting criminal damage to the clamp. In his defence, he tried to argue that the other party

had been trespassing on his property by applying the wheel clamp in the first place and used some very old authority to support his findings.

These arguments were not accepted by the court and his conviction was upheld.

Grey areas

In some cases, the article itself may not be damaged but, instead, an item which helps it to operate is harmed. In **Cox v Riley 1986**, the defendant was found guilty of criminal damage after he erased a programme from a plastic circuit card operating a saw to cut wood to specially programmed designs. **The court decided that, while no damage had been caused to the saw itself, there had been damage to the card.**

A similar approach was taken in **Whiteley 1991**. In this case, a computer hacker infiltrated JANET, the Joint Academic Network, altered and deleted files and changed some of the passwords. The computer was not damaged by this misuse, but it was rendered inoperable because of the damage to the magnetic particles on the disks.

The problem of computer misuse has now been recognised as a subject worthy of treatment in its own right and the passing of the **Computer Misuse Act 1990** has made it easier to obtain convictions for such offences. The Act is not only concerned about harm caused to the actual computer but also the harm caused by the unauthorised use of the material contained within.

S3 deals with this and creates an offence if a person intentionally does any act that causes any unauthorised modification of the contents of any computer.

Property

Under the Criminal Damage Act 1971, property encompasses all items of a tangible nature, including money and animals belonging to another person. Wild animals that have been tamed and/or kept in captivity will come into this category but wild mushrooms, flowers, fruit or foliage will not.

This definition of property appears very similar to the one in the **Theft Act 1968** but there are two important distinctions.

- **Land cannot be stolen but it can be damaged.**
- **Intangible property, including patents and copyrights, can be stolen but cannot be damaged.**

Belonging to another

Under the basic offence the property that is damaged or destroyed has to belong to someone else. (It will be noted, later, that this is not the case for the more serious offences which may arise under **ss1(2)** and **1(3)**.)

It is not, therefore, an offence under **s1(1)** to damage or destroy one's own property. The person may also be protected if he honestly but mistakenly believes that the property was his, provided, of course, that the jury believes his version of the events.

In **Smith 1974**, a tenant of a ground floor flat gave notice to quit but asked that his brother might be allowed to stay on. The landlord refused to entertain the idea. The tenant then damaged floor boarding, roofing and wall panels in a conservatory and was charged under **s1(1)**. He claimed that he had done this to remove some of his own electric wiring. This had been installed with the landlord's permission in order that the tenant's stereo equipment would function more effectively. He therefore argued that, because he believed that the property belonged to him, he had a lawful excuse. In fact, in law, the items had become fixtures that should not have been removed and he was convicted.

Despite this, the Court of Appeal quashed his conviction, deciding that:

no offence is committed under this section (i.e. s1(1)), if a person destroys or causes

damage to property belonging to another if he does so in the honest though mistaken belief that the property is his own, and, provided that the belief is honestly held, it is irrelevant to consider whether or not it is a justifiable belief.

This defence will be looked at in more detail below.

Temporary control by others

The term 'belonging to another' is given a wide meaning under s10(2). Property is treated as belonging to another if that other has custody or control of it, a proprietary right in it, a charge over it, or a right under a trust.

It would be an offence therefore if the defendant had lent goods to another and damaged them while they were under the latter's control. In relation to a proprietary interest, such a right must be clearly established. An insurer would not come into this category, so if a person destroyed or damaged his own property in order to claim from an insurance company, he would not be committing an offence under this section, as he would not be harming goods 'belonging to another'.

Before leaving this subject, it should be noted that, if the damaged property belongs to a spouse, the consent of the Director of Public Prosecutions is needed before a charge can be brought. The restriction would not apply where the parties are no longer under a duty to cohabit.

9.2.3 THE *MENS REA* OF THE BASIC OFFENCE

This is satisfied if the person unlawfully destroys or damages property belonging to another, either intentionally or recklessly.

The meaning of the word 'intention'
The defendant cannot be found guilty under this head unless he:

- possesses a clear intent to cause the damage
- intends to act unlawfully, and
- damages property belonging to another.

If, therefore, he is under the mistaken impression that the property is his own, as in the case of **Smith**, described above, he would lack the necessary *mens rea*.

The meaning of the word 'reckless'

In light of the changes that have been made in this area of law, it is important to recap on this issue. It was noted in Chapter 2 that recklessness is the taking of an unjustifiable risk. What has to be decided, however, is whether this point should be decided in a subjective or more objective way, i.e. via **Cunningham** or **Caldwell** recklessness. If the first view is taken, the jury can only convict if they believe that the defendant foresaw that he was taking an unjustifiable risk. Under the second approach, the jury would look at whether the risk would have been obvious to an outsider.

Cunningham recklessness prevails

Hopefully, it will be remembered that, in **G and another 2003**, the House of Lords overruled the case of **Caldwell 1982**, and re-introduced Cunningham recklessness for all offences under the Criminal Damage Act, bringing the *mens rea* of criminal damage in line with that required for offences against the person.

Students are strongly urged to re-read Chapter 2 on recklessness at this point and should study the more detailed explanations of some of the cases to be found in **s1(3)**. The important cases on criminal damage are, however, summarised in the following chart.

9.2.4 DEFENCES TO A CHARGE OF CRIMINAL DAMAGE

All the normal general defences, which are described more fully in Chapter 10, are *prima facie* available. **In addition to this, there is a special**

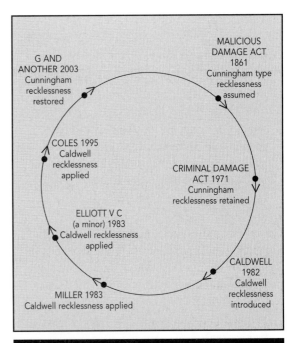

Figure 9.1 Recklessness in criminal damage

defence provided in the Act itself, the defence of lawful excuse. It is important to note that this special defence is not available for the aggravated offences under **s1(2)** and **(3)**.

◀ *Comment*

As noted in Chapter 2, there had been sustained academic criticism over the introduction of the more objective type of recklessness laid down in **Caldwell 1982**. The overruling of this case has brought the *mens rea* required for all offences of criminal damage in line with that required for offences against the person. For this and other reasons already mentioned in Chapter 2, this important decision is to be welcomed. This is particularly the case in relation to **s1(3) Criminal Damage Act**, if the accused is charged with arson in its aggravated form, i.e. with the intention to endanger life or being reckless as to whether life is endangered. Cases on this include **Caldwell itself,** discussed more fully under arson.

On the other hand, as Lord Diplock noted in **Caldwell,** the prosecution may well face greater difficulties in securing a conviction when Cunningham recklessness has to be proved. In **Shimmen 1987** and **Merrick 1995,** both defendants claimed that they did not believe that they were taking unjustifiable risks. It is hard to see how a jury could ignore these contentions and arrive at a different conclusion. An acquittal might seem a fairer result in the second case but is more questionable in the first instance. In **G and another 2003** however, the House of Lords made it clear that stupidity or lack of imagination should not be equated with recklessness.

The defence of lawful excuse

Under **s5(2) Criminal Damage Act 1971**, there are two situations where the defendant can claim this special defence:

- where he believes that the owner has consented to the damage or would have consented had he known of the facts
- where he destroys or damages the property of another in order to protect his own or another's property.

In the latter situation, two further points must be proved. He must also believe that:

- the property in question was in immediate need of protection, and
- the methods he adopted to do this were reasonable in the circumstances.

Rather surprisingly perhaps, s5(3) gives the defendant even greater protection. It states that 'it is immaterial whether a belief is justified or not if it is honestly held'.

Cases on s5

There have been many cases concerning the defence of lawful excuse, some successful, others not. Some of the more notable are discussed below.

In **Jaggard v Dickinson 1981**, the defendant was charged with basic criminal damage, after breaking into a house belonging to a stranger while under the influence of drink. She acted in the mistaken belief that the house belonged to her friend who would, she claimed, have consented to the breaking of the window if she had known of the facts. The magistrates stated that she could not rely on **s5(2)(a)** because she was intoxicated and her drunkenness was self-induced. Such a condition is normally fatal in relation to more general defences like mistake, (discussed in Chapter 11).

The Divisional Court refused to deny her the use of **s5** and her conviction was quashed. Mustill J stated:

> *. . . Parliament has specifically isolated one subjective element, in the shape of honest belief, and has given it separate treatment and its own special gloss in s5(3). This being so, there is nothing objectionable in giving it special treatment as regards drunkenness, in accordance with the natural meaning of the words.*

The decision in **Denton 1982** was even more surprising given the illegality of the defendant's act. He had deliberately started a fire at his employer's mill. He claimed that his employer had encouraged him to take this action so that the employer could make a fraudulent claim against his insurance company. **Denton's honest belief that the employer had authority to order such an action was sufficient to afford him the defence of s5.**

In **Chamberlain v Lindon 1998**, the defendant demolished a wall built by a neighbour because he believed that it threatened his own right of access and used **s5(2)(b)** in his defence.

The Divisional Court decided that the defendant had an honest belief that his property was in need of immediate protection and, provided such a belief was honestly held, he was entitled to use the defence.

Unsuccessful cases

The case of **Blake v DPP 1993** was an unusual one in that the defendant tried to argue that God himself had consented to the vicar's acts of criminal damage! The vicar had used a marker in order to write passages from the Bible on a stone pillar near to the Houses of Parliament. He was protesting against the possible use of force in the 'run up' to the Gulf War.

As well as trying to use **s5(2)(a)**, he also invoked **s5(2)(b)** by arguing that he was taking this action to protect the property of people in the Gulf States who would be affected by such military action.

Unfortunately for him, the Divisional Court of Queen's Bench Division was not prepared to accept either of these arguments. The court stated that there was no authority concerning consent given by God and also felt that, when viewed objectively, there was nothing in his action that could effectively protect the property of people so far away from the scene.

The defendant had been equally unsuccessful in the earlier case of **Hunt 1978**. He claimed that he had set alight some bedding in a block of old person's flats where his wife worked, because of his concerns over defective fire alarms. He argued that by drawing attention to the matter in this dramatic way, he was actually seeking to protect the property. **Despite this novel claim, his conviction was upheld.**

In **Mitchell 2003**, too, the trial judge decided that there was no lawful excuse under **s5** when the defendant illegally removed a clamp from his car. The judge took the view that the property was not in need of immediate protection and withdrew the defence from the jury.

Protests by anti-war demonstrators

Despite the genuine beliefs of the parties involved, the courts have been similarly unmoved by claims from anti-war protestors that their criminal actions have been taken to protect other property, either here or abroad, as seen in the case of **Blake**, above, and in **Hill and Hall 1989**. In the latter case, demonstrators were protesting against the presence of American military bases in this country and were hoping to drive them out. The defendants had gone to the site with equipment to cut the perimeter fences and tried to use **s5(2)(b)** in their defence. They argued that they were taking such action in order to protect other property in the neighbourhood, which might otherwise be destroyed by a retaliatory attack if military action were undertaken from the base.

The Court of Appeal upheld the convictions for criminal damage, despite the subjective

nature of s5(3). Rather unconvincingly, the judges decided that the test as to whether the property was actually in need of immediate protection, was a more objective one that the jury should decide upon after an appropriate direction on s5 from the trial judge.

A similar view was expressed by the Court of Appeal in the case of **Jones and another, Olditch and another and Richards, 2004,** concerning people protesting against the war in Iraq. The Court of Appeal was asked to give a preliminary ruling on several points being brought up by both the defendants and the Crown in relation to criminal damage inflicted on property at RAF Fairford. The defendants claimed that the attack on Iraq was an unlawful act that the defendants were attempting to prevent by damaging military property. They argued, therefore, that they were entitled to use the defence of public defence, the defences of necessity and duress of circumstances and that of lawful excuse under **s5 Criminal Damage Act 1971**. The trial judge had decided that the question of the legality of the war was not one for the domestic courts to try and the defendants were appealing against this. He had, however, been prepared to accept any defences that did not rely on this point, such as the defence of lawful excuse. The Crown appealed against this.

The Court of Appeal agreed with the trial judge that there was no international crime of aggression that could be determined in a domestic court. In relation to the defence of lawful excuse under the Criminal Damage Act, the defendants had more success. The Court of Appeal decided that this could be put forward without having to rely on the question as to whether the war was legal or illegal. The only objective element which the jury would have to consider was whether it could be said on the facts, as believed by the defendants, that the criminal damage alleged could amount to something that had been done in order to protect the property of another. Subject to that

element, the court and the jury were concerned simply with the question of a defendant's honestly held beliefs.

It can be seen from this rather obscure judgment that while the Court of Appeal upheld the rights of the defendant to use the defence of s5, it also agreed with the finding in **Hill and Hall** that there was an objective element in the defence of lawful excuse. This concerned the issue of whether the property was in immediate need of protection, a fact that would be decided by the jury.

◢ Comment

It is obvious that Parliament wanted to retain a subjective element in the special defence given under **s5(2)**, by the very precise nature of the wording in **s5(3)**, but it is equally clear that the courts are worried about the possible width of this and are seeking to curtail it, by introducing a two-fold test which is partly subjective and partly objective. The defendant's belief need not be reasonably held, provided that it is an honest one. The question as to whether the property needs immediate protection is, however, decided in an objective way by the jury. Some would argue that, if the courts declined to follow such a course, some defendants would be able to escape the consequences of their actions by putting forward all sorts of odd beliefs and might then have to be given the benefit of the doubt.

FIVE KEY FACTS ON BASIC CRIMINAL DAMAGE

- The basic offence is under s1(1) Criminal Damage Act 1971. It is committed when a person destroys or damages property belonging to another, intending to do this or being reckless about it. The maximum punishment is ten years' imprisonment if tried on indictment.

- The *actus reus* of the offence is destroying or damaging property belonging to another. It is not a crime under the basic offence to destroy one's own property.

- The property of others is destroyed or damaged if it is totally destroyed, made imperfect or inoperative or where it no longer serves a useful purpose. The damage may well be far slighter than this (Roper v Knott 1898, Samuels v Stubbs 1972, Hardman v C C of Avon 1986, Roe v Kingerlee), and can cover plastic circuit cards and computer disks, (Cox v Riley 1986, Whiteley 1991), but will not normally include spittle or simple trespassing (A 1978, Eley v Lytle 1885). The Computer Misuse Act 1990 now helps with some forms of damage. Property will include most tangible things but not wild flowers, fruit, fungi and foliage.

- The *mens rea* of the offence is to destroy or damage property intentionally or recklessly. In G and another 2003, the House of Lords decided that Cunningham recklessness must be proved, i.e. did the defendant foresee that he was taking an unjustifiable risk.

- A person will have a defence to a charge under s1(1), (but not for the more serious offences), if he mistakenly believes that the property is his (Smith 1974), or believes that the owner would have consented to the damage or successfully claims that the damage was necessary to protect his own or other property (s5(2), (Chamberlain v Lindon 1998). The belief does not have to be reasonably held and the defence can be used even when the defendant is intoxicated (Jaggard v Dickinson 1981), or performing an illegal act, (Denton 1982). The courts have, however, curtailed the width of the defence by deciding that the jury is entitled to take a more objective view as to whether the property is in need of immediate protection, (Blake 1993, Hill and Hall 1989, and Jones and Another 2004).

Activity

Decide whether the following have committed the offence of basic criminal damage and, if so, whether any defences in the **Criminal Damage Act** are available to them:

- Lenny, in retaliation for a practical joke played on him, decided to water down a crate of Billy's best malt whisky. To divert suspicion from himself, he also diluted two of his own cheap bottles of brandy.
- Jo knocked a policeman's hat from his head and it rolled into a puddle of water.
- Harry, a martial arts expert, was

demonstrating his skills outside the leisure centre in which he worked. He aimed a kick at the glass door of the centre, intending to stop just short of this, but smashed into it instead and broke it. He strongly maintains that his skill is normally of such a high standard that he believed that there was no risk in taking the action that he did.

● Griff covered the walls of the Town Hall with crayoned messages, strongly attacking the local council. The latter body was threatening to shut down the only theatre in the neighbourhood in order to build a car park. Griff claims that his acts were necessary to warn the public of this outrage.

● Jennifer missed the last train home after a lively Christmas party. She broke the lock and entered number 13 Railway Cuttings. Jennifer believed that the house belonged to her friend Dawn who would not object to her sleeping on the sofa. In fact, Dawn lived at number 15.

9.3 THE AGGRAVATED OFFENCE UNDER S1(2)

This offence is committed where a person destroys or damages property, either his own or another's, intending by the destruction or damage to endanger the life of another or being reckless about this.

It is not a requirement that someone's life must actually be put at risk; it is enough that a reasonable man would have believed this (**Sangha 1988**).

The maximum punishment for this offence is life imprisonment.

9.3.1 COMPARISONS BETWEEN S1(1) AND S1(2)

● The *actus reus* of the offence under s1(2) is very similar to the basic offence, i.e. destroying or damaging property, except that the property destroyed or damaged does not have to belong to another.

● The special defence of lawful excuse permitted in s5 does not apply to this more serious offence, although the more general defence of lawful excuse negativing *mens rea* in the first place could still be argued in appropriate circumstances.

● The *mens rea* for the aggravated offence is intention or recklessness, but with the added requirement that the defendant must intend by his destruction or damage to property, to endanger life or be reckless as to whether this will happen.

● The test for such recklessness is the same as for the basic offence, i.e. Cunningham recklessness.

9.3.2 DANGER TO LIFE

It is very important to realise that, with the aggravated offence, the danger to life must come directly from the damage to property and not from some other source. This is graphically illustrated in the case of **Steer 1988**. In this case, the danger was coming from the rifle that Steer was firing, not from the slight damage to the window.

The defendant had quarrelled with his former business partner and, in the early hours of the morning had gone to his bungalow, armed with an automatic rifle. He rang the bell and woke up the occupants and, when they looked out of the window, he fired one shot in that direction, plus two further shots, one at another window and the other at the front door. Mr and Mrs Gregory were not injured and it was not suggested that Steer had deliberately fired at them.

The defendant was charged under **s1(1)** and **s1(2) Criminal Damage Act** and also with possessing a firearm with intent to endanger life. He appealed against the conviction under **s1(2)**, stating that the judge had misdirected the jury about this. He argued that the danger to life in this case had been caused by the rifle shots, not by the damaged property.

The House of Lords agreed with this contention and quashed this conviction.

9.4 ARSON

When the Law Commission debated the changes to the law on criminal damage, it recommended that the original common law offence of arson should not be treated as a separate offence. Parliament, however, was not prepared to accept this and **s1(3)** was formulated.

A person can be charged under this section, in addition to s1(1) or s1(2) if there is any damage caused by fire.

- **The defendant would be charged under s1(1) and s1(3) if he destroys or damages property belonging to another by the use of fire, either intentionally or recklessly.**
- **The defendant would be charged under s1(2) and s1(3) if he destroys or damages property by the use of fire, intending by that destruction or damage to endanger life or being reckless whether life is endangered.**

9.4.1 CASES ON ARSON

It should be remembered that, in the case of **Caldwell 1982,** which has caused so much comment, the defendant was convicted of offences under both **s1(2)** and **s1(3)** of the **Criminal Damage Act 1971,** after setting light to

a residential hotel. Caldwell was prepared to plead guilty in relation to basic criminal damage and arson but strongly argued that he was not liable for aggravated arson because, in his drunken state, it had not crossed his mind that someone's life might be endangered.

Unfortunately for him, as noted earlier, the House of Lords at that time decided that the test for recklessness in the context of criminal damage should have a more objective element in it. The risk was felt to be an obvious one and therefore his conviction was upheld.

We also noted that in **Miller 1983**, the House of Lords upheld the charge of arson when the defendant accidentally started a fire and failed to take the necessary steps to put it out. **As the risk would have been obvious to a reasonably prudent person, the court decided that it was immaterial that the defendant had not have foreseen it.**

More controversially, in Elliott v C (a minor) 1983, a case mentioned in Chapter 2, the conviction under s1(1) and s1(3) Criminal Damage Act 1971, of the 14-year-old girl with learning difficulties, was upheld by the Divisional Court. A garden shed had been damaged after she had poured white spirit over the floor and thrown lighted matches onto it. The Caldwell test for recklessness was applied, despite the misgivings of the court.

This was followed in the case of Coles 1995, where a similarly afflicted 15 year-old boy set alight a haystack. His conviction under s1(1) and s1(3) was upheld by the Court of Appeal.

The changing law

We noted earlier in this chapter and in Chapter 2, that while the case of **G and another 2003** was very similar to the above two cases, a very different decision was reached, despite the fact that the damage was much greater. Here the defendants were even younger, aged 11 and 12. It will be remembered that, in the early hours of the morning, they entered the back yard of a Co-op shop, set alight some newspapers they found there and threw them under a wheelie-bin. They left the premises without waiting to see whether the fire went out. Instead, the fire escalated and travelled to the shop and adjoining buildings, resulting in damage in the region of £1,000,000. Following a definition of **Caldwell** recklessness, the boys were found guilty of criminal damage and their convictions were upheld in the Court of Appeal.

The House of Lords reversed this decision and returned to the former position, as stated in Cunningham, that foresight of the consequences was a necessary ingredient of recklessness. Therefore, if a defendant genuinely had failed to appreciate the risk because of his young age or some other characteristic, he should not be found guilty.

9.4.2 THE PUNISHMENT

The maximum penalty for arson is life imprisonment, should the offence be committed in its aggravated form.

This was the sentence imposed initially in **Simmonds 2001**. The defendant's wife was

Activity

Charlotte, aged 16, had a quarrel over money with her wealthy employer Will. She decided to teach him a lesson and, after seeing him leave for work in the morning, she entered his house, piled the silk cushions from the sofa into the middle of the room and set fire to them. She then emptied two bottles of Will's best champagne over the blaze to put it out and left the premises. The dense smoke and fumes from the remains of the cushions badly affected Britney, who was asleep in the next room. She had stayed the night with Will, a fact not envisaged by Charlotte. As a reult of her injuries Britney had to spend three days in hospital.

Advise Charlotte in relation to her liability for offences under the **Criminal Damage Act 1971**.

FIVE KEY FACTS ON S1(2) AND S1(3)

- The offence under **s1(2) Criminal Damage Act 1971** is committed where the party destroys or damages property intending by that destruction or damage to endanger life or being reckless as to whether life is endangered. The maximum punishment is life imprisonment.

- The danger to life must be caused by the destruction or damage **(Steer 1988)**.

- **S1(3)** states that if a person destroys or damages property by fire, this will be arson, for which the maximum punishment is life imprisonment.

- The *mens rea* for these offences is intention or **Cunningham** recklessness **(G and another 2003)**.

- The decisions in **Caldwell 1982** and **Elliot v C (a minor) 1983**, were overruled in **G and another 2003**. Caldwell recklessness, which introduces a more objective test for recklessness in relation to crimes of criminal damage, is no longer good law.

seeking a divorce. Despite an injunction prohibiting him from going near the matrimonial home, he visited the house, poured petrol all round it and then set fire to it. The house was not occupied at the time and the building and other houses in the terrace were saved. The contents however, were completely destroyed.

The defendant telephoned the police to tell them that he had no intention to hurt his wife but informed them that he had a shotgun which he was prepared to use against those who had hurt him in the past and against the police if they tried to pursue him. The weapon turned out to be a wooden-handled axe. Simmonds was sentenced to life imprisonment.

The Court of Appeal, following earlier guidelines, decided that while the defendant's conduct caused great concern, it did not justify an indeterminate sentence. A sentence of six years was substituted in its place.

Self-assessment questions on Chapter 9

1. Where is the law on basic criminal damage? State the elements of the offence.
2. Why were the convictions in **Samuels**, **Hardman** and **Roe** confirmed but not that in **A (a juvenile)**?
3. Why did interference with computer programmes cause difficulties for the courts and how was this problem resolved?
4. Which of the following constitutes 'property' that could be damaged under the **Criminal Damage Act**?
   A blackberry bush
   A farmer's field
   A patent
   A clump of wild mushrooms
   A £20 pound note belonging to the accused
5. Why was **Smith**'s conviction overturned?
6. What changes have taken place in relation to the *mens rea* of criminal damage?
7. Describe the defence of lawful excuse. Using decided cases to illustrate your answer, give two examples where the defence succeeded and two when it did not.
8. Distinguish between the offences under **s1(1)** and **s1(2)**.
9. Why was the conviction in **Steer** overturned?
10. What is arson and where is the law? Give two case examples.

Chapter 10

GENERAL DEFENCES I

10.1 INTRODUCTION

We noted when discussing substantive offences, that, in some instances, special defences could be used by the accused in relation to the particular crime in question, such as the limited defences of provocation and diminished responsibility in murder and the full defence of consent in assault and battery. This chapter and Chapter 11 look at the more general defences, which may also be of great help to the defendant in specific instances. You need to check carefully to see which defences are part of your particular course.

- Infancy (or lack of capacity)
- Insanity (or insane automatism)
- Non-insane automatism
- Intoxication
- Mistake
- Necessity (in very limited circumstances)
- Duress
- Duress of circumstances
- Marital coercion (rare!)
- Public and private defence

In this Chapter, the first four of these topics are examined:

- ✔ **Infancy or lack of capacity**
- ✔ **Insanity**
- ✔ **Automatism**
- ✔ **Intoxication.**

10.2 INFANCY OR LACK OF CAPACITY

The criminal law treats the matter of age in a different way to the civil law and, until very recently, put the liability of children and young persons into three categories, those under the age of 10, those between the ages of 10 and 14 and those of 14 and over. With regard to the first category, it is still comparatively rare for children of this age to be involved in serious criminal activity. It is not however, unknown and some very young children have been involved in horrific acts of violence. One example that resurfaced in recent years, when the question of payment for her life story hit the headlines, was the case of Mary Bell who, at the age of nine, murdered two very young children.

Fortunately, cases like this and the murder of James Bulger, a two-year old child, by two 11-year-old boys still remain rare. The latter case attracted a great deal of publicity because of the brutality and lack of compassion displayed by the young offenders.

It was established that they knew that they had done something seriously wrong and they were found guilty of murder. The case attracted more headlines when the European Court of Human Rights declared that it had been wrong for the Home Secretary to fix a period of years during which the boys could not be released. This matter was one for the courts. The boys have since been released on licence.

10.2.1 CHILDREN BELOW THE AGE OF TEN

However awful the circumstances, the law takes the view that very young children do not have the capacity to commit a crime. The Latin phrase 'doli incapax' is used, which means 'incapable of crime'. The law is to be found in s50 **Children and Young Persons Act 1933, as amended**.

It should be noted that, while such a young offender would not face a trial new rules are planned to fine parents instead. The child could well be subject to care proceedings if the crime is a serious one. Where the most serious offences are concerned, the child will not be released back into the community until he no longer poses a threat to society.

10.2.2 CHILDREN BETWEEN THE AGES OF TEN AND 14

This has been the subject of much debate in recent times. **The current position is stated in the Crime and Disorder Act 1998. This states that children of this age are now held to be criminally liable for their actions; the presumption that they are incapable of committing a crime, which had been affirmed by the House of Lords in C (a minor) 1996, has been removed.**

The case concerned a boy of 12, observed by the police on private property holding the handlebars of a Honda motor cycle while his friend tampered with the chain and padlock securing it. The boy ran away when challenged but was caught. He later appealed against his conviction on the grounds that the prosecution had not rebutted the presumption that he lacked criminal liability. The Divisional Court refused to entertain the appeal.

There was a further appeal to the House of Lords and this time it was successful. Their Lordships firmly upheld the existence of the presumption, deciding that it came from 'a long and uncontradicted line of authority'. Lord Lowry decided that the question of punishment for child offenders was a social and political matter as well as a legal one and believed, therefore, that if change were to be effected, this was a matter for Parliament.

The Divisional Court was obliged to follow the ruling of the House of Lords in this matter but in the following two cases, it took a robust attitude to the question of whether the young offenders knew they were doing something wrong.

In the case of A v DPP 1997, it decided that a 12-year-old boy had known he was doing

wrong, despite the fact that he had remained silent during questioning and throughout his trial. The court found the evidence of this because he had forced the girl in question to have sex with him even though her distress was obvious and he had later run away from the scene.

In **DPP v K&B 1997**, two girls of 14 and 11 had threatened, falsely imprisoned and robbed another 14-year-old girl. A boy, who had not been traced, had also raped her. The girls were charged, among other things, with aiding and abetting this rape. The magistrates were of the opinion that they could not convict on this count so the Crown appealed on a point of law to the Divisional Court.

The boy allegedly committing the rape was said to be between 10 and 14 years of age but, because he had not been traced, the prosecution had not had a chance to rebut the presumption about his lack of criminal liability. The Divisional Court decided that this was not fatal to the liability of the two girls. A rape had been established, the girls were present when it took place, had desired that it should happen and had helped to procure the result. The court was therefore of the opinion that a conviction on this count was possible.

In the interim period, a provision removing the presumption that children of this age do not have liability for their criminal acts was being put into statutory form. It finally appeared in s34 Crime and Disorder Act 1998.

10.2.3 CHILDREN OF 14 AND OVER

A child aged 14 or over has always been considered to be 'as responsible for his actions entirely as if he were 40'. This comment was made in **Smith 1845**, and the position is still the same today with regard to his actual liability for his criminal acts. The courts however, will recognise the youth of the offender when it

---

FIVE KEY FACTS ON INCAPACITY

- There is a conclusive presumption that children under the age of 10 are not criminally liable for their actions (**s50 Children and Young Persons Act 1933, as amended**).

- With children between the ages of 10 and 14, there used to be a rebuttable presumption that they were not criminally liable (**C (a minor) v DPP 1996**).

- The prosecution was then obliged to produce evidence that the child committed the act and also knew that the act was seriously wrong. Enough evidence of these two matters was shown in the cases of **A v DPP 1997** and **DPP v K and B 1997**, but not in **C (a minor) v DPP 1996**.

- This presumption has been abolished and children between the ages of 10 and 14 are now criminally responsible for their actions (**s34 Crime and Disorder Act 1998**).

- Children of 14 or over also have full criminal responsibility (**Smith 1845**), but along with children of 10 and over, they may well be tried in a Youth Court and receive a different sentence to that given to an adult.

---

comes to the choice of the court to be used for his trial and in the matter of sentencing him if he has been found guilty.

10.3 INSANITY (OR INSANE AUTOMATISM)

Most people would agree that someone suffering from insanity, who is completely unaware of his actions, should not be branded as a criminal. On the other hand, members of the public need reassurance that they will be protected from his violent acts. The criminal law therefore, has to strike a balance between these two principles and this section will examine how this is done.

The special verdict

The first point to note is that, if possible, such an offender should face trial. If it is then proved that he committed an unlawful act, he will not be found guilty; instead a special verdict will be recorded of 'not guilty by reason of insanity'. The public will normally be protected because the court then has the power to deal with the defendant. It possesses a range of special orders

to impose upon him. Before 1991 there was only one such order at the court's disposal; on a finding of insanity, the court was obliged to order that the defendant be admitted to a secure hospital without limitation of time. He could then only be released on the authority of the Home Secretary. In 1991 however, the **Criminal Procedure (Insanity and Unfitness to Plead) Act 1991** amended s5 of the **Criminal Procedure (Insanity) Act 1964**. This permits a wider range of disposals to be made when the defendant is found to have committed the crime but is also found to be insane. Figure 10.1 opposite shows this.

It is now necessary to look at the question of insanity in more detail.

10.3.1 INSANITY BEFORE THE TRIAL

If a person is in custody but is obviously insane, it may be considered unwise to bring him to trial, both because of the effect on his mental state and because the public needs to be protected. **The Home Secretary, therefore, has the power to detain him immediately in a mental hospital**

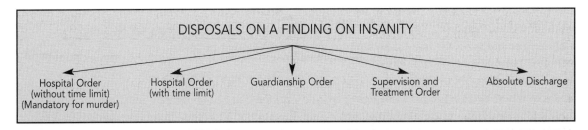

Figure 10.1 Disposals on insanity

provided that he has confirmation of the offender's state of mind from two doctors.

10.3.2 UNFITNESS TO PLEAD AT THE TIME OF THE TRIAL

If, because of his mental or physical state, the defendant is unable to appreciate the significance of the criminal trial, he may be found unfit to plead. Such a decision is not taken lightly. The Royal Committee on Capital Punishment recommended that, where possible, the defendant should have the benefit of a full trial.

In Podola 1960 therefore, even though the defendant could not remember anything at all about the crime because he was suffering from amnesia at the crucial time, the trial proceeded because, in all other respects, he was completely sane.

The question of unfitness to plead may be raised by the defence, the prosecution or by the judge himself. It may be claimed that the defendant is unable to understand the charges made against him, or is unable to appreciate the difference between the pleas of guilty or not guilty. Alternatively, he may be unable to instruct his defence. If the claims are felt to have merit, a special jury will be empanelled to decide upon the matter. This body is only permitted to find the defendant unfit to plead if reports from two doctors support this view and one of the doctors has been approved by the Home Secretary as having special expertise in the field of mental illness.

The *actus reus* must be established

If matters were left like this, it could result in unfairness to the defendant because the case has not been proved against him. Amendments made to the **Criminal Procedure (Insanity) Act 1964** now provide that a different jury must be empanelled to decide whether, on the evidence available, the *actus reus* of the crime has been established against the defendant. If the jury believes that it has, then the judge will decide what should happen to the accused. We noted earlier, that in all but murder cases, there is a variety of orders from which to choose when deciding how best to deal with the offender. If the jury is not convinced that the defendant did the act, he must be acquitted and no further action will be taken against him.

Not the same as a conviction

In the case of **Antoine 2000**, a special jury, after hearing psychiatric evidence, had decided that the defendant was unfit to plead. Another jury was then called upon to decide whether the accused had done the act that he was charged with. The question then came up as to whether he could put forward the defence of diminished responsibility under **s2 Homicide Act 1957**. The trial judge decided that he could not and proceeded to make an order that the defendant be admitted to hospital without a time limit. The defendant appealed and the case reached the House of Lords.

Their Lordships agreed that the defence of

diminished responsibility could not be brought up in such circumstances. This second jury was not there to judge on the mental element of the offence. The defence of diminished responsibility is only available as a limited defence where the defendant faces being found liable for murder. In a case of unfitness to plead, the first jury has decided that a trial for murder cannot go ahead, therefore the defendant does not face such a fate. If the second jury then goes on to find that the defendant did do the act charged against him, this finding is not classed as a conviction. The House of Lords did however hold that when deciding on whether the defendant committed the *actus reus* of the crime, the defences of mistake, accident, self-defence or involuntariness (i.e. non-insane automatism), could be brought up.

A similar appeal failed in **Grant 2001** where the defendant's counsel unsuccessfully argued that the possible defences of lack of intent and provocation should have been considered by the jury.

The Court of Appeal affirmed that this special jury was only empanelled to deal with the *actus reus* of the crime and not the defendant's state of mind. The Court of Appeal also stated that the mandatory hospitalisation without a time limit in cases where the *actus reus* of murder had been established did not infringe the perpetrator's rights under s6 Human Rights Act 1998.

10.3.3 INSANITY AT THE TIME OF THE CRIME

This is a completely different issue. In this situation the defendant is considered fit to plead, but either the defence, the prosecution or, on rare occasions, the judge, is claiming that he was insane at the time he committed the act in question. **In such a case, the question of whether or not the defendant is insane is** determined by reference to the rules laid down by the House of Lords after the case of M'Naghten in 1843.

The special verdict

If the defence of insanity is successful, an amended s2 of the offensively named **Trial of Lunatics Act 1883**, provides that a special verdict has to be recorded, stating that the defendant **'is not guilty by reason of insanity'**. Once this finding has been given, one of the orders mentioned above will then be put into force. If the crime is murder, then the judge is required to commit the defendant to a mental hospital at the discretion of the Home Secretary.

In practice, the defence of insanity is rarely used, although the changes made concerning treatment may alter this position. When the crime is homicide, most defendants prefer to use the limited defence of diminished responsibility, which, as noted in Chapter 4, reduces the offence from murder to manslaughter. Even if the defence is unsuccessful and the accused is sentenced to life imprisonment for murder, he may well be released on licence after serving a period of years in prison. If the defence of diminished responsibility is made out, the period of imprisonment may be considerably shorter. In both cases, prison is often felt to be a more acceptable alternative than incarceration in a mental hospital, and being labelled insane. It should however be noted that, with either diminished responsibility or insanity, the judge has the power to send the defendant to a secure mental hospital if the circumstances seem to warrant this, as seen in the article opposite.

10.3.4 THE DEFENCE OF INSANITY UNDER THE M'NAGHTEN RULES

As mentioned earlier, the rules relating to insanity were laid down after the case of **M'Naghten 1843**.

'Deal with Jesus' led to bomber's hate campaign

By Nigel Bunyan

A paranoid schizophrenic who claimed Jesus had told him to send a series of parcel bombs across Britain was sent indefinitely to a secure hospital yesterday.

Glynn Harding, 27, agreed to 'a deal' in which he would post 100 of the bombs in return for his stillborn baby being allowed to leave Hell and enter Heaven.

Harding, an animal rights sympathiser who searched the internet for information on how to make parcel bombs, had posted 15 by the time police arrested him near his home in Crewe, Cheshire, last February.

In the three months of his campaign he left one middle-aged woman disfigured and blinded in one eye, and transformed an outgoing six-year-old girl into a child who often cries when she is left at school.

Judge Elgin Edwards, the Recorder of Chester, told Harding he had admitted to crimes of 'pure evil'. Were it not for his illness, he would have been jailed for life.

Judge Edwards said that only the Home Secretary could authorise his release and added: 'I am bound to say . . . that I do not think you will be released for many, many years.'

Daily Telegraph, 22 September 2001

The accused, Daniel M'Naghten, tried to kill the Prime Minister at that time, Sir Robert Peel, but instead, shot and killed the Prime Minister's Secretary, Edward Drummond. M'Naghten was found not guilty of murder on the grounds that he was insane. This caused such an outcry that, after the case, the House of Lords consulted with all the judges and, from the responses to a series of questions, the **M'Naghten Rules** were formulated.

The **M'Naghten Rules** state that the jury should be informed that a person is presumed to be sane and responsible for his crimes unless it can be proved that, at the time of the offence:

he was labouring under such a defect of reason, from disease of the mind, as not to know the nature and quality of the act he was doing, or if he did know it, that he did not know he was doing what was wrong.

The burden of proof is on the defendant, who must prove his own insanity on the balance of probabilities. (This is the only general defence where the burden is not on the prosecution to disprove it, once it has been raised.)

It can be seen that the defendant has to prove three things:

- **a defect of reason**
- **caused by a disease of the mind**
- **so that he did not know what he was doing or, if he did know, he did not know that the act was wrong.**

A defect of reason

The courts have decided that this means a complete loss of the power of reasoning, not mere confusion or absentmindedness.

In **Clarke 1972**, the accused was charged with the theft of: a jar of coffee, a packet of butter and a jar of mincemeat, which she had transferred from the wire basket to her bag. Her defence rested on her forgetfulness, caused by depression. The trial judge decided that this raised the issue of insanity. The woman quickly changed her plea to one of guilty but then appealed against the judge's finding.

The Court of Appeal held that her behaviour 'fell very far short of showing that she suffered from a defect of reason'. The court decided that the rules are not meant to apply 'to those who retain the power of reasoning but who in moments of confusion or absent-mindedness fail to use their powers to the full'. Her conviction, therefore, was quashed.

Caused by disease of the mind

It is important to realise that it is the judges that must decide this. It is not a medical decision, although conditions such as schizophrenia are obviously covered. **Over the years, it has been decided that the term 'disease of the mind' is not merely confined to diseases of the brain alone; any malfunctioning of the mind caused by an inside source will be included.** In **Kemp 1957**, the accused inflicted grievous bodily harm on his wife with a hammer for no apparent reason. Evidence had been brought to show that he was normally a mild-tempered man and a devoted husband. He claimed that he had lost consciousness because he was suffering from arteriosclerosis, which had caused a congestion of blood in his brain. The prosecution argued that the defect of reason had been caused by a physical illness, not a mental one and was not, therefore, within the definition of the **M'Naghten Rules**.

The Court of Appeal upheld the trial judge's finding of insanity, arguing that the law 'is not concerned with the brain but with the mind, in the sense that "mind" is ordinarily used, the mental faculties of reason, memory and understanding'.

Other illnesses

It might cause surprise and concern to learn that, in addition to arteriosclerosis, the following states could also be classed as diseases of the mind and result in a finding of legal insanity if a crime has been committed:

- Epilepsy
- Diabetes
- Brain tumours
- Sleepwalking.

Such conditions can be temporary or permanent, curable or incurable.

Epilepsy and brain tumours

In Bratty v Attorney General for Northern Ireland 1963, Lord Denning affirmed that the question of insanity could be raised by the prosecution or the judge, in addition to the defence. He also agreed that conditions such as epilepsy and cerebral tumours could come under the definition of diseases of the mind, thus disapproving of the earlier case of Charlson 1955, where a contrary statement was made. He went on to state that:

any mental disorder which has manifested itself in violence and is prone to recur is a disease of the mind.

In **Sullivan 1984**, the accused kicked and injured an 80-year old man during an attack of psychomotor epilepsy and was charged with grievous bodily harm. The medical evidence showed that the defendant had committed the offence during the third stage of his epileptic fit when he was unaware of what was happening. The judge decided that he would have to direct the jury on the issue of insanity. The accused therefore, changed his plea to guilty of actual bodily harm and was sentenced to three years' probation. He then appealed against the judge's direction.

The House of Lords, although expressing sympathy for the defendant, nevertheless dismissed his appeal. The statements made in Kemp were approved of. Their Lordships decided that it was not important whether the impairment of the defendant was organic, as in epilepsy, or functional, or permanent or transient and intermittent, provided that the disease existed at the time of the act.

Diabetes

In this illness the blood sugar level has to be controlled by insulin. If not, the person may suffer from disorientation and aggression, which could end in loss of consciousness, a coma or even death.

Hyperglycaemia

If the sufferer forgets to take his insulin, this can lead to a high blood sugar level. This state is called hyperglycaemia. **As this arises from the diabetes itself, this comes under the legal definition of a disease of the mind and is classed as insanity, even though this is only a temporary state.**

Hypoglycaemia

If the defendant takes too much insulin, this may reduce his blood sugar level, a state known as hypoglycaemia. The courts take the view that because this state is caused by an outside source, i.e. the taking of too much medicine, this does not come under the heading of a disease of mind and is not insanity under the **M'Naghten Rules**. In such a case, the defendant may be able to put forward the defence of non-insane automatism, which, if successful, entitles him to a full acquittal. The following two cases illustrate the strange (and sometimes unfair) results of these conclusions.

In **Hennessy 1989**, the accused was charged with taking away a conveyance and driving while disqualified. He had diabetes and argued that he failed to take his dose of insulin because he was suffering from anxiety, stress and depression and that this affected his blood sugar level. He contended that this led to the condition of hyperglycaemia and a state of automatism, thereby allowing him this defence. The judge decided instead, that this state raised the question of insanity because the disease of the mind had arisen from the diabetes itself, not from any outside source. Like Clarke and Sullivan before him, Hennessy did not wish to be tainted with the stigma of insanity. He therefore changed his plea to guilty but then appealed against the judge's finding.

The Court of Appeal upheld the finding of the trial judge. Lord Lane stated that stress, anxiety and depression 'constitute a state of mind which is prone to recur' and could not be classed as outside factors. This meant the defence of automatism was not available to the defendant, only the defence of insanity because of his disease of the mind.

This case can be contrasted with **Quick 1973**. The accused was a nurse in a mental hospital and was convicted of occasioning actual bodily harm to a severely disabled patient. The defendant claimed that the attack occurred while he was suffering from hypoglycaemia and was unaware of his acts. He therefore argued that the defence of automatism could be used. The trial judge disagreed, stating that only the defence of insanity could be put forward. Once again, the defendant changed his plea to guilty but then appealed.

The Court of Appeal decided that Quick's mental condition was not caused by his diabetes but by his use of insulin and alcohol, which were outside sources. It followed, therefore, that the defence of automatism should have been put before the jury and because it had not been, the appeal had to be allowed, albeit reluctantly.

Why is the distinction upheld?

The courts make such a distinction between conditions caused by an outside source, like a blow to the head causing concussion or the wrongful use of medication, and diseases of the mind because, in the former case, the condition can easily be treated or avoided and is unlikely to recur. Where diseases of the mind are involved, which might well recur at a later time, the protection of the public is felt to be of paramount importance and the court needs to be able to make orders for suitable treatment and/or detention.

Sleepwalking

Such reasoning is apparent in the case of **Burgess 1991**, where the accused attacked his sleeping neighbour while watching television in her flat. The defendant hit her over the head with a bottle and video recorder and attempted to strangle her. When she cried out, he appeared to come to his senses and he voluntarily called an ambulance for her. At his trial for malicious wounding, he argued that he remembered nothing of the events and must have been sleepwalking during the attack. He therefore put forward the defence of automatism but this was rejected by the trial judge, who argued, instead, that the evidence suggested insanity under the **M'Naghten Rules**. After being found not guilty by reason of insanity, the judge ordered that Burgess should be detained in a secure hospital.

The Court of Appeal upheld this verdict. Lord Lane approved of the cases of Bratty and Sullivan and the views expressed in the Canadian case of Rabey 1980. The Supreme Court of Canada had stated that 'the ordinary stresses and disappointments of life which are the common lot of mankind, do not constitute an external cause constituting an explanation for a malfunctioning of the mind which takes it out of the category of a "disease of the mind".' Lord Lane's opinion of the law was not shaken by the later Canadian case of Parks 1992, where a man was acquitted when he allegedly drove over 20 kilometres while asleep and killed his mother-in-law! Lord Lane decided that while sleep is a normal condition, sleepwalking, and particularly violence in sleep, is not normal. He noted that the doctors for the defence and prosecution had given conflicting evidence. The prosecution had not believed that this was a case of sleepwalking at all but rather one of a 'hysterical dissociative state'. Lord Lane, therefore, upheld the judge's finding that this was 'an abnormality or disorder, albeit transitory, due to an internal factor, whether functional or organic, which had manifested

itself in violence' and decided that it needed to be treated, even if recurrence of serious violence was unlikely. He did however, agree that it was 'incongruous' to label such conditions as insanity and supported Lord Diplock's view, expressed in Sullivan, that Parliament should change the wording of the definition of insanity.

As not to know the nature and quality of the act he was doing . . .

The effect of the disease of the mind must be such that the defendant is unaware of what he is doing, or if he does understand this, he fails to appreciate that he is doing something wrong.

The first part of this statement covers situations where the accused does not understand the physical nature and quality of his act. In **Kemp 1957**, the defendant's attack occurred when he had lost consciousness and in **Burgess 1991**, the man claimed that he was asleep. Neither therefore, knew the nature and quality of their acts. This part of the Rules would also act as a defence if a man threw his girlfriend from the roof of a building, in the belief that he was flying a kite, or, conversely, his girlfriend chopped off his head, thinking that she was chopping down a tree!

The second part of this statement covers a person who is aware of what he is doing but does not realise that he is doing something wrong. This may be harder to prove.

In Codere 1916, the appeal court made it clear that the defendant will not be able to rely on such a contention just because he feels that he is not doing anything morally wrong, if he does know that his acts are legally wrong.

The case of **Windle 1952** also makes this position clear. The defendant, a 40-year-old man said to be of weak character, was married to a much older woman who was believed to be insane. She often spoke of suicide and a workmate of the defendant, irritated by Windle's constant complaints about his unhappy home-life, suggested giving her 'a dozen aspirins'. The defendant, instead, gave her 100. A defence doctor believed that the accused was suffering from '*folie à deux*', a form of communicated insanity, but both sets of doctors agreed that Windle knew that he was performing a wrongful act. He had also made the following comment to the police, '**I suppose they will hang me for this**?'

The Court of Appeal confirmed that the word 'wrong' in this context meant that the defendant knew 'that what he was doing was contrary to law, and that he had realised what punishment the law provided for murder'.

10.3.5 SUGGESTED REFORM OF THE DEFENCE OF INSANITY

As noted below, many people have strong reservations about the current law on insanity. *The Draft Criminal Code* provides for reform of this area. It adopts, with limited amendments, the recommendations made by the Butler Committee. It approves of that body's suggestion that the verdict should be changed to one of 'not guilty by reason of mental disorder'. Clause 35 states that this would be established if it is proved that the defendant, at the time he committed the offence, was suffering from severe mental illness or severe mental handicap. Two medical practitioners, who are experienced in this field, must give evidence to this effect. Clause 36 states that a mental disorder verdict should be brought where the defendant acts in a state of automatism due to mental disorder, or, more surprisingly, a combination of mental disorder and intoxication. It should also be brought where the fault for the offence cannot be established for this reason or where, because of his mental disorder, the defendant believes that an exempting circumstance existed.

◀ *Comment*

The law on insanity, particularly in relation to the **M' Naghten Rules** and the judges' interpretation of them, has been subjected to a barrage of criticism from a variety of sources. I have identified ten of these arguments:

1. The Rules were formulated in 1843 and have never been updated.

2. The Rules are restricted; they do not cover the defendant who is subject to an irresistible impulse that he knows is wrong but cannot control. The partial defence of diminished responsibility, reducing the liability from murder to manslaughter, does recognise this type of situation.

3. The Rules lay down a purely legal formula for establishing insanity; they have been criticised by the medical profession for not conforming to medical views of insanity.

4. They are also disliked by the people they were designed to protect, i.e. the defendants. The latter prefer to use the partial defence of diminished responsibility if the crime is murder. People suffering from epilepsy, diabetes and those who have committed crimes while sleepwalking are outraged to discover that the law labels them insane and, as shown in cases like **Clarke 1972, Sullivan 1984** and **Hennessy 1989**, often prefer to plead guilty rather than be tainted with such a stigma.

5. The judges themselves are uneasy about this development, as shown by the comments of Lawton L J in **Quick 1973. He stated that 'Common sense is affronted by the prospect of a diabetic being sent to such a hospital when in**

most cases the disordered mental condition can be rectified quickly by pushing a lump of sugar . . . into the patient's mouth'. It is felt that the condition of too much sugar in the blood could be put right just as quickly. Lord Diplock in **Sullivan 1984** and both the trial judge and Lord Lane, in **Burgess 1991** urged Parliament to look into this matter.

6. The very different results from a finding of an illness caused by an inside source, such as hyperglycaemia, and an effect on the mind caused by an outside source, such as the wrong dose of medication causing hypoglycaemia, appear to most people to be irrational and unfair. In the first instance, the defendant could be locked away without a time limit being set, whereas in the second case, if automatism is accepted, the defendant will have a complete defence and will walk free from the court. It is a valid argument that the public needs to be safeguarded against violence from offenders who have mental disorders but it may also need to be protected from those who have attacks because they have not followed their correct course of treatment.

7. This is the only general defence where the onus is on the accused to prove the defence.

8. The defence is not available for the defendant who believes that what he is doing is morally right but who knows that the act is legally wrong. Such a person is also in need of medical help.

9. The state of the law on insanity has been criticised by the Royal Commission on Capital Punishment, the Butler Commission and the Law Commission.

10. The old-fashioned terminology surrounding the law on insanity sounds offensive to modern ears. Those who cause harm while suffering from illnesses like epilepsy or diabetes are outraged when the courts label them insane; it must add further pain when they are then found 'not guilty by reason of insanity' under the **Trial of Lunatics Act 1883**. Surely it would not have been too difficult a task for Parliament to have repealed the act and modernised the law, rather than merely amending it in 1991.

10.4 NON-INSANE AUTOMATISM

We have just discussed the position where the defendant commits a crime but is completely unaware of this because he is suffering from a disease of the mind. This is an example of insane automatism. **If, however, an outside factor causes him to act like an automaton, he may be able to use the defence of automatism**.

The difference between insane and non-insane automatism

- With insane automatism, the verdict will be 'not guilty by reason of insanity'. The judge will then make an order regarding treatment for the defendant.
- Non-insane automatism, if proved, results in a complete acquittal. The defendant will walk free from the court.

The case of **Quick 1973**, noted under insanity, illustrates this. Another very similar example occurred in **Bingham 1991**.

The defendant, who had diabetes, was found guilty of the theft of a can of Coca Cola and a packet of sandwiches, worth just £1.16p. The trial judge would not permit him to put to the jury the defence that he was suffering from hypoglycaemia and had not been aware of any criminal activity.

The Court of Appeal stressed that the courts have made a clear distinction between hyperglycaemia (an excess of sugar in the blood), which is classed as a disease of the mind and gives rise to the defence of insanity, and hypoglycaemia (a deficiency of sugar in the blood), which is caused by an outside source. If the latter is satisfactorily established, it shows that the accused is in a state of non-insane automatism, which is a complete defence. The appeal, therefore, succeeded.

10.4.1 ESTABLISHING THE DEFENCE OF AUTOMATISM

The essence of the defence is that the defendant's actions are completely involuntary. Acts done after a blow to the head, or reflex actions after being attacked by a swarm of bees were cited as examples in **Hill v Baxter 1958**. In **Bratty 1963, Lord Denning stated that the defence was limited to reflex actions, acts done as a result of a spasm, or acts committed while unconscious or while having convulsions.**

It was made clear in that case that an act is not involuntary simply because the offender could not resist the impulse to act or did not intend the consequences to take place. Some of the examples given in earlier cases will now come under the heading of insane automatism, after decisions such as **Sullivan 1984** and **Burgess 1991**. In the latter case, the Court of Appeal firmly decided that sleepwalking came under the heading of a disease of the mind, and therefore the defence of insanity applied, not automatism. In the light of these decisions, which have limited the scope of automatism, it is rather surprising to note the

decision in **T 1990**. The court accepted that post-traumatic stress, which is surely a disease of the mind, could satisfy the criteria laid down for the defence of automatism, because this condition had been caused by the outside factor of a rape. A woman of 23 had allegedly been acting in a dream-like state during and after her involvement in a robbery. A psychiatrist diagnosed that, at the time of the crime, she was in a dissociative state and not acting with any conscious will.

The judge therefore allowed the defence of automatism to be put before the jury and the girl was acquitted of the crime. It is arguable whether this decision is in line with other authorities although it may well have been a just one in the circumstances.

In **Whoolley 1997**, the defendant admitted that he was driving very close to the car in front in a queue of slow-moving traffic on the M62. He alleged that he suddenly had a sneezing attack and lost control of his HGV wagon. He crashed into the car ahead and this caused a 'domino effect' involving seven other vehicles.

The appeal court decided that an attack of sneezing could be the type of involuntary act that came under the defence of automatism and affirmed that a verdict of not guilty by magistrates was allowable.

Limits on the defence

In **Broome v Perkins 1987**, the defence of automatism was not allowed to a person suffering from diabetes who still had some control over his vehicle and this position was affirmed in **AG's Reference (No 2 of 1992) 1994**. In the case that had given rise to this reference, the jury had found a lorry driver not guilty of the offence of causing death by reckless driving. He had driven 700 yards along the hard shoulder of a motorway before crashing into a parked car and killing two people standing in front of it. He alleged that he had been 'driving without awareness' after a long journey on a straight flat motorway. The acquittal caused concern and resulted in the *Reference*. **The Court of Appeal decided that the defence of automatism should not be available where there was merely reduced or imperfect awareness and some degree of control still existed. There had to be a 'total destruction of voluntary control' before the defence could apply.**

Self-induced automatism

In addition to the limitations noted above, the defence of automatism may not be available even in cases of hypoglycaemia, if it is the defendant's own fault that he is in such a condition.

In **Bailey 1983**, the defendant had suffered from diabetes for over 30 years and needed insulin to control his condition. He became very upset when his girlfriend ended their relationship and befriended another man.

Bailey visited this man to discuss the position and after ten minutes or so complained of feeling unwell and requested a drink of water and sugar. He then said that he had lost his glove and as the other man bent to look for it, Bailey hit him over the head with an iron bar, which he had brought with him. The jury found him guilty of malicious wounding.

The Court of Appeal made it clear that automatism arising from the voluntary consumption of drink or drugs is not covered by the defence because the party concerned has been reckless at putting himself in this position, a decision which will be discussed further in the next part of the chapter. The same approach however, is not normally taken towards someone who fails to take food after an insulin injection, unless he is aware that this might lead to 'aggressive, unpredictable and uncontrollable conduct', and it was felt that this fact was not generally known.

It was decided, therefore, that the jury had been misdirected on this point. Despite this finding the Court of Appeal held that there had been no miscarriage of justice. It was believed that the jury would still have convicted Bailey on the facts; there was ample evidence that he had deliberately gone to the victim's home, armed with an iron bar, in order to teach him a lesson.

10.4.2 REFORM OF THE DEFENCE OF AUTOMATISM

The Draft Criminal Law Bill 1989 upholds the defence in cases of spasms, reflex actions and convulsions. It would also allow automatism to be used when the defendant is in a state of unconsciousness or asleep, thus covering the **Burgess** type of situation, a change many would welcome.

Activity

- Do you agree with the contention that the law on insanity is outdated, unfair and in urgent need of reform?

- Romulus and Remus are twins. They both suffer from diabetes. Romulus was studying so hard for his examinations that he forgot to take his insulin. He became very ill-tempered and attacked his law lecturer after the latter criticised his revision plan.

  Remus is more of a 'party animal'. He did not have time to eat, but took an extra dose of insulin and went off to a club. He was later informed that he had overpowered two of the club 'bouncers' after they had objected to his unruly behaviour at the bar.

Advise the twins, who both face charges of grievous bodily harm. Neither has any recollection of the incidents in question.

10.5 INTOXICATION

In law, the phrase 'intoxication' covers both excessive drinking and various forms of drug taking.

There are rare occasions where the drunkenness or the drugged state is not the fault of the accused at all and, if this is shown to the satisfaction of the court, he may well have a defence. As a starting point, therefore, the law makes a distinction between voluntary and involuntary intoxication.

10.5.1 VOLUNTARY INTOXICATION

As a general rule, the defendant will not be able to rely on the defence of intoxication if he has voluntarily put himself into that state and then committed a crime. In **DPP v Beard 1920**, the Lord Chancellor of that time made the following statement:

Under the law of England as it prevailed until early in the nineteenth century voluntary drunkenness was never an excuse for criminal misconduct; and indeed the classic authorities broadly assert that voluntary drunkenness must be considered rather an aggravation than a defence.

TEN KEY FACTS ON INSANITY AND AUTOMATISM

- There are three possible times when the question of insanity arises, before the trial, at the time of the trial and at the time the offence was committed. If the case has reached the trial stage and unfitness is pleaded, a special jury must decide the issue. If the defendant is deemed insane, a separate jury will then examine the case against him and decide whether the *actus reus* has been established. If so, the judge will choose how to treat him from a range of orders although, in the case of murder, the defendant must be sent to a secure mental hospital **(Criminal Procedure (Insanity) Act 1964**, as amended).

- If the accused is thought to be insane at the time he committed the act (an issue that can be raised by the defence, prosecution or the judge), the **M'Naghten Rules** are used to decide whether legal insanity exists. These state that there must be a defect of reason, caused by a disease of the mind, so that the defendant did not know the nature and quality of his act or, if he did know what he was doing, he did not realise that his act was wrong. The defendant must prove his insanity on a balance of probabilities. If proved, a special verdict 'not guilty by reason of insanity' is recorded.

- The term 'defect of reason' means a complete loss of reasoning powers; forgetfulness is not enough **(Clarke 1972)**.

- The term 'disease of the mind' is wider than a disease of the brain; it includes any malfunctioning of the mind that affects reason, memory and understanding **(Kemp 1957)**. It includes criminal acts committed while suffering from arteriosclerosis **(Kemp 1957)**, in the midst of an epileptic fit **(Sullivan 1984)**, while suffering from hyperglycaemia caused by diabetes **(Hennessy 1989)**, and even where the defendant is sleepwalking or suffering from a blackout **(Burgess 1991)**. It does not include illnesses like hypoglycaemia which are caused by an outside source (**Quick 1973**). In such cases, the complete defence of automatism is available.

● Denning's statement that 'any mental disorder which has manifested itself in violence and is prone to recur is a disease of the mind' now seems to have been widened to admit diseases of the mind where the violence is unlikely to recur (**Burgess 1991**).

● The defendant must either be unaware of the nature and quality of his act or not realise that he is doing something wrong (**Codere 1916, Windle 1952**).

● Automatism is divided into insane automatism, to which the **M'Naghten Rules** are applied, and non-insane automatism, which is a complete defence, resulting in an acquittal. Non-insane automatism is sub-divided into involuntary automatism and self-induced automatism.

● Involuntary acts include blows to the head, reflex actions after being attacked by a swarm of bees (**Hill v Baxter 1958**), other involuntary spasms (**Bratty 1963**), a dissociative state caused by a rape (**T 1990**) and an attack of sneezing (**Whoolley 1997**).

● Automatism cannot now be pleaded for sleepwalking (**Burgess 1991**) nor for acts where the defendant still has the power to exercise some control over his actions (**Broome v Perkins 1987, AG's Reference (No 2 of 1992) 1994**).

● The defence will not be available if the accused has caused the situation by his own reckless conduct (**Bailey 1983**). Failing to take food after an insulin injection might not come into this category if it were not known that such inaction could cause aggression.

Specific intent crimes

During the nineteenth century however, the judges began to allow intoxication to be a limited defence in some circumstances where the most serious crimes were involved and the person would otherwise be put to death or, at the least, transported to the colonies. **It was gradually accepted that, while voluntary intoxication would never be a defence in crimes of basic intent, like assault, ordinary criminal damage, rape and manslaughter, it might be allowed as either a full or partial defence where crimes of specific intent are involved.** The following are examples of specific intent crimes:

● **Aggravated criminal damage with the intention of endangering life.**
● **Theft, where the offender dishonestly appropriates property belonging to another with the intention of permanently depriving the other of it.**
● **Gbh or malicious wounding under s18 OAPA 1861 with the intention to do some grievous bodily harm.**
● **Murder, where there is an unlawful killing with malice aforethought.**

All these crimes, with the exception of murder, which is treated as a special case, require some further intention to be established in addition to the basic offence. If this is not the case because of extreme drunkenness or a deeply drugged state negatives this, it is felt that the offender cannot be found guilty because he cannot be shown to possess the appropriate *mens rea*. It will be seen from the cases however, that, in many instances, he can be found guilty of a lesser offence, i.e. manslaughter instead of murder, basic criminal damage rather than the aggravated form and malicious wounding or grievous bodily harm under **s20**, instead of **s18**. The offence of theft causes difficulty, because no lesser offence exists to put in its place.

An example of the substitution of a lesser crime can be seen in **Lipman 1970**.

The defendant and the victim were both addicted to drugs and on the night in question, took LSD. The dead body of the girl was found a day later. She had suffered two blows to the head but had actually died of asphyxia from having part of a sheet crammed into her mouth. The man, an American citizen, had returned to his home country but was sent back to face trial for murder. He claimed that he had experienced a bad LSD 'trip', during which he had believed that he was descending to the centre of the earth and was being attacked by snakes, which he had tried to fight off. He argued that he had no knowledge of the real events and had not intended to harm the girl. Despite his claims, the jury found him guilty of manslaughter.

The Court of Appeal upheld this verdict. The court decided that he could not be found guilty of murder, a specific intent crime, if the intention to kill or cause grievous bodily harm could not be established. On the other hand, he could be found guilty of manslaughter; there had been an unlawful act and a death had resulted. Manslaughter was a basic intent crime for which self-induced intoxication was no defence.

In contrast, in **AG for Northern Ireland v Gallagher 1963**, the defendant was not able to show that he lacked the intention to kill. The prosecution claimed that the defendant harboured a grudge against his wife because she had been instrumental in arranging for him to be detained in a mental hospital. He therefore decided to kill her and bought a knife for this purpose. He also bought a bottle of whisky, either to give himself 'Dutch Courage' or to drown his conscience after the event. The jury convicted

him of murder but this was quashed by the Northern Ireland Appeal Court.

The House of Lords restored the conviction. Lord Denning gave the main speech. He decided that there were only two possible defences; the first was insanity, the second, intoxication. Denning decided that insanity was not applicable here because, although the man was a psychopath, this state of mind was not active at the time he conceived of the plan to kill his wife. He affirmed that the defence of intoxication was not available in a crime of basic intent and added that, even in a specific intent crime, it had to be shown that the degree of drunkenness was such that the defendant 'was rendered so stupid by drink that he does not know what he is doing'. Denning agreed that this had been established in an early case where a nurse at a christening had been so drunk that she had put the baby onto the fire, instead of a log of wood. He also quoted with approval a later case where a man had stabbed his friend several times, in the mistaken belief that it was a theatrical dummy in his bed, not a real person. In Gallagher however, the defendant obviously knew what he was doing and had formed the clear intent to kill. Lord Denning made the following pronouncement:

> *My Lords, I think the law on this point should take a clear stand. If a man, whilst sane and sober, forms an intention to kill, and makes preparation for it, knowing it is a wrong thing to do, and then gets himself drunk so as to give himself Dutch courage to do the killing, and whilst drunk carries out his intention, he cannot rely on this self-induced drunkenness as a defence to a charge of murder, nor even as reducing it to manslaughter.*

He did take pains to note that the defence of insanity would be available for both specific intent and basic intent crimes if the drunkenness was so acute that it had led to a 'disease of the mind', as where the defendant was suffering from delirium tremens.

Basic intent crimes

As stated in **DPP v Beard 1920**, intoxication cannot be used as a defence for these crimes. A basic intent crime is a crime where the *mens rea* does not exceed the *actus reus* of the offence. This was stated in **DPP v Morgan 1976**. Examples of basic intent crimes include:

● Manslaughter
● Rape
● Malicious wounding or grievous bodily harm under s20 OAPA 1861
● Actual bodily harm
● Common assault and battery.

◀ *Comment*_____

The reasoning behind the refusal to allow intoxication as a defence is that the act of getting drunk or putting oneself into a drugged state is felt to be a reckless course of conduct which, combined with a criminal act, will amount to recklessness in law and thus satisfy the *mens rea*. It is probably best to think of this as a policy decision on the part of the courts, rather than trying to reason it through, because there are difficulties with this in cases where **Cunningham**-style recklessness has to be shown.

Despite these problems, and despite what is stated in **s8 Criminal Justice Act 1967**, the rule that drunkenness is no defence in crimes of basic intent was categorically affirmed by the House of Lords in the case of **DPP v Majewski 1977**.

The defendant was convicted of three counts of actual bodily harm and three counts of assault on a police constable. Majewski was a drug addict and claimed that on the day in question he had consumed such large quantities of drugs and

alcohol that he 'completely blanked out' and had no recollection of committing assaults in the pub in Basildon or later at the police station. The judge told the jury to disregard the fact that there could be a defence on this ground and the defendant appealed.

The House of Lords unanimously upheld the conviction. Their Lordships were obviously concerned about the social as well as the legal implications of allowing such a defence. Lord Salmon stated: 'If there were to be no penal sanction for any injury inflicted under the complete mastery of drink or drugs, voluntarily taken, the social consequence could be appalling'. Lord Elwyn-Jones stated that self-induced drunkenness had long been a problem. He went on to say that 'voluntary drug-taking with the potential and actual dangers to others it may cause has added a new dimension to the old problem'.

Majewski's convictions, therefore, were upheld and the defence denied him. Lord Elwyn-Jones approved of the case of Beard, and stated clearly that it was only in crimes of specific intent that drunkenness could ever provide a defence. Lord Salmon admitted that it could seem illogical to allow the defence in one class of case and not in another but felt that treating specific intent crimes differently was justified in order to alleviate the harshness that might otherwise be caused. He did not agree that basic intent crimes should be allowed the defence as the law had been clear on this subject for about 150 years and had not been seen to cause injustice. He believed that the rules were more necessary today, because of the increase in drug taking.

In **Fotheringham 1989**, the defendant was appealing against his conviction for the rape of a 14-year-old girl. She had acted as a babysitter for Fotheringham and his wife and had gone to sleep in the matrimonial bed. The defendant claimed that he was very drunk and had got into bed and had sexual intercourse in the mistaken belief that the girl in the bed was his wife. He was appealing because the judge had directed the jury to disregard this fact.

The Court of Appeal upheld the rule that self-induced intoxication cannot be used as a defence to a crime of basic intent and stated that neither could the defence of mistake be raised, if this mistake were caused by self-induced intoxication. The case of O'Grady 1987 (see later in this chapter) was held to be authority for this.

10.5.2 INVOLUNTARY INTOXICATION

In the aforementioned cases, the offenders had deliberately taken alcohol or drugs. We now need to look at the position where the intoxication is involuntary. Examples would be where drink or drugs were given to the offender without his knowledge, as where his drink has been 'spiked'. In such a case, the defendant might well have a defence, both in cases where the crime is a specific intent one and also where it is a basic intent one, provided that in the latter situation the defendant is not found to have been careless.

In the early case of Pearson 1835, it was stated that 'If a party be made drunk by stratagem, or the fraud of another, he is not responsible'.

Calming drugs

In some circumstances, the courts have gone further than this. The intoxication also may be classed as involuntary even if taken deliberately, if it can be shown that the defendant believed that he was taking a drug to calm himself when, in reality, it had the opposite effect.

In **Hardie 1985**, the defendant's long-term relationship broke down and he was asked to leave the flat he shared with his girlfriend. He became very upset and during the day took several Valium tablets, after being reassured that

they would not do him any harm. He later fell asleep and claimed that he could remember very little after this time but while in this state, he started a fire in a wardrobe at the flat he was vacating. The jury found him guilty of arson.

The Court of Appeal quashed the conviction. Parker L J stated: 'It is true that Valium is a drug and it is true that it was taken deliberately and not taken on medical prescription, but the drug is, in our view wholly different in kind from drugs which are liable to cause unpredictability or aggressiveness. It may well be that the taking of a sedative or soporific drug will, in certain circumstances, be no answer, for example in a case of reckless driving, but if the effect of a drug is merely soporific or sedative the taking of it, even in some excessive quantity, cannot in the ordinary way raise a conclusive presumption against the admission of proof of intoxication for the purpose of disproving *mens rea* in ordinary crimes, such as would be the case with alcoholic intoxication or incapacity or automatism resulting from the self-administration of dangerous drugs'.

Limitations on involuntary intoxication

The courts are not prepared to extend this licence too far.

In Allen 1988, it was affirmed that the defence was not available to a defendant who had been drinking wine in a voluntary way but had failed to realise the strength of it and had acted out of character as a result.

Even a defendant that has been intoxicated by another unknowingly, might not be able to use the defence if it is believed that he has still retained the ability to form the intent to commit the crime in question. **The House of Lords decided this in Kingston 1995, and overturned the controversial quashing of the decision by the Court of Appeal. The final court upheld the opinion of the trial judge that 'a drugged intent is still an intent'.**

The defendant was involved in a business dispute with another couple and the latter decided to blackmail him. They knew that he had paedophiliac tendencies and arranged for him and their accomplice to visit a flat to which a 15-year-old boy had been lured. The latter had been given drugs and was asleep on the bed. The defendant was then invited to abuse the boy and was photographed and taped as he did so. Kingston claimed that he, too, had been drugged and had performed the unlawful acts while in this state. He asserted that, if he had not been so intoxicated, he would have been able to control his actions. The Court of Appeal decided that, if this were indeed the case, the defence of involuntary intoxication should be open to him.

The House of Lords was clearly worried about the implications of such a move, and refused to allow this. The current state of the law, therefore, is that provided that an intent to commit the crime in question seems to have been established from the facts, intoxication is no defence, whether the offence is one of basic intent or specific intent and whether the intoxication is voluntary or involuntary.

10.5.3 POSSIBLE REFORM OF INTOXICATION

Over the years, various suggestions have been put forward to reform this area of law. Some reformers are concerned about the fact that intoxication often causes severe social problems and therefore recommend making it a separate offence. The Butler Committee suggested one called dangerous intoxication, which would come into play when the defendant was acquitted of the main charge and which would carry a penalty of one year's imprisonment for a first offence or three years for subsequent ones. This proposal did not find favour with the Criminal Law Revision Committee. This body did not like the idea of the same penalty being applied, whatever the offence against the person and suggested, instead, clarifying the present rule laid down in **Majewski**.

Other reformers believe that it is unfair to treat an intoxicated person in the same way as if he were not drunk or drugged, and disapprove of the current restrictions put upon the defence of intoxication. The defence is more widely available in other jurisdictions, including Australia, Canada, New Zealand and South Africa. The Law Commission, in a consultation paper in 1993, suggested that UK law should follow similar lines and abolish the basic intent/specific intent distinction and allow the defence to be put forward in all instances. The responses to this were unfavourable so the Commission now proposes to codify and clarify the present law, with only minor amendments. (See Law Com No 229 1995 Legislating the Criminal Code: Intoxication and Criminal Liability.)

FIVE KEY FACTS ON INTOXICATION

- The defence of intoxication is available for specific intent crimes if the defendant is so drunk or drugged that he is not able to form the *mens rea* for the offence in question (**DPP v Majewski 1977**). In most cases, the defendant will be found liable for a lesser crime instead, such as manslaughter instead of murder (**Lipman 1970**), basic criminal damage instead of aggravated criminal damage or gbh under **s20** instead of **s18**. If intoxication completely negatives *mens rea* in a case of theft, the defendant is entitled to an acquittal.

- If the accused still retains the ability to form an intent to commit the crime, the defence of intoxication will not be available, as in **AG for Northern Ireland v Gallagher 1963** and **Kingston 1995.**

- Specific intent crimes are normally those for which an extra intention has to be established beyond that required for the *actus reus*, although murder has been included in this category. The offences include grievous bodily harm under **s18 OAPA 1861**, criminal damage with intent to endanger life, theft and burglary.

- The defence of intoxication is not available for basic intent crimes (**DPP v Beard 1920, DPP v Majewski 1977, Fotheringham 1989**).

- If the intoxication is involuntary, the defence may be available for both basic intent crimes and specific intent crimes (**Pearson 1835**). It may also be pleaded where the drugs are taken deliberately, if they are believed to be calming drugs rather than stimulants (**Hardie 1985**).

Activity

- Roxie was upset when she was passed over for promotion. She had a sleepless night so took some amphetamines to help her get through the following day. She then visited a local bar and consumed eight glasses of vodka in quick succession. She later regained consciousness at the local police station and was told that she had hit the barman over the head with her laptop computer because he wasn't serving her quickly enough and had assaulted PC Flynn who had been summoned to take her away. Advise Roxie who has been charged with actual bodily harm, in relation to the defence of intoxication.

- Decide how your answer would differ in the following unrelated circumstances:

a) Billy the barman had died and Roxie was charged with his murder.

b) A colleague, Velma, had given Roxie several Valium pills, which had an adverse effect on her. She later discovered that she had set fire to the office before she left.

Self-assessment questions on Chapter 10

1. What degree of criminal liability do the following groups possess?
   Children under 10?
   Children between 10–14?
2. What changes were made by the **Criminal Procedure (Insanity & Unfitness to Plead) Act 1991**?
3. Why are the decisions of **Antoine** and **Grant** important?
4. Define insanity under the **M'Naghten Rules** and state where the burden of proof lies.
5. Using decided cases to illustrate your answer, explain why the effects of illnesses such as arteriosclerosis, epilepsy and diabetes might come under the **M'Naghten Rules**.
6. Why were the convictions of **Codere** and **Windle** upheld but **Clarke**'s finding of guilt quashed?
7. Why were the defendants in **Whoolley**, **Quick** and **Bingham** entitled to an acquittal but not **Bailey**?
8. Distinguish between basic intent crimes and specific intent crimes, giving three examples of each.
9. Discuss the outcomes of the cases of **Majewski** and **Fotheringham**.
10. Why did the appeals fail in **Gallagher** and **Kingston** but succeed in **Hardie**?

Chapter 11

GENERAL DEFENCES II

11.1 INTRODUCTION

Our investigation of general defences continues with study of the following topics:

- ✔ Mistake
- ✔ Necessity
- ✔ Duress
- ✔ Duress of circumstances
- ✔ Marital coercion
- ✔ Self-defence and prevention of crime.

11.2 MISTAKE

11.2.1 MISTAKES ABOUT THE LAW

Generally, making a mistake about the law will not provide a defence. In 1982, Lord Bridge stated that a fundamental principle existed that ignorance of the law is no defence in criminal law. If, for example, the defendant had led a very sheltered life and then killed someone who disagreed with his views, he would not have a defence to the crime of murder even though he might have been unaware that such an offence existed.

11.2.2 MISTAKES OF FACT

With this type of mistake, the defence is possible in limited situations:

- Where the mistake prevents the formation of the *mens rea* necessary for the crime.
- Where there is justification or excuse for the defendant's actions, as seen in the cases of Williams (Gladstone) and Beckford, mentioned later.
- Where a statute provides for this, as in the Theft Act 1968, and the Criminal Damage Act 1971, where the defence of lawful excuse is available.

The courts will have the task of deciding whether a mistake has been made in any of these circumstances. Until the 1970s, the defence was only possible if the defendant could prove that his mistake of fact was reasonable in the circumstances. In **Tolson 1889**, this was established.

The defendant's husband had deserted her and she later heard from others that he had been aboard a ship bound for America that had sunk with no survivors. Six years later, she went through a ceremony of marriage with another man. The husband then turned up again.

Mrs Tolson's conviction for bigamy was quashed on appeal. Stephen J stated:

The conduct of the woman convicted was not in the smallest degree immoral, it was perfectly natural and legitimate. Assuming the facts to be as she supposed, the infliction of more than a nominal punishment on her would have been a scandal. Why, then, should the legislature be held to have wished to subject her to punishment at all?

Tolson, while recognising the existence of the defence of mistake, nevertheless put restrictions on its use by deciding that the mistaken belief had to be both honestly and reasonably held. This view of the law held sway for many years but later became subjected to attack, culminating in the landmark House of Lords decision in **DPP v Morgan 1976**. This case widened the use of the defence and, in cases where subjective recklessness or intention had to be proved, allowed it to be used where the mistake was genuine but the belief was not necessarily a reasonably held one. It should be noted that while this wider proposition was clearly stated, it did not help the defendants in this particular appeal for reasons that are stated below. The facts of this extraordinary case were as follows:

The defendants were all in the RAF and spent the evening drinking together. Morgan then invited the others to have intercourse with his wife and stated that, if she protested, she did not really mean this and was doing so to increase her pleasure. This was shown to be completely untrue. The men were all convicted of rape but tried to argue on appeal that they believed that the woman was consenting and that the judge had misdirected the jury that their belief had to be a reasonable one.

Their Lordships admitted that there had been a misdirection and clearly stated that, in cases where intention or recklessness has to be proved, an honest mistake, even one that is not reasonably held, could provide a defence. In this particular case, however, the convictions were not quashed because the judges held that the jury would not have believed such a story and would still have convicted even if the point of law had been correctly put to them.

In **W (a minor) v Dolbey 1989**, a 15-year-old defendant was able to take advantage of this rule when he was convicted of malicious wounding. He successfully argued that he honestly believed that the air rifle he carried no longer had any pellets in it.

Back to a reasonable belief?

The changes made in the **Sexual Offences Act 2003** in relation to rape and several offences relating to children, now emphasise that any mistake as to the victim's consent or age has to be a reasonable one. The decision in **Morgan**, therefore, as it relates to the offence of rape, is no longer good law. How this overruling will affect other cases of mistake, such as those described in the section below, is unclear.

Mistake in relation to other defences

- **Self-defence**
  The widening of the defence of mistake as a result of the decision in **Morgan** was utilised in two cases where the defendants were claiming that they acted in self-defence as a result of a mistake of fact. The first was **Williams (Gladstone) 1987**, where the defendant mistakenly believed that he had observed a mugging. He therefore attacked a man who was forcibly holding a youth and, following this, was convicted of actual bodily harm. The real situation was that his victim had grabbed hold of the youth because the latter had just robbed a woman.

  The defendant's appeal against his conviction was successful on the grounds that he had made an honest mistake.

- **Defences**
  Similarly, in Beckford 1988, a policeman who shot a man who had been terrorising his family, was able to use the defence of mistake because he had believed, wrongly as it transpired, that the victim was armed.

- **Intoxication**
  While the decision in **Morgan** opened up the defence of mistake, it was still not available for mistakes made while drunk or drugged. This was noted in the case of **Fotheringham 1989**, discussed in Chapter 10. The defendant unsuccessfully claimed that he was entitled to an acquittal because he mistakenly believed that the babysitter was his wife. **In O' Grady 1987, noted later in this chapter, the Court of Appeal would not allow the defence of self-defence to be used where, because of his intoxication, the defendant mistakenly believed himself to be in danger.**

FIVE KEY FACTS ON MISTAKE

- There is normally no defence for mistakes about the law.

- When a mistake of fact exists, the defence can be used if the mistake means that the *mens rea* of the crime cannot be established. It is also available if the mistake provides an excuse for the acts committed, as in **Williams 1987** and **Beckford 1988.** In addition, some statutory offences specifically allow the defence of mistake (**Theft Act 1968, Criminal Damage Act 1971**).

- At common law, the original view was that only an honest and reasonable mistake about the facts would provide a defence (**Tolson 1889**). In **Morgan 1976**, the House of Lords decided that in crimes where intention or subjective recklessness had to be proved (in this case rape) the mistake did not need to be a reasonable one, provided that the belief was honestly held. This new view of the law was applied in **W (a minor) v Dolbey 1989** and in **B (a minor) v DPP 2000** (see Chapter 2). The specific defences relating to mistake in the **Theft Act 1968** and the **Criminal Damage Act 1971** also take this approach.

- The **Sexual Offences Act 2003** reverts back to the old position in relation to sexual offences. It clearly states that any mistakes about consent, in rape cases, and age, in offences against minors, must be reasonably held. This contrasts with the statutory defences of mistake. In other cases, such as assault, it is possible that the **Morgan** principle could still be used but it should be remembered that **Tolson** was never specifically overruled. The law is far from clear on this point.

- The defence of mistake may be available in cases where another defence is being claimed like self-defence or prevention of crime (**Williams (Gladstone) 1987, Beckford 1988**), but it cannot be used if the accused made the mistake as a result of voluntary intoxication (**O'Grady 1987, Fotheringham 1989**).

11.3 NECESSITY

The defences of necessity, duress and duress of circumstances are all connected and, for this reason, the key facts chart and the activities will encompass all three defences. In particular, duress of circumstances, only recognised by that name since the 1980s, is felt to be an extension of the defence of necessity rather than duress. In all three offences, the defendant is claiming that he did not want to commit the crime in question but either the circumstances or other people were forcing him to do this.

11.3.1 THE SCOPE OF THE DEFENCE OF NECESSITY

There has always been some doubt as to the actual extent of this defence in English law and this uncertainty was reflected in the comments of members of the Commission drafting the Criminal Code. They stated: '**We are not prepared to suggest that necessity should in every case be a justification; we are equally unprepared to suggest that necessity should in no case be a defence**.' The cases that have come before the courts also show this ambivalence.

In early times, the defence was available in specific instances. For example, it was felt to be justifiable to pull down a house to prevent a fire spreading to others, to jettison the cargo of a ship to save lives or for a prisoner to escape if the jail in which he was kept imprisoned caught fire. Before the passing of the **Abortion Act 1967**, there was a defence to a charge of carrying out an illegal abortion if this was necessary to safeguard the life of the mother or, as in the case of **Bourne 1939**, a 14-year-old girl who had been raped.

In **Johnson v Phillips 1976,** it was held that a police officer acting in the course of his duty, was permitted to order a motorist to disobey traffic regulations, if this action was felt to be necessary for the protection of people and property.

Extension of the defence

In **Re F (Mental Patient: Sterilisation) 1990**, West Berkshire Health Authority, acting with the permission of the girl's mother, sought a declaration that it was not unlawful to sterilise a patient suffering from a very serious mental disability, after the girl had formed a sexual relationship with another patient. It was believed that a pregnancy would be disastrous to her precarious mental health. The Official Solicitor, acting on behalf of the girl who was not able to give her own consent to this operation, challenged the action, doubting its legality.

The House of Lords came out strongly in favour of the Health Authority. Lord Brandon stated:

In many cases . . . it will not only be lawful for doctors, on the ground of necessity, to operate on or give other medical treatment to adult patients disabled from giving their consent; it will also be their common duty to do so.

In 1992, a doctor was allowed to perform a caesarean operation on a pregnant woman who, because of her beliefs, had specifically refused to give her consent to it. The doctor claimed that the operation was necessary to save the life of the unborn baby.

Similarly, in **Re A (children) 2000**, as discussed in Chapter 3, an operation was again considered to be necessary in order to save the life of Jodie, one of the famous conjoined twins. In this case, however, it would also lead to the death of Mary, the other twin. The twins both had a heart, a brain and a set of lungs but Mary's were not functioning properly and she only stayed alive because blood was being pumped through her body by Jodie's heart through their common aorta. If the twins were separated, Mary would die. The Court of Appeal had to decide whether the doctors would be killing this twin unlawfully if they embarked on such an operation or whether this action could be justified in the eyes of the law.

As we have already noted, the three judges came to a unanimous decision that the operation would be lawful. This seems to imply that their minds were as one on this subject but in fact, the routes by which each of them came to their conclusions were very different. Walker L J seemed to be of the opinion that the operation would be lawful, either because there was no intention at all to kill Mary or, at any rate, no murderous intent on the part of the doctors. The other two judges believed that, following Woollin, an intention to kill was present and that the operation would therefore be considered to be a murderous act unless a defence could be found.

Ward L J discussed several defences, including necessity but appeared to favour the defence of private defence, which will be examined later in this chapter. Brooke L J preferred the defence of necessity. With reference to the latter, he decided that the three requirements for its use, as put forward in 1887 by Stephen L J had been made out:

- The act was necessary to avoid inevitable and irreparable evil (harm).
- No more was planned to be done than was

reasonably necessary for the purpose to be achieved.

- **The evil to be inflicted was not disproportionate to the evil to be avoided.**

It was acknowledged that principles of modern family law led to the conclusion that the interests of the stronger twin had to take precedence over those of the weaker one. The defence of necessity therefore was, as the reporter of the case stated, **'uniquely available to provide justification of what would otherwise be an offence of murder'.**

◀ *Comment*

The result of this decision is that the defence of necessity has been extended quite considerably. For example, it was previously believed that the defence could never be used to justify a case of murder, as noted below. The Court of Appeal dealt with this by deciding that this prohibition does not apply where the victim has already been decided by the circumstances and is not being picked out as an alternative to another party. There has also been a development from what has been termed 'rights-based' doctrine of necessity, where the defence was used in the best interests of the person involved, as in **Re F** to cases of 'utilitarian' necessity. Here the victim's rights may be overridden for the sake of another party. The Court of Appeal took pains to state that the case of **Re A** was an exceptional one but, as the late Sir John Smith remarked, **'the decision is, whether it likes it or not, a precedent, and a very important one for the criminal law'.**

11.3.2 LIMITATIONS ON THE DEFENCE OF NECESSITY

While allowing the defence in specific situations (and, at its narrowest, the case of **Re A (children)**

could be seen as just one more specific example), the courts have been wary of expanding the defence in a more general way. Lord Hale, an early writer, made it clear that the defence was not available just because a person was hungry or unclothed. In the latter half of the last century, Lord Denning, normally a champion of the underdog, was equally forthright when he stated: **'. . . if hunger were once allowed to be an excuse for stealing, it would open a door through which all kinds of lawlessness and disorder would pass'.** He was even less inclined to allow the defence to homeless people, arguing that, if it were allowed **'no one's house could be safe. Necessity would open a door which no man could shut'.**

Until the case of **Re A (children)**, the courts were strongly influenced by the infamous case of **Dudley and Stephens 1884**, where the Divisional Court decided that necessity was not allowed as a defence to murder. Lord Coleridge claimed that if necessity was once allowed in such circumstances, it might **'be made the legal cloak for unbridled passion and atrocious crime'.**

The two defendants, another man and a 17-year-old cabin boy had been adrift in the ocean in an open boat, 1600 miles from land. They had been without food for eight days and without water for six. They therefore decided to kill and eat the cabin boy, who had become very weak. Four days later, a passing ship discovered them. The men were charged with murder. The jurors obviously had some sympathy for the plight of the shipwrecked crew because, although they decided that the defendants had indeed killed the boy, they wished to record a special verdict. This recognised the fact that the men had little hope of an early rescue and would probably have died if they had not committed the act. It was also acknowledged that the boy was likely to have died anyway although it was stressed that there was no greater necessity to kill him rather than one of the men.

The Divisional Court was not prepared to

allow a defence in these circumstances. Lord Coleridge had sympathy with the suffering of the defendants and appreciated the difficulties of resisting temptation in such a dreadful situation but stated that the judges were:

> *often compelled to set up standards we cannot reach ourselves and to lay down rules which we could not ourselves satisfy. But a man has no right to declare temptation to be an excuse, though he might himself have yielded to it, nor allow compassion for the criminal to change and weaken in any manner the legal definition of the crime. It is therefore our duty to declare that the prisoners' act in this case was wilful murder, that the facts as stated in the verdict are no legal justification of the homicide; and to say that in our unanimous opinion the prisoners are upon this special verdict guilty of murder.*

The men were sentenced to be hanged but the sentence was later commuted to just six months' imprisonment without hard labour.

Rather surprisingly, in **Buckoke v Greater London Council 1971**, Lord Denning decided that the defence of necessity was not even available for firefighters and other rescuers, if they contravened the traffic regulations in their race to the scene of danger. He did go on to say that they should be congratulated rather than condemned for their action and expressed the hope that they would not be prosecuted in the first place. One example of this noted by Smith and Hogan, of where a prosecution did not take place, concerned the behaviour of an army corporal at the time of the sinking of the Herald of Free Enterprise at Zeebrugge. He told the inquest that he had ordered people near a young man on a rope ladder to push him off it, as he was preventing the rescue of others. The man had become petrified through cold and fear, and would not move despite all attempts to persuade him. The corporal and others involved were never prosecuted.

It should be noted that firefighters have now been given a special defence under the **Road Traffic Act 1988** in certain situations. Other statutes also lay down specific defences akin to necessity as, for example, the **Criminal Damage Act 1971**, which allows a defence under **s5(2)** if the accused acted as he did in order to protect property he thought in immediate need of protection.

Conversely, the courts have decided that the common law defence is not available if the statutory provision expressly or impliedly precludes this, as shown in **DPP v Harris 1995**, a careless driving case.

Similarly, in **Cichon v DPP 1994**, the defendant was unsuccessful in his attempt to use the defence of necessity because the notorious **Dangerous Dogs Act 1991** (now amended) laid down an offence of absolute liability. The defendant, a nephew of the dog's owner, claimed that he had taken off the muzzle of the pit bull terrier in the park to allow it to be sick because it had kennel cough. Despite this, he was still found guilty, fined £50 and the dog ordered to be destroyed. Dog lovers will be pleased to note that the animal later won a reprieve from its death sentence.

Despite the limitations noted above, it can be seen that the defence of necessity has expanded in several ways in recent years and differing views have been expressed about such developments. Along with this has come the recognition of a new defence, that of duress of circumstances, discussed below after duress of threats, which again tries to cater for situations where a defence is felt to be justified.

11.3.3 POSSIBLE REFORM OF THE DEFENCE OF NECESSITY

At present, there are no plans to change the common law rules on this defence, uncertain though they are. In 1977, the Law Commission had been in favour of abolishing the defence altogether. It was felt that it only covered rare cases and, where such a defence was felt to be necessary, it could be included in the relevant statute. In other cases, it was argued that the matter could be dealt with when deciding whether or not to charge the offender or when the defendant was sentenced. This view was strongly criticised at the time, causing the Law Commission to rethink the matter.

Their altered view has now been strengthened in the light of the development of the defence of duress of circumstances, for which they have given the seal of approval. In the Law Commission's Report No 218, *Legislating the Criminal Code – Offences Against the Person and General Principles, 1993,* and the Draft Bill accompanying it, special provisions are included relating to duress of circumstances. None have been drafted concerning the wider defence of necessity but the Commission does recommend

that it should remain as a common law defence, to be developed by the judges, as required.

11.4 DURESS (OF THREATS)

Prima facie, the defence of duress by threats is available if the defendant is forced to commit a criminal act because another person is using force against him or another or threatening to do so.

In **AG v Whelan 1934,** it was stated that the defence of duress exists where the accused is subjected to **'threats of immediate death or serious personal violence so great as to overbear the ordinary powers of human resistance'.** If the case is heard in the Crown Court, the jury will decide this matter. With regard to magistrates' courts, it was decided by the Divisional Court in **A v DPP 2000,** that the magistrates should adopt a two-fold test. They should first decide whether the defence could be brought, but at this stage they should only consider whether the defendant had raised a defence fit to be tried; they should not try the case on its merits. This should only be done after hearing all the evidence. In this case therefore, the appeal succeeded.

11.4.1 THE ELEMENTS OF THE DEFENCE OF DURESS

The definition in **Whelan** now needs further examination:

'Threats'

The defendant must be subjected to force or the threat of it. This could be aimed at the accused himself but it could cover threats to his family and others close to him, as suggested in **Hurley and Murray 1967,** an Australian case. This was affirmed by the Court of Appeal in **Wright 2000,** where the defendant's non live-in boyfriend was threatened. The court held that it was wrong of the trial judge to limit the defence to the girl herself or her immediate family. The Law

Commission favours the view that there should be no restrictions at all on the person's actually threatened, but it cannot be said with certainty that this is the current position.

'of immediate death'

The word **'immediate'** requires investigation. Normally, if there is plenty of time to obtain help and protection from other sources, the defendant will not be able to use the defence of duress. In some circumstances however, the courts may take a more sympathetic view of the fears of the accused, as in **Hudson and Taylor 1971**. Hudson, a young girl of seventeen and Taylor, aged nineteen, were the principal prosecution witnesses in a malicious wounding case but, through fear of retaliatory action from associates of the accused, changed their stories in court and ensured the acquittal of the defendant. The girls were later charged with perjury and put forward the defence of duress, claiming that they had been threatened with serious physical violence if they testified. In addition, they had seen one of those threatening them sitting in the public gallery at the trial, which reinforced their decisions to change their evidence. The judge made it clear to the jury that the defence was not available because the threats **'were not sufficiently present and immediate'** and the girls were convicted.

The Court of Appeal decided that the prosecution needed to prove that the girls could have obtained protection. It should then have been up to the jury to decide the matter after considering the age of the offenders, the circumstances in which they found themselves and any risks that may have been involved.

The question of the immediacy of the threats was again at issue in **Abdul-Hussain 1999**. The case actually concerned the defence of duress of circumstances, which the court first confirmed was available for a hijacking case. The defendants were fugitives, having fled to the Sudan from Iraq, where they had fallen foul of Saddam Hussein. They feared that they would be put to death if they were deported back to Iraq and they believed this to be imminent. They therefore decided to hijack an aeroplane bound for Jordan and effected this by the use of imitation weapons. The plane eventually landed at Stansted and after negotiations lasting eight hours, the defendants surrendered to the police. At their trial, the judge refused to put the defences of necessity and duress to the jury because the threat was not seen by him as **'sufficiently close and immediate to give rise to a virtually spontaneous reaction to the physical risk arising'**. The defendants appealed against their convictions.

The Court of Appeal affirmed the view taken in Hudson and Taylor that the threat must be imminent but need not be immediate, and questioned the later decision in Cole 1994, which had suggested otherwise. As a result, the court allowed the appeals on the grounds that the defence of duress of circumstances should have been left to the jury.

On the other hand, in Heath 1999 the appeal was rejected. The court decided that the defendant had ample time to seek police protection after being threatened by drug dealers. He had not done so because he was a heroin addict and did not want the police to be involved.

'or serious personal violence'

It is obvious from the definition in **AG v Whelan** that the threat must be a really serious one. In **Valderrama-Vega 1985**, the defendant gave three reasons for becoming involved in a drug smuggling operation against his will. He claimed that he and his family were threatened with death or injury if he did not comply, he was under severe financial pressure and that threats had been made to divulge his homosexual leanings. The judge told the jury to discount the last two fears, as they were not serious enough to constitute duress. He then told them that they should only allow the defence if they were convinced that the defendant committed the crimes solely because of the threats of violence.

The Court of Appeal agreed that the second and third threats had been rightly excluded but decided that the threat of violence did not have to be the only reason for his criminal activities. This part of the judgment, therefore, had been a misdirection but not a grave enough one to upset the conviction.

Similarly, in **Ortiz 1986**, the judge had again told the jury that duress was only available if the defendant acted as he did solely as a result of the threats. A threat had been made to harm the defendant's wife and child but, earlier in the proceedings, substantial inducements had also been given to the defendant to persuade him to carry out the crime. He had received business advantages, nearly £90,000 in cash, a family holiday and a flat in Chelsea. The jury refused to accept the defence of duress and convicted him of drug dealing.

The Court of Appeal upheld the conviction despite the judge's misdirection but did suggest that such a ruling should not be given in future.

'so great as to overbear the ordinary powers of human resistance'.

This question was looked at in the case of **Graham 1982**. He was a homosexual who lived with his wife and his homosexual lover, King. Graham claimed that he was frightened of King, because he had been violent towards both Graham and his wife. This had driven the wife from the matrimonial home, shortly before the crime took place. Graham also alleged that the Valium he was taking had increased his fear and made him agree to help in the murder of his wife. Mrs Graham was lured back to the house and strangled by King with a flex from the coffee percolator. The prosecution claimed that Graham had assisted in this action and with the disposal of the body afterwards. The defences of intoxication and duress were rejected and he was convicted of murder.

The Court of Appeal held that, if anything, the judge had been too favourable to the accused in his summing up and dismissed his appeal. It decided that the following two-fold test should be used with regard to duress:

- Was the defendant impelled to act as he did because, as a result of what he reasonably believed the other had said and done, he had good cause to fear that, if he did not act as he did, death or serious injury would result?
- Would a sober person of reasonable firmness, sharing the characteristics of the defendant have acted in the same way?

This can be broken down further into three separate points:

- The defendant's belief in the threat must have been a reasonable one
- he must have had good cause to fear that death or personal injury would result if he failed to participate
- a sober person of reasonable firmness, sharing the characteristics of the defendant, would have reacted in a similar way

Rejected characteristics

The question as to which characteristics of the accused can be attributed to the sober person of reasonable firmness has occupied the attention of the court in the last few years.

In **Bowen 1996**, the defendant had obtained goods on credit from over 40 electrical outlets and sold them to others. He claimed that he had only committed the offences because of threats to use petrol bombs against him and his family, and had not gone to the police because of his fear of retaliation. Evidence was put forward by the defence that Bowen only had an IQ of 68 and was especially vulnerable to threats.

The Court of Appeal rejected his appeal on the grounds of duress. The judges decided that his low intelligence fell short of mental impairment and characteristics such as excessive vulnerability, pliability and timidity were not factors shared by a person of reasonable firmness.

In the earlier cases of Hegarty 1994 and Horne 1994, the characteristics of a personality disorder in the first instance and vulnerability in the second case had also been rejected.

In **Bowen** however, an extension of the defence had taken place even though this did not help the defendant in question. **The court accepted that a recognised mental illness or psychiatric condition like post-traumatic stress disorder leading to learned helplessness, was among the characteristics that could be taken into account, along with age, severe physical disability, pregnancy and perhaps the person's sex.**

11.4.2 LIMITATIONS ON THE USE OF DURESS

Voluntary participation in a criminal enterprise

Even if both parts of the test in Graham are satisfied, the defence will not be allowed to a person who has voluntarily joined a gang or voluntarily taken part in a criminal exercise and is then forced to take part in activities of which he does not approve. This point was established in **Fitzpatrick 1977**, where the defendant had voluntarily joined the IRA but had later tried to leave the organisation. Threats were then made against both him and his mother so he was 'persuaded' to take part in an armed robbery in which he shot and killed an innocent person.

The Court of Appeal for Northern Ireland said that:

if a person voluntarily exposes and submits himself . . . to illegal compulsion, he cannot rely on the duress to which he has voluntarily exposed himself as an excuse either in respect of the crimes he commits against his will or in respect of his continued but unwilling association with

those capable of exercising upon him the duress which he calls in aid . . .

It was also made clear that the ruling was not confined to proscribed organisations like the IRA and this was affirmed in the case of **Sharp 1987**. The latter had been involved in a series of armed robberies on sub-post offices and in the latest attack the shop owner had been killed by another member of the gang. Sharp tried to argue that he had only remained involved because the ringleader had threatened to kill him.

The Court of Appeal reiterated that where the defendant:

voluntarily, and with knowledge of its nature joined a criminal organisation or gang which he knew might bring pressure on him to commit an offence and was an active member when he was put under such pressure, he cannot avail himself of the defence of duress . . .

This view of the law has been extended to certain defendants who consort with drug dealers and then cannot pay their suppliers, as in the cases of **Ali 1995, Flatt 1996, Heath 1999,** and **Harmer 2001**. In all these cases the defence of duress failed.

The decision in **Harmer** was criticised on the grounds that while the defendant knew that he was consorting with criminals for his drug supply, he did not know that he would be forced to commit a crime of the type he was forced to undertake.

This point was addressed in the case of **Z 2003**. The defendant, a former minder for a prostitute, claimed that he had been forced to commit a burglary because of threats made against him and his family by the girl's current minder and boyfriend. The latter was known as a man of violence, who boasted that he had already committed three murders. Immediately after the threats, he sent one of his armed associates with the defendant, to the scene of the burglary. The defendant was convicted of aggravated burglary but appealed.

Among other matters, the Court of Appeal decided that the judge had misdirected the jury on the question of the defendant voluntarily exposing himself to the risk of violence. That, on its own, was not sufficient to deprive him of the defence. He must have voluntarily exposed himself to the risk that he might be required, under threat of violence, to commit crimes of the seriousness of the type charged on the indictment.

This decision appears to lessen the strictness of the rule but even if the defence is put forward, the jury may not believe the defendant's account of the crime.

The crimes of murder and attempted murder

The courts have also had to decide whether the defence of duress should be made available for all crimes even the most serious one of murder. Judicial opinion on this has changed over the years.

In **DPP for Northern Ireland v Lynch 1975**, the defendant was ordered to drive a group of terrorists to the scene of the crime where they then murdered a policeman. The defendant took no part in this but later drove the men away. He claimed that he would have been shot if he refused to help but despite this, was convicted of murder.

The case reached the House of Lords where it was decided that the defence of duress was available for a secondary offender; a retrial was therefore ordered. Lord Wilberforce stated: 'Heinousness is a word of degree, and that there are lesser degrees of heinousness, even of involvement in homicide, seems beyond doubt. An accessory ... may (not necessarily must) bear a less degree than the actual killer.'

In **Abbott 1977**, the Privy Council had to decide whether the defence of duress was ever available for a principal offender. It was stated that this position had never been argued in an English court, although early legal writers had declared that it should not be.

In the present case, the defendant had taken part in a particularly horrible murder where the woman in question had been stabbed with a cutlass and then buried alive. The defendant alleged that he was forced to help because of threats made against him and his mother.

The Privy Council upheld the conviction, stating that it was **'incredible ... that in any civilised society, acts such as the appellant's, whatever threats may have been made to him, could be regarded as excusable or within the law'.**

No defence for secondary offenders

The precedent in **Abbott** was not actually binding on the English courts but was clearly affirmed in **Howe and Bannister 1987**. The defendants had been involved in the vicious murders of two young men, who were alleged to have 'grassed' on other gang members. The defendants had kicked and punched the first victim until he was near death but had not been involved in the final act of strangulation. In the second case however, they had been the actual killers. After their conviction for murder, they argued that the defence of duress should have been allowed.

The House of Lords unanimously disagreed. Lord Griffiths stated: 'We are facing a rising tide of violence and terrorism against which the law must stand firm recognising that its highest duty is to protect the freedom and lives of those who live under it'. He was strongly of the opinion that the defence should not be available to the actual killer. He then went on to decide that it should not be allowed for a secondary offender either, saying that it was neither rational nor fair to make such a distinction. This was because, in many cases, the latter was just as blameworthy as the actual

killer or often, as in the case of a contract killer, more so. He said that those who were obviously innocent of wrongdoing, as where a woman was forced to drive criminals to the scene of the crime, would not be prosecuted in the first place. He concluded his argument in the following way:

> As I can find no fair and certain basis upon which to differentiate between participants to a murder and as I am firmly convinced that the law should not be extended to the killer, I would depart from the decision of this House in DPP for Northern Ireland v Lynch 1975 and declare the law to be that duress is not available as a defence to a charge of murder or to attempted murder.

The judges also rejected the idea that duress should be a partial defence which, if successful, would reduce the offence from murder to manslaughter.

No defence for attempted murder

In **Gotts 1992**, a boy of 16 alleged that he had been ordered by his father to kill his mother otherwise he, instead, would be shot. He therefore stabbed his mother and seriously injured her but fortunately, she survived. The defence of duress was not allowed at his trial so the boy pleaded guilty and was put on probation for three years. The House of Lords was eventually called upon to decide the matter.

Lord Jauncey, for the majority, after reviewing the case of Howe, stated 'I can therefore see no justification in logic, morality or law in affording to an attempted murderer the defence which is withheld from a murderer'.

11.4.3 POSSIBLE REFORM OF DURESS BY THREATS

There has been little consensus on this subject and the judges in the cases of **Howe** and **Gotts** felt strongly that it was time for Parliament to intervene in relation to the defence of duress and clarify when it should, or should not be available. Some judges favour the complete abolition of the defence and believe that any circumstances excusing the defendant could be looked at when the defendant was sentenced. The minority in the case of **Gotts** felt that the defence should be available for all cases of duress, including murder. Similar confusion is apparent in the views of the Law Commission. This body has been looking at possible reforms on this subject since 1974 and, currently, takes a similar view of the defence to that of the minority in the cases mentioned above. In its latest proposals, found in the Law Commission Report No 218, *Legislating the Criminal Code: Offences Against the Person and General Principles 1993*, it suggests that the defence should be available for all crimes, including murder and attempted murder. It does however, recommend that the burden of proof for this defence should be shifted to the defence, as it is with insanity.

Under these proposed reforms, a person will have a complete defence if the crime was committed because of duress of threats. The defendant must have committed the crime because he knew or believed that he or another was being threatened with immediate death or serious injury or before he or another could obtain 'effective official protection'. A threat to damage property would not suffice. He must also have believed that there was no other way of preventing the threat being carried out. When assessing the seriousness of the threat, the courts would be asked to take both a subjective and objective approach. The threat to the defendant must be 'one which in all the circumstances (including any of his personal characteristics that affect its gravity) he cannot reasonably be expected to resist'. The Commission felt that the more restrictive test in **Graham** was not in line with other defences, especially self-defence, and also felt that the present separation of characteristics that could be taken into account, and those that could not, was unsatisfactory. The amended law would therefore change this. There would be no requirement to show 'good cause' for the fear and all the defendant's characteristics could be taken into account.

The amended defence would not however, be available to someone 'who knowingly and without reasonable excuse exposed himself to the risk of a threat', so presumably the existing rules on the voluntary joining of a criminal enterprise would remain.

◀ *Comment* _____

The proposals are a mixture of the current law and new additions. The main proposal is to make the defence available for murder and attempted murder. This would obviously make the law more rational but it also has certain drawbacks:

- It conflicts with the view taken by the majority of the Law Lords in **Howe** and **Gotts**.
- If the defence succeeded, someone who killed intentionally would be entitled to a complete acquittal. This might well cause extra distress to the victim's family.
- An awareness of the latter point might make the jury more inclined to reject the defence and find the accused guilty of murder. He would then be sentenced to life imprisonment, despite the threats made to him.
- The changes might lead those who otherwise would have taken a heroic stand to take the easier option.
- Even where there is an obvious threat of harm to the defendants and more sympathy for their plight, many would argue against a full acquittal. They would take the view that the vicious

behaviour of defendants like **Abbott, Howe, Bannister** and even **Gotts** should not be allowed to go unpunished completely, however horrible the circumstances in which they found themselves.

- The more subjective approach taken in the proposals could result in more acquittals of less deserving defendants, who would not be required to prove the reasonableness of their belief in as strict a way as in **Graham**. In addition, more of the defendant's characteristics could be taken into account. The 'sober person of reasonable firmness' would disappear which, it could be argued, might widen the defence in an unacceptable way. In **Lynch**, Lord Morris had forcibly stated that **'Duress must never be allowed to be the easy answer of those who can devise no other explanation for their conduct'**. It should however, be noted that the burden of proof would change and the onus would be on the defendant to establish the duress.

If Parliament failed to approve of such a change, another suggestion was to make duress a partial defence, allowing the charge to be reduced to manslaughter. This would deal with some of the concerns expressed above but this proposal, too, has its critics.

The main misgiving is that a person who has been subjected to the most awful threats, which few could be expected to resist, would still be charged with a very serious crime. Even those prepared to give up their own lives rather than take the life of another, might well succumb to threats directed at their children or other loved ones and it could be unfair to brand them as convicted killers.

It should also be noted that other alternatives have been put forward. One of these is to abolish the defence completely and make allowance for the duress in the sentencing process. This move would be out of line with most other common law jurisdictions and, arguably, would be a step backwards, rather than a reform. Another solution would be to retain the rule that duress cannot be used as a defence in cases of murder but change the mandatory aspect of the sentence, so that life imprisonment is not the only option. People against such a move would argue that the deterrent aspect would then be lessened.

It remains to be seen whether any of these changes will be effected in the foreseeable future. The current trend in Parliament is to increase criminal liability rather than to reduce it, so the Law Commission's proposals might not be welcomed.

11.5 DURESS OF CIRCUMSTANCES – AN EXTENSION OF NECESSITY

The defence of duress was, until recently, confined to threats against the person or someone close to him. Any other kind of pressure on him was felt to come under the possible defence of necessity and, as has been noted, was not often allowed.

Since the late 1980s, however, a special defence has sometimes been permitted which has become known as duress of circumstances. The following cases show where it can or cannot be used.

11.5.1 THE CREATION OF THIS NEW DEFENCE

Its origins began with the case of **Willer 1986.** The defendant believed that he was going to meet a fellow radio enthusiast but was directed instead down a very narrow alley, where he and his friends were confronted by a gang of youths. The latter surrounded the car, uttering death threats and trying to drag out the occupants. Willer managed to escape by mounting the pavement and driving through a small gap in the road but then discovered that one of his friends was missing. After an unsuccessful rescue attempt, he sought help from the police station but ended up being charged with reckless driving. He was convicted after being refused the defence of necessity. Fortunately, his run of bad luck ended when he appealed.

The Court of Appeal decided that necessity was not the appropriate defence; this, they argued should have been duress. Watkins L J concluded: 'the assistant recorder upon those facts should have directed that he would leave to the jury the question as to whether or not upon the outward or return journey, or both, the appellant was wholly driven by force of circumstance into doing what he did and did not drive the car otherwise than under that form of compulsion, ie under duress'.

11.5.2 THE DEVELOPMENT OF DURESS OF CIRCUMSTANCES

The defence was developed further in the case of **Conway 1989,** another reckless driving case, although arguably one with less merit. The accused had driven off erratically and at high speed after two plain clothed policemen in an unmarked car approached him. His version of events (substantially different to that of the prosecution) was that one of his passengers strongly believed that this was a second attempt to cause him serious harm and had urged the driver to try to evade the attackers. The defendant was convicted of reckless driving but appealed.

The Court of Appeal confirmed that:

necessity can only be a defence to a charge of reckless driving where the facts establish 'duress of circumstances' as in R v Willer . . . i.e. where the defendant was constrained by circumstances to drive as he did to avoid death or serious bodily harm to himself or some other person.

The same rules as duress of threats

In the above case, the judges agreed that 'a defence of duress of circumstances is a logical consequence of the existence of duress as that term is ordinarily understood, i.e. 'do this or else'.' Rather confusingly, however, they went on to state: 'This approach does no more than recognise that duress is an example of necessity. Whether 'duress of circumstances' is called 'duress' or 'necessity' does not matter. What is important is that, whatever it is called, it is subject to the same limitations as 'do this or else' species of duress.'

After **Conway** therefore, it was clear that the new defence had been recognised but also that it was subject to the same limitations as duress, i.e. it was only possible to use it where there was a fear of death or personal injury.

This point was confirmed in the odd case of **Martin 1989**, yet another driving case. The defendant claimed that, even though he had been disqualified from driving, he had been forced to drive his stepson to work because his wife had threatened to commit suicide if he did not comply! Doctors supported the view that his wife did have suicidal tendencies and was capable of carrying out the threat. She had been shouting and screaming and making such threats because her son had overslept and she had feared that he would be sacked if he were late for work.

Once again, although the Court of Appeal was sceptical as to the success of the defence, it decided that it should have been put before the jury. The court stated that the authorities were now clear and that:

English law does recognise a defence of necessity. Most commonly this defence arises as duress, that is pressure on the accused's will from the wrongful threats or violence of another. Equally however it can arise from other objective dangers threatening the accused or others. Arising thus it is conveniently called 'duress of circumstances'.

The Court of Appeal stressed that the defendant had to pass the two tests established in Graham for duress of threats:

- That he had good cause to fear death or serious injury unless he acted in the way that he had.
- That a sober person of reasonable firmness, sharing the same characteristics as the accused, would have responded in the same way.

The defendant in **DPP v Bell 1992** was able to establish this when he drove off while under the influence of alcohol, because of his fear that those pursuing him intended to harm him. **In addition, the fact that the defendant had only driven a short way before stopping, rather than all the way home, showed that he was acting reasonably. It was on this latter point that the drink/driving appeals failed in the cases of DPP v Davis and DPP v Pittaway in 1994.**

In the case of **Cole 1994**, the defendant claimed that he had robbed two building societies because he needed the money to repay moneylenders. He alleged that they had attacked him with a baseball bat and had threatened him, his girlfriend and their child with further violence if he did not find the money.

The Court of Appeal decided that the defendant could not rely on duress by threats because the moneylenders had not ordered him to rob the banks, i.e. the person making the threats had not nominated the crime to be committed. Neither could he put forward the defence of duress of circumstances, because the connection between the threat and the criminal act was not as close or immediate as in Willer, Conway and Martin, 'where the offence was virtually a spontaneous reaction to the physical risk arising'.

The appeal court may have been alarmed at the escalation in the use of this defence because they echoed an earlier call for Parliament to legislate on the matter and decided that, in the meantime, the defence of duress should be rigidly confined.

It therefore comes as somewhat of a surprise to note the decision in **Pommell 1995. In this case, the Court of Appeal confirmed that, prima facie, the defence of duress of circumstances was available for all crimes except murder, attempted murder and some forms of treason.**

In **Cairns 1999**, the defence was allowed for charges of dangerous driving and wounding with intent. The victim, who had been drinking, spread-eagled himself across the bonnet of the defendant's car with his face up against the windscreen and, fearing for his safety, the defendant drove off with him still in this position. The driver, who was said to be small and rather timid, claimed that he was also afraid of the victim's friends who chased after the car, shouting and waving their arms. They alleged that they were merely trying to stop the defendant driving away. When the car came to a hump in the road, the victim fell off the bonnet and the defendant drove over him, breaking his spine. The trial judge advised the jury that the defence was only available if **'actually necessary to avoid the evil in question'** and the accused was convicted.

The Court of Appeal decided that this was a

misdirection and the conviction was quashed. After Martin, the jury was asked to look at the defendant's perception of the threat and then consider whether he had acted reasonably and proportionately with regard to it. The Court also approved its direction in Abdul-Hussain 1999, mentioned earlier.

The defence succeeded on a similar point in **Safi and others 2003.** The defendants were members of the Organisation of Young Intellectuals of Afghanistan who had hijacked a plane there and eventually landed it at Stansted Airport, as reported in the newspaper article opposite, at the beginning of the trial. The men were fleeing from the brutal Taliban regime and argued that they were in imminent fear of their lives if they stayed. The jury in the first trial could not agree on a verdict but the men were convicted after a second trial. They then claimed that the judge had misdirected the jury by stating the elements of duress differently from the first judge, who had relied heavily on the direction in **Graham**. The second judge believed that there had to be evidence that the defendants were, in fact, in imminent peril, rather than whether they genuinely believed this. This was important because the passengers had been kept in the aircraft at Stansted for four days. The prosecution alleged that once the defendants had reached England, they should have released the passengers and given themselves up as they were no longer in imminent peril. The defendants claimed that they were still in fear that they would be returned to Afghanistan or that the police would storm the plane, right up to the time the requested United Nations representative arrived.

The Court of Appeal decided that there had been a material misdirection on this point, which could have made a difference to the jury's decision. Longmore LJ stated:

'We have reached the conclusion that the suggested direction in Graham continues to be the law in relation to duress and that Sir Edwin, (the trial judge), was, with respect,

incorrect to hold that there must be a threat in fact, rather than something the defendant reasonably believed to be a threat, before the defence of duress can be invoked.'

The appeal was allowed but the court took pains to note that their decision was not to be seen as a charter for future hijackers. The judge ended by saying: 'We have every confidence that future juries given a correct direction, in accordance with the law set out in Graham in 1982, will convict in appropriate cases and acquit if it is right to do so.'

Limits on the defence

We have seen that the potential scope of the defence of duress of circumstances is now wide enough to cover many different situations but as it shares the same principles as duress of threats, it is not available for murder or attempted murder. It may also not be allowed for conspiracy or certain forms of treason, as suggested in **Abdul-Hussain 1999. In the latter case, the Court of Appeal made its fourth plea to Parliament to put the defence on a statutory footing and thus set its boundaries.**

'We seized plane to flee Taliban horrors'

STANSTED HIJACK TRIAL

By Paul Cheston, Courts Correspondent

An Afghan university lecturer today told an Old Bailey jury how the horrors of the Taliban regime drove him to lead the armed hijacking of a plane and hold 170 passengers hostage at Stansted airport.

Ali Safi, 38, described how he was forced to watch a woman being stoned to death as her eight-year-old daughter begged for mercy for the 'crime' – in the eyes of the Taliban – of leaving the house without being accompanied by a man.

He claimed the local authority arranged for lorry-loads of stones to be brought in and the leader of the Taliban's 'department of prevention of crime and promotion of virtue' cast the first stone.

The father-of-three said his own son had died from a simple respiratory problem because the young boy was taken ill when he was away and the Taliban, under their hardline moral code, would not permit his wife to leave home alone to take the child to hospital. Safi himself was arrested for playing chess and as a punishment was beaten so

badly with cables and a metal bar that his back turned the colour of an aubergine, the court heard.

On Fridays, he said, the local football stadium was turned into a punishment block where arms and legs were hacked off those who had offended the regime. He claimed the amputated limbs were hung from trees.

When the Taliban took control of the country in 1996, Safi said he saw death squads roaming the streets shooting on sight. They broke into a hospital next to his home and indiscriminately shot nurses and patients. Bodies were ordered to be left lying in the streets as deterrents despite the 40 degree heat and the threat of disease.

A few years earlier in Kabul he had seen the bullet-ridden body of President Najibullah, who had been overthrown by the Mujahideen, and his brother, hanging from a traffic pole in the middle of the street.

Safi is one of 11 defendants, aged between 20 and 38, said to have seized the plane which was originally on an internal flight from Kabul in February last year. They were armed with four handguns and explosive grenades.

They are accused of forcing it to fly across several former Soviet countries before eventually landing at Stansted where – in an operation costing £2 million – it was surrounded by armed police before the siege ended after 77 hours.

Safi, from the northern city of Masar-i-Sharif, said women who had once enjoyed the normal freedoms of the West were liable to be arrested and either stoned to death or subjected to public lashings for any breach of the ruthless and extreme moral code enforced by the Taliban.

'In one of the worst experiences of my life I saw a woman stoned to death who I knew because she lived in our area,' he told the jury through an interpreter.

'I saw a hole being dug and the judge decide that she had left her house without permission of her husband. They placed her in the hole.'

He said that the head of the 'prevention of crime and promotion of virtue' committee was the first person to throw a stone and that the people who had been ordered to watch were forced to stone the woman to death.

Safi added: 'They stoned her until the hole was full, then a doctor pronounced she was still alive so they kept on stoning her until she died. Her eight-year-old daughter was running around her begging people not to thrown stones at her mother.'

Safi and nine other defendants deny hijack. The 11th defendant, who does not face that charge, has pleaded not guilty to possessing explosives and arms. The case continues.

Evening Standard, 31 October 2001

Meanwhile, the defence continues to develop. **In Shayler 2001**, it was decided that the defences of both necessity and duress, as developed, were *prima facie* available under the **Official Secrets Act 1989**. In the case at issue however, the appeal failed.

No half-way house

If the defence of duress of circumstances succeeds, it is a complete defence, entitling the defendant to an acquittal. In **Symonds 1998**, the Court of Appeal decided that it was not correct in a dangerous driving case, merely to reduce the offence to careless driving.

11.5.3 POSSIBLE REFORM OF DURESS OF CIRCUMSTANCES

The Law Commission has recognised the value of this defence and has included it in its Draft Criminal Law Bill 1993. These current proposals differ from what is in the *Draft Criminal Code*. The newer version would permit the defence to be used in crimes of murder and attempted murder, but would change the burden of proof, which would now be on the accused. This would bring this defence in line with duress of threats. Under Clause 26, the defence would be available for a defendant who only commits a crime because 'he knows or believes that it is immediately necessary to avoid death or serious injury to himself or another. The danger that he knows or believes to exist must be such that in all the circumstances (including any of his personal characteristics that affect its gravity) he cannot reasonably be expected to act otherwise'.

Comment

It will be seen from the suggested reforms that the defence of duress of circumstances has been accepted as good law by the Law Commission and would be extended to cover all offences including murder and attempted murder. The merits and possible problems with this are the same as those discussed under duress by threats. It can also be seen that the test in **Martin** has been watered down, although there is still an objective element when assessing the actions that the defendant has taken in response to the threat. Hopefully the clarification by the Court of Appeal in **Safi** of the test to be used for establishing this form of duress will lessen the appeals in this area.

Activity

- In small groups, or individually in written form, discuss the following question:

  'At the present time, English law recognises the three separate, but related defences of necessity, duress and duress of circumstances. Is this a satisfactory state of the law?'

- Decide whether a defence of necessity, duress or duress of circumstances is available in the following scenarios:

  Charles took part in the killing of James after Mary threatened to commit suicide if he refused to help.

  Anne found herself surrounded by a hostile crowd in the middle of town. She saw George's Mercedes parked nearby, with the keys still in the ignition, so jumped in and sped away at 60 miles per hour. She has been charged with theft and dangerous driving.

  William and Victoria were the only survivors of a plane crash. After 15 days without food, William killed and ate Victoria.

- Critically examine whether a relaxation of the current limits on the defence of duress, on the lines suggested by the Law Commission, would open the floodgates to a rush of possibly unworthy claims.

11.6 MARITAL COERCION

This very limited defence only applies to a wife who can prove that she committed an offence other than treason and murder in the presence of, and under the coercion of, her husband.

The defence was originally formulated at common law, where it was presumed that a wife was acting under the coercion of her husband unless the prosecution could prove otherwise. In 1925 this presumption was abolished by **s47 Criminal Justice Act 1927. Currently, marital coercion only exists as a defence in such a situation. Wives need to show that they are validly married. In Ditta 1988**, Lord Lane expressed doubts as to whether the defence could be extended to polygamous marriages.

In Cairns 2003, the Court of Appeal decided that the trial judge had misdirected the jury on the elements of this defence after a wife had been convicted of conspiracy to supply heroin and her appeal was successful.

 Comment

Probably, most people would agree with the late Sir John Smith when he declared that the defence of marital coercion **'is a relic of the past which ought to have been abolished long ago.'** The Law Commission recommended its abolition back in 1977 but, as yet, no reform has been effected.

TEN KEY FACTS ON NECESSITY, DURESS OF THREATS AND DURESS OF CIRCUMSTANCES

- The defence of necessity is a very limited defence, confined to specific situations (**Bourne 1939, Johnson v Phillips 1976, Road Traffic Act 1988 (as amended), Re F (Mental Patient: Sterilization) 1990** and **Re A (children) 2000**). Apart from exceptional circumstances, such as those in the latter case, it is not available for the crime of murder (**Dudley and Stephens 1884**), nor where statutes do not intend the defence to be available (**Cichon v DPP 1994, DPP v Harris 1995**).

- Duress of threats provides an excuse for the commission of a crime. It is definitely available if the person or his family is threatened (**Hurley and Murray 1967**), and may well apply if others are at risk.

- It can only be used where the defendant reasonably fears death or serious injury, and a sober person of reasonable firmness, sharing the characteristics of the accused, would have acted in the same way (**AG v Whelan 1934** and **Graham 1982**). The word 'characteristics' would include age, sex, mental impairment and post-traumatic stress disorder (**Bowen 1996**), but not a personality disorder (**Hegarty 1994**), excessive vulnerability, timidity or pliability (**Horne 1994, Bowen 1996**) or a low IQ (**Bowen 1996**). Threats to reveal someone's poor financial position or his homosexual tendencies are not enough (**Valderama-Vega 1985**), but the threat of death or serious injury need not be the sole reason for the defendant's act (**Valerama-Vega 1985, Ortiz 1986**).

- The threat must be imminent, without the prospect of getting official protection (**Heath 1999**), although the courts may look at extenuating circumstances, such as the age of the defendant and the belief that official protection is inadequate (**Hudson and Taylor 1971, Abdul-Hussain and Others 1999**).

- Even if the requirements for the defence are satisfied, it is not normally available for those who voluntarily join gangs or other illegal enterprises (**Fitzpatrick 1977, Sharp 1987, Ali 1995, Flatt 1996**). It might be allowed in cases where the defendant has not anticipated that he might be pressurised into committing a crime, as in **Z 2003**. The defence cannot be used in cases of murder, by either a principal offender (**Abbott 1977**) or a secondary offender (**Howe 1987**). Neither is it a defence for attempted murder (**Gotts 1992**).

- Duress of circumstances is an extension of the defence of necessity but has the same rules and limitations as duress of threats. There is no actual threat from a person; instead it comes from the circumstances. If successful, the defendant is entitled to a full acquittal (**Symonds 1998**); it cannot be used to reduce a charge.

- The defence is available where the defendant fears that death or personal injury will result if he does not commit the crime. The fear need not exist in fact but the defendant must reasonably believe it (**Graham 1982, Safi 2003**). The jury must also be satisfied that a sober person of reasonable firmness, sharing some of the characteristics of the defendant, would have acted in a similar way (**Graham 1982, Martin1989**). Such a defence was first suggested in **Willer 1986**, although it was not specifically named as such until **Conway**

1989. Early cases concerned driving offences but in **Pommell 1995, Abdul-Hussain 1999, Shayler 2001** and **Safi 2003**, the Court of Appeal decided that the defence can be used for nearly all crimes, the exceptions being some forms of treason, murder, attempted murder and possibly conspiracy.

● Despite this extension, it was stated in **Cole 1994** and on three other occasions that Parliament should legislate on the defence of duress and meanwhile it should be 'rigidly confined'.

● As in duress by threats, normally duress of circumstances can only be used if the threat is perceived by the defendant to be imminent (**Bell 1992, Safi 2003**). It was felt that the danger had passed in **DPP v Davis 1994** and **DPP v Pittaway 1994**.

● In **Pommell 1995**, however, the Court of Appeal stated that if there were possible explanations for the delay, the matter should be put before the jury.

11.7 PUBLIC AND PRIVATE DEFENCE

The defences described below, particularly self-defence come under this blanket heading because a party may lawfully use force, provided that this is not excessive, in the defence of both public and private interests. He is therefore allowed to use such force in defence of the following:

● To prevent crime or assist in the lawful arrest of an offender
● To prevent a breach of the peace
● To protect his property or to prevent a trespass
● To protect himself from unlawful violence
● To protect himself from unlawful detention

11.7.1 PREVENTING A CRIME OR ASSISTING AN ARREST

The law on this was developed at common law but is now found under **s3 Criminal Law Act 1967. This states:**

a person may use such force as is reasonable in the circumstances in the prevention of crime or in assisting in the lawful arrest of offenders or suspected offenders, or of persons unlawfully at large.

In the case of **Renouf 1986**, the defendant had been working on the forecourt of his garage when the occupants of a Volvo car drew up and threw things at him. He suffered an injury to his arm and his car windscreen was damaged. After calling to his wife to call the police, he followed the men in his car and eventually forced them onto a grass verge. He was convicted of reckless driving (still in existence at that time), but appealed.

The Court of Appeal held that the possible defence under s3, that he was trying to assist in the lawful arrest of offenders, should have been put before the jury and quashed the conviction.

This statutory defence is also open to a person who is personally threatened, in addition to the common law defence of self-defence, discussed below. While he is defending himself against the attack on his person or the person of another, he will, in most cases, also be preventing a crime being committed. The **Criminal Law Act** makes it clear that the common law defence remains in areas where the act does not provide a defence and in **Cousins 1982**, it was stated that both defences exist and can be used in tandem with each other.

Defending property

In earlier times, a person was allowed to stand firm and fight against the loss of his property whereas if the attack were against him personally, he was supposed to retreat from the danger. In **Hussey 1924**, the Lord Chief Justice quashed the conviction of a man who barricaded himself in when threatened with alleged unlawful eviction. He then fired a gun through the door at the three people armed with household tools who were seeking to remove him, wounding two of them. It is extremely unlikely that a similar decision would be arrived at today but it is still clear that a person can seek the help of the law in protecting his property. In **AG's Reference (No 2 of 1983) 1984**, the Court of Appeal decided, rather surprisingly, that it was not unlawful for a person to make up petrol bombs to try to prevent crime and defend his property in an area where there had been extensive rioting and further threats were imminent.

11.7.2 SELF-DEFENCE AT COMMON LAW

The judges have decided that a person may use reasonable force to protect himself or another person if he fears an attack or one actually occurs. This involves a two-part test, involving both subjective and objective elements:

● Did the defendant believe that he needed to defend himself in this way?
● Was the force he used reasonable?

In Shaw 2002, the Privy Council upheld the defendant's appeal against a conviction of murder because these two elements had not been separated in a clear enough way.

The subjective element

The jury should decide this point by looking at the circumstances from the view of the accused. This could mean that the belief need not always be a reasonable one. The cases of **Williams (Gladstone) 1987** and **Beckford 1988**, discussed earlier in this chapter, show this aspect of the rule in operation. The courts are not so generous if the defendant is merely making the mistake about his need to defend himself because he is intoxicated.

This point was made clear in **O'Grady 1987**. The defendant was addicted to drink and, on the night in question had consumed eight flagons of cider! He then retired to his flat with two friends. In the morning, one of these friends found him covered with blood and the other friend dead. O'Grady claimed that he and the victim had been involved in a fight in the night and when he had felt the victim he was cold. The defendant reported the matter to the police and argued that he had only acted in self-defence. When he was examined, a number of cuts and bruises were noted which might have supported his version of events, but he was still convicted of manslaughter.

The Court of Appeal confirmed that the defence of self-defence would be available to a 'sober man who mistakenly believes he is in danger of immediate death at the hands of an attacker' but not to a person whose mistake was caused by voluntary intoxication.

No need to retreat

In the older cases of common law self-defence the defence sometimes failed unless the defendant showed that he had tried to retreat from the danger.

In **Julien 1969** the Court of Appeal decided that instead:

what is necessary is that he should demonstrate by his actions that he does not want to fight. He must demonstrate that he is prepared to temporise and disengage and perhaps to make some physical withdrawal.

In the following case, the Court of Appeal went further. In **Bird 1985** a 17-year-old girl became very upset when an ex-boyfriend appeared at her party with a new girlfriend in tow. He left after a heated argument but later returned alone and the argument continued. The defendant threw a glass of Pernod over him and a physical fight developed. Bird alleged that she was held up against a wall and had then lunged at the victim. The glass was still in her hand when she hit him in the face, causing him to lose an eye.

The Court of Appeal decided that the case of Julien had placed too great an obligation on the defendant to demonstrate that he did not wish to fight, which was not reflected in the later Privy Council decision in Palmer 1971. This case had decided that 'there are no prescribed words which must be employed in or adopted in a summing up'. The court also stated that the courts had gone too far when they said that the defendant must demonstrate a desire not to fight. This was not consistent with the rule that a person can use force, not merely to counter an attack, but also to ward off an attack honestly and reasonably believed to be imminent. It was felt that the defendant's demonstration that he did not want to fight was the best evidence that he was acting reasonably and in good faith in self-defence; but was no more than evidence to this effect. Bird's conviction for wounding was therefore quashed.

The objective element

It has just been noted that the defendant's belief that he has to act in self-defence need not be a reasonable belief. **With regard to the actual force used, however, the courts have now made it very plain that only reasonable force can be used to counter the threat and that this is an objective test.** This had been felt to be the law but some doubt was cast upon this view in the case of **Scarlett 1993**. A pub landlord forcibly ejected a drunken customer who then fell down the steps and was killed. The judgment seemed to imply that the test for deciding whether the force used was excessive was also subjective.

This was firmly denied by the Court of Appeal in Owino 1996. The court said that if such a view were taken, it would allow a person who was merely threatened with a punch, to shoot the other and plead self-defence. The court concluded 'That clearly is not, and cannot be, the law'.

The use of excessive force

It has therefore been made abundantly clear that an objective view is taken when assessing whether the defendant has used reasonable or excessive force. Should the force be found to be excessive by this standard, the defence will fail and the defendant will be guilty of whatever crime has been committed. This is shown clearly in the cases of **Clegg** and **Martin**.

In **Clegg 1995**, the defendant had been on a night patrol in West Belfast, in order to catch joy riders. He had not been informed of the reason for the patrol but it was established at his trial that he did not believe the offenders were terrorists.

The car containing the victim was initially stopped at the checkpoint but then accelerated away in the centre of the road with its headlights full on. Someone in the checkpoint team shouted that it should be stopped and all four members of Clegg's team fired at it. Clegg's evidence was that he fired four bullets into the windscreen and one into the side of the car as it passed. He alleged that a fellow soldier had been struck by the speeding car and his life was in danger. Scientific evidence, on the other hand, showed that the last shot had been fired when the car had already passed and was over 50 feet further along the road. The 18-year-old passenger had been hit in the back. It also emerged later that the speeding car had not caused Private Ainbow's injuries and he was later convicted of conspiring to pervert the course of justice.

There were no juries in such cases in Northern

Ireland in view of the political situation; therefore it was a single judge who found Clegg guilty of murder. He found that there was insufficient evidence for him to use **s3 Criminal Law Act** in his defence. The Court of Appeal disagreed but went on to decide that there had been no miscarriage of justice because the force used by Clegg with regard to the fourth shot had not been reasonable; it had been fired with the intention to kill or seriously injure the victim.

Nevertheless, the Court of Appeal called on Parliament to consider making a change in the law on this subject and, meanwhile, put a point of law to the House of Lords. This was whether a killing by a police officer or soldier in the course of his duty should be regarded as manslaughter rather than murder where the force used is excessive and unreasonable.

The House of Lords decided that it would be impractical to make a distinction between excessive force used in trying to prevent a crime or apprehend a suspect and any excessive force used in self-defence, particularly as the two often overlap. Their Lordships then reviewed authorities such as Palmer 1971, a Privy Council decision, McInnes, a Court of Appeal decision in the same year, and Zecevic v DPP 1987, an Australian case. They came to the conclusion that 'there is no half-way house. There is no rule that a defendant who has used a greater degree of force than was necessary in the circumstances should be found guilty of manslaughter rather than murder. . . . The defence either succeeds or it fails. If it succeeds the defendant is acquitted. If it fails, he is guilty of murder.' Clegg's conviction for murder therefore, was upheld.

He was later allowed a retrial when fresh forensic evidence was produced and, in March 1999, his conviction was quashed. **The judge decided that while much of Clegg's testimony was 'a farrago of deceit and lies' it could not be proved conclusively that he had fired the fatal shot.**

The Norfolk farmer, Tony Martin, was only partially successful in his appeal. He had been found guilty of murder after using excessive force in self-defence when fatally shooting a 16-year-old burglar and injuring another.

The Court of Appeal agreed with the jury that the force used to repel the burglars had been excessive, no matter how great Martin's fears. The court was prepared instead to accept fresh evidence, allowing the partial defence of diminished responsibility to be put forward and, as noted in Chapter 4, the life sentence for murder was reduced to five years for manslaughter.

◀ *Comment*

In **Clegg**, their Lordships had the opportunity to 'bite the bullet' and change the rules so that a manslaughter verdict could be substituted for murder, in cases where excessive force was used in self-defence or prevention of crime. They preferred to maintain the status quo but if they had acted more radically, they would not have faced the criticism that they were acting alone or against informed opinion. Back in 1958, in the case of **Howe** (not the same **Howe** as in duress), the Australian courts had decided that a killing by excessive force in self-defence should be treated as manslaughter, not murder (although they later brought their law into line with the English courts). Our Criminal Law Revision Committee also favoured a more liberal defence and suggested a change in the law, as did a Select Committee of the House of Lords when its members looked into the question of murder and life imprisonment.

Whether such a change should only be effected in relation to the police and armed services, as some have argued or apply more universally is a contentious issue. Perhaps a stronger case can be made out for the police and armed services because of the tense situations in which they may find themselves, where the need for a split-second decision is vital. On the other hand, it could be an unwise move to give more licence to limited groups in the community.

At the time of writing, the matter is once again in the spotlight as a result of the support given to the Householder Protection Bill, a Private Members' Bill, by the Metropolitan Police Commissioner and the Conservative Party. The Government, too, originally was of the opinion that the law needed to be amended, but after a change of Home Secretary, has rethought the matter, as seen in the newspaper article below.

Blair U-turn on right to tackle intruders

By Joe Murphy

Tony Blair today shied away from new laws to guarantee the right of homeowners to fight back against burglars.

The Government announced it would not support Tory proposals to change the law to give people stronger rights to use physical force to protect their homes and families.

Home Secretary Charles Clarke is believed to be behind the decision, which comes only a month after Mr Blair told the Commons he was minded to change or clarify the law. Tory leader Michael Howard has promised a Bill to amend it in favour of crime victims.

Under existing law, the public must limit themselves to 'reasonable force'. The Tory Bill, which had its first reading in the Commons today, would change this to allow all but 'grossly disproportionate force'. Mr Clark said the month-long government review had concluded the current law was 'sound'. He said new guidance would be issued to police and the public explaining that householders can use force, though strictly only in self-defence and not against a fleeing criminal.

He said the Crown Prosecution Service, the Director of Public Prosecutions and the Association of Chief Police Officers back the new guidance, which will say people should not be arrested or prosecuted unless they are deemed to have caused unnecessary harm. It will be made clear to the public that the law ensures 'appropriate steps to protect themselves, their family and property will always be justified'.

Evening Standard, 12 January 2005

FIVE KEY FACTS ON SELF-DEFENCE

- Most of the law on this subject comes from two main sources. **S3 Criminal Law Act 1967** allows a party to use reasonable force to prevent a crime or to assist in the apprehension of offenders and the common law defence of self-defence is available where a person uses reasonable force to protect himself or another or their property. The two areas can be used in conjunction with each other (**Cousins 1982**). In both, a defendant may use reasonable force to avert the danger, and the jury will decide the matter (**Renouf 1986**).

- The belief that an attack is imminent is decided on a subjective basis, so an honest but unreasonable belief will suffice (**Williams (Gladstone) 1987, Beckford 1988**), although this rule will not apply if the mistake is caused by intoxication (**O'Grady 1987**).

- There is no longer a need for the defendant to retreat from the danger (**Julien 1969, Palmer 1971** and **Bird 1985**), nor need he demonstrate that he has no desire to fight (**Bird 1985**).

- The question of whether the force used is reasonable is decided objectively (**Owino 1996, Martin 2001**), and will apply equally to the police and armed services (**Clegg 1995**).

- If the defence is successful, it results in a full acquittal; there is no half-way house, allowing the crime of murder to be reduced to manslaughter (**Clegg 1995**). The defendant would need to find another defence, as in **Martin 2001.**

Activity

Fred had an argument with Wilma. He picked up some pebbles and indicated that he was going to throw them at her. Wilma could have deflected the blow quite easily but instead, picked up a boulder and hit Fred with it, fracturing his skull in two places. Fred later died in hospital.

Advise Wilma on the issue of self-defence.

11.7.3 POSSIBLE REFORM OF THE DEFENCE OF SELF-DEFENCE

Clause 27 of the *Draft Criminal Law Bill* states that a person may use force to protect himself or another from harm or from damage to their property or to prevent a crime or breach of the peace. The use of force must be 'such as is reasonable in the circumstances as he believes them to be', which largely restates the present position, with its objective and subjective elements.

As described more fully in Chapter 4, the Law Commission's Provisional Conclusions on Partial Defences to Murder, dated May 2004, suggested amending the defence of provocation to include cases where the defendant killed because he feared serious violence directed towards himself or another. The Commission added in its report **'Since our proposal for provocation is that it should be recast in a way which would include (subject to safeguards) excessive force in self-defence, we would not propose a separate partial defence of that kind'.**

Self-assessment questions on Chapter 11

1. Describe the principle regarding mistake laid down in the case of **Tolson** and show how this was altered by the cases of **Morgan** and **B (a minor) v DPP** and, more recently, by the **Sexual Offences Act 2003**.
2. Why were the appeals in **Williams** and **Beckford** successful but not those of **Fotheringham** and **O'Grady**?
3. Why did the defence of necessity fail in the case of **Dudley and Stephens**? Why then did it succeed in **Re A (children)**?
4. Distinguish between duress of threats and duress of circumstances.
5. It was previously believed that the threat had to be an immediate one. How has this been affected by the decisions in **Hudson and Taylor**, **Abdul-Hussain and Others** and **Safi**?
6. Examine the different elements of the test for duress, as laid down in the case of **Graham**.
7. Using cases to support your answer, describe two groups of people who are unable to benefit from the defences of duress of threats and duress of circumstances.
8. Explain why the defendants were successful in their claims of duress of circumstances in **Willer, Martin** and **Safi** but failed in **Davis, Cole** and **Cairns**.
9. Distinguish between **s3 Criminal Law Act 1967** and self-defence at common law. With regard to the latter, describe the two elements that have to be established.
10. Why was the defence of public and private defence not originally available for **Clegg** and **Martin**? What was the eventual outcome of these two high profile cases?

Chapter 12

PARTIES TO A CRIME

12.1 INTRODUCTION

As the title of the chapter suggests, more than one person may be involved in a crime. For example, two or more people may decide to carry out an armed robbery on a bank or to break into a house in order to steal. **If they commit the offence together, they are considered in law to be joint principals. If one party merely helps the other to commit the crime, he is known by a variety of names. He is normally known as a secondary offender, but could also be called an accessory or an accomplice. In some of the older cases, he may have been classed, rather confusingly, as a principal in the second degree.**

This chapter looks at both types of offenders in the following way:

✔ The law on participation
✔ The principal offender
✔ The different types of secondary offender
✔ The *actus reus* of accomplices
✔ The *mens rea* of secondary offenders
✔ Problem areas
✔ Suggested reform on secondary offenders.

12.2. THE LAW ON PARTICIPATION

By whatever title an accomplice is known, the law takes a very strict attitude towards him. The law is to be found in a very old statute, which was amended by the **Criminal Law Act 1967.**

- **S8 Accessories and Abettors Act 1861, as amended, states that 'Whosoever shall aid, abet, counsel and procure the commission of any indictable offence .... shall be liable**

to be tried, indicted and punished as a principal offender'
- **S44 Magistrates Courts Act 1980 takes the same approach with regard to summary offences.**

If this is the case, we need to examine why a distinction is made between principal offenders and accomplices.

- **It could be important when sentencing because in most cases the judge has some flexibility.**
- **The *actus reus* and *mens rea* of secondary participation is different to that required for the principal.**
- **Even if liability is strict in relation to the principal, the prosecution will still need to prove some form of *mens rea* in relation to any secondary offenders.**

12.3 THE PRINCIPAL OFFENDER

It has been noted that the person who directly brings about the *actus reus* of the offence, i.e. the main perpetrator of the crime, is known as the principal.

It has also been seen in many cases throughout this book, that it is possible to have more than one principal. A shocking example is shown in the newspaper article, opposite.

The test to decide whether an offender is a principal or a secondary offender is to discover whether his act is the most immediate cause of the *actus reus* or whether he is merely helping that cause to be effected.

Jail for pair who poisoned boy to death with salt

By Patrick McGowan

A childless couple were found guilty today of killing a three-year-old boy they had planned to adopt when he failed to meet their expectations of comfortable family living.

Ian and Angela Gay were both sentenced to five years' jail after being convicted at Worcester Crown Court of poisoning Christian Blewitt with salt and causing him a fatal head injury.

The couple were cleared of murder and found guilty of manslaughter.

The child was admitted to hospital five weeks into a trial placement with the couple at their former home in Bromsgrove, Worcestershire.

Christian had been taken from his biological mother, who had neglected him, shortly after his first birthday and was placed with the Gays with his younger brother and sister in November 2002.

The couple had been told about his difficult start in life during the adoption process managed by Sandwell Social Services, However, only days into the 13-week placement, Mr Gay 37, who quit his job to become a full-time househusband, rang his caseworker to complain about the child whom he said was uncommunicative.

He described Christian as 'brainless', 'a vegetable' and 'a zombie'.

On 8 December, the child was taken to hospital in Dudley, West Midlands, suffering from high sodium levels and head injuries, from which he later died.

The court heard evidence from medical experts but it may never be known what happened to Christian.

In the hours before former engineer Mr Gay carried him into casualty, the only people with him were himself and his wife.

The prosecution claimed the couple, who bought a five-bedroom house for their new family, became disenchanted with Christian when he rejected Mr Gay. In police interviews, Mr Gay said his wife, who returned to work as an actuary earlier than agreed with social workers, became upset by Christian's behaviour and had wanted to send the children back.

On 7 December, Christian had bitten, headbutted and kicked Mrs Gay. The following day, after Mr Gay returned from tending his cabin cruiser, the boy had smeared gravy over his face and thrown food on the kitchen floor.

Mr Gay said: 'He had an expression on his face which I described as smiling, laughing at me.'

Christian was taken upstairs by Mr Gay who put him in his baby sister's cot to confine him. The next thing, the court heard, was that Mrs Gay found Christian comatose.

The couple said they did not know how Christian came to have a raised sodium level in his blood.

The prosecution suggested he had been force-fed up to four teaspoons of salt as a punishment for being naughty and shaken or hit, causing a brain injury.

Evening Standard, 13 January 2005

Innocent Agents

It is usually a simple matter to discover the principal but there are some difficult areas. One of these is where the apparent principal is unaware that he is involved in wrongdoing, another is where he is too young to be apprehended. **In such cases, the perpetrator of the crime is known as an innocent agent and the person instigating the crime will be treated as the principal.**

An example of the first type of innocent agent might be where a courier personally delivers a letter bomb to the victim, believing it to be a harmless parcel. Obviously, it would be very unjust to convict the courier of this crime; he is merely the innocent agent. **The principal, therefore, would be the person sending the bomb.** Similarly, in an unnamed case in 1665, a daughter was instructed to give her father a potion to cure his cold. In fact, it was poison with which his wife intended to kill him. **The wife was held to be the principal and the daughter was the innocent agent.** The second type of innocent agency would exist if a modern day Fagin co-opted several children under the age of ten to engage in shoplifting on his behalf. **The children could not be charged as principals because they would be under the age of criminal liability. The adult, therefore, would be the principal.**

12.4 THE DIFFERENT TYPES OF SECONDARY OFFENDER

It can be seen from the **Accessories and Abettors Act 1861** that secondary offenders are those who **aid, abet, counsel or procure the commission of a crime. It was stated in AG's Reference (No 1 of 1975) 1975 that these words should be given their ordinary meaning.** The judges of the Court of Appeal went on to state that Parliament must have intended each of the four terms to have their own, distinct meaning, otherwise one or two words would have sufficed. They now need to be examined in more detail.

12.4.1 TO AID

The term 'to aid' **has been interpreted as 'to give help, support or assistance'.** Normally, such help will be given at the time the crime is committed, although the cases show that this is not always the position.

12.4.2 TO ABET

This means 'to encourage, incite or instigate'. Again, it is felt that such encouragement would normally be at or near the scene of the crime. In this way it can be distinguished from the term 'to counsel', which has a similar meaning but takes place before the crime is committed.

The terms 'aiding and abetting' imply some sort of action on the part of the secondary offender; a merely passive presence at the scene of the crime will not normally make a person liable. In **Bland 1988**, the defendant's conviction for aiding and abetting a dealer in drugs was quashed.

The appeal court decided that merely living with such an offender and perhaps having knowledge of his activities was not enough to incur liability; a more active involvement was required.

In the much earlier case of **Coney 1882**, the defendant's conviction for abetting a battery had also been quashed. The judge had not made it clear to the jury that a simple attendance at an illegal prize-fight was only evidence that the spectator might have been involved and was not, in itself, conclusive. If the jury had not been misdirected on this point and there had been some evidence that he had actively participated in the event, as, for example, by cheering and clapping, the jury could have rightly convicted him.

In **Wilcox v Jeffrey 1951**, a more active involvement was found by the Divisional Court.

The defendant was the proprietor of a magazine called *Jazz Illustrated*. He had attended a concert at which a celebrated American jazz musician had played his saxophone, in direct contravention of an **Aliens Order** that prevented him from performing while in the UK. There was no direct evidence that the magazine owner had actively participated at the concert, but he had attended and had later written an article for his magazine, describing the performance in glowing terms.

Taken together, these actions by the defendant were considered to be enough to constitute aiding and abetting the contravention of the Order.

A party could also be an aider and abettor in cases where he is under some sort of duty to control the other party, as in **Tuck v Robson 1970**. The defendant was a licensee of a public house which was visited by the police after closing time. Three people were subsequently charged and convicted of consuming intoxicating liquor out of hours. The licensee was charged with aiding and abetting the crime.

The Divisional Court decided that he had knowledge that the offence was being committed. A more difficult matter was whether he could be said to have assisted in its commission. The court decided that there was enough evidence that he had aided and abetted the offenders. He had failed to eject the customers or even to withdraw their permission to be on the premises, when he possessed the requisite authority to take such a course of action.

12.4.3 TO COUNSEL

This also involves the giving of advice and encouragement but usually takes place before the crime.

An example of counselling can be seen in the case of **Calhaem 1985**. The defendant was infatuated with her solicitor and wished to remove his girlfriend from the scene. She therefore hired a private detective called Zajac to murder her. Zajac claimed that he had no intention of committing the crime but was going to pretend that he had attempted the murder but was unsuccessful. He alleged that he visited the girlfriend's house with this plan in mind but then panicked and killed her in response to her screams.

Despite this contention, Zajac was convicted of murder and Calhaem was found guilty of being a secondary offender. She appealed on the grounds that the judge had not directed the jury that her counselling of the contract killer had to be a substantial cause of the killing. She unsuccessfully tried to argue that it was not her words or actions that had persuaded the killer to commit the crime.

The Court of Appeal agreed with the trial judge that the word 'counsel' merely meant to 'advise, solicit or something of that sort' and decided that there was no implication in this word that there had to be a causal connection between the counselling and the crime. It will be noted below that a different view is taken with regard to the word 'procure'.

12.4.4 TO PROCURE

In **AG's Reference No 1 of 1975 (1975), this term was held to mean 'to produce by endeavour'.** Lord Widgery then added: 'You procure a thing by setting out to see that it happens and taking the appropriate steps to produce that happening'.

The same case decided that that procuring may also take place when the principal offender has no knowledge of this. In most cases of aiding, abetting and counselling there will have been some form of contact between the principal and secondary offenders, 'some meeting of the minds', as stated by Lord Widgery C J.

He decided that this was not necessary in the case of procuring. The judge stated, 'there are plenty of instances in which a person may be

said to procure the commission of a crime by another even though there is no sort of conspiracy between the two, even though there is no attempt at agreement or discussion as to the form which the offence should take. In our judgment the offence described in this reference is such a case'.

What is felt to be necessary, however, is some sort of connection between the acts of the secondary offender and the actual crime committed.

In this case, the defendant had 'spiked' the drinks of his friend with spirits, knowing that the other would later be driving home. The friend was charged with a drink driving offence and the defendant was charged as an aider, abettor, counsellor and procurer. The friend was convicted but the judge decided that there was no case to answer in relation to the secondary offender.

The Attorney General's Reference was a result of the disquiet felt about this decision. The Court of Appeal decided that a person acting in such a way should have faced trial for two reasons. First, he had acted secretly in lacing the drinks of his friend. The latter was therefore unaware of the alcohol consumed and was unable to take precautions to avoid committing an offence. Secondly, as a direct consequence of the added spirits, the friend had driven with the excess alcohol in his blood. This provided the causal link between the actions of the alleged secondary offender and the principal offender, which was felt to be essential in cases of procuring.

To sum up, therefore, a secondary offender can be charged with all four types of secondary participation, aiding abetting, counselling and procuring but can be found guilty if just one of these is satisfied. Normally, the accomplice will counsel and procure before a crime is committed and will aid and abet during the course of an offence. With aiding, abetting and counselling there is usually some contact between the principal and the accessory in relation to the

crime to be committed but this is not necessary for procuring. What is required here is some sort of connection between the acts of the secondary offender and the eventual crime.

12.5 THE *ACTUS REUS* OF PARTICIPATION

It has to be proved that the secondary offender has done something positive to assist or encourage the committing of the offence or has taken some steps to procure its commission. It was noted above that a passive presence at the scene of the crime would not, on its own, be enough to constitute liability.

In Clarkson 1971, the conviction of two soldiers for abetting a rape was quashed because they had not participated in any way; they had merely been present at the time the crime took place.

It is not necessary, however, to prove that the actions of the accomplices had any utility in the committing of the crime or even to prove that any incitement or encouragement was heeded, as was shown in the case of **Calhaem**, mentioned earlier.

Attempts to withdraw from the crime

The very early authority of **Saunders and Archer 1573** suggests that this is possible. It appears however, that in pre-planned crimes, a mere show of repentance will not be sufficient and the offenders will need to take positive steps to indicate that their assistance is at an end. It was stated in **Whitehouse 1941** that they will need to:

serve unequivocal notice upon the other party to the common unlawful cause that if he proceeds upon it he does so without the further aid and assistance of those who withdraw.

In some cases, the accomplice will need to go further and neutralise the effect of any aid he

has given, such as taking back the car he has stolen or making the other surrender the weapon that was supplied. He will find it more difficult to avoid liability if his change of heart comes about at the scene of the crime. In **Becerra and Cooper 1975**, the defendants and another man broke into the house of an elderly woman and attacked her, after hearing that she kept large sums of money there. Becerra was not engaged in the attack but used a knife to cut the telephone wires. Cooper later took control of this knife and moved towards the kitchen to look for the money. The men were then disturbed by the arrival of the tenant of the first floor flat who had come to investigate. Becerra called to the others 'Come on, let's go!' and he and the third man escaped through a window. Cooper was unable to get away and, in the ensuing struggle, the tenant was stabbed. Becerra tried to argue that his withdrawal from the scene of the crime meant that he was not liable for this murder.

The Court of Appeal refused to accept this and his conviction was upheld, as it was in Baker 1994, where the defendant had taken part in the stabbing of the victim before stating that he wanted nothing more to do with the violence.

If the attack is not pre-planned and the violence of the perpetrator is more spontaneous, the other party may be able to withdraw more easily. This was suggested in **Mitchell and King 1999** and approved of by the Court of Appeal in **O'Flaherty 2004**. In the latter case, there had been a street fight and an exchange of blows between the deceased and the three defendants, F, R and T, involved in this appeal. The last two defendants, armed with a bottle and claw hammer respectively, had not then pursued the victim, while others, including O'Flaherty, had done so. The latter, still armed with his cricket bat, watched as the victim was assaulted further by these other participants but took no further part in the attack and was the first to move away. The victim died after sustaining both head

injuries and stab wounds. The three appellants and others were all charged with murder.

The Court of Appeal decided that the trial judge had misdirected the jury concerning the issue of possible withdrawal from the crime and quashed the murder convictions of R and T. In relation to O'Flaherty however, the conviction was upheld, despite the misdirection. It was decided that any reasonable jury would have concluded from the fact that he was holding a cricket bat as the group attacked the deceased, that he was present and, at the very least, providing encouragement or prepared to lend support to the criminal activity.

In addition, the court made the following points in relation to withdrawing from a joint enterprise:

- **While a strict approach could be taken, it was not correct to state that there could never be a withdrawal from a joint enterprise of this sort.**
- **The question of whether a party had done enough to show that he had withdrawn was ultimately a question of fact and degree for the jury. In this respect it was not necessary to have taken steps to prevent the crime.**
- **In cases where there was doubt as to whether the violence consisted of one continuing act or two separate incidents, this was relevant in deciding whether the particular defendant had withdrawn from the criminal acts or had joined in after they were caused.**

12.6 THE *MENS REA* OF SECONDARY OFFENDERS

For the *mens rea* of secondary liability to exist, the prosecution must show two things:

- That the accomplice had knowledge of the type of crime to be committed.

- That he had the intention to aid, abet, counsel or procure the principal offender.

12.6.1 KNOWLEDGE THAT A CRIME IS TO BE COMMITTED

It was stated in **Johnson v Youden and Others 1950** that, before a person can be convicted of aiding and abetting the commission of an offence, **'he must at least know the essential matters which constitute that offence'**. In **Bainbridge 1960** it was decided that the defendant need not know of the precise crime that is to be committed, provided that he possesses, not mere suspicion **'but knowledge that a crime of the type in question was intended'**.

Six weeks before any criminal activity took place Bainbridge used a false name and address to purchase oxyacetylene-cutting equipment. This was used later by the principal offenders to cut through the windows, the doors, and the safe of a bank. Bainbridge was charged with being an accessory to the burglary but tried to argue that he did not know the purpose for which the equipment was being used. He claimed that while he suspected that something illegal was going on, he believed that his purchases were merely being used for the breaking up of stolen goods or something similar.

The Court of Appeal held that while it was not enough merely to show that the defendant knew that some sort of illegal activity was planned, it was not necessary to show that he knew the exact time and place of the intended crime. The court decided that the judge had explained the matter well to the jurors, who had obviously not believed the defendant's story. His conviction, therefore, was upheld.

The House of Lords took the matter further in the case of **DPP for Northern Ireland v Maxwell 1978**. The defendant was a member of a prohibited terrorist organisation and, being a local man had guided other terrorists to a public house called the Crosskeys, which was owned by

a Catholic. A bomb was planted and the fuse ignited. The defendant was not involved in that activity and had not, at any time, had the bomb in his possession. Despite this, he was convicted.

The House of Lords was called upon to decide whether an accomplice could be convicted if **'the crime committed by the principal, and actually assisted by the accused, was one of a number of offences, one of which the accused knew the principal would probably commit.'** Their Lordships firmly held that the answer was 'yes'.

Viscount Dilhorne explained their decision in the following way:

An accessory who leaves it to his principal to choose is liable, provided always the choice is made from the range of offences from which the accessory contemplates the choice will be made.

He acknowledged that the lower court had gone further than earlier cases but added that 'it is a sound development of the law and in no way inconsistent with them. I accept it as good judge-made law in a field where there is no statute to offer guidance'.

Would recklessness on this point be enough?

The law seems to be undecided on this point but it appears unlikely.

In **Blakely, Sutton v DPP 1991**, there was a clear statement by the Divisional Court that objective or inadvertent recklessness is not sufficient to constitute liability but less certainty as to whether subjective recklessness would suffice. In this case, the two women defendants had 'spiked' the drink of the first defendant's lover to stop him returning home to his wife. They intended to tell him what they had done but he left before they could do so. He was convicted of a drink driving offence and the defendants were found guilty as accessories. The women obviously intended that the defendant should drink the alcohol but, equally obviously, did not intend that the man should drive and thereby commit the offence. The court had to decide whether their convictions should be upheld on the grounds that they should have contemplated the possibility that the man might leave and drive away.

The Divisional Court quashed their conviction because the magistrates had used the Caldwell test of recklessness. The court was definite that this type of recklessness was insufficient to create liability. The judges were less clear with regard to Cunningham-type recklessness, although they did suggest that it was best to avoid the word 'reckless' altogether when deciding upon the *mens rea* of secondary offenders.

While the position with regard to subjective recklessness may be in doubt, mere negligence on the part of the alleged secondary offender is definitely insufficient to incur liability. In

Callow v Tillstone 1900, a vet was negligent in his examination of a carcass of meat and declared it to be sound. The meat was later offered for sale and the owner was convicted of the strict liability offence of selling unfit food. **The vet's conviction as an accessory, however, was quashed. He had not intended to be an accomplice and, as noted below, this point must also be shown for a secondary offender, even when the offence in question is a strict liability one.**

12.6.2 THE INTENTION TO AID, ABET, COUNSEL OR PROCURE

In addition to the knowledge that a crime will be committed, **the prosecution must also prove that the accomplice had the intention to do the acts that assisted or encouraged the commission of the crime.**

In **National Coal Board v Gamble 1959,** the Coal Board, via the actions of one of its employees, was found guilty of aiding and abetting because the intention to assist the principal offender was apparent, even though there was no benefit to the accomplices. The employee of the Coal Board operated a weighbridge and informed a lorry driver that his load was nearly four tons overweight. The driver decided to take the risk and the operator supplied him with a ticket permitting him to leave the premises.

The driver's employers were later found guilty of contravening the Motor Vehicles (Construction and Use) Regulations 1955 and the National Coal Board was convicted as a secondary offender.

An equally strict line was taken in Garrett v Arthur Churchill (Glass) Ltd 1970, where the defendant's conviction for knowingly being involved in the exportation of goods without a licence was upheld, even though he was merely an agent and the goods actually belonged to the other party.

Is motive relevant?

It was noted in Chapter 2 that, provided that an intention to commit the crime is proved, the offender's motive is normally irrelevant. This position does not appear to have been followed in **Gillick v West Norfolk Area Health Authority 1986.** Victoria Gillick, the intrepid campaigner for support of family values, sought a declaration that doctors would be acting illegally if they prescribed contraceptives to girls under the age of 16 without obtaining the consent of their parents. It was contended that, by such an action, the doctors were aiding and abetting the commission of unlawful sexual intercourse.

The House of Lords decided that the doctors would not have the intention to commit such a crime if they followed the guidelines that had been laid down, limiting such provision to exceptional cases. Lord Scarman stated:

> The **bona fide** *exercise by a doctor of his clinical judgment must be a complete negation of the guilty mind which is an essential ingredient of the criminal offence of aiding and abetting the commission of unlawful sexual intercourse.*

This was clearly a policy decision and he did go on to say that if a doctor gave the contraceptive treatment merely to facilitate the girl's unlawful sexual intercourse, he might well be guilty of secondary liability.

12.7 PROBLEM AREAS

12.7.1 IF THE PRINCIPAL OFFENDER IS ACQUITTED

Even if the principal is acquitted, it is still possible for the secondary offender to be found liable if **the *actus reus* of the main offence has been committed and the secondary offender has the *mens rea* for participation. The courts are then prepared to combine the two elements and convict him.** This complicated principle is best

understood by looking at the appalling behaviour of the two husbands in the cases described below and the obvious desire of the courts to convict them.

In the case of **Bourne 1952**, a man forced his wife to have sexual intercourse with a dog. This is illegal but mercifully the wife was not charged. If she had been brought to court, she would have been able to plead the defences of marital coercion or duress and, hopefully, would have been acquitted. **Because the *actus reus* of the crime was held to exist however, the court was able to convict the husband for aiding and abetting the illegal act.**

The decision in **Cogan and Leak 1976** is perhaps less easy to justify, although it is clear why the Court of Appeal was reluctant to quash the conviction. Leak wished to punish and humiliate his wife after she had refused him money so on his return from a drinking session, he forced her to have sexual intercourse, first with him and then with his drinking partner, Cogan, while the husband looked on. The unfortunate woman was said to be sobbing quietly throughout the ordeal. Later, Cogan was charged with rape and Leak with procuring this offence. Leak could not be charged with his own rape of his wife because, at that time, it was not an offence for a husband within a marriage to have sexual intercourse without his wife's consent.

Both men were convicted at first instance but appealed. Cogan's appeal was successful, following the questionable decision of the House of Lords in **Morgan 1976** in the interim period, which held that an honest belief that the other had consented could be a defence to a charge of rape; the belief did not have to be a reasonable one. Leach tried to argue that, as the principal had been acquitted, his conviction as an accomplice could not then stand. As Cogan's conviction was quashed, it was arguable whether the crime of rape still existed.

The Court of Appeal refused to quash Leak's

conviction. Lawton L J took a robust approach to this problem, roundly declaring that an acquittal would be 'an affront to justice and to the common sense of ordinary folk'. He found that a rape had, indeed, been committed and confirmed that Leach had procured this offence. He rejected the appellant's arguments and stated, 'Here one fact was clear – the wife had been raped. . . : The fact that Cogan was innocent of rape because he believed she was consenting does not affect the position. . . In the language of the law the act of sexual intercourse without the wife's consent was the *actus reus*; it had been procured by Leak who had the appropriate *mens rea*, namely his intention that Cogan should have sexual intercourse with her without her consent'.

This possible expansion of the law was followed in the case of **Millward 1994**. The defendant was charged with aiding, abetting, counselling and procuring his employee to commit the offence of causing death by reckless driving. The vehicle in question was a tractor, with a trailer attached. The hitch on the tractor was defective and during the journey, the trailer became detached from the tractor and hit another vehicle. The driver of this car was killed. Both employer and employee were originally convicted but the employee's conviction was quashed on appeal. Millward tried to argue that the acquittal of the principal meant that the *actus reus* of the offence had not been committed because the recklessness of the employee had not been made out.

The Court of Appeal decided that the *actus reus* did still exist; i.e. taking of the vehicle onto the road in a defective condition so as to cause the death. It was stressed that procuring does not require a joint intention between the accessory and the principal, thus allowing the accessory to be convicted even when the principal is acquitted.

The court approved of the reasoning in **Cogan and Leak** and distinguished the earlier case of

Thornton v Mitchell 1940, where the facts were somewhat similar. A conductor had given inadequate signals to the driver of a bus who was trying to reverse and this had resulted in a fatal injury to a pedestrian. In this instance, the driver of the bus had been acquitted and the conductor's conviction for aiding and abetting the careless driving of the principal had also been quashed by the Divisional Court.

12.7.2 WHERE THE LIABILITY OF THE SECONDARY OFFENDER IS DIFFERENT

Liability of the secondary offender for a different offence to that of the principal is possible, provided that both offences share the same *actus reus*. This was not held to be the case in **Dunbar 1988**. It was alleged that Dunbar wanted to see her lover dead but she claimed that this comment had been made while she was intoxicated. It was shown that she suspected that the co-defendants might break into the flat of her lover and, in the course of the burglary, might inflict some harm upon the woman. Dunbar argued strongly however, that she had not envisaged that death or grievous bodily harm might result.

The Court of Appeal quashed her conviction for manslaughter. The trial judge had not made it clear to the jury that, if the defendant had not contemplated the possibility that death or grievous bodily harm might occur and had only suspected that some lesser harm might be inflicted, she could not be found guilty of manslaughter. The crime that she was contemplating was different to the one actually committed by the other offenders.

12.7.3 WHEN THE SECONDARY OFFENDER IS A VICTIM

It was established in the early case of **Tyrell 1894**, that the alleged accomplice cannot be found guilty of aiding and abetting if the offence in question was actually created to protect her. In this case an under-age girl was charged with aiding and abetting a man to have incestuous sexual intercourse with her but was acquitted. The court felt it to be wrong that she should face criminal proceedings because the Act had been passed to protect such girls from themselves.

12.7.4 WHERE A JOINT ENTERPRISE IS SAID TO EXIST

In many of the situations mentioned in this chapter, the question of who is the principal offender and who is a mere accessory, has usually been obvious. In some instances, the position is not so clear, especially where two or more parties embark together on a criminal activity. The late Sir John Smith stated that the essence of such a joint enterprise **'is that the parties have a common purpose to commit an offence'**. In such a case, the general rule is that if one of the parties commits a crime, the others, too, will be liable, even if events go beyond the common purpose, provided that the offence committed is one that could have been foreseen by the other parties.

Smith strongly believed that the ordinary rules of primary and secondary liability should be applied in such cases. Where one party is claiming that he is less at fault than the other, all that then needs to be worked out is whether he is, on the facts, a secondary participator or a joint principal.

In the case of Stewart and Schofield 1995, the Court of Appeal refused to uphold such a view and decided that the law should take a stricter approach in cases of joint enterprise where the parties involved have set out together on a criminal escapade. Hobhouse L J stated:

> The allegation that a defendant took part in the execution of a crime as a joint enterprise is not the same as an allegation that he aided, abetted, counselled or procured the commission of that crime. A person who is a mere aider or abettor is truly a secondary party to the commission of whatever crime it is that the principal has committed . . . In contrast, where the allegation is joint enterprise, the allegation is that one defendant participated in the criminal act of another. This is a different principle. It renders each of the parties to a joint enterprise criminally liable for the acts done in the course of carrying out that joint enterprise.

Criminal acts going beyond the original plan

In some instances, one party may commit a greater crime than was planned by the parties to a joint enterprise. The courts then have to decide whether the changed circumstances are enough to absolve the others from liability. Hobhouse took the view that this matter was a question of fact, rather than law, but also stressed that not all variations of the original plan would be enough to excuse them.

- In Chang Wing-Siu 1985, the Privy Council stated that when assessing the possible *mens rea* of the unwilling participant, a subjective approach should be used. Under this test, liability would not arise unless it was shown that the accused believed that the risk of the greater harm happening was a real or substantial one. Nevertheless, the court added the rider that the defendant's state of mind could be inferred from his conduct and any other evidence throwing light on the matter.
- In Hyde and others 1991, the Court of Appeal upheld the convictions for murder of the three defendants, who had kicked and punched another person outside a pub, despite the fact it was impossible to say who had inflicted the fatal blow.
- The Privy Council went further still in Hui Chi Ming 1992, and upheld the defendant's conviction for murder, even though the

others in the venture were only found guilty of manslaughter in an earlier trial.

- In Powell and Daniels 1997, the Law Lords took an equally uncompromising attitude. They made it clear that despite the fact that only intention will suffice for *mens rea* in relation to the actual perpetrator of a murder, such a strong degree of blameworthiness did not have to be proved for the other parties in a joint enterprise. They could be found guilty if they merely foresaw the possibility of the perpetrator commiting such an offence. In this case therefore, the convictions for murder were upheld for all three of the members of the joint enterprise, after one of them shot and killed a drug dealer.

Criminal acts that were not foreseen

In such cases, the others in the joint enterprise will not be fixed with equal liability, as can be seen in the following cases:

- In **Mahmood 1994**, the 15-year-old defendant and the even younger driver were 'joy-riders', being chased by the police after their erratic driving was noted. The driver jumped out of the car while it was still moving and Mahmood followed. The empty car, still in gear, mounted a pavement and struck a child's pram, killing the ten months' old baby inside.

  The Court of Appeal thought that the passenger may well have contemplated that someone could be killed or injured by the other's dangerous driving but not that the car would be abandoned in such a way. The conviction for manslaughter was quashed.
- In **English 1997**, the defendant and another attacked a policeman with wooden posts but the other party suddenly pulled out a knife and fatally stabbed the victim.

  The House of Lords followed an earlier Northern Ireland decision in Gamble 1989, where the defendant had been expecting to

take part in a 'knee-capping' and had not foreseen that the victim would have his throat cut. Their Lordships decided that English's conviction for murder could not be sustained.

Differing ways of dealing with the defendant in a joint enterprise

The appeal courts have various options:

- To release the defendant from all blame by quashing the conviction and leaving it at that.
- To order a retrial and let a new jury decide on the matter.

  This approach was taken in **Uddin 1998**.
- To find the defendant guilty of a lesser offence instead

This option was favoured in **Gilmour 2000**. The defendant had driven three others to a housing estate, and waited for them while they threw a petrol bomb into a house where the six occupants were asleep. Three children died in the resulting blaze. The defendant was found guilty of the three murders. On appeal, it was claimed that, as a normal rule, the throwing of petrol bombs did not cause such serious injuries, only minor fires, and it was therefore possible that the defendant had not foreseen the tragic consequences that actually occurred. He may also have been unaware that a larger bottle than average had been used to make the bomb.

The Court of Appeal quashed the murder convictions but went on to decide that the defendant could be found guilty of manslaughter instead because he had foreseen that a petrol bomb would be thrown in order to cause a fire. While questioning some of the statements made in Stewart and Schofield, the court decided that the basic principles laid down in that case could be relied upon and applied to this new situation.

Comment

The late Sir John Smith challenged the correctness of this decision. He argued that the facts of the case are comparable to **Gamble**, **Powell** and **English**, where a manslaughter conviction was not imposed. He also questioned whether this was truly a case of joint enterprise, claiming that it fell more easily into the category of secondary liability. It was debatable whether the accused had been involved in any pre-arranged plan, because, according to him, he was not a willing participant. He had been roughly awakened in the middle of the night and ordered to take part in this operation. It could therefore be argued that he was merely giving reluctant assistance rather than joining the others in a common purpose.

It should be noted that the Law Commission has recognized that the law on participation, particularly in relation to joint enterprise, is 'complicated, uncertain and anomalous', and has undertaken to review this, (see below).

Activity

- Barry recruited two children to steal mobile phones for him from a local store. Peter was 12, Wendy was 9.
  Assess the possible liability of Barry, Peter and Wendy in relation to participation.
- Thelma is jealous of her friend Louise, who has just passed her advanced motoring test. She secretly laces Louise's orange juice with vodka,

12.7.5 INDEPENDENT ACTS

For any of the above principles to apply, some form of joint enterprise or secondary liability must first be established. It was confirmed in **Petters and Parfitt 1995** that if two parties act independently of each other rather than as a joint enterprise or as principal and accessory, they cannot then be held liable for the acts of the other party. If a killing took place in such circumstances, and it was impossible to establish who actually did the act then, as the law stands today, both parties must be acquitted. This means that a serious crime could go unpunished, as seen in cases where a child has been killed but it is impossible to prove which of the parents is responsible. Calls for reform in this area have now been heeded by the Law Commission. In its Report No. 282, in 2003, with the rather inelegant title of *Children: Their Non-Accidental Death or Serious Injury* (Criminal Trials), the Commission proposes two changes to the present law:

An aggravated form of the existing offence of child cruelty. This would arise where the cruelty has contributed significantly to the child's death.

A new offence that would arise where a person of 16 and over who had responsibility for a child was aware that there was a real risk that the child might be harmed yet failed to take steps to prevent it.

knowing that the latter will be driving home. Louise is later charged with driving a motor vehicle with excess alcohol in the blood.
  Discuss Thelma's involvement.
- In **Rook 1993**, the defendant was convicted of being a secondary offender to the crime of murder. The case involved a contract killing in which the taxi driver, Afsar, arranged for three men to kill his wife. The men had at least two meetings in which

they discussed the ways of carrying out the crime and Rook had asked for money 'up front' to help pay for the new clothes they would need after the event. He then had second thoughts about being involved and did not turn up at the pre-arranged murder spot. The other two men dragged the unfortunate woman from the car in which she was travelling with her husband and brutally murdered her. Rook was convicted with the others but appealed. He argued that he had never intended the woman to be killed and that he had merely tagged along to see how far the others would go. He then claimed that he had tried to stall them and had believed that if he did not turn up at the appointed place, the others would not go ahead with the crime.

Imagine that you are a judge of the Court of Appeal and decide whether Rook's appeal should succeed. Give clear reasons for your answer.

TEN KEY FACTS ON PRINCIPAL AND SECONDARY OFFENDERS

- The main perpetrator of a crime is called the principal offender; in some cases, there may be more than one principal. If an innocent agent is involved, a person may be convicted as a principal even though he is not at the scene of the crime. Innocent agents are those without knowledge of the crime or those who lack capacity. People with less involvement are called secondary offenders. They may also be known as accomplices or accessories. Secondary offenders are liable to be tried and punished in the same way as principal offenders (**s8 Accessories and Abettors Act 1861**, as amended and **s44 Magistrates Courts' Act 1980**).

- They will fulfil this role if they have aided, abetted, counselled or procured the offence. In **AG's Reference (No1 of 1975) 1975**, it was stated that these words should be given their ordinary meaning. All four terms may appear on the indictment but the secondary offender can be convicted if just one of these forms of assistance is proved.

- Aiding and abetting usually takes place at the scene of the crime. Aiding means giving help, support or assistance; abetting means encouraging, inciting or instigating the crime. A purely passive presence will not incur liability, unless the person is involved in other ways or has the authority to control the others (**Coney 1882, Clarkson 1971** and **Bland 1988**, and contrast with **Wilcox v Jeffrey 1951** and **Tuck v Robson 1970**).

- Counselling means inciting or encouraging, or 'to advise or solicit or something of that sort' (**Calhaem 1985**). This will arise before the crime takes place. Liability may still be incurred even where the principal offender does not heed the advice (**Calhaem 1985**). The term 'to procure' means 'to produce by endeavour', i.e. to set out to see that the crime happens, but there is no requirement that the principal has to know of these actions. There must, however, be some causal connection between the steps taken by the alleged accomplice and the actual crime committed (**AG's Reference (No 1 of 1975) 1975**).

- The *actus reus* of participation requires the activities of aiding, abetting, counselling or procuring, i.e. something active to assist the commission of the crime, although it is not necessary for the help to have been of any use. A secondary offender may still be liable even when the principal offender has been acquitted, so long as the *actus reus* of the crime is still held to exist. This will then be merged with the *mens rea* of the accomplice (**Bourne 1952, Cogan and Leak 1976** and **Millward 1994**).

● Accomplices may be able to withdraw from their criminal activity without incurring liability, but must take steps to make this position clear to the others involved in the crime (**Whitehouse 1941**). In many cases, they will need to go even further and neutralise the effects of any help already given. The later the withdrawal, the less likely it is that the courts will believe it is genuine (**Becarra 1975, Baker 1994** and **O'Flaherty 2004,** but this may be possible if the violent acts are more spontaneous, **Mitchell and King 1999**).

● Two points have to be established before the *mens rea* of participation is satisfied. First, there must be knowledge that the crime is to be committed (**Johnson v Youden and Others 1950**) or, at the very least, **Cunningham**-style recklessness that an offence might happen (**Blakely, Sutton v DPP 1991**). It appears from the cases of **Bainbridge 1960** and **DPP for N.I. v Maxwell 1978**, that it is enough for the accused to be aware of the type of crime committed. Secondly, there must be an intention to assist the principal (**NCB v Gamble 1959, Garrett v Arthur Churchill Glass Ltd 1970**). Such intention must exist even if the offence committed is a strict liability one, as in **Callow v Tillstone 1900**. The defendant need not intend that the actual crime should be committed. **Gillick** appears to have been decided on its own facts.

● When two or more people embark upon a joint criminal venture, this is known as a joint enterprise. Despite the misgivings of the late Sir John Smith, the appeal courts have decided that these cases must be treated differently to those of ordinary secondary liability (**Stewart and Schofield 1995**).

● The participator in the joint enterprise will still be liable, even where the crime of the other party varies from what was originally planned, provided that it was in the range of acts contemplated by him (**Stewart and Schofield 1995**). The test however is subjective. The defendant must have believed that the risk of the harm occurring was a substantial one but the jury can deduce this from his conduct and any other evidence (**Chan Wing-Siu 1985, Powell 1997**).

● If the act is outside the contemplation of the defendant, he cannot be found liable (**Gamble 1989, Mahmood 1995, English 1997**). If no joint enterprise is found, and it cannot be established who inflicted the injury, both parties must be acquitted (**Petters and Parfitt 1995**).

12.8 SUGGESTED REFORM ON SECONDARY OFFENDERS

The Law Commission has studied the law relating to accessories on several occasions. The most recent proposals were in their 1993 Consultation Paper No. 131, entitled *Assisting and Encouraging Crime*. The Commission invited comments on their proposals for radical changes in this area. It was suggested that two new offences should be created in the form of inchoate offences. This would mean that they would not be dependent on the main crime having to take place.

● First, a person would be guilty of assisting crime if he knows or believes that another party is doing an act (or will do one), which will involve the commission of a crime and he does any act to assist this. To widen liability, the clause states that assistance includes the giving of advice about how to commit the offence and advice on how to avoid detection or arrest.

The person will also be liable if he assists a principal and knows or believes that the latter intends to commit one of a number of offences (i.e. the **Bainbridge** type of situation).

● The offence of encouraging crime will arise where the offender solicits, commands or encourages the principal to do acts which would involve the commission of an offence by the principal and intends that such acts should be done.

The help should be brought to the attention of the principal but the latter does not need to be influenced by it. It is also not necessary that the offender should know the identity of the principal, nor even have any particular group in mind, provided that he intends that his communication will be acted upon by any person to whose attention it comes.

If effected, these changes would mean the abolition of aiding, abetting and counselling and also the abolition of the common law offence of incitement, which is dealt with in Chapter 13. The Commission believed that there might also be a need for another new offence to cover procuring, in cases where there is no communication about this with the principal. It remains to be seen whether any of these far-reaching proposals will be acted upon.

The Commission hoped to publish a report in 2004 but at the time of writing, this has not yet materialised.

Self-assessment questions on Chapter 12

1. State three other names for an accomplice.
2. Give two examples of innocent agents.
3. Define the following expressions, giving examples of each:
   To aid
   To abet
   To counsel
   To procure
4. Using decided cases to illustrate your answer, explain how the *actus reus* of participation is established.
5. Describe the two elements that have to be shown before the necessary *mens rea* of a secondary offender is proved. Give cases to support your findings.
6. What steps must a secondary offender take in order to withdraw from the crime without incurring liability?
7. Citing case examples to back up your answer, decide when it is possible for the secondary offender to remain liable after the acquittal of the principal.
8. What is meant by the term 'a joint enterprise' and why is this treated differently from secondary liability?
9. Why were the convictions upheld in the cases of **Hyde** and **Powell** but quashed in **Mahmood** and **English.**
10. Why were the defendants acquitted in **Petters** and **Parfit** and how would the Law Commission deal with such cases?

Chapter 13

INCHOATE OFFENCES

13.1 INTRODUCTION

Inchoate offences are incomplete offences. The parties involved may well have desired that a crime should go ahead, but circumstances could prevent this. For example, an offender may have planned to murder another, he may have raised the gun to shoot him, taken careful aim but then, for some reason, the gun does not fire. In another case, an armed robbery may have been plotted but the sudden re-routing of the security van may have prevented the planned ambush. In yet another scenario, a person may have been pressurising his friend to blackmail a business acquaintance, but this friend may have had 'cold feet' and decided to pull out of the venture. Not unnaturally, even though the main crimes did not go ahead, the law still takes the view that the people involved in these activities should be punished. In the first instance, therefore, the offender would be charged with attempted murder. In the second case, the wrongdoers might also be charged with attempt or might, instead, be charged with conspiracy. In our last example, the party exerting the pressure on his friend might be guilty of incitement. These three offences, therefore, are the subject of this chapter and will be considered in the following way:

✔ Atempts to commit a crime
✔ Statutory conspiracy (an outline only)
✔ Incitement (an outline only)
✔ Suggested reform of inchoate offences.

13.2 ATTEMPTS TO COMMIT A CRIME

The law of attempts is now governed by the Criminal Attempts Act 1981. S1(1) Criminal Attempts Act 1981 states that a person will be guilty of attempt if:

> with intent to commit an offence to which this section applies, a person does an act which is more than merely preparatory to the commission of the offence.

S4(1) goes on to state: 'the attempt is punishable to the same extent as the substantive offence'.

13.2.1 THE *ACTUS REUS* OF ATTEMPT

This will exist where the party 'does an act which is more than merely preparatory to the commission of the offence'.

The law makes a clear distinction therefore, between acts which are undertaken merely to prepare for the crime in question and acts done after this time which will amount to an attempt. With regard to earlier acts, the party may be guilty of other less serious offences, as, for example, obtaining a gun and ammunition unlawfully or stealing a car, but he will not, at this stage be guilty of the attempt to commit the main crime. For this to occur, he must do something more substantial and with a closer connection to the crime in question. Before the **Criminal Attempts Act** codified the law on attempts, the Court of Appeal in **Davey v Lee 1968** took the view that it had to be **'a step towards the commission of the specific crime, which is immediately and not merely remotely connected with the commission of it'.** In DPP v Stonehouse 1978, the House of Lords approved of the early description in Eagleton 1855 that **'Acts remotely leading towards the commission of the offence are not to be considered as** attempts to commit it; but acts immediately connected with it are'. Their Lordships therefore decided that 'the offender must have crossed the Rubicon and burnt his boats'. The Law Commission, when formulating the changes in the law of attempt, decided that there was 'no magic formula' to work out when enough has been done to amount to an attempt but decided that it must be **'more than merely preparatory'**. With this as a guide the question could then be left to the jury's good sense.

The meaning of more than merely preparatory

In **Jones 1990**, the defendant was unable to accept that his ex-mistress had formed a serious relationship with another man. Jones purchased four guns and shortened the barrel of one of them. He drove to the school where his rival was dropping off his child and jumped into the victim's car. He then pointed the loaded gun at the man and stated 'You are not going to like this'. The victim managed to grab the gun, throw it out of the window and escape. The police later arrested the defendant who also had a knife with him. They recovered his holdall, which contained a hatchet, ammunition and a length of cord and his car, where they found a large quantity of English, French and Spanish money.

Jones claimed that he had only intended to kill himself and appealed against his subsequent conviction. He argued that he had at least three more acts to do before he could be said to be ready to kill anyone; i.e. he had to remove the safety catch on the gun, to put his finger on the trigger and thirdly, he had to pull that trigger.

The Court of Appeal agreed that the acts of obtaining the gun, shortening it, loading it, putting on a disguise and going to the school were merely preparatory to the commission of the offence but added that 'once he had got into the car, taken out the loaded gun and pointed it at the victim with the intention of killing him there was sufficient evidence for the

consideration of the jury on the charge of attempted murder'. The appeal therefore, was dismissed.

In other cases, the matter is less clear-cut. In **Gullefer 1990**, the defendant had placed a bet at a greyhound stadium. The dog was not performing well so, in the final stages of the race, the defendant climbed over the fence and onto the track and tried to distract the dogs. He hoped that this action would result in the race being declared null and void and in the eventual return of his stake money from the bookmaker. Unfortunately for Gullefer, he was no more successful in this plan than he was with his gambling and he was charged with attempted theft. His luck changed for the better, however, when his appeal was heard and his conviction was quashed.

Lord Lane decided that the attempt could not be said to begin until the defendant embarked upon 'the crime proper'. Gullefer's actions when he jumped onto the track, therefore, were merely acts in preparation for the later crime of theft and, at that time, he could not be said to be guilty of an attempt.

The decisions in the case of **Campbell 1991** and **Geddes 1996** are rather more disquieting. In the first case, the defendant was arrested within yards of a post office, armed with an imitation gun and was convicted of attempted armed robbery. In the second case, Geddes had been discovered by a teacher in the boys' lavatory block at a school in Brighton. He had no authority to be there and left when challenged, discarding his rucksack as he went. This was found to contain a large kitchen knife, ropes and a roll of masking tape. He was later convicted of attempted false imprisonment.

Both convictions however, were quashed on appeal on the finding that the acts were not more than merely preparatory. While the appeal court appeared to be convinced that the defendants had the necessary intention to commit the crimes in question, they

nevertheless felt bound to conclude that the actions were not advanced enough to merit a conviction.

The Court of Appeal took a more robust approach in Attorney General's Reference (No 1 of 1992) 1993 and decided that a defendant could be found guilty of rape without the need to show that he had tried to penetrate the woman's vagina, provided that there was enough other evidence of attack.

13.2.2 THE *MENS REA* OF ATTEMPT

- This consists of an intention to bring about the offence.

S1(1) states that a person will be guilty of attempt if **'with intent to commit an offence'**, he does an act which is more than merely preparatory to its commission. In relation to the attempt to commit the actual crime, reckless behaviour is not sufficient to incur liability.

This was clearly affirmed by the Court of Appeal in **Millard and Vernon 1987**. The defendants were football supporters who were convicted of attempted criminal damage. They had pushed repeatedly against a wooden wall at the ground. The prosecution alleged that they had done this in conjunction with each other in order to damage the line of planking, whereas the defendants strongly denied that they were acting with intent to damage the stand, or that they were acting in cohort. They appealed on the grounds that the judge had not made it clear that recklessness was insufficient *mens rea* for an attempt, even though it would suffice for the full crime of criminal damage.

The Court of Appeal agreed with this reasoning and quashed their convictions.

The same view would be taken if the defendant was charged with attempted grievous bodily harm under **s20 Offences Against the Person Act 1861**. If the offence had been carried out, the offender could be convicted if he either intended to inflict grievous bodily harm or was reckless about this. For the charge of **attempting** to inflict grievous bodily harm to succeed, however, only intention will suffice. With the crime of murder, the defendant can be found guilty if it is proved that he intended to kill or to cause grievous bodily harm. For the crime of attempted murder, the wrongdoer must be shown to have had the intention **to kill**; the intention to cause grievous bodily harm is not enough and, if this is all that can be proved, the defendant must be acquitted.

We now need to see how this can be established. It is primarily a jury matter. **In Mohan 1976, decided before the Criminal Attempts Act 1981, the Court of Appeal said that intention meant:**

a decision to bring about, in so far as it lies within the accused's power, the commission of the offence which it is alleged the accused attempted to commit, no matter whether the accused desired the consequence or not.

In attempted murder, therefore, the fact that the defendant foresaw that his actions might cause the death of the victim would not be enough. As in the full crime of murder, however, if the defendant foresaw that death was a virtually certain consequence of his actions, this would be strong evidence from which the jury would be entitled to find that the wrongdoer had the necessary intention. In **Walker and Hayles 1990**, discussed in Chapter 2, the Court of Appeal was prepared to accept a direction of the trial judge that the jury could infer that the defendant had the necessary intention if he foresaw that there was a very high degree of probability that death would result, although it was made clear that the court preferred the words 'virtually certain'.

In this case, the convictions for attempted murder were upheld. The appellants had thrown the victim from a third floor block of flats because it was believed that he had ill-treated Walker's sister.

The Court of Appeal confirmed that it was necessary to show that the appellants had intended to kill the victim and that the intention to cause really serious harm was insufficient for attempted murder. The court found that this had been proved and that the statements made by the trial judge did not amount to a misdirection. This case now needs to be read in the light of the judgment of the House of Lords in Woollin 1998, mentioned in Chapter 2. It is almost certain that the words 'highly probable' would now be considered insufficient; the defendant must have foreseen that death was a virtually certain consequence of his actions.

It is clear from the Law Commission's report that it was envisaged that intention had to be proved for **all** criminal attempts and with regard to all aspects of the offence in question. Despite this, a uniform approach has not always been followed and a different view has been taken in respect of the offences of attempted rape and attempted arson, as will be noted below.

Crimes where lesser *mens rea* will suffice

In cases of rape and aggravated criminal damage, intention still has to be proved with regard to the actual conduct, but a lesser degree of blameworthiness, i.e. recklessness, may suffice in relation to the circumstances in which the crime was committed. These exceptions are best explained by looking at the cases of **Khan 1990** and **AG's Reference (No 3 of 1992) 1994**.

In **Khan and Others 1990**, a 16-year-old girl had gone to a house with five boys after a visit to a disco and other boys had joined them. It was alleged that three of the boys had raped the girl and that four others, the defendants in this case, had attempted to do so.

The defendants were convicted of attempted rape but claimed that the judge had misdirected the jury on the *mens rea* required for this offence. They said that it had not been proved that they had intended to commit all aspects of the offence. They agreed that they intended to have intercourse with the victim, but argued that they thought that the girl was consenting.

The Court of Appeal decided that the *mens rea* necessary for attempted rape was the same for the complete offence: *namely an intention to have intercourse plus knowledge of or recklessness as to the woman's absence of consent. No question of attempting to achieve a reckless state of mind arises; the attempt relates to the physical activity; the mental state of the defendant is the same.* **The court believed that this interpretation of the law was desirable because it 'did not require the jury to be burdened with different directions as to the accused's state of mind, dependant on whether the individual achieved or failed to achieve sexual intercourse'.**

The same approach was taken and expanded upon in **AG's Reference (No3 of 1992) 1994**. The offence in question was attempted arson, being reckless whether life be endangered under **s1(2) Criminal Damage Act 1971**. The defendants were acquitted because the judge ruled that, on a charge of attempt, intent to endanger life was required; recklessness was not sufficient. **The Court of Appeal decided that this was wrong and said that it was enough for the defendants to be in one of the states of mind required for the commission of the full offence.**

To sum up, therefore, the *mens rea* required for attempt is intention in relation to committing the actual crime but in certain limited circumstances, recklessness will suffice with regard to the circumstances in which the crime is committed.

Comment

One can see why the Court of Appeal was reluctant to see the offenders go unpunished in the situations described above. It has to be admitted however, that the two decisions have 'muddied the waters' and made the law less certain regarding the *mens rea* of attempt. In respect of the offences of rape and aggravated arson the court appears to have changed the law clearly laid down by Parliament. With regard to other crimes, the courts have been definite in their opinion that intention only will suffice so, at present, a two-tier system operates which is difficult for juries (and students!) to understand and may lead to further appeals.

One solution would be for Parliament to make it clear that the *mens rea* required for an attempt should be the same as for the full offence. Another would be for the House of Lords to overrule the decisions in **Khan** and the **Reference** and state that intention is needed for all aspects of every offence. This, however, is unlikely to happen. After the appeal in **Khan** was dismissed, the Appeal Committee of the House of Lords rejected the defendants' application to appeal to that House, thereby tacitly agreeing with the decision of the lower court. The third way is to accept the different treatment for these crimes. The Law Commission was originally in favour of demanding intention for all the aspects of a crime but came to believe that this approach was too narrow and now agrees with the changes effected by case law.

The amended Draft Criminal Code reflects this and states (rather obscurely!) that 'an intention to commit an offence is an intention with respect to all the elements of the offence other than fault elements, except that recklessness with respect to circumstances suffices where it suffices for the offence itself'.

13.2.3 ATTEMPTING TO COMMIT THE IMPOSSIBLE

Before leaving the subject of *mens rea*, it has to be decided whether a person can be guilty of an attempt to commit a crime, even though the crime itself is, for some reason, impossible to commit. The following examples illustrate the problem:

- **A gang member attempts to shoot and kill an informer while he is asleep in his bed but, unbeknown to him, another gang member has already strangled the man.**
- **A wrongdoer might be attempting to smuggle 50 crates of whisky into the country but the plan has been discovered and the bottles now contain cold tea.**

The question that needs to be asked is whether such people should be charged with attempting to commit a crime because, as has been noted, the crime itself is now impossible. **The House of Lords has made it clear that the answer to this question is 'yes'** but over the last two decades, the decisions of that court have swung alarmingly from one view to the other on this subject.

Earlier decisions

In **Haughton v Smith 1975**, which was decided before the law on attempts was put into statutory form, the police seized a quantity of stolen corned beef but allowed the lorry to continue on its journey under the control of a disguised policeman. At the end of its route, the people unloading the consignment were arrested and later convicted of attempting to handle stolen goods.

The case reached the highest appeal court where their Lordships decided that the conviction for attempt could not be sustained if the crime itself was not possible.

The **Criminal Attempts Act 1981** clearly intended to reverse such decisions. **S1(2)** states that: *a person may be guilty of attempting to commit an offence to which this section applies even though the facts are such that the* *commission of the offence is impossible*. Despite this plain wording however, the House of Lords considered the matter again in the case of **Anderton v Ryan 1985**.

Mrs Ryan had confessed that she had bought a video cassette recorder for £110 in the belief that it was a stolen one and was charged with both handling and attempted handling of stolen goods. In the event, the prosecution felt unable to establish that the goods had been stolen, so the first charge was dropped and only the attempted handling charge pursued. The magistrates refused to convict but the Divisional Court supported the prosecution's appeal on the point of law.

The House of Lords quashed the conviction, obviously believing that it would be unjust to find liability in a case such as this, despite what was laid down in s1(3).

The current law

In **Shivpuri 1987**, the House of Lords overruled this decision, made less than two years earlier. The defendant had been arrested by customs officials on his return from a visit to India. While there, he had been approached by a dealer in drugs who had offered him £1,000 to take control of a suitcase in Cambridge, the contents of which he was later to distribute to others. He believed that the drugs were either heroin or cannabis. He was later arrested in London, as he handed over a packet to a third party. This packet and the others in the lining of his suitcase were found to contain a harmless vegetable matter like snuff, rather than harmful drugs. The defendant argued that his conviction for attempting to deal with a prohibited drug should be quashed on the grounds that the complete offence was impossible. The case reached the House of Lords.

Lord Bridge felt it was necessary to start with the Act itself (although he did not really explain why he had not taken that approach in Anderton!). He said it had to be decided whether the defendant had intended to deal with drugs, to which the answer was clearly

yes. It then had to be established whether he had done an act which was more than merely preparatory to the commission of the offence and, again, the answer was yes. Lastly, it had to be examined whether this act required anything further than this. S1(2) indicates that the answer to this is no; the defendant, therefore, must be found guilty.

The learned judge then questioned whether this result could stand with the earlier decision in Anderton v Ryan and decided that it could not. His conclusion was that the latter case was wrongly decided and that he and his fellow judges 'fell into error' in their desire to avoid convicting Mrs Ryan and others in her situation. He was obviously influenced by the strong criticism of this ruling given by Professor Glanville Williams in the *Criminal Law Journal* in 1986. Lord Bridge stated ruefully,

'The language in which he criticises the decision in Anderton v Ryan is not conspicuous for its moderation, but it would be foolish, on that account, not to recognise the force of the

But this isn't the white powder I had in mind!

FIVE KEY FACTS ON ATTEMPTS

- The law on attempts is in the **Criminal Attempts Act 1981**; the maximum punishment is the same as for the complete offence.

- The *actus reus* exists where a party does an act which is more that merely preparatory. The jury will decide this issue but the conviction may be quashed if that body has not been directed properly on the matter or the acts cannot be said to be directly connected to the crime (**Gullefer 1990, Campbell 1991, Geddes 1996**).

- The mental element needed for the attempt is intention, which was said in **Mohan 1976** to mean a decision to bring about the commission of the offence whether or not desired. Intention must be proved for attempted murder, attempted assault in all its forms, attempted theft and attempted basic criminal damage. For attempted murder, there has to be an intention to kill, not merely to cause serious harm, as is possible in the complete offence, and it appears that the direction in **Woollin** may now be required. This would mean that the jury is not entitled to find intention unless the defendant foresaw that death was a virtually certain consequence.

- Recklessness about the actual commission of the offence is not normally enough (**Millard and Vernon 1987**). In attempted rape and attempted aggravated arson however, although the offender must intend to commit the sexual intercourse or criminal damage, he may still be convicted if he is reckless about the woman's consent in the first instance or reckless about endangering life in the second situation (**Khan 1990, AG's Reference (No 3 of 1992) 1994**).

- The House of Lords in **Shivpuri 1987** clearly affirmed **s1(2) Criminal Attempts Act** and upheld that it is possible to be convicted of attempting to commit a crime, even though the actual offence may not have been possible.

criticism and churlish not to acknowledge the assistance I have derived from it'.

Their Lordships unanimously decided to overrule Anderton v Ryan, using the rights given under the Practice Statement of 1966 to do so and dismissed the appeal in Shivpuri.

The position is, at last, crystal clear; a person can be found guilty of attempt, even though the actual crime is impossible.

Before leaving the question of attempts, it is important to note that certain crimes cannot be attempted. These are attempting to conspire, attempting to aid, abet, counsel or procure and attempting to assist an offender after the commission of a crime.

13.3 STATUTORY CONSPIRACY (AN OUTLINE ONLY)

A conspiracy is an agreement between two or more people to do an unlawful act. Until the passing of the **Criminal Law Act 1977**, conspiracy was a common law offence and covered a wide range of activities, including a conspiracy to commit a tort such as trespass. The Law Commission believed that the offence should be confined to agreements to commit crimes but felt that certain areas of the law needed to be discussed more fully. When the

Criminal Law Act was passed therefore, two forms of common law conspiracy were retained for what was supposed to be an interim period. Over 30 years later, this position remains, so the law on conspiracy is an uncomfortable mix of statute law and common law. The following three forms of conspiracy still exist:

- Conspiracy to commit a crime, an offence defined in the **Criminal Law Act 1977**.
- Conspiracy to defraud, a common law offence.
- Conspiracy to corrupt public morals or outrage public decency, also created at common law.

A Level students that are required to study this topic may be relieved to discover that only statutory conspiracy has to be examined, the principles of which are detailed below.

13.3.1 CONSPIRACY TO COMMIT A CRIME

As stated, this offence is to be found in the **Criminal Law Act 1977**, as amended by the **Criminal Attempts Act 1981** and the **Criminal Justice Act 1987**.

S1 states that the offence of conspiracy to commit a crime will take place when a party agrees with another or others to pursue a course of conduct which, if carried out, will amount to or involve the commission of an offence, or would do so if something had not happened to make the offence impossible to commit.

These are often known as **s1** conspiracies. The punishment is laid down in **s3** but this, too is complicated. In cases of murder and other very serious crimes, the maximum is life imprisonment; in other cases punishable by imprisonment, the maximum sentence should not exceed the maximum for the main offence.

The *actus reus* of conspiracy

Three points need to be established:

- **An agreement with others**
- **to pursue a course of conduct**
- **which, if carried out, will amount to or involve the commission of an offence.**

Although an agreement with others must be shown, it is only necessary for the offender to have agreed with one of them. Normally this would not include a spouse or a child or the intended victim. In **Chrastny 1991** therefore, the defendant tried to argue that she had only discussed the matter of supplying Class A drugs with her husband.

The Court of Appeal refused to accept this claim, as the evidence implied that she had been aware that other conspirators were involved in the plan.

The *mens rea* of conspiracy

This requires intention.

The Law Commission made it clear that liability would only be incurred if the defendant intended to commit the offence. The Bill introduced into Parliament originally stated that the defendant and his fellow conspirators 'must intend to bring about any consequence which is an element of the offence'. Unfortunately, this clause was deleted from the statute because the whole phrase, of which this was only a part, was felt to be too complicated. **Instead, intention can be implied from the wording of s1(1), when it states that a person must agree with another to pursue a course of conduct. S1(2)** also states that, in cases where the full offence can be committed without the offender having knowledge of any particular fact or circumstance necessary for the commission of the crime, such a person cannot be found guilty of conspiracy unless **'he and at least one other party to the agreement intend or know that the fact or circumstance shall or will exist at the time when the conduct constituting the offence is to take place'**. This means that even in cases where recklessness, negligence or strict liability suffices for the complete offence, this is not enough for conspiracy to commit such crimes; here, an intention must be proved.

Difficulties arising from Anderson

Given the statements above, it is very surprising to note the comments of the House of Lords in **Anderson 1986**.

The defendant, while in Lewes prison, had agreed with others to help a temporary cellmate facing very serious charges, to effect an escape from prison. After his own release, Anderson had provided some diamond wire but was then involved in a car accident and took no further part in the plan. He tried to argue that he did not possess the *mens rea* for conspiracy. He claimed that he had never intended for the agreement to go ahead and had never believed that it could succeed. He stated that, instead of giving any additional help, he was going abroad with the money paid up-front.

The House of Lords dismissed his appeal against his conviction but the reasoning of Lord Bridge when reaching such a decision has been seriously questioned. He came to the rather startling conclusion that the conspirator did not need to intend that the pre-arranged plan should actually take place.

He accepted that it was a necessary ingredient to agree that a course of conduct should be pursued, which would then lead to the committing of an offence. Nevertheless, he decided that it was not necessary to prove that each and every conspirator should intend that the crime should be committed.

This view of the law ensured that Anderson's conviction could be upheld. It also makes it easier for the prosecution to convict those who only play a subordinate role in the planning of a crime and who do not really care whether or not the offence is carried out, so long as they are paid for their part in the proceedings. It has however, been sharply criticised by academics. **S1(1)** implies an intention to pursue a course of conduct which, if carried out would involve the commission of an offence. In addition, **s1(2)** specifically demands knowledge or intention for conspiracy to commit strict liability offences and ones for which recklessness might suffice for the full offence. It would therefore, be extremely odd if intention were required for these offences but not for all the others where a higher degree of *mens rea* is needed for the complete offence.

Anderson was distinguished on this point by the Court of Appeal in Northern Ireland, in the case of **McPhillips 1990**, concerning conspiracy to murder.

His conviction was quashed because it was believed that he had intended to give a warning that a bomb was primed to go off at a disco at 1am, the busiest part of the night, while the other conspirators had not.

If the statements in **Anderson** had been followed, it would have been immaterial that McPhillips did not intend the crime to go ahead.

The court however, seized on another part of Lord Bridge's judgment, where he suggested that special consideration should be given to honest citizens who might find themselves caught up in a conspiracy and feel obliged, for a time, to go along with the plot. The court conveniently overlooked the fact that McPhillips was far from innocent in other respects and had definitely been involved in the criminal activities.

Lord Bridge's *dicta* was also ignored in **Edwards 1991**. There was a conspiracy to supply amphetamines, an illegal drug, but there was some doubt as to whether the defendant intended to supply another drug instead, which was not illegal.

The Court of Appeal held that a direction by the trial judge that the defendant could only be convicted if he intended to supply amphetamines was held to be correct. If Anderson had been followed, a different answer would have been given.

Must the conspirator play a part in the proceedings?

Another part of Lord Bridge's judgment that has also given rise to problems was his contention that the defendant is only guilty of conspiracy if he intended to play some part in the proceedings.

The late Sir John Smith called this **'a novel dictum'** and noted that it is unsupported by authority. It also creates a loophole through which many offenders could escape, especially ringleaders, and others in a similar position, who organise events and then leave it to others to carry out the 'dirty work'. In **Siracusa 1990**, the Court of Appeal decided to address the issue, even though it was not directly pertinent to the appeal it was hearing.

The court decided in this drug smuggling case that participation in a conspiracy could be passive as well as active. The judges decided tactfully that Lord Bridge could not have meant what he said! O'Connell L J remarked:

> 'We think it obvious that Lord Bridge cannot have been intending that the organiser of a crime who recruited others to carry it out would not himself be guilty of conspiracy unless it could be proved that he intended to play some part himself'.

Unfortunately, his words were quite clear. He stated that the *mens rea* for **s1** conspiracy would only be established if 'the accused, when he entered into the agreement, intended to play some part in the agreed course of conduct in furtherance of the criminal purpose'. This statement may cause problems in the future.

◀ *Comment*

It can be seen that the Court of Appeal has been making valiant efforts to limit the effect of these two statements by Lord Bridge and, that, so far, their attempts to do this have gone unchallenged and may be said to represent the law as it currently stands. It may have been clearer if the Court of Appeal had noted that Lord Bridge's second statement was merely *obiter* and that the court did not feel able to follow it.

13.3.2 CONSPIRING TO COMMIT THE IMPOSSIBLE

S1 Criminal Law Act 1977 makes it clear that a statutory conspiracy can take place even though the full offence is impossible.

13.3.3 CONSPIRACIES WHERE A FOREIGN ELEMENT IS INVOLVED

Where the conspiring is done abroad, but the crime is to be committed in the UK, it will obviously be of great advantage if the enforcers of law and order can act as soon as possible to prevent the crime taking place. The courts have done their best to help this process.

In **DPP v Doot 1973, the House of Lords held that a conspiracy could, in some circumstances, be a continuing process.** Where an unlawful arrangement was made abroad to import cannabis into the UK, it was decided that all the conspirators could be charged with the offence when one of their group landed in England.

Their Lordships stated:

> A conspiracy does not end with the making of the agreement. It will continue so long as there are two or more parties to it intending to carry out the design.

FIVE KEY FACTS ON STATUTORY CONSPIRACIES

- The rules are laid down in the **Criminal Law Act 1977. S1(1)** defines the offence.

- The *actus reus* is agreeing with another or others that a course of conduct will be pursued, which if carried out will amount to the commission of an offence (or would do so if the crime were not impossible).

- From the rather obscure wording of the statute, it appears that the defendant must intend that the offence should be carried out, but the House of Lords in **Anderson 1986** decided that the defendant was guilty even when this was not established. The Court of Appeal did not follow this reasoning, in either **McPhillips 1990 or Edwards 1991** so the law on this point is far from clear.

- In **Anderson**, the House of Lords also stated, *obiter*, that the alleged conspirator must have intended to play some part in the commission of the offence. The Court of Appeal in **Siracusa 1990** decided that the House of Lords did not really mean to state this! The law on this point also remains uncertain. Academics appear to favour the views of the Court of Appeal on these issues.

- The Criminal Law Act makes it clear that the offence of conspiring to commit a crime can be committed even the offence itself is impossible.

This very useful interpretation enabled the conspiracy to be thwarted and the crime prevented.

In Liangsiriprasert v Government of the USA 1991, the Privy Council took this reasoning a stage further and decided that even if an overt act like the above could not be proved, it was still possible to decide that a conspiracy existed. The court argued:

The only purpose of looking for an overt act in England in the case of a conspiracy entered into abroad, can be to establish the link between the conspiracy and England or possibly to show that the conspiracy is continuing. But if this can be established by other evidence, for example the taping of conversations between the conspirators showing a firm agreement to commit the crime at some future date, it defeats the preventative purpose of the crime of conspiracy to have to wait until some overt act is performed.

The Court of Appeal approved of this extension in Sansom 1991.

13.4 INCITEMENT (AN OUTLINE ONLY)

Incitement is mainly a common law offence, although there are some specific offences of incitement which have been put in statutory form. Examples are inciting a person to commit murder, inciting others to mutiny or inciting racial hatred.

The remaining part of this chapter will examine common law incitement. The current position is that incitement to commit a summary offence is only triable summarily, whereas an incitement to commit an indictable offence is triable on indictment. This might seem obvious but it was not always the law. An odd feature which does remain is that, while the punishment for an incitement to commit a summary offence cannot exceed that given for the full offence, the courts have the discretion to set the punishment when the offence is tried on incitement. This means that, theoretically at least, the inciter could receive a higher sentence than the person committing the offence. This could be a useful deterrent in combating terrorist attacks.

13.4.1 THE *ACTUS REUS* OF INCITEMENT

Incitement occurs where:

- a person urges another to commit a crime or
- 'reaches or seeks to influence the mind of another'.

The courts have decided that incitement can be effected by suggestion, argument, persuasion or, as stated in **Race Relations Board v Applin 1973, even by threats or other pressure.** Incitement will often be verbal but it is possible to put the words in writing and thereby incite members of the public.

In the early case of Most 1881, the incitement seemed obvious when the defendants urged certain members of the community to rise up and assassinate the heads of state. In Invicta Plastics Ltd v Clare 1976, a conviction was also upheld when an advertisement was placed in a motoring magazine drawing attention to the company's product which could be used to help evade police speed traps.

The Divisional Court held that, when looking at the advertisement as a whole, there was clear evidence of incitement.

The incitement does not have to be successful but there must be incitement to commit an actual offence known to law. In **Whitehouse 1977**, a loophole was disclosed when a man was accused of inciting a young girl of 15 to have incestuous intercourse with him. **S11 Sexual Offences Act 1956** stated that it was an offence for a woman of 16 or over to permit her father and other close

relatives to have sexual intercourse with her but under-age girls were not included. Therefore, Whitehouse could not be found guilty because he was charged with inciting a girl to commit a crime which, under statute, she was incapable of committing. The judges were understandably reluctant to decide that young girls in these appalling situations should be tainted with the suggestion that they, also, had done wrong.

The defendant, therefore, was found not guilty in the current case but the judges suggested that Parliament should step in and plug this loophole in the law. This was effected very speedily and s54 Criminal Law Act 1977 lays down that it is an offence for a man to incite to have sexual intercourse with him a girl under the age of 16 whom he knows to be his grand-daughter, daughter or sister.

Another offender who escaped liability when he was obviously guilty of wrongdoing was **Curr 1968**. The defendant ran a highly lucrative business of advancing money to women with large families and in return taking their Family Allowance books to cover the debt, plus a large sum in interest. He handled between 40 and 80 such books a week and made a profit of around 800 per cent on the deals. He employed a team of women to cash the signed vouchers for him and was charged with inciting them to commit offences under the **Family Allowances Act 1945**.

The Court of Appeal quashed the man's conviction, arguing that while it was obvious that the defendant knew that he was acting illegally, the prosecution also needed to establish that the women agents knew that they were committing a crime. This matter had not been properly put before the jury so the court felt obliged to quash the defendant's conviction for incitement. He must have been laughing all the way back to the Post Office!

The team drafting the *Criminal Code* strongly criticised this decision, arguing that it was not necessary to prove that the person who was being incited had to know that an offence was being committed. It was felt to be enough that the *defendant* had such a belief. **Curr however, is a Court of Appeal decision that has not been overruled. It must, therefore, reflect the state of the law at the present time.**

13.4.2 THE *MENS REA* OF INCITEMENT

The accused must be shown to have:

- intended to bring about the criminal result
- used persuasion or pressure to do this

although it is not necessary for the offence to be committed. The early decision in **Higgins 1801** made this position clear and the judges affirmed this in **Whitehouse 1977. From the decision in Curr 1968, discussed above, the defendant must also believe that the person incited will have the necessary *mens rea* to commit the crime in question or, at least, another crime requiring the same *mens rea*.** If he does not believe this, they could be in the position of innocent agents and he could be the principal offender, provided that he was charged correctly.

13.4.3 INCITEMENT OF CRIMES WHICH ARE IMPOSSIBLE TO COMMIT

The law on this is rather confused. **Since the case of Fitzmaurice 1983, it is also out of line with the statutory position taken for the crimes of attempts and conspiracy to commit a crime. We need to see how this position arose.**

In **McDonough 1962**, the defendant's conviction for inciting a number of butchers to handle stolen meat carcasses which he believed were in a cold store, was upheld. He tried to argue that his conviction should be quashed because, at that time, the carcasses were not, in fact, in that place and there was some doubt as to whether they had ever existed.

The Court of Appeal held that the essence of the offence lay in his suggestion to the other parties that they should receive the meat that he believed was stolen.

The Law Commission felt that this was a sensible line to take and, with regard to attempts and conspiracy, Parliament made it clear when it passed the **Criminal Attempts Act 1981** that the defendant may still be liable even if the actual offence is impossible.

Confusion resulting from Fitzmaurice

Despite the comments made above, the wording of the decision in the strange case of **Fitzmaurice 1983** appears to allow a defence of impossibility in some instances where the planned crime has not taken place. The defendant was convicted of inciting three men to commit a 'wages snatch'. At his father's request, he had recruited the men allegedly to rob a woman walking from her workplace to the National Westminster Bank. In fact, the defendant's father had hatched a complicated plot to recover reward money by informing the authorities that there was an impending raid on a security van. He had therefore dissuaded his son from taking part but had arranged for him to assemble a gang. He then intended that this gang would be discovered outside the bank, wearing masks and carrying imitation firearms. The son was completely unaware of his father's plot but after it was discovered, he was charged with incitement. He tried to argue that he could not be guilty of inciting the other men to commit a crime that could not, in fact, be committed. **The Court of Appeal held that it was immaterial that the defendant's father was not planning a real offence because the defendant believed that he was arranging for the men to commit a robbery and such an offence was still possible to perform. The conviction, therefore, was upheld.**

Despite the upholding of the conviction, the judges did not take this opportunity to bring the law on incitement in line with that of attempts and statutory conspiracy. They failed to lay down a general rule that an offender would still incur liability even though the crime he was inciting was impossible. Instead, a far more limited rule now seems to exist in relation to incitement. If the incitement is of a general nature, then the defence of impossibility will not prevail, as seen in **Fitzmaurice,** and the inciter can be convicted. If however, the incitement concerns a specific issue, such as inciting another to kill a third party when in fact, that person is already dead, the inciter cannot be found guilty, as the specific crime has proved impossible to commit.

 *Comment*

It is difficult to understand why the Court of Appeal did not take this chance to put the law on incitement, in respect of crimes that are impossible to commit, on the same footing as attempts and conspiracy. It was clearly the intention of both the Law Commission and Parliament that the defence should not be available for inchoate offences.

FIVE KEY FACTS ON INCITEMENT

- Incitement is a common law offence. If tried on indictment, the courts have the discretion to set the punishment.

- The *actus reus* is committed when the offender suggests, urges, persuades, threatens or pressurises the other to commit a crime (**Race Relations Board v Applin 1973**). Incitement can be effected orally or in writing (**Most 1881, Invicta Plastics v Clare 1976**). The offender must be inciting the other to commit a crime known to law; if there is no such offence he cannot be found guilty (**Whitehouse 1977**). If the crime does exist, then it does not matter if the inciter is unsuccessful in his attempts to persuade the other to commit it (**Higgins 1801**).

- The *mens rea* of incitement is an intention to bring about the required result, plus persuasion or pressure on the person targeted.

- The controversial case of **Curr 1968** also decided that the person incited must have the *mens rea* to commit the offence in question. While this decision has been criticised, it has not been overruled.

- **Fitzmaurice 1983** appears to decide that an inciter may have a defence in cases where a specific crime was the subject of the incitement but the crime has proved to be impossible. This approach differs to the one taken in the offences of attempt and conspiracy. If, however, the incitement is of a more general nature, the law mirrors that of these last two crimes and the fact that the more general type of crime has proved to be impossible will not prevent a conviction for incitement.

13.5 SUGGESTED REFORM OF INCHOATE OFFENCES

It has been seen that a measure of reform of the law on conspiracy to commit a crime was effected by the **Criminal Law Act 1977** and changes made to the law on attempts made in the **Criminal Attempts Act 1981**. The offence of incitement has not been the subject of such a degree of scrutiny. The Draft Code team did investigate whether to change the name of the offence but at that time, decided to retain it. Clause 47 of the Draft Code defines incitement. This states that a person will be guilty of incitement if:

(a)   **he incites another to do or cause to be done an act or acts which if done, will involve the commission of the offence or offences by the other; and**

(b)   **he intends or believes that the other, if he acts as incited, shall or will do so with the fault required for the offence or offences.**

Clause 50 of the Code, if ever enacted, provides for a common approach to be taken with regard to impossibility. It states that **'a person may be guilty of incitement, conspiracy or attempt to commit an offence although the commission of the offence is impossible'**.

As noted in Chapter 11 the Law Commission is now in favour of abolishing the crime of incitement altogether and is, instead, in favour of creating two new inchoate offences of assisting and encouraging crime.

Activity

Decide whether the following wrongdoers can be charged with an inchoate offence, giving full reasons for your answers:

- Pablo, Gustav and Salvador met to enjoy their weekly drink together and discussed the possibility of stealing the Crown Jewels from the Tower of London. Salvador, a glass merchant, promised to provide the equipment to cut the glass behind which the jewels were kept. The friends were unaware that the jewels had been transferred to Windsor Castle the month before. They also failed to realise that their conversation had been taped and they were arrested. Salvador claimed that he had never intended to take part in the crime itself and had never really believed that it was going to take place.

- Claude was at a racing track. The horse he had backed, called Monet's Folly, was trailing at the back of the field. Claude fired an air pistol close to the track, trying to distract the leading horses. He was hoping to get the race called off and thereby retrieve his stake money. His plan failed miserably and he was later charged with attempted theft.

- Jacques is a student activist, who fiercely opposes the contraction of art courses at Chagall University. He placed an advertisement in the Student Quarterly Review urging students to rise up and kill the Chancellor. The Chancellor, however, is aware of the strength of feeling that his reforms have engendered and has employed a team of bodyguards to keep a 24-hour watch over him.

Self-assessment questions on Chapter 13

1. Where is the law on attempts to commit a crime and what is the punishment?
2. Giving cases to support your answer, describe the test for deciding whether an attempt has been made.
3. What is the *mens rea* for attempt in cases of murder, grievous bodily harm under **s18** and gbh under **s20**?
4. Why have the decisions in **Khan 1990** and **AG's Reference (No 3 of 1992) 1994** caused difficulties with regard to the *mens rea* of attempt?
5. What is the position if a person attempts to commit a crime but the actual crime turns out to be impossible?
6. Define a criminal conspiracy and state where the law is to be found.
7. Why did the House of Lords decision in **Anderson** cause problems with regard to the *mens rea* of conspiracy.
8. How has this problem been dealt with in subsequent cases?
9. Using cases in support, describe the *actus reus* and *mens rea* of incitement.
10. Explain why the case of **Fitzmaurice** has caused problems.

Chapter 14

THE SYNOPTIC MODULES

14.1 INTRODUCTION

The year 2001 saw the end of the more traditional type of A Level that had existed in this country for 50 years and the introduction of a new modular system, comprising six modules. The old examination had been held in high esteem but concerns had been expressed over the fact that students who were unable to complete their two years of study or who failed the end of course examinations had nothing to show for their efforts. The new modular A Levels were designed to deal with this problem, provide increased motivation and enable students to build on work already undertaken. They gave students the chance to achieve shorter-term goals. For example, the passing of the first three modules could endow the student with an Advanced Subsidiary qualification, which would exist in its own right, the standard being that expected of students halfway through a two-year course. On the other hand, it was also envisaged that success at this point would provide an incentive for many to continue onwards towards the final A Level qualification and, hopefully, beyond. The Welsh Joint Education Committee, for example, stresses that their A Level Law qualification may be followed by candidates of any age, **'irrespective of their gender, ethnic, religious or cultural background ... and provides opportunities for candidates to extend their life-long learning'**. It is to be hoped that all students reading this book and studying A Level Law, will find this to be the case.

This chapter now goes on to discuss the following subjects:

✔ **The synoptic element in A Level Law**
✔ **Differences in approach**

✔ **Module 6 of the AQA qualification**
✔ **The Special Studies Module devised by OCR**
✔ **The LW6 paper set by WJEC.**

14.2 THE SYNOPTIC ELEMENT

Critics of the proposed new system had claimed that the modular approach could lead to a loss of understanding of the wider issues and principles connected to the particular subject. To counteract this, the sixth module in the A Level specification is designed to be a synoptic one, aimed at drawing together aspects of the whole two year course. For students studying criminal law in A2, this requires you to show how this topic operates within the wider context of the English legal system.

The AQA specification states that the subject of law **'is one that lends itself to such connections by its very nature'**. This Board encourages students undertaking Module 6 to draw on material from any of the other modules.

The OCR board, when sending their selected material (discussed below), emphasises that students are expected to demonstrate more than an understanding of the criminal law aspects of the data sent to them. They must also **'use legal methods and legal reasoning to analyse legal material, to select appropriate legal rules and apply these in order to draw conclusions'**.

WJEC requires A Level students **'to make synoptic connections'** between a wide range of topics and to **'sustain an argument which reflects the complexities of the issues'**.

14.3 DIFFERENCES IN APPROACH TAKEN BY THE EXAMINATION BOARDS

It can be seen from the above comments that the three examination boards all welcome the requirement that students should remain aware of the wider issues inherent in their study of criminal law. The Boards have however, devised different methods to deal with this, as shown in the next three sections where each of these approaches is examined in more detail.

14.4 MODULE 6 OF AQA

Students studying the AQA specification should be aware that the questions set on Module 6 are based on pre-defined concepts. Despite this, the Board stresses that the examination questions **'will be drawn widely to allow for a range of responses. Thus, although each question will be based around a specified concept, any appropriate subject matter will be valid as a basis or illustration to support the student's argument and discussion'**. It can be deduced from this, that you have a large measure of autonomy in the choice of the material you can use to answer the questions set. You can therefore select appropriate topics from those in which you have the greatest interest and/or the most material at your disposal.

The examination lasts for 90 minutes and you are expected to answer two questions out of four. Module 6 comprises 20% of the total A Level Marks, so students doing well here will enhance their marks considerably. Careful pre-planning is therefore strongly recommended and this will be made easier by the fact that the questions do not vary greatly for each sitting. Examples of Module 6 questions can be seen on the AQA website.

Five concepts have been pre-selected for examination of this module. In alphabetical order they are:

- **Balancing conflicting interests**
- **Fault**
- **Judicial creativity**
- **Law and justice**
- **Law and morals.**

It is proposed to give a brief mention of each and to indicate a few areas that could be investigated. Note that these are mere suggestions in order to give you some indication of the range of material available. You and your tutors may well select completely different areas of study. Be aware that examiners delight in original answers, provided that they demonstrate a proper understanding of the subject matter and are related to the question set.

Balancing conflicting interests

In criminal law, the greatest conflict arises in the decision of the criminal to break the law, often for personal gain, and the State's desire that the law should be enforced for the protection of the majority of law-abiding citizens. You could examine some of the methods used to deal with such problems. For example, a range of punishments has been devised by the State reflecting the degree of seriousness of the offence but care is also taken to ensure that these sanctions are just. The offender's interests are safeguarded in many ways, including:

- **The right to a fair trial**
- **Non-custodial sentences for most first-time offenders**
- **The growth of community sentences**
- **Drug treatment orders where applicable**
- **Early release programmes, including possible release on licence for those serving a mandatory life sentence for murder.**

These attempts to give justice to the offender need, in turn, to be balanced against the need to protect and reassure the public. There are increasing fears concerning street robbery, burglary and drug related crime and a widely held view that the above methods were really introduced in order to reduce prison overcrowding, without enough thought being given to the possible consequences.

There are many examples of other, more specific conflicts in criminal law, among them the following:

- Balancing the rights of a party to do as he wishes in private, as seen in the decriminalisation of homosexual activities, against the desire of the State to ensure that the participant does not harm himself or others. Note the restrictions on the use of consent in Brown and Others and Dica.
- The desire to be fair to a party who is forced to commit a crime against his will. This has been achieved by the development of the defence of duress. Balanced against this is the need to put some controls on the defence in order to protect possible victims, hence the decision not to allow the defence on a murder charge. The possible consequences of the more radical changes proposed by the Law Commission could be discussed.
- The need for laymen to become involved in the criminal justice system against the reluctance of many to sit as magistrates or serve on a jury. Possible reform of the system to make it more attractive to them could be examined, as could alternatives, such as appointing more paid magistrates and abolishing more jury trials.
- The perceived need for strict liability offences for the protection of the public against the possible injustice to some of those convicted.

Judicial Creativity

This is one of the most popular options as it allows Year 1 work to be built upon. It nearly always appears on the examination paper in one form or another. AQA states that the inclusion of this concept:

requires candidates to develop their previous studies into a more abstract examination of how judges are involved in issues of policy when fulfilling these functions. Candidates should therefore be able to explain what might be meant by the word 'policy' and to illustrate their discussions by reference to appropriate examples and illustrations from any appropriate areas of law studied in any of the modules.

The explanatory note goes on to stress that such policy decisions relate to both the judges' own rules and those laid down by Parliament so you are expected to 'be aware of the ways in which the judges attempt to balance the roles of each'. There is a great deal of material to draw upon here but it is advisable to study the following issues:

- The operation of our system of binding precedent, particularly in relation to the position of the House of Lords, the Privy Council, the Court of Appeal (Criminal Division) and the Divisional Court of QBD. Note also the benefits and failings of such a method.
- Examples of rules of criminal law developed entirely by the judges, e.g. in relation to murder, constructive and gross negligence manslaughter and general defences, including necessity and duress.
- Examples of overruling of past decisions by the House of Lords using powers given under the Practice Statement of 1966, and the impact of these cases in the field of criminal law. Cases could include Howe and Bannister, Shivpuri and, in particular, G and another.
- The general aim of judges when interpreting statutes, i.e. to discover the intention of Parliament, but the widely different approaches taken to achieve this, e.g. Whiteley v Chappell, (words taken literally) and Smith v Hughes, (purposive approach). Note that the trend is towards the latter, allowing extrinsic material to be

examined, but be aware that this approach can lead to more uncertainty in the law.

- Difficulties caused by some of the judges' interpretation of words in a statute, whether or not they have been defined by Parliament, e.g. Caldwell (recklessness), Moloney, (intention) and Gomez and Hinks (appropriation).

Fault

This is a popular and fertile area that many of you might choose to study.

- You could note that most offences require some form of blameworthiness on the part of the defendant, in the form of intention, recklessness or negligence, before criminal liability can be imposed. You could investigate various problem areas in this respect, among them the difficulties with the definitions of intention and recklessness and the burden put on the jury where gross negligence resulting in death is at issue. There is so much material here that each of these areas could be developed in its own right.
- Many of you will choose to examine strict liability offences where liability is imposed without the need to prove fault. This is a good area to study because it can also be used for most of the other concepts. Note examples of such offences and the possible justification of them, (protection of public by keeping standards high etc), but note more adverse criticisms. Be aware also of the reluctance of judges to convict in 'truly criminal' cases, unless some degree of fault is shown or the imposition of strict liability has been made clear by Parliament.
- At the opposite end of the scale, be aware that in rare cases, no liability will arise whatever the degree of fault, e.g. in relation to children under 10. You could note the alternative ways of dealing with such offenders. You could also assess the comparatively recent changes made by

Parliament concerning children aged between 10 and 14, who now have the same liability as adults. A few offenders may escape the stigma of a criminal conviction by being labelled insane instead, often an unappealing alternative. Be aware of the special verdict and the fact that in cases of murder, they would be placed in a mental institution without a time limit being set. A wider range of disposals is now possible for lesser crimes.

- You could note that even where fault is established, the judges could decide that this is of a lesser degree than that possessed by other parties, as where secondary offenders are involved.
- Alternatively, there may be some justification or excuse for the criminal behaviour and a full or partial defence could be accepted, such as self-defence, mistake, necessity, duress, or defences under the Homicide Act 1957.

Law and Justice

You could start by describing the different meanings of these two words and examine some of the many areas where justice may not be 'seen to be done'. These could include:

- The imposition of a mandatory life sentence for murder, regardless of the circustances, e.g. in mercy killings and where excessive force has been used in self-defence.
- The inability to secure convictions in cases of corporate killings.
- The classification of illnesses like epilepsy and diabetes as insanity.
- The imposition of liability without fault.
- The stance taken by the courts and Parliament that ignorance of the law is no defence while the rules are increasing at an alarming rate.

You could continue by noting some examples of where the criminal law and notions of justice do appear to be moving more closely together.

- **The development of the defences of necessity, duress of threats and, more recently, duress of circumstances.**
- **The acceptance that men and women react differently to threats.**
- **The recognition that rape can exist within a marriage.**
- **The decision in G and another ensuring that a uniform approach is taken with regard to reckless behaviour.**
- **More victim support schemes and better treatment of witnesses.**

Law and morals

Once again, the words need to be defined and distinguished, although there is, of course, a good deal of overlap between the two. This is because the vast majority of people would believe that a just legal system should be based on strong moral principles. This can be seen in the sanctions against unlawful killing and theft. These crimes could then be defined and examined to show why such behaviour is considered to be so unacceptable. Many would also include the infliction of serious bodily harm and deception in the same category. These areas seem to be clear cut, but you could go on to note other areas where legal rules and ideas of morality do not co-exist so easily.

For example, some people (and religions) believe that all forms of suicide are morally wrong. English law however is less definite about this and makes a distinction between those who choose to die alone and those who enlist the aid of others. Since 1961, the law has taken the view that it is not criminal behaviour in the first instance but it would be in the second. This is graphically illustrated by the refusal of the House of Lords to allow Diane Pretty the right to 'die with dignity', because she would have required the assistance of her husband to effect this. The law might also penalise those who survive a suicide pact and they could face a charge of manslaughter. In addition,

there are those who believe that any homosexual activity is morally wrong but the law now takes a very different view to the stand taken in the days of Oscar Wilde, provided that any such sexual activity takes place in private and involves consenting adults.

In addition, there are no sanctions against lying, so long as this is not done under oath or to damage a person's reputation in the eyes of right thinking members of society, whereas many would argue that all forms of lying are morally wrong. Similarly, the law does not condemn adultery but many religions take a very different view.

On the other hand, with the imposition of strict liability offences, the law may punish those who are morally blameless, such as the unfortunate shop owners in **London Borough of Harrow v Shah** and the luckless publican in **Cundy v Le Cocq** and you could examine why this approach is taken.

14.5 THE SPECIAL STUDIES PAPER DEVISED BY OCR

The Special Studies Paper in Unit 6 is, like the other two OCR A2 papers, of 90 minutes duration. It does, however, attract 40% of the A2 marks, as opposed to 30% in the other two papers, so it is very important to do well in this if you are seeking the higher grades. This will entail careful preparation in advance of the examination.

The OCR Board decided that an effective way of dealing with the synoptic requirement would be to send out a booklet of selected material, which the students could then study prior to the examination. This information has a shelf life of two years. At the time of writing, the current material gives extracts from 12 pieces of data, the majority of them on the elements of robbery and burglary. Previous pre-released packs have covered the subjects of involuntary manslaughter and selected general defences.

The data given out will provide you with basic material from which to undertake further study, in anticipation of the questions that might arise on the examination paper. These questions will not be known in advance. Because it is synoptic paper, it is important to remember that, in addition to criminal law topics, other questions will be set requiring you to draw on your wider knowledge of the workings of the English legal system. These often involve topics relating to sources of law, such as the doctrine of precedent and statutory interpretation, plus the work of the law reform bodies, although, in addition to this, knowledge of other areas could be sought. The specification states that in addition to knowledge of criminal law,

> *there is source material on topics contained in the specifications for the AS Units. This material thus indicates the legal structures and/or legal processes and/or legal issues which candidates will be expected to draw together and make connections between these and the substantive law.*

Many of you will be given course time in which to look at the data sent out but do not despair if you are studying alone. Provided that you have studied the information carefully, your work is likely to stand out as being both original and fresh. Even those of you examining the material via class discussions would be advised to undertake more in-depth solitary study, particularly as, in the final question, you will often be required to apply your knowledge of the rules to specific unknown scenarios. This necessitates the acquisition of specific skills, which increase greatly with practice. Hopefully, some of these will have been developed in Year 1, while preparing for the Unit 3 examination on Sources of Law and in your answers to the problem scenarios seen throughout this book.

Primary and secondary sources

Included in your pre-released booklet, you are likely to find extracts from primary (or original)

sources of law. These could include extracts from Acts of Parliament, delegated legislation or from important cases, perhaps developing, refining or even overruling existing precedents. In rare cases, the judgment may be setting an entirely new precedent, a precedent of first impression. In addition, there may be passages from secondary sources, such as well-respected textbooks, articles from legal journals and reports from other legal bodies. You may be required to distinguish between these two sources in relation to the data you are given. In addition, some of this information may, in turn, refer to other sources. If so, you are urged strongly to study these, too, to aid your preparation.

The current OCR paper

This material has been released for use in June 2005, January 2006, June 2006 and January 2007 and consists of 12 pieces of data, 11 of them relating to robbery and burglary. The points mentioned below are only some suggestions of areas that could be examined. Your tutors may well decide that different areas need investigation so be careful to take these on board..

The first extract looks at the operation of binding precedent in English law, but also explains how the law can grow within such a system. You are reminded that this matter is discussed in Chapter 1 of this book, as well as in your Year 1 material.

The passage goes on to state that, in addition to Parliament, our judges also develop legal principles and even make new law when the necessity arises. You need to be aware of examples of such development and creation in the field of criminal law. In source 8, for example, Lord Justice Edmund Davies observed that the phrase 'having entered as a trespasser' was **'one which has not, to the best of our knowledge been previously canvassed in the courts'**.

The first extract also looks at law made by Parliament and highlights the distinction between the interpretation and construction of statutes. It informs us that our judges may have widely different opinions on how flexible they should be if faced with ambiguous or unclear statutory provisions. Some judges take a very restrictive view of this, believing that the words laid down by Parliament should not be tampered with, whereas others feel far less constrained. Be able to quote examples of each type of approach. A layman might assume that a more liberal attitude should always be taken by judges, in order to avoid injustice, absurdity or uncertainty, but the matter is less clear-cut than first appears and you should recognise that there are strong arguments for and against both these views. Since 1969 however, and the criticisms of the Law Commission regarding too wide a use of the literal rule, there has been a gradual move towards a more purposive approach to statutory interpretation, including a greater readiness to use outside material connected to the statute. This could involve looking at recommendations made in earlier Government reports, or those made by one of the law reform bodies. In Source 3, the recommendations of the Criminal Law Revision Committee are referred to by the Court of Appeal, in connection with the word 'force' used in the **Theft Act 1968**. You could examine the status of the Criminal Law Revision Committee and its influence in developing the criminal law and note that its role now appears to have been usurped to a large extent by the Law Commission.

Outside material could also include authoritative textbooks. In Source 6, the opinions of three different legal academics were examined to help the Court of Appeal reach its decision on the meaning of the phrase 'the entry must be as a trespasser'. In the case of **Pepper v Hart**, the House of Lords also permitted the use of Hansard, but placed conditions upon this. You could note these and look at other benefits and drawbacks of using extrinsic aids.

The extract ends by noting that 'hard cases make bad law'. Be able to discuss the meaning of this term and give examples.

Sources 2–6 relate to the crime of robbery and the definition of certain words within **s8** and within the definition of theft. Students are urged to study Chapter 7 very carefully in relation to the meanings of the words 'force' in the definition of robbery and 'appropriation' in theft.

Sources 3, 4 and 6 discuss the meaning of the word 'force' and it should be noted how this has been developed through different cases, On the suggestion of the Criminal Law Revision Committee, this replaced the word 'violence' under the old law. One of the aims of that body and of Parliament when reforming this area of law, was to put more of the words into everyday language that juries would understand, rather than giving statutory definitions. Other examples in the same Act include the word 'dishonest' and 'the intention of permanently depriving the other of the property'. Analogies also can be drawn with the **Criminal Damage Act 1971**, with its change of wording from 'malicious' to 'reckless'. You could investigate whether this lack of Parliamentary assistance is to be desired or whether it puts too much responsibility on the jury. It can also lead to judges giving their opinion of the words, when giving a direction to the jury, as seen in **Dawson**. You could decide whether the judges should have this freedom or whether they are usurping Parliament's role. One rather dubious advantage of giving such help is that, should the judge's interpretation be thought to be wrong, there is the possibility of an appeal on the grounds of a misdirection. If the matter is left to the jury without further guidance, and they arrive at what is later perceived to be the wrong decision, the actual verdict cannot be challenged. An **Attorney-General's Reference** would have to be made should a change in the law be felt to be necessary.

Sources 4 and 5 examine the meaning of the word 'appropriation'. This word is defined in the Act but has still caused problems in cases of theft and robbery. Be able to quote examples and note that in **Hale**, the Court of Appeal appeared to be widening the meaning of the word, despite arguing that they were looking at the 'natural meaning of the words' and using a common sense approach. They interpreted the word 'appropriation ' to cover a continuous act, which could be contrasted with the case of **Atakpu**, noted under theft.

Sources 8–11 look at the crime of burglary and the possible meanings of the phrases, 'entry', 'as a trespasser' and 'building'. There are no statutory definitions, although partial help is given with the word 'building'. You are advised to refer back to Chapter 7 for further information on this to see how these words have been developed via case law, (although in Source 11, the judge emphasises that all the help he requires is within the Act itself, i.e. an intrinsic aid to interpretation).

This material would be ideal for the setting of problem situations in which you would need to apply the law to a specific set of facts.

The jury is mentioned several times in this collection of data. It is stressed more than once that the final decision rests with them. It is therefore possible that a wider question could be set on the benefits and disadvantages of having juries in criminal cases.

14.6 THE LW6 PAPER SET BY WJEC

The A Level Law option for this Board is entitled **Criminal Law and Justice** and therefore takes a wider approach to the subject than the other two Boards. In addition to standard criminal law topics, it also includes an examination of crime and society, police powers and the prosecution process. Paper LW6 of this option consists of one compulsory question either in the form of an essay or as a case scenario. It is shorter than the papers set for LW4 and LW5 and therefore attracts 20% of the A2 marks, as opposed to 40% for the other two modules. As with the other

Boards, because this is the synoptic part of the examination, you should be aware that any aspect of the two-year course could be examined. In practice, however, more of the questions in a case scenario are likely to be based on the A2 elements and it would be rare for an essay to be set purely on AS material, although obviously you will need to revise key areas. **The wording in the Specification is as follows: 'The question will be drawn from the A2 specification and elements of the AS specification as required.'**

14.7 CONCLUSION

This part of the A Level course may well involve most of you in extra study, whichever Board you are dealing with. Despite this, it is to be hoped that at the end of the two year period, you will have gained, not only knowledge of the rules of criminal law, but also a wider appreciation of how those rules fit into the legal system as a whole.

Chapter 15

BRINGING IT ALL TOGETHER

15.1 INTRODUCTION

Well, you've made it! Hopefully, by now, you will have a good knowledge of the key topics in your particular modules and be ready to embark on your revision programme. This last chapter is designed to help you with this. Remember that the chapters in this book are set out in a distinctive way to help you in your studies. Apart from general defences, all the law on a particular topic will be found in one chapter. In addition to revising the legal content, remember that:

● **The key facts charts summarise the current state of the law.** This knowledge is essential as a basis for your revision programme.

● **The comment sections discuss some of the problems arising from the state of the law.** This additional material will help you obtain a wider view of some of the more controversial aspects of the law for use in essay questions.

● **The proposals for reform are indicated separately in the text.** An awareness of these is vital for some examination questions, as they indicate the changes that might be made in the future.

This chapter deals with your revision programme in the following order:

✔ **Main points of Chapters 1–13, with past examination questions**
✔ **A revision plan**
✔ **Answering examination questions**
✔ **Examination day hints.**

15.2 HIGHLIGHTS OF CHAPTERS 1 TO 13

Chapter 1

The material in this chapter helps put the criminal law in context and recaps on some of the information relating to the English Legal system, which most of you will have studied in Year 1. For example, you are reminded of the importance of the doctrine of binding precedent.

Precedents laid down by the House of Lords obviously bind all the lower courts. Their number is not vast because, in criminal matters, the House will only consider points of law of general public importance. Before 1966, the House of Lords also was bound by its own earlier decisions, but the Practice Statement in that year gave the court the freedom to overrule its own earlier decisions if they were felt to be wrong or outdated. This power has been used sparingly but effectively, as can be seen in the cases of **Howe, Shivpuri** and **G and another**.

The Court of Appeal lays down precedents that bind the Crown Court. In turn, it is bound by decisions of the House of Lords, even though it might, on occasion, prefer not to follow them. It can, however, choose not to follow precedents laid down by the Privy Council, as can be seen under provocation. In addition, it can refuse to follow its own earlier decisions if they are based on a misapplication of the law, as noted under actual bodily harm or one of the three exceptions in **Young's Case** applies. The rulings of the Divisional Court of Queen's Bench Division bind the magistrates' courts but the former court, in turn, must obey higher court precedents.

Chapter 1 also summarises the various 'rules' the judges have adopted when trying to interpret the meaning of key phrases in Acts of Parliament, which should be of use when dealing with non-fatal offences against the person, property offences and the synoptic papers. In addition, knowledge of the various reform bodies could be important, particularly the suggestions for reform recommended by the Law Commission.

Chapter 2

Actus reus

Note the 'state of affairs' cases, like **Larsonneur**, and, particularly, the area on omissions. There could be a problem scenario similar to the one in the Activity section or an essay on the following lines:

OCR question 1999.

'In general, the criminal law prohibits the doing of harm but does not impose criminal liability for a failure to do good.' Assess the truth of this statement by reference to the situations where a person may incur criminal liability by reason of a failure or omission to act and the arguments used to justify it

Suggested answer
This question does not seek an explanation of the first part of the statement; by the inclusion of the words 'by reference to...' it is confined to cases and statutes where liability for omissions has been laid down. You could start by noting that, in general, the statement is true in English law and quote Stephen L.J. You could then go on to describe specific situations where the judges have decided not to follow this general approach and explain clearly why a different view was taken. For example, liability has been imposed where a contractual duty has been broken, **Pittwood**, where a duty exists at law, **Dytham**, where a special relationship exists between the parties, **Instan**, where a party has assumed responsibility for another,

---

(**Gibbins and Proctor, Stone and Dobinson**), and where a dangerous situation has been created by the defendant and he has then failed to address it, as in **Miller**. You should also quote instances where liability has been imposed by statute, particularly in relation to motoring offences, in order to keep standards high. You could then go on to note more 'grey area' situations, as in **Khan**, where the defendants escaped liability because the jury had not been properly directed on the issue of possible liability and **Fagan**, where liability was imposed in another way. You could then contrast English law with other jurisdictions where a tougher line is taken and come to an effective conclusion.

Mens rea – Intention in murder

Remember that the question of intention is to be decided by the jury and that **Moloney** has established that in cases of direct intent no extra help on the meaning of the word need be given, only if there is an oblique intent. In **Woollin,** the House of Lords approved of the direction in **Nedrick,** which confirmed that the jury should decide on the question of intention. In cases of murder, however, where an oblique intent is argued, their discretion is limited and

'they are not entitled to find the necessary intention unless they feel sure that death or serious bodily harm was a virtual certainty (barring some unforeseen intervention) as a result of the defendant's actions and that the defendant appreciated that this was the case'.

A question on the lines of whether foresight of consequences actually amounts to intention is a very popular one. You are, therefore, urged strongly to study the Comments' Section in Chapter 2, discussing the implications of the House of Lords' decision in **Woollin** and that of the Court of Appeal in **Matthews and Alleyne,** which should provide you with enough material to deal effectively with such an essay.

Recklessness

Note that two types of recklessness came to be recognised in English law, **Cunningham** and **Caldwell recklessness** and remember that the first, more subjective type of recklessness was always needed for non-fatal offences against the person. **Caldwell** recklessness became confined to cases of criminal damage. Know how this came about. Be able to discuss the strictness of **Caldwell** in cases like **Elliott** and also be aware that the House of Lords was only prepared to recognise a lacuna, or loophole, in very limited circumstances. Be aware of the important House of Lords' decision in **G and another,** where the more objective form of recklessness, introduced by **Caldwell,** was abolished. Note carefully, their Lordships' reasons for overruling **Caldwell** and the Comments' section regarding this decision. This very topical subject may well come up as an essay question on the lines of **'Chart the rise and fall of Caldwell recklessness'** or be combined with a problem on criminal damage.

Strict liability

Questions on this subject are very popular. There could be a problem on the lines of the one set in Chapter 2 but, more frequently, such questions take the form of an essay, as noted below.

WJEC question 2004

Examine critically the approach taken by the courts in determining whether an offence is one of strict liability, illustrating your answer with reference to decided cases.

Suggested answer

The word 'examine' suggests an in-depth study of the subject and use of the word 'critically' indicates that the merits and failings of the approaches taken by the courts must be investigated. An effective way would be to start by distinguishing between the more minor regulatory offences and 'truly criminal' cases. You could then give several examples of the

---

former and note that they are often statutory offences, with which the courts cannot normally interfere. Despite this, some defendants have appealed, (nearly always unsuccessfully), and you need to quote examples. These have included cases on polluting rivers, (**Alphacell v Woodward**), unsafe buildings, (**Atkinson v Sir Alfred McAlpine**), unintentionally supplying drugs, (**Pharmeceutical Society Society of Great Britain v Storkwain**), selling unfit food. (**Smedleys v Breed**), being in possession of wild birds, (**Kirkland v Robinson**) and illegal broadcasts, (**Blake**). The courts may take the view that the imposition of such liability helps to protect the public, acts as a deterrent and thus keeps standards high and also results in other benefits, such as being able to secure a conviction in less easily proved areas. You could also mention that, while liability is strict, it is not always absolute, and give examples. You could then discuss the failings of strict liability, the most important being the imposition of liability without any fault being proved, even negligence, and the attendant sense of injustice felt by some defendants, who through no fault of their own, suffer the stigma of a criminal conviction. This is compounded by a lack of consistency in certain areas, (contrast **Cundy v Le Cocq** and **Sheras v De Rutzen**) and some rather confusing judgments, seen in **Warner.** You could then go on to note that these criticisms would be particularly acute in more 'truly criminal' cases. The House of Lords appears to have recognised such concerns and has moved away from the imposition of strict liability in such cases unless this has been clearly expressed in the relevant statute. This approach can be seen in the cases of **Sweet v Parsley, B (a minor) v DPP** and **K.** You need to know these cases well and the opinions expressed therein. Finally, you need to end your answer with an effective conclusion.

Chapter 3

Murder

Be aware that murder is a common law offence and learn the current definition, after the abolition of the year and a day rule. The *actus reus* is the unlawful killing of a human being under the Queen's peace and the *mens rea* exists where there is malice aforethought, which means the intention to kill or cause serious injury. Link this information up with that given in Chapter 2 regarding the meaning of intention. Note the difficulties of establishing birth and death. In **AG's Ref (No 3 of 1994) 1998,** the House of Lords decided that it could be manslaughter but not murder, when a foetus is injured, the baby is then born alive and later dies.

Remember that in **Re A (children),** the Court of Appeal recognised an extension of the situations where a homicide may be lawful, i.e. where the killing is necessary to save the life of another. Note the interaction of several areas here. Under **Woollin,** the death would have been unlawful unless a defence could be found and two of these were suggested; utilitarian necessity and private defence. Study these points by linking the information found in Chapter 2 (intention after **Woollin,** Chapter 3 (lawful homicide) and Chapter 11 (the defences of necessity and private defence). The **Mental Capacity Bill** may well add further instances where others may be involved in accelerating a death. The decision in **Pretty** however, where the House of Lords laid down that assisting another to commit suicide is unlawful, indicates that a line is being drawn here, although, if the help is merely preparatory, no prosecution may be brought in the first place. No court action resulted after a well-publicised report of a wife helping her terminally ill husband to travel abroad for such assistance.

Causation and transferred malice

The subject of causation, often in the form of a problem, is a very popular area, either on its own as an essay or combined with murder or manslaughter in a problem. One of the most important points to remember is that it will take a very special event to break the chain of causation, as in **Jordan.** Note key cases where this

was not established, particularly **Blaue, Malcherek, Dear, Smith, Cheshire** and **Mellor.**

There could also be a problem situation in which a third party is killed or injured, instead of the intended victim, as noted in Chapter 2. If so, the latter person and the actual victim are treated as if they are one, under the doctrine of transferred malice. The crime must be of the same type (**Latimer**), which was not the case in **Pembliton,** and the victim must be in existence. In **AG's Reference (No 3 of 1994) 1998** the House of Lords was not prepared to extend the doctrine to an unborn child.

Chapter 4

This deals with voluntary manslaughter and is a fertile ground for both problems and essays. Be aware that the law is **ss2–4 Homicide Act 1957** and provides a limited defence reducing murder to manslaughter if one of three situations is shown.

Diminished responsibility

This could be linked to the general defence of insanity, which is available for all crimes but has a stigma attached (see Chapter 10). Note that in **Martin**, the Court of Appeal accepted the defence of diminished responsibility, after a self-defence plea failed. Learn the three elements of diminished responsibility, an abnormality of mind, caused by an inside source, which substantially affected his responsibility for his actions, with cases in support of each. Be aware of the important case of **Dietschmann,** where the House of Lords decided that the abnormality of the mind did not have to be the sole cause of the killing. The judges also decided that even if the defendant would not have killed if he had not been drinking, the pre-existing abnormality of mind should still be taken into account.

Know some of the criticisms that have been expressed about this partial defence but note that, in May 2004, the Law Commission decided not to recommend any changes to it.

Provocation

Know the three elements of provocation, i.e that there must be some form of provocation, the defendant must have suffered a sudden and temporary loss of self-control and a reasonable (or ordinary) man would have acted in the same way. Be aware that, at present, almost anything said or done can amount to provocation and should be put before a jury, even where this is self-induced, as in **Johnson.** The concepts of a sudden and temporary loss of self-control and that of the reasonable man continue to give trouble, so note carefully, the cases on this, particularly in relation to 'slow burn' cases regarding the former issue and that of **Smith (Morgan)** in relation to the latter. The House of Lords has decided that the Court of Appeal was right to extend the characteristics, even mental ones, that may be attributed to the reasonable man, in respect of both the gravity of the provocation and the defendant's loss of control. **Camplin** is still regarded as good authority but has been significantly extended by **Smith (Morgan).** Study the Comments' section on this for help in essay questions and note, very carefully, the Law Commission's proposals, published in 2004, for reform of this area of law. If enacted, the defence would be narrowed to acts of grave provocation that are not self-induced but extended to cover those who act in fear of violence, such as someone suffering from long-term abuse or a party reacting to a threat of violence with excessive force. In a problem question, provocation could be combined with diminished responsibility and even involuntary manslaughter, as noted below.

OCR question 2004

Victoria is the wife and assistant of a knife-throwing expert, Carl, who both work for a circus. Carl is renowned for his hot temper and has recently been off work suffering from depression. Their act consists of Victoria being strapped to a board whilst Carl throws 20 knives all around her from a distance of five metres to within as little as 15 centimetres of her body. They have been doing this for many years without a single mistake and Carl regards his technique as perfect. One evening, just before their act begins, Victoria tells Carl that she is having an affair with the lion tamer, Wayne. Carl is shocked and enraged but, at that moment, the fanfare strikes up for the start of their act and Carl and Victoria enter the ring for their performance. The third knife Carl throws goes straight into Victoria's heart, killing her instantly.

Discuss Carl's liability for Victoria's death

Suggested answer

It is advisable with a question like this to take each of the possible offences in turn, describe the points to be proved and apply the law very precisely to the facts. You need to arrive at some sort of conclusion in relation to each issue. You could then look at any general defences that might assist the defendant. To start, Carl could try to argue that the death was a result of an unfortunate accident but might not be believed. You could then investigate the crimes of murder, voluntary manslaughter and involuntary manslaughter. The *actus reus* of the common law offence of murder may exist, i.e. an unlawful killing of a human being within the Queen's peace. The *mens rea* of murder is malice aforethought, which means the intention to kill or cause serious injury. Carl has never made such a mistake before and considers that his technique is perfect so might find it difficult to prove a lack of direct intent. He could therefore be liable for this offence unless he could plead provocation, diminished responsibility or involuntary manslaughter in either of its two forms.

If Carl puts forward the partial defence of provocation, it is up to the prosecution to disprove this. With regard to a possible provoking event, Victoria's words are likely to be sufficient, **s3 Homicide Act 1957.** Carl's performance took place immediately after this news and he is known for his hot temper, so he might be able to establish a sudden and temporary loss of self-control, as required by **Duffy**. On the other hand, it was the third knife that killed Victoria, so this could be evidence of some pre-mediation and/or time for a 'cooling-off period', as in **Ibrams**, although a 'slow burn' effect may be argued, as in **Ahluwalia**. Carl might also succeed in showing that an ordinary man with a hot temper and depression would have acted in the same way. Cases such as **Camplin, Morhall, Smith (Morgan**), and **Weller**, have decided that both physical and mental elements relating to the accused should be put before the jury.

In relation to diminished responsibility, note where the law is to be found and the three different points that would have to be proved by Carl. Depression has been accepted as an abnormality of mind, as noted in **Seers** and **Ahluwalia** and is an inside source, but this depression must be shown substantially to have affected Carl's responsibility for his actions. The question does not tell us how long he has been off work or whether his depression is severe so he will need the evidence of doctors to convince the jury.

Carl might be able to show that he had no direct intent to kill and that it was merely the shock of the news that affected his knife throwing. The prosecution would have difficulty in establishing constructive manslaughter, because, while the act was dangerous and caused Victoria's death, it was not, originally, an unlawful act. As in **Lamb**, Victoria was not put in fear of an assault.

In the alternative, manslaughter by gross negligence might be put forward. It could be argued that Carl's act in continuing with the performance in such circumstances was so bad as to amount to a criminal act, as laid down in **Adomako**. It appears to show a reckless disregard for Victoria's safety, despite Carl's confidence in his ability. In **Adomako**, the House of Lords decided that it would not be misdirection for a judge to use the word 'reckless' if the situation warranted the ordinary use of the word, a point taken up by the Court of Appeal in **Lidar**.

Carl might wish to bring up the general defence of consent and argue that dangerous exhibitions were included in **AG's Reference No 6 of 1989**, but should be informed that it has been established that a party cannot consent to serious harm (**Brown**), let alone to being killed, as noted in **Leach** and affirmed in **Pretty**.

Chapter 5

Constructive manslaughter

If a death was not intended but arises from an unlawful and dangerous act, this could be a case of constructive manslaughter. Be careful to discuss all three elements of the offence, with supporting cases, as noted in the examination question shown below under Chapter 6.

Gross negligence manslaughter

Currently, this has replaced reckless manslaughter. Be aware of how this occurred and note the approval of the earlier cases of **Bateman** and **Andrews**. As noted above, know that this offence will only be found if, having regard to the risk involved, the conduct of the accused is so bad as to amount to a criminal act, as decided by the House of Lords in **Adomako**. Give other examples, such as **Edwards** and **Kite**.

Be aware of the Law Commission's wish to abolish this offence and that of constructive manslaughter and create instead two new offences of reckless killing, and killing by gross carelessness. Note that the Home Office might add a third. This information is vital should you be asked to comment on the current deficiencies of involuntary manslaughter (see below in the AQA question).

Corporate killing

Be aware of the difficulties in establishing a manslaughter conviction against a large company. At present, it is necessary to use the identification principle with all its attendant difficulties, as affirmed in **AG's Reference (No 2 of 1999)**, rather than the aggregation principle that could now help establish evidence of gross negligence in some cases. It is a very relevant topic so could well come up. In an essay, discuss the reforms suggested by the Law Commission and Home Office and the adoption of a possible new offence called corporate killing, where an individual does not have to be identified.

Chapter 6

Chapter 6 is a large chapter containing all the non-fatal offences against the person. You need to note precisely the *actus reus* and *mens rea* of each one, from assault and battery up to grievous bodily harm with intent. Be aware that the harm can be indirectly inflicted. Note that abh can be established with the *mens rea* of a common assault and that the *mens rea* for a **s20** offence is merely 'some harm' but for liability under **s18**, there must be an intention to cause gbh. Be able to pinpoint the other differences between **s18 and s20**. Note the general defence of consent and when this may be put forward but be aware also of the restrictions on this, particularly after the decisions of the House of Lords and the European Court in **Brown,** and the Court of Appeal in **Dica.** Note that the courts have been prepared to accept that words can amount to an assault as can psychiatric harm (**Constanza, Ireland),** but note that the **Protection from Harassment Act** now provides a more direct way of obtaining help against stalkers.

AQA question 2004

Unknown to Alan, whilst he was out celebrating with his friends, someone slipped a drug into his drink. Going into a crowded underground station on his way home some time later, he suddenly felt a great rush of energy. He pushed people around him out of his way and this created a surge of movement amongst those in front, which resulted in Bob falling from the platform. Initially, Bob avoided the electrified line but, in panic when he heard the sound of an approaching train, he tried to jump up onto the platform again but fell back onto the electrified line and was killed.

Alan was identified and chased by other members of the public, including Chris and Dave. Alan hit Chris and gave him a black eye. Dave then wrestled Alan to the ground and Alan's elbow ligaments were badly damaged in the struggle. Whilst Alan was sitting on the floor nursing his injury, Chris caught him with a swinging blow to the face. Chris was wearing a ring which ripped across Alan's cheek, causing it to bleed heavily.

a) Discuss Alan's criminal liability for the death of Bob.

(25 marks)

b) Discuss the criminal liability of Alan, Chris and Dave arising out of the incidents during the chase.

(25 marks)

c) Discuss the suggestion that reform of the current law on involuntary manslaughter is unnecessary because it is easy to understand and it correctly identifies the conduct which should be punished as unlawful homicide.

(25 marks)

Suggested answer

Unlike the other boards, AQA questions are of 75 minutes duration and normally comprise several different issues, relating to offences against the person or offences against property, combined with selected defences. Each part of the question should be dealt with separately, first looking at the substantive offences before ascertaining whether any defences can be argued. If the marks are evenly distributed, 25 minutes are available for each part.

You are asked to discuss Alan's liability for the death of Bob. The offences of murder and manslaughter need to be examined. Murder and voluntary manslaughter can be discounted because there is no malice aforethought, as discussed under highlights of Chapter 3, above. Liability for gross negligence manslaughter can also be ruled out so only constructive manslaughter remains. For this offence, there must be an unlawful act, that is also dangerous, and which has caused a death. The unlawful act could be a battery. This offence was developed at common law, but it was decided in **DPP v Taylor** that it should now be deemed a statutory offence, under **s39 Criminal Justice Act 1988**. The *actus reus* is established where the defendant applies physical force to another, (**Ireland**). The *mens rea* arises where the defendant does this intentionally or recklessly. In our case, we need to consider whether Alan has inflicted a battery on the persons he pushed out of the way, which ultimately affected Bob. The case of **Collins v Wilcock** decided that the ordinary contacts of every day life should be tolerated but also noted that 'the least touching of another in anger is a battery'. This law needs to be applied to Alan. It has been decided that a battery need not be directly inflicted, as seen in **Scott v Shepherd**, **Martin** and **Fagan**. Pushing in a crowded underground station could be classed as dangerous and, in this instance, a death has resulted. It would have to be decided whether Alan intended to do the pushing or was **Cunningham** reckless, as confirmed in **Venna**. If so, the elements of constructive manslaughter might have been made out. You should now assess whether the defence of intoxication could be used. The scenario states that Alan has been celebrating, which indicates that he might have been drinking. Prima facie, the defence is not available for a basic intent crime, as affirmed in **Majewski**. Alan's intoxication, however, was partly involuntary and in such a case the defence might still be used, as stated in **Pearson**. A further point that might be argued is whether the chain of causation was broken by Bob's own later action when he heard the train approaching. The 'but for' test and the legal cause of death needs to be discussed, with supporting cases. The finding of a new intervening act is unlikely, as seen in **Roberts**, as a reasonable man might well have acted as Bob did.

In the second part of the question, non-fatal offences against the person need to be looked at, plus the defences of self-defence and preventing crime. In relation to Alan, the

definition, *actus reus* and *mens rea* of actual bodily harm under **s47 Offences Against the Person Act 1861** should all be discussed and applied. A black eye is not 'so trivial as to be wholly insignificant', (**Chan-Fook**), so provided that Alan intended a mere assault or battery or was subjectively reckless about this, the offence would be established, as decided by the House of Lords in **Savage and Parmenter**. Alan could try to argue self-defence, as discussed under Chapter 11 below. His belief that he was being attacked must have been an honest one but did not have to be reasonable (**Williams (Gladstone)**) but the force used should not have been excessive, a point that is judged objectively (**Owino, Clegg,** and **Martin**).

Dave could be charged with inflicting grievous bodily harm under **s20** of the same act. The *actus reus* and *mens rea* of this offence need to be described and applied. It was confirmed in **Ireland and Burstow** that the damage need not be directly inflicted and the *mens rea* is satisfied if Dave intended or was **Cunningham** reckless about inflicting some harm (**Mandair**). Dave could be advised to put forward the defence of preventing crime under **s3 Criminal Law Act 1967**. The force he used, however, must have been reasonable in the circumstances.

Chris might have committed offence of malicious wounding, either under **s20**, as above, or under **s18**, the most serious non-fatal offence. The words 'wounding' and 'malicious' need to be examined and applied. Alan's cheek was 'ripped open', thereby satisfying the definition of wounding affirmed in **JJC (a minor) v Eisenhower**. The word 'malicious' merely means the intention to cause some harm or being reckless about this, (**Cunningham**). Chris could be charged with the more serious offence under **s18** if it were established that, in addition to the malicious wounding, he actually intended to cause grievous bodily harm. The word 'intention' has the same meaning as in murder cases. Chris, too, could try to use the defence of prevention of crime but might find this more difficult than Dave because Alan was sitting on the floor, rather than escaping, and the force used by Chris was greater.

The third part of the question is phrased in a provocative way, considering the deluge of criticism that has been levelled at both types of involuntary manslaughter and you may well choose to disagree with all or part of the statement. You should describe the elements of each offence, or in the case of constructive manslaughter, refer back to Part a) and then discuss some of the criticisms, as noted in Chapter 5. For example, the offence of constructive manslaughter is said to be unfair to the accused and, as noted by the late Sir John Smith, is 'in a discreditable state of uncertainty', which hardly suggests that it is easy to understand. The different decisions in relation to drug addicts that are involved in another's death and those concerning indirect harm show problems in identifying the conduct that should be punished in this way. In addition, the objective approach taken in **Church**, as to what constitutes a dangerous act does not sit easily with other parts of the law on offences against the person, where a more subjective approach is taken.

With regard to manslaughter by gross negligence, Lord Mackay's definition in **Adomako** was very vague. It is the jury that has the task of deciding whether the conduct was 'so bad in all the circumstances as to amount to a criminal act or omission' which, it could be argued, is asking too much of that body. You could bring in the difficulties in securing such a conviction against large companies. You should end your account by noting that the Law Commission proposed that the two existing types of involuntary manslaughter should be abolished and replaced with two new offences in the form of reckless killing and killing by gross carelessness. You need to discuss the changes that would ensue if these changes were brought into law but also be aware that while the Home Office has adopted these recommendations, it also is considering another new offence to plug a possible loophole. You could also note the proposed new offence of corporate killing.

Chapter 7

Theft

There is nearly always a question on theft in the exam. It is important to understand the *actus reus* and *mens rea* and be able to apply **ss2-6** to problem situations. Be aware also of the specific defences laid down in the Act. Appropriation of property is still a favourite area and is discussed below. You should also be able to decide whether someone is or is not dishonest under the Act and really has the intention to deprive the other of it permanently. Look at **ss 1 and 2**, the case of **Ghosh** and **s6**.

Part AQA question 2004

Write a critical evaluation of either the *actus reus* or the *mens rea* of any one property offence of your choice

Suggested answer

A good choice would be to examine the *actus reus* of theft, to be found in **ss3, 4**, and **5** of the **Theft Act 1968**, as there is ample material to use. You first need to describe this as 'appropriating property belonging to another'. The word 'appropriation' is defined in **s3** as assuming the rights of an owner, but the judges have confused the issue over their changing opinions of what this phrase means. In **Morris**, the House of Lords held that an appropriation occurs when just one of the rights of an owner is assumed, and, in **Gomez**, decided that the appropriation would take place the first time this happened. You could note that this interpretation obviously made it easier to secure a conviction but also caused problems, as seen in **Atakpu and Abrahams**. More problems arose from the affirmation by the House of Lords in **Gomez** that **Lawrence** was rightly decided and that an appropriation can take place even if the other has consented to the taking. You should note that this view of the law has attracted great criticism from legal academics because of its width and overlap with **s15**. You may well have your own opinions on this but note, also, the relevant Comments' section in Chapter 7. Go on to discuss the cases following **Gomez**. The Court of Appeal appeared to be narrowing the scope of the word in **Gallasso** and **Mazo** but, despite this, the House of Lords extended it again in **Hinks**. This case decided, (but only on a 3–2 decision, with powerful dissenting judgments), that there can be an appropriation even where a valid gift has been made, which clearly conflicts with principles of civil law and has caused renewed concern. The Court of Appeal refused to go further in **Briggs**, and decided that the word 'appropriation' requires a physical act. A remote act triggering a payment was deemed insufficient.

You could go on to examine the other key words in the definition of the *actus reus*. The word 'property' has caused less upheaval but you could discuss the decision in **Oxford v Moss**, which revealed a possible loophole in the law. You should also note that there has been extensive case law, and some conflicting decisions, on the interpretation of the phrase 'belonging to another', particularly in relation to people holding money for a particular purpose, under **s5(3)**, as seen in **Hall, Davidge v Bennett** and **Wain**. You always need to end your answer with an effective conclusion.

The *mens rea* of theft has caused less confusion, but note some difficulties, particularly in relation to the word 'dishonest' which has not been defined by statute but instead, rather obscurely, in **Ghosh**. Note, however, the help given in **ss1(2)** and **s2(2)** as to specific situations where a person would be dishonest and the three situations in **s2(1)** where he would not be. You should note that a party would have the intention to deprive the other permanently of property under **s6**, if he treated it as his own to dispose of. Be able to quote cases in support, especially those deciding whether the value in the property has been used up, as in **Lloyd** and **Bagshaw**.

Robbery and Burglary

Know that all the elements of theft must first be satisfied for both these offences and the extra elements then added. Under **s8**, you might have to decide whether the force or threat of it is sufficient for a robbery, for which the maximum sentence is life. It must be more than a mere snatching, as there must be some resistance to the taking **(Clouden)**. The violence must have occurred at the time of the theft or preceding this, although the courts have decided that theft can be a continuing act, as in **Hale**.

Remember that under **s9**, burglary, which attracts a maximum sentence of 14 years, can be committed in two ways. Both require a trespass by making an effective, but not necessarily substantial, entry **(Ryan)**. This will also be satisfied if a party enters a prohibited part of a building or exceeds his permission to be there. Note also that the word 'building' has been interpreted liberally. It is also burglary under **s9(1)(a)** if, instead of stealing, a party enters with the intent to inflict gbh or cause criminal damage and under **s9(1)(b)** where, having entered as a trespasser, he goes on to steal or inflict gbh. Note that if the burglar commits the offence with a real or imitation firearm or other offensive weapon, this will be aggravated burglary under **s10**, with a maximum of life.

Chapter 8

This examines making off without payment under **s3 Theft Act 1978**. The *actus reus* exists when the defendant makes off without having paid as required or expected, **(Aziz)**. The *mens rea* requires knowledge that payment on the spot is expected, being dishonest and having an intention to evade payment altogether **(Allen)**.

The chapter also covers deception offences under **s15** *and* **s16 Theft Act 1968** and **ss1 and 2 Theft Act 1978**. It should be remembered that, after **Gomez**, anyone satisfying the definition of **s15** would also be guilty of theft but not those in the reverse position. Be aware of the differences between theft and deception. The two often come up together. You also need to memorise carefully the *actus reus* and *mens rea* of **s15** and the two deception offences in the **Theft Act 1978**. With regard to obtaining services by deception under **s1**, the new **S1(3)** makes it very clear that mortgages and other loans are included, thus overruling the controversial decision in **Halai**. Note also, the recent case of **Sofroniou,** where the Court of Appeal decided that dishonestly inducing a bank or building society to provide banking or credit card services, dishonestly operating such an account and dishonestly using a credit card over a period of time, are all covered by **s1**. Be aware that the offence of evading a liability by deception is in three parts. **S2(1)(a)** operates where the defendant, by deception, dishonestly secures the remission of the whole or part of a debt, like paying with a stolen credit card **(Jackson)**. **S2(1)(b),** arises where the defendant dishonestly and by deception persuades the creditor to wait for payment or to forgo it entirely, with the intention never to pay, as in **Holt and Lee**. **S2(1)(c)** comes into play where the defendant, by deception, dishonestly gains an exemption from paying a debt, as in **Firth**. Note that, under **s5**, these different types of deception can be done deliberately or with **Cunningham** recklessness.

Chapter 9

This gives detail on basic criminal damage and the aggravated offences under **S1(2)** and **1(3)**. With regard to the *actus reus*, know the meaning of the terms 'damage' and 'destruction', with cases in support, and note the wide interpretation of the words 'belonging to another'. Be aware that all three offences can be committed intentionally or recklessly and make it clear that **Caldwell** was overruled by the House of Lords in **G and another**. **Cunningham** recklessness must now be proved. This may well have made a difference in the case of **Elliott v C** and ensured that the convictions were set aside in **G**. Know the difference in the definition of property

between this offence and the offence of theft. Have a good knowledge of lawful excuse under **s5** but note that this defence is confined to the basic offence. A person will have a defence if he mistakenly believes that the property is his, as in **Smith,** believes that the owner would have consented to the damage or successfully claims that the damage was necessary to protect his own or other property, **(Chamberlain v Linden)**. Be aware that, on the wording of **s5(3)**, the belief does not have to be reasonably held and is available even when the defendant is intoxicated, **(Jaggard v Dickinson),** or performing an illegal act **(Denton)**. In certain circumstances however, the courts have interpreted **s5(3)** more narrowly and have decided that the jury is entitled to take a more objective approach when assessing whether the property is in need of immediate protection, as seen in **Blake, Hill and Hall**, and **Jones and others**.

Note that in the aggravated offence under **s1(2)**, the property need not belong to another but know that the intent or recklessness of endangering life must be caused by the damaging or destroying of property, which was not the case in **Steer**. Be aware that, under **s1(3)**, damage or destruction by the use of fire is classed as arson. If this is done with the intention of endangering life or being reckless about this, it will be treated as aggravated arson, as in **Caldwell** and **Coles**. Remember however, that these two decisions were overruled in **G and another** and it is now necessary for the prosecution to establish a subjective form of recklessness in all cases of criminal damage. Refer back to Chapter 2 for comment on the implications of this.

Chapter 10

This covers the first four of the 10 general defences. Note that the presumption that no liability exists for 10–14 year-olds has been removed by Parliament so only those under 10 will escape liability altogether. Note that, in relation to insanity, the cases of **Antoine** and

Grant have decided that diminished responsibility cannot be brought up if the defendant has been found unfit to plead through insanity. Know that under the **M'Naghten Rules,** people are presumed to be sane unless at the time of the crime they were labouring under a defect of reason caused by disease of the mind so that they did not know what they were doing or if they did, they were unaware that they were doing wrong. Be able to quote cases on all three aspects, especially the judges' interpretation of what constitutes a disease of the mind. This includes cases of epilepsy **(Sullivan),** arteriosclerosis **(Bratty),** diabetes **(Hennessy)** and even sleepwalking, **(Burgess)** a view that has been roundly criticised. The consequences of this defence, which results in a finding of not guilty by reason of insanity, should be contrasted with that of non-insane automatism, which is a complete defence. Note the very different results where the defendant is suffering from hyperglycaemia, as in **Hennessy,** which is caused by an inside source and classed as insanity, and hypoglycaemia which is caused by an outside source and where the defence of automatism is available. In **Quick,** the defendant took too much insulin and had his conviction quashed. The defendants were also successful in **T** and **Whoolley** but be aware that the defence may be refused if the automatism is self-induced, as discussed in **Bailey.**

Intoxication is popular with examiners! Remember that the rules differ for basic intent crimes, for which intoxication is no defence, as seen in **Majewski** and **Fotheringham** and specific intent crimes, where it may be, although it will normally only reduce the crime, as in **Lipman.** Note the important ruling in **Kingston** however, that a drunken intent is still an intent, as is one formed before the intoxication **(Gallagher).** Involuntary intoxication, as in the case of 'spiked' drinks, could be a defence. The defence is also possible where the defendant takes supposedly calming drugs, with adverse results, **(Hardie).**

Chapter 11

This concerns the other general defences. The limited defence of mistake may be available if a mistake of fact prevents the *mens rea* of the crime being established or provides an excuse for the acts committed, as in **Williams** and **Beckford.** In addition, certain statutory offences specifically allow the defence, as seen in the **Theft Act 1968** and the **Criminal Damage Act 1971.** This defence could be combined with intoxication or self-defence, with strict liability (**B (a minor) v DPP**), theft or criminal damage.

The defences of necessity, duress of circumstances, which is an extension of necessity, and duress of threats, should all be learned together and the elements of each known well to deal with a question such as the following:

WJEC question 2004

To what extent, if at all, are duress and necessity recognised as defences to a criminal charge?

Suggested answer
You could begin by stating that both necessity and duress have been developed at common law but also have strong limitations imposed upon them. When considering necessity, you could note the ambivalent attitude taken by the drafters of the Criminal Code in their statement that 'We are not prepared to suggest that necessity should in every case be a justification; we are equally unprepared to suggest that necessity should in no case be a defence.' The judges appear equally undecided. A limited defence was accepted in early times to deal with specific circumstances, such as to prevent a fire spreading or a ship sinking and later to safeguard the health of a child who was raped, **(Bourne).** It has continued in this case by case fashion in more recent times, as seen in **Re F (Mental Patient: Sterilisation)** and in the important case of **Re A (children)**, where an operation to separate conjoined twins was allowed even though one

of them would die. The death of Mary was felt to be necessary to avoid the death of the other twin. Special circumstances have also been recognised by Parliament, as seen in **s5 Criminal Damage Act 1971** if property is in need of immediate protection, and in the **Road Traffic Act**, which gives special dispensation to speeding fire fighters.

You need to note however, that the defence has not been accepted in a more general way, especially not as a defence to an ordinary murder charge, as noted in the notorious case of **Dudley and Stephens,** even though the jury had expressed sympathy for the starving shipwrecked sailors. Rather surprisingly, even the famously liberal judge Lord Denning, was against its general use. Note also that no reform is planned in this area of law. The Law Commission seems content to allow the defence to expand very gradually on a case by case basis.

You could go on to state that the judges have made it clear that duress of circumstances is an extension of necessity, rather than duress of threats. It was developed to provide a defence in cases where the defendant was forced to commit the crime in question because he feared death or serious injury would otherwise follow from the circumstances in which he found himself. Be aware that the defence started in a small way, in relation to driving offences, as in **Willer, Conway** and, perhaps more surprisingly, in **Martin**. It has since expanded to cover wounding with intent, (**Cairns**), and even hijacking, as seen in **Abdul-Hussain** and **Safi**, but note also that the judges have made repeated calls to Parliament to put this defence, and that of duress of threats, on a statutory basis.

Know that the latter defence may be available if the defendant is forced to commit a criminal act because someone is using more direct force against him or another or threatening to do so. The elements of the defence need to be stated in a precise way and the case of **Graham** used in support. Be aware that the courts have taken a pragmatic view of the word 'immiediate', as seen in the cases of

Hudson and Taylor, Abdul-Hussain and **Safi.** Stress, however, that in this defence and that of duress of circumstances, which shares many of the same criteria, the fear must be one of death or serious injury, nothing less, (**Valderama-Vega, Ortiz** and **Graham**). As in provocation, the question of which of the characteristics of the accused can be taken into account when deciding whether a person of reasonable firmness would have acted in the same way, has occupied the courts. Note that they have not been quite as generous in this complete defence. Excessive vulnerability, pliability, timidity and personality disorders have not been accepted, but mental illness and psychiatric conditions like post-traumatic stress disorder leading to learned helplessness have been, as have age, severe physical disability, pregnancy and perhaps sex (**Bowen, Hegarty**).

You should then note that, as with necessity, strong restrictions have been put on the use of the last two defences. They cannot normally be used by those already engaging in a similar type of criminal activity, as seen in **Fitzpatrick** and **Sharp,** but be aware of the more sympathetic attitude taken in **Z**. In **Howe and Bannister,** the House of Lords unanimously decided that the defences are not available for a charge of murder, for either the principal or an accomplice. The comments made in this case would enhance any answer. The same rule was extended to cases of attempted murder (**Howe Gotts**). You could, however, note that despite the unease expressed by the judges over the possible width of these defences, the Law Commission has recommended the removal of the restriction in cases of murder, although it would tighten up certain other aspects of the defence.

You could end your answer by referring back to the title of the question and state that, while the defences of necessity and duress in its two forms have been recognised by the judges, they have also been careful to place restrictions upon them. In addition, Parliament has shown a reluctance to become involved at all, ignoring several pleas from the judiciary to legislate in this area.

Self-defence and the prevention of crime are also popular areas and may well be the subject of a problem question, in which too much force is used and a death results. At present, this is still murder unless another defence can be put forward, as in **Martin**. Stress that there are two aspects to establishing self-defence. The defendant must have believed that his action was necessary in order to defend himself. Be aware that this point is decided in a subjective way. This means that provided that the belief was an honest one, it does not have to be reasonably held. Nor is it necessary for him to retreat, **(Bird)**. In contrast, the decision as to whether the force used against the attacker was reasonable, is decided objectively, as noted in the cases of **Clegg** and **Martin**. Note that, at the time of writing, (January 2005), the government has now decided that the present law on the subject is satisfactory and it will not therefore, be reviewing the law in relation to the use of excessive force in self-defence or the prevention of crime. Note, however, the possible reforms of provocation which would affect this area, if ever enacted.

Chapter 12

This chapter concerns parties to a crime and you need to learn the differences between principal and secondary offenders. The latter could be aiders, abettors, counsellors and procurers and you should know the meanings of these words and be able to give cases in support. This could be the subject of an essay in its own right as seen on a 1999 OCR paper or be part of a larger problem question. Be careful to distinguish between secondary offenders and those who conspire or incite. You should be aware that detailed knowledge of the actual crime to be committed is not vital for establishing *mens rea*, as noted in **Bainbridge** and **Maxwell** but there must be an intention to act as an accessory in one or more of the four ways **(NCB v Gamble)**. Note that the law is hard on those who embark on a joint enterprise. They will be liable along with the main perpetrator unless the latter does something

completely unexpected or they make a truly effective withdrawal. Know the latest cases on this fertile area, such as **O'Flaherty**.

Chapter 13

Chapter 13 describes the different types of inchoate offences, attempt, conspiracy to commit a crime and incitement. Know that, under the **Criminal Attempts Act 1981, a**n attempt is treated in the same way as a complete crime but must involve an act that is more than merely preparatory, as was the case in **Jones** but not in **Gullefer, Campbell** and **Geddes**. In most cases, it is necessary for a clear intent to be shown, **(Millard and Vernon)**, rather than any lesser form of *mens rea*, but note the exceptions with regard to attempted rape and attempted arson, where recklessness was accepted in relation to part of the offences in question. Be sure to note that the House of Lords' decision in **Shivpuri** has clearly established that there can still be an attempt even though the crime in question is not possible.

Be aware that the law on conspiracy to commit a crime is in **s1 Criminal Law Act 1977, as amended.** The defendant must have agreed with others, (not a spouse), to enter into a course of conduct that if carried out will amount to the commission of a crime. Use of the word 'must' in **s1** implies intention and this is reinforced by **s2(1)**. Study the case of **Anderson** however, to note the problems it has caused with regard to intention and note how these were adroitly avoided by the Court of Appeal, in **McPhillips** and **Edwards**. Another part of Lord Bridge's judgment suggested that the defendant must have intended to play a part in the proceedings but this statement, too, was not accepted by the lower court in **Siracusa**. What is clear is that a conspiracy can exist even if the crime contemplated proves to be impossible.

Be aware that incitement is a common law offence and takes place where a party urges or otherwise influences another to commit a crime, **Race Relations Board v Applin, Invicta Plastics)**. The *mens rea* is an intent to do this, although it is not necessary for the crime to occur. Note the difficulties caused by the case of **Curr**, which suggested that those incited need to possess *mens rea*, as well as the inciter, and **Fitzmaurice** which refused to lay down a general rule that incitement would still exist where the main crime is impossible. The Draft Criminal Code, if ever enacted, would bring this into line with the other inchoate offences.

Hopefully, the above information, together with photocopies of the Key Facts' Charts, will form a good basis for your revision programme.

15.3 DEVISING A REVISION PLAN

The most important point is to try to enjoy your revision and you can do this if you don't leave it all until the last minute. Most successful revision entails careful planning to avoid last minute panics and attendant loss of confidence. I have known a few bright students who have managed to learn the whole of the course in just three or four weeks, but one of these was a policeman! Such a course is not to be recommended, if you wish to keep your health, looks and sanity!

If you are undertaking the activities and the end of chapter revision questions, you should be pleasantly surprised to discover just how much you know already. I would suggest that, before you begin your concentrated revision, you should re-read as much of your work as possible, to gain an overview of the whole subject. After this you should write down all the areas you need to learn, to know from the start the revision route that you are going to take. You can then condense down and down and, by examination day, just have cards of the main points, to trigger your memory. It is important, when dividing up your work, not to set yourself impossible tasks:

- **Take a small area at a time, read the information, take notes and ask yourself what you have learned.**

- **Have periodic breaks and give yourself treats. The diet can be reactivated after the exam!**
- **Work with friends. One excellent way to revise is to teach the subject to another. Your positions can then be reversed and you can take notes as your friend explains the matter to you. Remember, you are not in competition; you are all hoping to obtain high grades.**
- **Do not however, discuss your progress with your friends on the day of the examination, either before or afterwards. This can cause unnecessary and usually unfounded panic or depression if you come to believe that you have left out something important.**

15.4 ANSWERING EXAMINATION QUESTIONS

15.4.1 COPING WITH ESSAYS

Structure

A good essay should always contain an informative first paragraph, clearly indicating to the examiner the path your essay is to take, a more detailed block of relevant information in the middle and a very effective conclusion.

It is surprising how many students start writing immediately they are given the signal to turn over their paper. They are eager to get the information they possess down on paper as soon as possible and hope that further inspiration will follow when this dries up. Sometimes this practice works well but more often it does not. It is far better to read the question slowly, take in all the salient points and then jot down some preliminary notes. After this, you can begin to assemble the material in a more logical sequence and draw up a brief plan of your answer. (It is important to keep this brief. Some plans are so extensive that too little time is left for the real answer!)

- The first few words of your essay should be chosen carefully because these will give the examiners their initial impression of your ability and, hopefully, help influence them as they then read on.
- The middle part of your work should contain the bulk of your facts and argument and needs to be presented well. Use short, punchy sentences where possible and divide these into manageable paragraphs, perhaps leaving gaps between the latter for extra clarity. Large blocks of uninterrupted text, especially if your handwriting is not as clear as it could be, can be daunting to the most conscientious examiner.

  Remember to put in linking phrases, connecting up these paragraphs, to ensure that your work flows seamlessly from one point to the next. You should also refer back to the essay title at appropriate intervals to make it clear that your argument is still on track.
- The conclusion of your essay is also of great importance. If you have managed to bring in some of the words of the essay title, so much the better! Remember that the examiners are often marking hundreds of scripts. You need to remind them in the last few words of your answer that you have dealt diligently and effectively with the question posed.

Content

When first choosing a particular question on your examination paper, ensure that you really do understand all the issues raised and have the necessary knowledge and wider understanding to answer the question properly. Too many students try to turn the question round to what they were hoping the examiner would ask! Another failing is the use of the *'scattergun'* approach, i.e. where the student is determined to write all he knows about the subject, whether relevant or not!

Most essay answers will require a combination of facts and comment. With regard to the latter, watch out for words like **'discuss'**, **'evaluate'** or **'analyse'** and appreciate that, in addition to possessing knowledge of the subject matter, you will also be expected to comment on that information, preferably including well-respected outside source material to support your arguments. When the word **'criticise'** is mentioned, remember that this can include both favourable and adverse comments.

Length

Students often ask how much they should write in an essay but this question is extremely difficult to answer. So much depends on the *quality* of the work. A rather trite answer is to tell them not to write too little or far too much. A very brief response can indicate a lack of knowledge or, alternatively, an inability to develop the points appropriately. When you make a statement therefore, try to elaborate upon it or qualify it in some way and you will then find that your answers are getting longer. At the other end of the scale, some gifted students have the ability to write reams of prose of such a dazzling brilliance that you want it to go on forever! In other overlong answers, however, there is evidence of repetition, irrelevance and waffle, which, instead of enhancing the work, detracts from it, as the main points become less clear. Most answers should fall between these two extremes. If you have been completing the activity sections in this book at regular intervals and/or doing other homework set by your school or college, you should be able to assess whether you are getting the balance right.

15.4.2 DEALING WITH PROBLEMS

In Year 2, these appear as frequently as essays in the examinations. As with the latter, it is vital to study the question carefully before embarking on your answer.

A good approach is to read through the scenario, underlining key words and making notes as you go through it. Remember that many of the words in the questions have been selected specifically to draw out your knowledge on the subject. In other cases, the opposite approach might have been taken and the information left deliberately inconclusive. This normally suggests that you should look at the issue from more than one angle.

Analogies with existing cases

It is important to realise that many problem questions on exam papers in law are loosely based on one or more real-life cases that have come before the courts. **The facts will obviously be changed to some degree but the examiner will be hoping that you will be able to identify the case and use it to support your arguments. In some instances, however, there may be greater differences between the two scenarios than normal and this, too, will be deliberate. The examiner will be hoping that the sharper students will pick this up and go on to ascertain whether the differences are material enough for the cases to be distinguished.**

The correct mix of law and application

When answering problem questions, it is essential to state the law on the subject first and then go on to apply that law to your facts. Too many students fail to deal with these issues in an equally effective way. The majority spend too much time on the knowledge part, giving long descriptions of all the various rules connected to the topic, coupled with the facts of supporting cases, whether directly relevant or not. They may then be left with too little time to spend on application, confining this to a mere few lines at the end of the answer. This is insufficient proof of their ability to *apply* the law carefully to a given situation.

Other students will take exactly the opposite

approach and, from the outset, start to apply the rules to the facts without having first described them. This, too, is inadvisable because it is very difficult to give details of a rule at the same time as it is being applied. More often than not, important points are omitted and valuable marks lost.

It is therefore essential to remind yourself at the start of your homework or examination of the need to keep the two matters separate. Remember to:

- **Identify the general area of law**
- **Describe the relevant rules**
- **Apply those rules to your facts, quoting cases or statutes in support**
- **Advise the relevant party.**

If several different issues are involved, it might be advisable to describe each set of rules in turn and apply those to the facts before continuing with the next topic. This often results in a clearer, more precise answer, and avoids the possibility of repetition or omissions.

With regard to giving advice to a party, you might not always feel able to reach a firm conclusion on this. If so, make this clear. On the other hand, you might find in later discussions that you have come to a different conclusion to others. Provided that you have argued the points well, and the authorities are equally ambivalent on the issue, this is perfectly acceptable. Remember that the judges, too, can be equally divided over the outcome of a case, so you are in good company! You might have noted, as you travelled through this book, that several important principles of law have only come into existence on a 2–1 majority of the Court of Appeal or a 3–2 majority of the Lords.

15.5 EXAMINATION DAY ASSISTANCE

The following 10 points might help you in the exam room:

✔ **List the subjects covered**

In those first tense moments when you are waiting to start, jot down all the topics in your module. Examiners are not tricksters; the questions set are sure to relate to some of these areas. You will then be able to identify them more quickly.

✔ **Read the paper carefully**

When the signal to start is given, spend several minutes reading the paper, remembering to turn over the page if appropriate. There may well be a 'doddle' of a question lurking there!

✔ **Draw up plans of the questions chosen**

✔ **Make an effective start**

The examiner may be marking hundreds of scripts so you need to make an impact with your first words. A brief explanation of the course your answer is to take works wonders, as it puts the examiner on the same track as you immediately.

✔ **Cite authority**

Remember that the examiner is looking for your knowledge of the law, so it is vital to back up your answer with appropriate case law or relevant Acts of Parliament. As mentioned earlier, don't use valuable time writing out the facts of a case in too much detail, a brief explanation to convince the examiner that you know your stuff will do. Remember, it is the principle of law that is the most important part. If you can't remember the name of the case, don't panic; put in brief facts and quote the principle coming from it. If you can't even remember that, put in general information and you may pick up some marks. You cannot get any from a blank page!

✔ **Time yourself properly**

Should you run short of time, be ruthless! Stop one question and continue with the next and finish with notes if you are completely out of time at the end. It is surprising how much information you can put down in this way in roughly the same time as writing one complete sentence. The latter will only give you minimal marks, whereas examiners are sympathetic if there appears to be a genuine problem, especially if you have written a lot before this!

✔ **Leave some space after each question**

You can then return to the answer at a later time if you have something extra to add.

✔ **Structure your answer**

Hopefully, you will have taken on board the advice given in **15.4** in relation to dealing with essays and problems.

✔ **Check your answers**

Try to leave enough time to read through and correct your answers. You might be surprised at the odd things you have written in the stress of the moment!

✔ **Forget about it!**

Finally, after having finished the exam, put it all behind you until result time. The very best of luck to all of you! I hope that your study of Criminal Law has been a worthwhile experience.